Principles of Web Design

Fourth Edition

Joel Sklar

COURSE TECHNOLOGY
CENGAGE Learning

Australia • Brazil • Japan • Korea • Mexico • Singapore • Spain • United Kingdom • United States

COURSE TECHNOLOGY
CENGAGE Learning™

Principles of Web Design, Fourth Edition
  by Joel Sklar

Executive Editor: Marie Lee

Acquisitions Editor: Amy Jollymore

Managing Editor: Tricia Coia

Development Editor: Lisa Ruffolo

Editorial Assistant: Patrick Frank

Marketing Manager: Bryant Chrzan

Content Project Manager: Jill Braiewa

Print Buyer: Julio Esperas

Art Director: Marissa Falco

Compositor: Value Chain International Ltd.

Copyeditor: Camille Kiolbasa

Proofreader: Chris Smith

Indexer: Liz Cunningham

International Student Edition:
ISBN-13: 978-0-538-74757-8
ISBN-10: 0-538-74757-9

Course Technology
25 Thomson Place
Boston, MA 02210
USA

Disclaimer
Course Technology Cengage Learning reserves the right to revise this publication and make changes from time to time in its content without notice.

Cengage Learning is a leading provider of customized learning solutions with office locations around the globe, including Singapore, the United Kingdom, Australia, Mexico, Brazil, and Japan. Locate your local office at: **international.cengage.com/region**

Cengage Learning products are represented in Canada by Nelson Education, Ltd.

For your lifelong learning solutions, visit **course.cengage.com**

Visit our corporate website at **cengage.com**

Printed in Canada
1 2 3 4 5 6 7 14 13 12 11 10 09

Brief Contents

Contents

Chapter Summary

Key Terms

Review Questions

Hands-On Projects

Individual Case Project

Team Case Project

CHAPTER 4

Planning Site Navigation

Chapter Summary

Key Terms

Review Questions

Hands-On Projects

Individual Case Project

Team Case Project

CHAPTER 5

Working with Tables

Preface

Principles of Web Design, Fourth Edition leads you through the entire Web site creation process, from start to finish, while developing and enhancing your HTML, CSS, and visual design skills along the way. You will learn how to create accessible Web sites that let users easily and quickly navigate through your information, regardless of browser type, connection speed, or computing platform. Whether you are building a site from scratch or redesigning an existing site, the principles presented in this text will help you deliver your Web content in a more interesting, accessible, and visually exciting way.

This edition of the book includes two new chapters. Chapter 10 discusses Cascading Style Sheets (CSS) positioning properties, which take advantage of current browser features that let you build innovative, well-designed Web pages without using cumbersome tables to control page layout. Chapter 13 provides a Web site design studio—an opportunity to work as a Web site designer and create a mock-up layout design for a fictional Web site, building the design from preliminary sketches to a completed HTML version of the conceptual site for content testing and browser compatibility.

This edition of the book is printed in full color, allowing you to better see how designers use color in the example Web sites that illustrate Web design principles. Updated illustrations and screen shots throughout the book reflect current browsers and Web design trends.

The Intended Audience

Principles of Web Design, Fourth Edition is intended for anyone who has a working knowledge of HTML and wants to apply those skills to the task of designing attractive, informative Web pages. To work effectively with the content of this book, you need to understand the basics of HTML at the code level. You may have taken an introductory class in HTML, or taught yourself HTML with the help of a book or the Web. You should be able to build a simple Web page that includes text, hyperlinks, and graphics. Additionally, you should be comfortable working with computers and know your way around your operating system, whether Windows, Macintosh, or UNIX.

The Approach

As you progress through the book, you will practice the design techniques by studying the supplied coding samples, looking at the example pages and Web sites, and applying the principles to your own work. Each chapter will conclude with a summary, individual and team project ideas, and a review section that highlights and reinforces the major concepts of each chapter. To complete a case project, you should complete each chapter in sequence.

Overview of This Book

The examples and exercises in this book will help you achieve the following objectives:

- Apply your HTML skills to building designed Web pages
- Effectively use graphics, typography, color, and navigation in your work
- Understand the effects of browser and computing platform on your design choices
- Learn to build portable, accessible Web sites that clearly present information
- Gain a critical eye for evaluating Web site design

In **Chapter 1** you will explore the variables in Web design and learn how Web browser, connection speed, and other factors affect your work. You will also explore the current state of HTML and preview the new markup languages that will change the future of the Web. **Chapter 2** covers the basic design principles that you will apply as you work through the book. You will look at a variety of Web sites and learn to focus on both the user's needs and information requirements of your site. In **Chapter 3** you will learn about the process of planning your Web site before you start coding. You will also learn about important file naming and directory conventions, as well as create a flowchart that depicts the information structure of your site. You will also learn how to publish your site to the Web and plan for ongoing site maintenance and updates. **Chapter 4** discusses basic navigation principles and how to build navigation schemes that meet your user's needs with the creative use of hypertext linking. **Chapter 5** explains how you can use the HTML table elements to create page templates and take a page concept from design to HTML code.

Chapter 6 introduces CSS, including its basic syntax, and explains how to control style information in a single file or across and entire Web site. **Chapter 7** demonstrates the principles of using creative typographic design in the Web environment, and focuses on using Cascading Style Sheets to manipulate a wide variety of type properties. **Chapter 8** explains the effective use of images and color on your Web site, including image file formats, correct use of the <img> element, and computer color basics. **Chapter 9** covers the CSS box model, which controls the margin, padding, and border characteristics of block-level elements. You will also learn about the special box properties that allow you to create floating text boxes and images. **Chapter 10** discusses how to use CSS2 properties to create positioned layouts. **Chapter 11** explains how to organize information and create effective Web sites using frames. In **Chapter 12**, you will learn how to work with HTML form elements to build interactive Web pages that collect information from a user and process it on the Web server. Finally, in **Chapter 13**, you will apply a wide variety of skills you learned in the book to building a mock-up layout design for a fictional Web site.

Features

Principles of Web Design, Fourth Edition contains many teaching aids to assist the student's learning.

- **Chapter objectives:** Each chapter in this book begins with a list of the important concepts to be mastered within the chapter. This list provides you with a quick reference to the contents of the chapter as well as a useful study aid.
- **Illustrations, tables, and screenshots:** Illustrations help you visualize common components and relationships. Tables list conceptual items and examples in a visual and readable format. Updated screen shots reflect the latest technology being used in Web design.

■ **Notes:** Chapters contain Notes designed to provide you with practical advice and proven strategies related to the concept being discussed.

■ **Two new chapters covering Web page design:** The CSS positioning properties offer creative ways to design Web sites. The final chapter lets you practice the skills and principles you learned to build an appealing, useful Web site. The coverage of the new chapters in this book is outlined in more detail above.   NEW!

■ **Full color Web page illustrations**: Web page figures and other illustrations are shown in full color so you can assess how color affects Web page content and how designers use color effectively in sample Web sites.   NEW!

■ **Chapter summaries:** Each chapter's text is followed by a summary of chapter concepts. These summaries provide a helpful way to recap and revisit the ideas covered in each chapter.

■ **Review Questions:** End-of-chapter assessment begins with a set of approximately 15 to 20 review questions that reinforce the main ideas introduced in each chapter. These questions ensure that you have mastered the concepts and have understood the information you have learned. Some questions have been updated for the Fourth Edition.

■ **Hands-On Projects**: Although it is important to understand the concepts behind Web design topics, no amount of theory can improve on real-world experience. To this end, along with conceptual explanations, each chapter provides Hands-On Projects related to each major topic aimed at providing you with practical experience. Some of these include researching information from people, printed resources, and the Internet, as well as installing and using some of the technologies discussed. Because the Hands-On Projects ask you to go beyond the boundaries of the text itself, they provide you with practice implementing Web design skills in real-world situations. Many projects have been updated for the Fourth Edition.

■ **Case Projects**: The individual and team case projects at the end of each chapter are designed to help you apply what you have learned to business situations much like those you can expect to encounter as a Web designer. Depending on instructor preferences, you can work on your own or with a team to independently synthesize and evaluate information, examine potential solutions, and make recommendations, much as you would in an actual design situation. These have also been updated for the Fourth Edition.

Online Companion

The online companion to accompany *Principles of Web Design* has been an important component to this book since the First Edition. For the Fourth Edition, it offers greater enhancement to textbook learning by providing updated information and Web links for further research. Please visit this FREE Web site by going to *www.course.com*, and then searching for this book by title or ISBN.

Teaching Tools

The following supplemental materials are available when this book is used in a classroom setting. All of the teaching tools available with this book are provided to the instructor on a single CD-ROM.

Electronic Instructor's Manual. The Instructor's Manual that accompanies this textbook includes additional instructional material to assist in class preparation, including Sample Syllabi, Chapter Outlines, Technical Notes, Lecture Notes, Quick Quizzes, Teaching Tips, Discussion Topics, and Key Terms.

ExamView®. This textbook is accompanied by ExamView, a powerful testing software package that allows instructors to create and administer printed, computer (LAN-based), and Internet exams. ExamView includes hundreds of questions that correspond to the topics covered in this text, enabling students to generate detailed study guides that include page references for further review. The computer-based and Internet testing components allow students to take exams at their computers, and also save the instructor time by grading each exam automatically.

PowerPoint Presentations. This book comes with Microsoft PowerPoint slides for each chapter. These are included as a teaching aid for classroom presentation, to make available to students on the network for chapter review, or to be printed for classroom distribution. Instructors can add their own slides for additional topics they introduce to the class.

Data Files. Files that contain all of the data necessary for the Hands-On Projects and Case Projects are provided through the Course Technology Web site at *www.course.com*, and are also available on the Teaching Tools CD-ROM.

Solution Files. Solutions to end-of-chapter Review Questions, Hands-On Projects, and Case Projects are provided on the Teaching Tools CD-ROM and may also be found on the Course Technology Web site at *www.course.com*. The solutions are password protected.

Distance Learning. Course Technology is proud to present online test banks in WebCT and Blackboard, as well as MyCourse 2.0, Course Technology's own course enhancement tool, to provide the most complete and dynamic learning experience possible. Instructors are encouraged to make the most of your course, both online and offline. For more information on how to access your online test bank, contact your local Course Technology Cengage Learning sales representative.

Read This Before You Begin

The following information will help you as you prepare to use this textbook.

To the User of the Data Files

To complete the steps and projects in this book, you will need data files that have been created specifically for this book. Your instructor will provide the data files to you. You also can obtain the files electronically from the Course Technology Web site by connecting to *www.course.com* and then searching for this book title. Note that you can use a computer in your school lab or your own computer to complete the steps and Hands-On Projects in this book.

Using Your Own Computer

You can use a computer in your school lab or your own computer to complete the chapters, Hands-On Projects, and Case Projects in this book. To use your own computer, you will need the following:

- A **Web browser,** such as Microsoft Internet Explorer 7.0 or later, Mozilla Firefox version 2.0 or later, or Opera version 6.0 or later.
- A **code-based HTML editor,** such as Adobe Dreamweaver, one of the many shareware editors, or a basic text editor such as Notepad on the PC or SimpleText on the Macintosh.

To The Instructor

To complete all the exercises and chapters in this book, your users must work with a set of user files, called the data files, and download software from Web sites. The data files are included on the Teaching Tools CD-ROM. They may also be obtained electronically through the Course Technology Web site at *www.course.com*. Follow the instructions in the Help file to copy the user files to your server or standalone computer. You can view the Help file using a text editor, such as WordPad or Notepad.

After the files are copied, you can distribute the data files for the users yourself, or tell them where to find the files so they can make their own copies of the data files. Make sure the files are set up correctly by having students follow the instructions in the "To the User of the Data Files" section.

Course Technology Data Files

You are granted a license to copy the data files to any computer or computer network used by individuals who have purchased this book.

Visit Our World Wide Web Site

Additional materials designed especially for this book might be available for your course. Periodically search *www.course.com* for more information and materials to accompany this text.

Acknowledgments

Thanks to the team at Course Technology Cengage Learning for their hard work and honest desire to produce the best book possible.

Thanks to Tricia Coia who manages projects with aplomb.

Thanks to Lisa Ruffolo, developmental editor extraordinaire (and astute football fan), whose hard work and insights make this a better book.

Thanks to the reviewers who provided plenty of comments and positive direction during the development of this book:

Charles Cash, Griffin Technical College; Ric Heishman, George Mason University; Sammy J. Van Hoose, Wayland Baptist University

As always, thanks to Diana, whose love and support make it easier when I'm staring at a blank page and can't write a thing. I couldn't do it without you, honey.

To Sammy, thanks for your enthusiasm, your sharp design eye, and all your help on the project Web site. Go Corsairs!

To my Mom and Dad, who instilled in me a love of reading and books that (I hope) comes through in my writing.

Thanks and a biscuit to my girl Kallie, who suggested content and Web site examples that I wouldn't have thought of on my own. Time to go out, girl!

1

Understanding the Web Design Environment

When you complete this chapter, you will be able to:

- Describe the current state of HTML
- Move from HTML to XHTML
- Use good coding practices
- Describe browser compatibility issues
- Consider for connection speed differences
- Design for multiple screen resolutions
- Address operating system issues

In this chapter, you explore the variable factors that affect Web design. You learn how **Hypertext Markup Language (HTML)**, the language used to create documents on the World Wide Web, is constantly evolving, and preview the new markup languages that are changing how you design for the Web. You learn how to use good coding practices to create HTML code that is valid and based on current acceptable standards. You see how Web browsers affect the way users view your content, and how variations in the user's browser choice, screen resolution, and connection speed pose specific challenges to creating Web pages that are displayed properly in different computing platforms. Finally, you consider what type of software tool you can use to create your HTML code.

The Current State of HTML

In this section, you explore the evolution of HTML and its future as a markup language for creating Web documents. You analyze the structural nature of HTML, the need for style sheets that allow you to separate presentation from content, and the use of hypertext as a means for organizing information.

HTML: Then and Now

When Tim Berners-Lee first proposed HTML at the European Laboratory for Particle Physics (CERN) in 1989, he was looking for a way to manage and share large amounts of information among colleagues. He proposed a web of documents connected by hypertext links and hosted by computers called hypertext servers. As the idea developed, Berners-Lee coined the term, "the

World Wide Web." He created a simplified application of the **Standard Generalized Markup Language (SGML)**, a standard system for specifying document structure, and called it the Hypertext Markup Language. HTML greatly reduces the complexity of using SGML to facilitate transmission of documents over the Internet.

When Berners-Lee created HTML, he adopted only the elements of SGML necessary for representing basic office documents such as memos and reports. The first working draft of HTML included elements such as titles, headings, paragraphs, and lists. HTML was intended for simple document structure, not for handling today's varied and complex information needs. As the Web evolved and expanded, the demand to transport data for transactions such as shopping and banking has far outgrown the capabilities of HTML. The need for new markup languages and standards to address these demands is handled by the **World Wide Web Consortium (W3C)**.

HTML and the World Wide Web Consortium

HTML has progressed significantly since it was first formalized in 1992. After the initial surge of interest in HTML and the Web, a need arose for a standards organization to set recommended practices that would guarantee the open nature of the Web. To meet this need, the W3C was founded in 1994 at the Massachusetts Institute of Technology. The W3C, led by Tim Berners-Lee, sets standards for HTML and provides an open, nonproprietary forum for industry and academic representatives to add to the evolution of this new medium. The unenviable goal of the W3C is to stay ahead of the development curve in a fast-moving industry. The various committees that make up the W3C look to expand and set standards for the many new Web technologies that have emerged. These include Extensible Hypertext Markup Language (XHTML), Extensible Markup Language (XML), Cascading Style Sheets (CSS), and other markup and style languages. You will learn more about these new companion technologies to HTML later in this chapter.

NOTE
Visit the W3C site at *www.w3.org* to find out more about HTML, XHTML, XML, CSS, and the history and future of the Web. You can look up individual element definitions, test your code for validity, or keep up to date on the latest Web developments.

Using HTML for Structure

HTML is a **markup language**, a structured language that lets you identify common sections of a document such as headings, paragraphs, and lists. An HTML file includes text and HTML markup (or element) tags that identify these sections, as shown in Figure 1-1.

The HTML markup tags indicate how the document sections appear in a browser. For example, the <h1> element tags in the following code indicate that the text is a first-level heading:

```
<h1>What is HTML?</h1>
```

Figure 1-1

Structural elements in an HTML file

The browser interprets the HTML markup elements and displays the results, hiding the actual markup tags from the user. The user sees only the text "What is HTML?" formatted as a level-one heading and the paragraph text formatted as a paragraph. Figure 1-2 shows the browser's rendition of the HTML code.

Figure 1-2

The browser interprets the HTML markup elements and displays the results

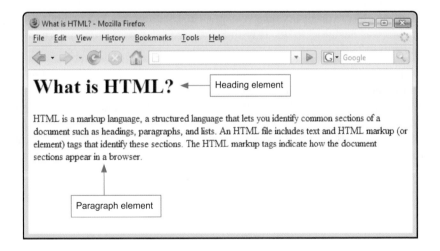

HTML adopts many features of SGML, including the cross-platform compatibility, which means it allows different computers to download and read the same file from the Web. Because HTML is cross-platform compatible, it does not matter whether you are working on a Windows PC, Macintosh, or UNIX computer. You can create HTML files and view them on any computer platform.

HTML is not a What You See Is What You Get (WYSIWYG) layout tool. It was intended only to express logical document structure, not formatting characteristics. Although many current HTML editors let you work with a graphical interface, the underlying code they create is basic HTML. However, because HTML was not designed as a layout language, many editing programs create substandard code to accomplish a certain effect. You cannot rely on the HTML editor's WYSIWYG view to test your Web pages. Because users can view the same HTML file with different browsers and on different machines, the only way to be sure of what your audience sees is to preview your HTML files in the browsers you anticipate your audience will use.

HTML is ideal for the Web because it is an open, nonproprietary language that is cross-platform compatible. All of the markup tags are included with every document and usually can be viewed through your browser. Once you are familiar with the HTML syntax, you will find that one of the best ways to learn new coding techniques is to find a Web page you like and view the source code.

NOTE
All of the major browsers now support a similar action to view the source code. Right-click a blank spot in the browser window and choose either View Page Source or View Source. Internet Explorer opens source code in the Notepad text editor. Firefox and Netscape open the page source in a secondary window.

Using Style Sheets for Presentation

Style elements such as <font> were introduced by browser developers to help Web designers bypass the design limitations of HTML. Designers and writers who are accustomed to working with today's full-featured word processing programs want the same ability to manipulate and position objects precisely on a Web page just as they can on a printed page. Again, this is not what HTML was designed to do; as with SGML, HTML was intended to represent document structure, not style.

Mixing style information within the structure, as is the case in most early Web development, limits the cross-platform compatibility of the content. The display information that is embedded in Web pages is tailored towards one type of display medium, the computer screen. With style sheets, the presentation properties are separate from the content. This accommodates the variety of devices and users that browse the Web. The Web server can determine the type of requesting device and supply a style sheet that matches the device. Figure 1-3 illustrates this concept.

Figure 1-3
Formatting data for multiple destinations

The W3C's recommendation for a Web style language, named **Cascading Style Sheets (CSS)**, allows authors to create style rules for elements and express them externally in a document known as a **style sheet**. CSS eliminates the need for nonstandard coding practices, that until recently have dominated Web design. For example, assume that you want all of your <h1> headings to appear green and centered everywhere on your Web site. Without CSS you would need to include the following code for every instance of an <h1> element:

```
<font color="green"><h1 align="center">Some Heading Text</h1></font>
```

Using a CSS rule, you can express the same style as follows:

```
h1 {color: green; text-align: center;}
```

You can place this rule in an external style sheet and then link every page on your site to that style sheet; the single rule controls every <h1> element in your Web site. Later, if you want to change the <h1> color to red, you simply revise the style sheet rule to change every page on your site.

Until recently, the adoption of CSS as a standard for style has been limited because of poor and uneven support by the major browsers. The newer browsers, such as Internet Explorer 7.0, Firefox 2.0, and Netscape Navigator 8.0, offer more complete and consistent support for CSS, freeing designers to work with this powerful style language. You will learn more about CSS in later chapters of this book.

Organizing Information with Hypertext

The most engaging aspect of browsing the World Wide Web is the linking of information on related topics using **hypertext**, a nonlinear way of organizing information. When using a hypertext system, you can jump from one related topic to another, quickly find the information that interests you, and return to your starting point or move onto another topic. As a hypertext author, you determine which terms to create as hypertext links and where users end up when they click a link.

On the Web, clickable hyperlinks, which can be text or images, can connect you to another Web page, for example, or allow you to open or download a file, such as a music, image, movie, or executable file. Although the basic one-way nature of a hypertext link has not changed since the Web was developed, the nature of the destination content has changed greatly. The different types of linked content and media continually evolve as the Web grows into a richer, more interactive environment. Taking advantage of these new technologies in any Web site often requires users to have faster connection speeds than dial-up modems. You will read more about connection speed as a design variable later in this chapter.

Moving from HTML to XHTML

HTML has progressed through a number of versions since its inception in 1989. The latest standard is version 4.01, which was released by the W3C in late 1999. This is the last release of HTML in its current state. The next generation of HTML is called the **Extensible Hypertext Markup Language (XHTML)**. The W3C released version 1.0 of XHTML in January 2000; a revised version was released in August 2002. XHTML 2.0 is currently under development.

A Brief Introduction to XML

To understand XHTML, a brief introduction to XML is necessary. Like HTML, XML is also a subset of SGML, but has no predefined elements such as <h1> or <p>. The major difference between XML and HTML is that HTML is a predefined set of elements that the browser understands, while XML is a **metalanguage**. The PC Webopedia defines the "meta" prefix as meaning "about," so a metalanguage is a language about a language. XML is thus a language that lets you describe a markup language, allowing you to create your own elements to meet your information needs. This flexibility provides:

- The ability to add new elements or attributes to extend the capabilities of HTML
- The ability to design new browsers or applications for different methods of accessing the Internet

XML code looks very similar to HTML code, with some syntactical differences that you will read about in the next section. The major difference between the two languages is that XML allows you to create elements that describe any type of information you desire. For example, consider that poets might want to create a markup language that expresses the different parts of a poem, as shown in the following code sample:

```
<poem>
<title>An Ode to the Web</title>
<stanza>
<line>So many Web sites</line>
<line>So little time</line>
<line>And all I want to do</line>
<line>Is critique their design!</line>
</stanza>
</poem>
```

Notice that this code looks very much like regular HTML code, except that the tags are not standard, but specific to the type of content they contain. Unlike standard HTML, the browser does not know how to display this information unless a style sheet is supplied that specifies, for example, that the contents of the <line> elements should be displayed in the browser as 12-point Helvetica text.

Benefits of Moving to XHTML

One of the significant advantages of applying XML rules to HTML is that XML has stricter code syntax. As more sites adopt XHTML, they will have to clean up code that does not match the standard, including removing **deprecated elements**, which are elements that the W3C has identified as obsolete and consequently will not be included in future releases of HTML. With more Web sites using standardized code, browsers will more easily judge what is correct code and what is not. In addition, XHTML is designed to appear properly in browsers that support HTML 4.01.

HTML was originally designed for limited document expression and has not adapted well to the exploding interest in the Web. On the other hand, because XHTML is based on XML, it is extensible, which means that designers can extend its capabilities, allowing developers to address future markup needs easily. XHTML is also designed to support the variety of new devices that will access the Internet as new technologies emerge. Any XHTML-compliant software must access and display XHTML regardless of the computer or display type.

Because XML allows better data handling, the new version of XHTML promises to work smoothly with database and workflow applications. The next generation of HTML will include advanced support for form elements, defining them more for data handling than presentation, and allowing data to pass between applications and devices with greater ease. Tables will emphasize a data model that can render their content based on the presentation device. For example, tabular data for stock pricing information could be sent to multiple destinations and displayed to best fit the user's individual display type, such as a personal digital assistant (PDA) or cell phone. This arrangement gives the same data greater value; though it only needs to be generated once, it can be displayed in many ways.

XHTML Syntax Rules

XML, and therefore XHTML, contain a number of syntax rules that are different from those in HTML. XHTML conforms to the following XML syntax rules:

- Documents must be well-formed.
- Elements must nest symmetrically.
- Element names are case sensitive.
- End tags are required.
- Empty elements are signified by a closing slash.
- Attribute values must be contained in quotation marks.

Documents Must Be Well-Formed

A **well-formed document** is one that adheres to the syntax rules described in this section. Any document that does not meet the syntax rules will not be accepted as an XHTML document.

Elements Must Nest Correctly

You can nest XHTML tags, but they must not overlap. Each set of opening and closing tags must completely contain any elements that are nested within the set. For example, the following is incorrect XHTML syntax:

```
<p><strong>some text... </p></strong>
```

The closing tag for the bold attribute must come before the closing tag for the paragraph element. The correct nesting syntax follows:

```
<p><strong> some text... </strong></p>
```

XHTML Is Case Sensitive

XHTML, unlike HTML, is case sensitive. An XHTML-compliant browser interprets <BLOCKQUOTE> and <blockquote> as two different elements. Although not required, the accepted convention in XHTML is to use all lowercase characters for element and attribute names.

End Tags Are Required

In HTML, certain elements such as the <p> element had optional closing tags. This is not allowed in XHTML, where nonempty elements need a closing tag. For example, the following two <p> elements do not have closing tags:

```
<p>This is the first paragraph.
<p>This is the second paragraph.
```

In XHTML, the following example is correct:

```
<p>This is the first paragraph.</p>
<p>This is the second paragraph.</p>
```

Empty Elements Are Signified by a Closing Slash

Empty elements must either have a closing tag or be marked "empty" by a slash (/) in the single tag. For example, the <br> element, when rendered in XHTML, becomes <br />. The <img> element looks like the following:

```
<img src="photo.jpg" />
```

Notice the closing slash. Older browsers ignore this, so you can convert empty elements to be XHTML-compliant without worrying if your pages are displayed properly.

 NOTE

To be certain that older browsers ignore the XHTML closing slash, make sure to leave a space in front of the slash. For example, your <br> tags should look like this:

Attribute Values Must Be Contained in Quotes

All attribute values in XHTML must always be contained within quotes, unlike those in HTML. The following is incorrect XHTML syntax:

```
<h1 align=center>Heading</h1>
```

The correct syntax follows:

```
<h1 align="center">Heading</h1>
```

Adopting XHTML Syntax Rules

If you anticipate working with XHTML in the future, you should begin to follow these syntax rules in your HTML code now. This ensures that the HTML you are creating today will work with XHTML in the future. If you have legacy HTML code, consider revising it to meet XHTML syntax standards. The following code shows an example of HTML code that is common on the Web today. Although not syntactically correct, this code is displayed properly in the browser:

```
<H1>Some plain HTML code</h1>
    <P>This is a paragraph of text.
    <IMG SRC="xml.gif">
```

```
<H3>A bulleted list</H3>
<UL>
<LI>Item one
<LI>Item two
<LI>Item three
```

Converting this code to syntactically correct XHTML means applying the stricter syntax rules listed earlier, resulting in the following code:

```
<h1>Some plain HTML code</h1>
    <p>This is a paragraph of text.</p>
    <img src="xml.gif" />
    <h3>A bulleted list</h3>
    <ul>
    <li>Item one</li>
    <li>Item two</li>
    <li>Item three</li>
    </ul>
```

NOTE

Many shareware and commercial software programs can assist you in bringing your code up to XHTML standards. These include HTML Tidy at *http:// tidy.sourceforge.net/* and Tidy GUI at *http://perso.wanadoo.fr/ablavier/TidyGUI/*.

Style Sheets Are Required

Because XHTML is an application of XML, you must use style sheets to render presentation information in XHTML. Separating data from style means that the same information can be directed to various display devices simply by changing the style sheet. When different style sheets are used, the contents of the same Web page can be displayed on a computer monitor, TV screen, handheld device, or cellular phone screen. This data-once, destination-many format liberates the data and structure of XHTML documents to be used in a variety of applications. A script or applet (a small program written in Java that runs in a browser) redesigns the data presentation as it is requested from the server and applies the proper style sheet, based on the user's device choice.

The following two style sheet languages are currently available for use with XML or XHTML:

- *Cascading Style Sheets*—CSS has recently gained much wider use due to increasing browser support. CSS is an easy-to-use style language that controls only how documents are presented. The W3C released the second edition of CSS, called CSS2, in 1998.

- *Extensible Style Language (XSL)*—As an application of XML, XSL both describes page formatting and allows XML documents to be transformed from XML to XSL and vice versa. XSL supports the use of CSS style rules within an XSL style sheet, so the two style languages complement each other.

Migrating from HTML to XHTML

When should you choose to adopt XHTML for your Web site rather than HTML? If you are building a new site from scratch, you can start by coding well-formed XHTML, using CSS for display information. If you have an existing site, you have a larger job ahead of you. Adopting XHTML for existing sites should be a gradual process rather than an abrupt shift to the new language. The transitional flavor of XHTML lets you start to adopt the newer syntax while keeping legacy HTML code such as attributes that control page and link colors. As you migrate closer to strict XHTML, you will be cleaning up code on existing pages, planning coding conventions for new pages, removing deprecated elements, and moving display information to CSS. Eventually you will be creating Web pages that contain only structural information, with all display information kept separately in CSS files. Chapters 6 through 10 discuss CSS in detail.

The following list contains steps you need to take to migrate from HTML to XHTML:

1. *Evaluate existing code*—Check for basic compliance with XHTML syntax rules. Are closing tags included? Are all tags lowercase? Are attributes quoted? How much cleanup work is necessary to make the code well-formed? Most of this work can be automated in the various HTML editing programs.

2. *Evaluate existing presentation information*—How much of your code includes deprecated elements such as <font> and deprecated attributes such as "bgcolor," "face," and "size"? On many sites, this information can make up as much as 50% of the existing code. Start thinking about how you can convert these presentation characteristics to CSS.

3. *Create coding conventions*—Create coding conventions and follow them throughout the site. Make sure that new content added to the site follows the new coding and CSS standards. The more you standardize, the easier your maintenance chores become.

4. *Start using CSS*—Start by building simple style sheets that express basic characteristics such as page colors, font family, and font size. Consider using more advanced CSS options such as classes that allow you to name and standardize the various styles for your site. As you build style rules, start to remove the existing display information in the site.

5. *Test for backward compatibility*—Older browsers ignore new XHTML syntax rules, but you still need to test in older browsers to make sure that your content is legible and readable. Test carefully with your CSS style rules to make sure that they are supported in older browsers; if they are not, either adjust with the older browsers in mind, or consider serving a different set of style sheets for older browsers, which some Web servers are capable of doing.

Choosing an HTML Editor

You can create or generate HTML code to build Web pages in many ways. In the earlier days of the Web, the most widely accepted tool was Notepad, the simple text editor that comes with Windows versions from 95 to Vista. On the Macintosh, the equivalent tool is TeachText or SimpleText. Many sites on the Web are coded using these text-editing tools, which are easy to use and still relied upon by many HTML authors. They also are the best way to learn HTML because you have to enter every tag by hand. However, fewer designers use simple text editors now that increasingly robust HTML authoring packages have appeared.

There are a variety of HTML editing programs, such as Adobe Dreamweaver, Adobe GoLive, and Microsoft Expression Web (which replaces FrontPage), to name a few. Some code-based HTML editors, such as Adobe HomeSite, forgo a WYSIWYG approach. They have become popular because they include many powerful enhancements that Notepad lacks, such as multiple search-and-replace features and syntax checking, while still allowing you to manipulate code at the tag level. The most recent authoring tools offer syntax validation and code conversion as well, which can greatly lessen the tasks of cleaning up older code to match the newer XHTML syntax rules.

NOTE

A variety of lower-cost HTML editors are available on the Web as shareware, which is software you can try before you buy. Visit *www.download.com* and search for "HTML editors" to view a list of software you can download.

Many of the latest office applications also convert documents to HTML. For example, you can create a flyer in your word processor and export it to create an HTML page. You can even create slides in Microsoft PowerPoint and export them to HTML. This hands-off approach leaves much to be desired for an HTML author, however, because you give up control over the finished product. In addition, the practice of converting content from a program such as Microsoft Word to HTML is notorious for creating substandard HTML code. You are better off moving away from one of the office applications to a dedicated HTML authoring package if you are serious about creating attractive, standards-compliant Web sites.

As with browsers, authoring packages interpret tags based on their own built-in logic. Therefore, a page that you create in an editing interface may look quite different when displayed in a browser. Furthermore, many editing packages create complex, substandard code to achieve an effect specified by the user. This complex code can cause compatibility problems across different browsers. HTML authors who are accustomed to coding by hand (in Notepad or another text editor) often are surprised to see the complexity of the code an HTML editing package has generated.

To code effectively with HTML, you must be comfortable working directly at the code level. Though you may choose to use one of the many editing packages to generate the basic layout or structure for your page or to build a complex table, be prepared to edit the code at the tag level to fix any discrepancies. You probably will end up working with a combination of tools to create your finished pages.

Using Good Coding Practices

In the past, Web designers wrote nonstandard code, employing a "whatever works" mentality to trick the browser into presenting the results they wanted. Some examples of this are using the heading tags <h1> through <h6> solely for their font sizes rather than as logical headings, or manipulating the <table> elements into a layout tool instead of a container for data as they were intended.

These are bad habits that are best left behind. This section provides guidelines for creating code that ensures the greatest standards-compliance, presentation, and usefulness of your content.

- Stick to the standards
- Use semantic markup
- Choose the correct document type
- Validate your code

Stick to the Standards

The best way to create well-coded Web sites is to strictly follow the standards set by the World Wide Web Consortium. This approach provides the greatest acceptance and uniform display of your content across multiple browsers and operating systems. This "best practices" method of coding is widely supported among sites that are interested in the greatest accessibility. Following the W3C standards does not mean that your site has to be visually uninteresting, although you may have to sacrifice the latest multimedia enhancements. Reliable visual and information design techniques, along with the use of Cascading Style Sheets, can let you overcome many functional limitations.

Coding with standards and respecting the W3C mandate to separate content structure from presentation information makes your content more accessible and portable to different devices and destinations. Who would have envisioned that, at the outset of the Web, content would be delivered on cell phones or televisions? Who can imagine what devices will be used in the future? Content that is designed to standards is more meaningful to search engines, displays more consistently in multiple browsers, and has a longer life and greater chance of being accessible in future applications.

NOTE

The Web Standards project (*www.webstandards.org*) is "a grassroots coalition fighting for standards that ensure simple, affordable access to Web technologies for all." This site is a good place to get started on reading more about the history, trends, and current state of Web standards development.

Use Semantic Markup

Semantic markup is descriptive markup that identifies the intended use of different document sections. Semantic markup accurately describes each piece of content. Although this may sound like an obvious use of markup elements, until recently this logical use of the HTML elements was largely ignored by the Web development community. For example, HTML authors know that an <h1> element signifies a block of text as a first-level heading, but many times this element is used simply for its ability to increase the font-size of text. The <ul> element, which indicates a bulleted list, was used for its indenting characteristics. When you use semantic markup, the document elements match the meaning and usage of the document sections; a <p> signifies a paragraph, a <blockquote> is for a lengthy quotation, and so on. Semantically correct markup is readable not only by humans but by machines as well, lending itself to improved recognition by search engines, news agents, and accessibility devices.

NOTE

Semantic markup is the basis for the evolution of the Web into a universal medium for data, information, and knowledge exchange as described by the W3C in their Semantic Web Activity group (*www.w3.org/2001/sw/*). Although this vision of the Web is still in early development, the emphasis on correct usage of markup elements benefits the accessibility and longevity of your Web content.

Choose the Correct Document Type

The W3C is working towards a vision of the Web where all content is coded correctly and separate from presentation information, but the organization also realizes that this is not the state of the Web today. The current state of markup on the Web is very haphazard, nowhere near the W3C's recommended stricter standards. Very few Web sites are valid and actually conform to W3C standards. To ease the transition to a more standardized Web, three document types, or "flavors," of both HTML and XHTML are available: Strict, Transitional, and Frameset.

- *Strict*—Use this flavor when you want clean, structural markup code, free of any markup tags associated with layout. Use Strict with Cascading Style Sheets to get the font, color, and layout effects you want. This document type does not allow any deprecated elements and attributes.

- *Transitional*—This document type is the most common, because it allows obsolete elements from older versions of HTML and newer features such as style sheets and well-formed markup. The benefit of the Transitional type is that it allows you to gradually migrate from existing HTML code that may still contain font and presentation information to the more syntactically correct, cleaner markup code necessary to match the Strict type.

- *Frameset*—Use this type when you want to use frames to partition the browser window into two or more sections. The Frameset specification is only important if you plan to use frames to partition the browser window, as described in Chapter 11 "Working with Frames."

When you choose a document type, you are actually pointing to a set of rules, called a **Document Type Definition (DTD)**, that contains all the elements, attributes, and usage rules for the markup language you are using. You can select a document type for your Web pages with the Doctype statement. This code was often omitted in the earlier days of the Web, but with browsers maturing, choosing the correct document type is essential to making sure that your Web pages are displayed properly and match the W3C standards. Doctype statements should always be the first line of code in your file, as shown in Figure 1-4.

Figure 1-4
The Doctype statement

```
<!DOCTYPE HTML PUBLIC "-//W3C//DTD HTML 4.01 Transitional//EN">

<html>
<head>
<title>Example File</title>
</head>

<body>



</body>
</html>
```

DOCTYPE
statement

NOTE

When you include a document type, the browser operates in "standard mode," presenting the document using W3C rules. If there is no document type, the browser operates in "quirks mode," which renders the page like an older browser, allowing the "quirky" code from the earlier days of Web development.

To select a document type, either choose one through your HTML editing software or add code directly to the document. Most HTML software lets you choose the document type when you create a new file. Alternately, you can enter the code directly, but as you can see in the following list, the syntax is complicated and easy to mistype. It is always best to copy and paste these document type statements from an existing document whenever possible.

Which is the best document type to use? If you are working with older code or want a more "relaxed" standard, use HTML 4.01 Transitional. If you are coding to the latest standards, using Cascading Style Sheets to express presentation information, you can use XHTML Transitional.

NOTE

Doctype code is complicated and easy to mistype. Consider creating a template that contains the Doctype statement so you can reuse it every time you start a new document.

HTML 4.01 Strict

```
<!DOCTYPE html PUBLIC "-//W3C//DTD HTML 4.01//EN"
    "http://www.w3.org/TR/html4/strict.dtd">
```

HTML 4.01 Transitional

```
<!DOCTYPE html PUBLIC "-//W3C//DTD HTML 4.01 Transitional//EN"
    "http://www.w3.org/TR/html4/loose.dtd">
```

HTML 4.01 Frameset

```
<!DOCTYPE html PUBLIC "-//W3C//DTD HTML 4.01 Frameset//EN"
```

```
    "http://www.w3.org/TR/html4/frameset.dtd">
```

XHTML 1.0 Strict

```
<!DOCTYPE html PUBLIC "-//W3C//DTD XHTML 1.0 Strict//EN"
    "http://www.w3.org/TR/xhtml1/DTD/xhtml1-strict.dtd">
```

XHTML 1.0 Transitional

```
<!DOCTYPE html PUBLIC "-//W3C//DTD XHTML 1.0 Transitional//EN"
    "http://www.w3.org/TR/xhtml1/DTD/xhtml1-transitional.dtd">
```

XHTML 1.0 Frameset

```
<!DOCTYPE html PUBLIC "-//W3C//DTD XHTML 1.0 Frameset//EN"
    "http://www.w3.org/TR/xhtml1/DTD/xhtml1-frameset.dtd">
```

Validate Your Code

Another step towards standards compliance is to validate your code. **Valid code** conforms to the rules of the W3C. The lack of valid code is a major problem for the future of a standards-based Web. In a 2004 study, a survey of 2.4 million different Web pages found that 99% did not meet W3C standards. Although this number may have decreased, a quick survey of most any Web site's code shows that few are valid.

Valid code enhances browser compatibility, accessibility, and exchange of data. Whether you write HTML or XHTML code, you should validate your code to make sure it conforms to W3C standards. Validation is so easy to perform, it is hard to understand why many Web designers apparently ignore it. To validate your code, simply use a software program called a validator to read your code and compare it to the rules in the DTD. The validator generates a list of validation errors. Many HTML editors contain built-in validators, or you can use a Web-based validator such as the W3C validation service at *http://validator.w3.org/*.

Using a validator is an eye-opening experience for any Web designer. The most common mistakes that make your code invalid include:

- No doctype declaration
- Missing closing tags, most commonly on paragraphs
- Missing alt attributes in <img> elements
- Incorrect tag nesting
- Unquoted attributes

If you compare this list to the XHTML syntax rules listed earlier in this chapter, you can see how moving to standardized coding practices helps clean up most of these common coding errors.

Browser Compatibility Issues

One of the greatest challenges facing HTML authors is designing pages that multiple browsers can display properly. Every browser contains a program called a **rendering engine** that interprets the markup tags in an HTML file and displays the results in the browser. The logic for interpreting the HTML tags varies from browser to browser, resulting in potentially conflicting interpretations of the way the HTML file is displayed. As a Web page designer, you must test your work in as many different browsers as possible to ensure that the work you create appears as you designed it. Although your work might seem cross-browser compatible, you may be surprised to see that the results of your HTML code look very different when viewed with different browsers.

NOTE

To ensure the greatest compatibilities of your Web pages across multiple browsers, follow these guidelines:

- Follow W3C standards
- Validate your code
- Know your audience
- Test your work in multiple browsers

Most HTML authors do not have the luxury of knowing the age, type, or operating system of the browsers that will be used to view their Web pages. Browser and version choices can vary widely based on a number of variables. Many individuals and organizations are reluctant to upgrade software simply because a new version has been released. Other users may have older computers that do not have the processing speed or disk space to handle a newer browser. Although it is a good idea to test with the latest browsers, it also is prudent to test your work in older browsers to maximize the number of people reached with your Web pages.

Knowing your audience is a major step towards correctly implementing your site. For example, you may be building a site that discusses the latest in programming language trends. This site will attract computer-savvy users, so you can code for the latest browsers. On the other hand, if you are creating a site that will attract the general public, you need to test in older browsers to make sure your pages appear as designed in older and newer browsers alike. If you want to include animations or effects that require a plug-in, use a development tool that already is supported by the major browsers. Make sure that the most important content on your site is rendered in a way that does not rely on new technology so that users with older browsers still get your message. Finally, if you are designing for an intranet and can mandate the type of software your viewers use, you can work with only one browser in mind.

As discussed earlier, not only are new browsers released frequently, but older browsers still are used by many Web users. The newer browsers support desirable features, such as Cascading Style Sheets, that are not supported by older browsers. Including newly supported features in your page design may significantly affect the way your page is viewed if the older browsers cannot interpret the latest enhancements. Browsers exhibit subtle differences across computing platforms as well.

The newer browsers such as Internet Explorer 7.0, Firefox 2.0, and Netscape 8.0 offer much better support for the standards released by the W3C. These browser software companies have found that, as part of the Web development community, they, too, benefit from the increased support of the standards. More consistent browsers allow better visual design and increased interactivity for all users.

NOTE

If you would like to download a particular browser, or find out which browser is currently the most popular, visit one of these Web sites:

- BrowserNews at *www.upsdell.com/BrowserNews/*
- CNET Browser Info at *www.browsers.com*

Considering Connection Speed Differences

Connection speed is another variable that should influence your Web page design. Most users simply will not wait longer than 10–20 seconds for a page to load. If your pages download slowly, your users probably will click to go to another site before they see even a portion of your content. Many designers make the mistake of not testing their pages at different connection speeds. If you do not test, you cannot appreciate what it is like for users to connect at different speeds to your site, and you may lose valuable visitors.

Although a majority of U.S. computer users now have high-speed access to the Web, approximately one-quarter still access the Web with a dial-up modem. According to Nielsen//NetRatings, (*www.netratings.com/*) "U.S. broadband penetration among active Internet users grew to 78.45% in December 2006. Narrowband users connecting at 56Kbps or less now comprise 21.55% of active Internet users." Around the world, broadband access has grown sharply. According to the Organization for Economic Development (OECD) at *www.oecd.org*, "the number of broadband subscribers in the OECD member countries increased 33% from 136 million in June 2005 to 181 million in June 2006." Access via cable modem had been the most reliable high-speed connection to the Web for home users, but Digital Subscriber Line (DSL), the service offered by telephone companies, has gained in popularity. Corporations still rely primarily on T1 or Integrated Services Digital Network (ISDN) connections. Table 1-1 describes the more common types of connection technologies.

Technology	Speed	Notes
Regular telephone line	Up to 56 Kbps	About 20 percent of U.S. computer users still connect to the Internet using this method; however, you're lucky if you can consistently maintain a connection speed over 44 Kbps
ISDN basic	64 Kbps to 128 Kbps	ISDN offers good speed and allows a constant connection to the Internet, but is fairly expensive; ISDN is more common in urban areas and is primarily used by business
DSL	512 Kbps to 8 Mbps	DSL uses a single existing phone line to carry both voice and data, and allows a constant connection to the Internet
Cable modem	512 Kbps to 52 Mbps	Cable modems are fast, allow a constant connection to the Internet, and you don't have to dial up to connect

Table 1-1   Common types of connection technologies

Even though more users have high-speed access, Web designers should still strive to keep their page designs simple enough for the pages to load quickly. The single biggest factor influencing the speed at which your pages are rendered is the size and number of graphics on your Web pages. As a rule of thumb, no single image on your Web site should exceed 10 to 15 KB. If you know all your users have faster access, you can design your pages to match. For the general public, you can consider 56 Kbps as a base connection speed because many users still use dial-up modems. You will learn more about how to prepare your images to download quickly in Chapter 8.

Working with the Cache to Improve Download Time

All Web pages are stored on computers called Web servers. When you type a Uniform Resource Locator (URL) address in your browser, it connects to the appropriate Web server and requests the file you specified. The server serves up the file so your browser can download it. The first time you visit a site, the entire contents of the HTML file (which is plain text) and every image referenced in the HTML code is downloaded to your hard drive. The next time you visit this site, your browser downloads and parses the HTML file. The browser checks to see if it has any of the specified images stored locally on the computer's hard drive in the **cache**. The cache is the browser's temporary storage area for Web pages and images. The browser always tries to load images from the cache rather than downloading them again from the Web.

You can make use of the browser's caching capabilities by reusing graphics as much as possible throughout your site. Once an image is downloaded, it remains in your user's cache for the number of days specified in the user's preference settings. Most users do not change the settings, so there is a good chance your graphics will remain on the user's hard drive a while. Every time the user revisits your site, the cached graphics load locally rather than from the Web server. The browser's caching capability is a great argument for standardizing the look of your site by using the same navigation, branding, and background graphics throughout. Not only does the consistency increase the usability of your site, but also your pages load faster.

Designing for Multiple Screen Resolutions

No matter how carefully you design pages, you can never know how users view your work because you do not know their monitors' screen resolutions. A computer monitor's **screen resolution** is the width and height of the computer screen in pixels. Most monitors can be set to at least two resolutions, whereas larger monitors have a broader range from which to choose. User screen resolution is a factor over which you have no control.

Screen resolution is a function of the monitor's capabilities and the computer's video card. The current most common screen resolution (traditionally expressed as width × height in pixels) is 1024 × 768, replacing 800 × 600 as a standard. As larger monitors become less expensive, some users are choosing even higher resolutions of 1280 × 1024 and above, allowing them to display more on the screen. As a Web designer you still have to consider users with older computers who use an 800 × 600 screen resolution. Although more Web sites are redesigning to a 1024 × 768 standard, many others still retain an 800 × 600 design.

Fixed Design

Figures 1-5 and 1-6 show the same L.L. Bean Web site viewed at different screen resolutions, using fixed design.

Notice in Figure 1-5 that the page is designed to display its content specifically within an 800 × 600 screen resolution. The content entirely fills the browser window, indicating that 800 × 600 is the base screen resolution of this Web site. Users viewing the same page at 1024 × 768, as shown in Figure 1-6, see the content aligned to the left side of the page, and the passive white space on the right side of the page fills in the remainder of the screen. You will read more about the use of active and passive white space in Chapter 2.

Figure 1-5

Fixed design at 800 × 600 resolution

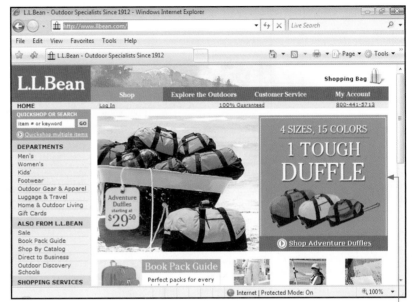

Content fills the browser window

Figure 1-6

Fixed design at 1024 × 768 resolution

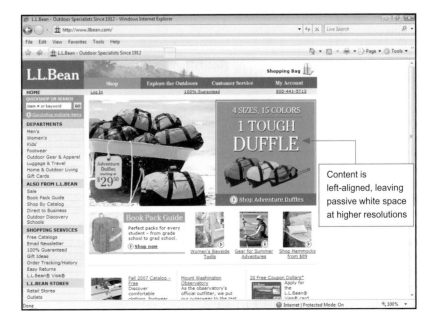

Content is left-aligned, leaving passive white space at higher resolutions

Flexible Design

In contrast, Figures 1-7 and 1-8 show a Web page that has been designed to adapt to different screen resolutions.

Figure 1-7

Using flexible design, content fills window at 800 × 600

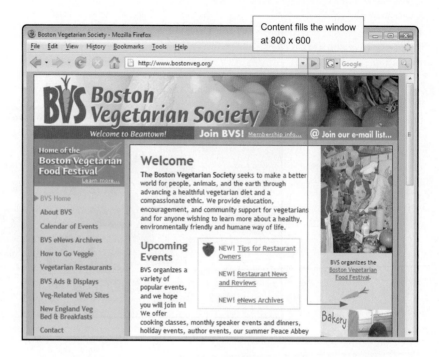

Figure 1-8

Using flexible design, middle column expands to fit at 1024 × 768

The Web page shown in Figures 1-7 and 1-8 was designed for an 800 × 600 resolution, but is adaptable to other resolutions as well. As the screen resolution changes, the middle column expands or contracts to accommodate the varying screen width, while the outside columns remain fixed. The designers accomplished this adaptability through variable rather than absolute table widths. You will learn about this technique in Chapter 5. The challenge in using this type of design is that the content must remain organized and legible at all screen resolutions, requiring more testing by the Web developer to ensure success.

Centered Design

A third choice for handling different screen resolutions is shown in Figures 1-9 and 1-10. These figures show a Web page that has been designed to adapt to different screen resolutions by remaining centered in the user's browser.

Figure 1-9

Centered design at 800 × 600

The Web page shown in Figure 1-9 fills the browser window at 800 × 600 resolution. As the screen resolution changes, the Web page stays centered in the browser window, splitting the remaining space into equal amounts on the left and right side of the browser window. Figure 1-10 shows the same page at 1024 × 768. This technique creates a border for the page with the leftover space, resulting in more active white space than the left-justified technique shown in Figure 1-6. The benefit of centering a page is that the layout of the content remains unchanged no matter what the user's screen resolution.

Figure 1-10

Centered design at
1024 × 768

Leftover space is equally distributed
on both sides of the browser window

As a Web designer, you decide how to code your Web site to handle different screen resolutions. Most Web sites were once coded to the lowest possible screen resolution, which is 640 × 480. Now that monitors are getting bigger and less expensive, the majority of Web users probably have their screen resolution set to 1024 × 768, which is greater than the current standard 800 × 600 resolution for most Web sites. If you know your audience is consistently using a higher resolution, you can code to it. Otherwise, decide whether to use 1024 × 768 or 800 × 600 as your base resolution. Look at examples of other sites to see which design best suits your audience. Consider using flexible design or centered design, both of which will adapt to multiple resolutions. Remember to test at different resolutions to ensure that your users can view your pages properly.

Operating System Issues

The user's operating system is the variable over which you have the least control. People use endless combinations of monitors, computers, and operating systems on desktops around the world. In today's computing environment, three operating systems dominate: the Windows PC platform, the Apple Macintosh platform, and various flavors of UNIX. The best method for dealing with this variety is to test your content on as many operating systems as possible, although this is not realistic for the student or beginning Web designer. Remember the following points about different operating systems:

- *Monitors and display software*—For many technical and physical reasons, the colors you choose and images you prepare for your site can look vastly different on different machines. Screen resolutions and sizes, color depth, and video hardware and software all affect the look of your Web pages. Follow the guidelines on colors in Chapter 8 to make sure your designs are as cross-platform compatible as possible.

- *Browser versions*—Not all browsers are the same on all operating systems. Often software companies release different versions of their browsers based on the popularity of the operating system. For this reason, Internet Explorer is often a release behind on the Macintosh platform. Furthermore, Microsoft does not even make a UNIX version of its browser, although Netscape and Mozilla do. The only solution to this problem is to test your work in as many browsers as possible.

- *Font choices*—Installed fonts vary widely from one computer to another. Choose fonts that are commonly used; otherwise, the font you choose, if not installed on the user's machine, will appear in a default typeface. Read Chapter 7 for more information on this subject.

Chapter Summary

Many variables affect the way users view your Web pages. As an HTML author, your goal should be to code pages that are accessible to the largest audience possible. As you plan your Web site, make the following decisions before implementing your site:

▶ Use Cascading Style Sheets. The style enhancements and control offered by this style language are impressive, but are not evenly supported by older browsers. Implement CSS gradually, testing for browser compatibility as you go.

▶ Decide whether to code to the XHTML standard. If you are starting a new Web site, your best choice is to code to this new standard. If you are working with an existing Web site, decide on the most expedient method for upgrading your existing code to XHTML standards to ensure future compatibility with new tools and browsers.

▶ Use good coding practices by writing standards-based markup that includes a document type and validates correctly.

▶ Choose the type of editing tool needed to create your HTML code. If you choose a WYSIWIG editor, make sure it creates standards-based code. Avoid using word processing programs to create Web pages.

▶ Choose the suite of browsers and operating systems you will use to test your site. Although you will include the latest versions of Firefox, Netscape, and Internet Explorer, consider testing in older versions of each browser as well.

▶ Decide how browser-specific your site will be. In most cases, your goal is to create a site that is widely accessible to multiple browsers. However, if you have a narrow audience or specific requirements, you may want to specify one browser as the primary method for viewing your site.

▶ Resolve to test your work continually as you build your site. Test with multiple browsers at different screen resolutions and at different connection speeds. If you can, view your site on multiple platforms such as Windows, Macintosh, and UNIX.

Key Terms

cache	rendering engine
Cascading Style Sheets (CSS)	screen resolution
deprecated element	semantic markup
Document Type Definition (DTD)	Standard Generalized Markup Language (SGML)
Extensible Hypertext Markup Language (XHTML)	
hypertext	style sheet
Hypertext Markup Language (HTML)	valid code
markup language	well-formed document
metalanguage	World Wide Web Consortium (W3C)

Review Questions

1. HTML is a subset of which markup language?
2. List three characteristics of HTML that make it ideal for the World Wide Web.
3. What are the benefits of viewing source code on the Web?
4. What work does the World Wide Web Consortium perform?
5. What is a deprecated element?
6. What style language allows the separation of style from structure in HTML?
7. What are the advantages of using an external style sheet?
8. What feature distinguishes XML from HTML?
9. What are the two types of style languages designed for use with XML?
10. Explain how XML lends itself to customized data applications.
11. What improvements does XHTML promise over existing HTML?
12. Explain how different browsers affect the display of a Web page.
13. Describe the benefits of semantic markup.
14. Describe some common reasons HTML code might not validate correctly.
15. What is the most common screen resolution?
16. Explain how screen resolution affects the display of a Web page.
17. List four common types of Internet connection technologies.
18. Explain how the browser's caching capability improves download time.
19. Explain the three issues you should consider when designing for multiple operating systems.

Hands-On Projects

1. Visit the World Wide Web Consortium Web site and find the Web-based validator at *http://validator.w3.org*. Using a favorite Web site or your own HTML code, run the validator and view the validation errors. If you are working with your own HTML code, correct the errors in your code until the validator reports no errors.

2. In this project, you edit an existing HTML file to conform to XHTML coding standards.

    a. Copy the **project1-2.htm** file from the Chapter01 folder provided with your Data Files to the Chapter01 folder in your work folder. (Create a Chapter01 folder, if necessary.)

    b. Using a text editor such as Notepad, open **project1-2.htm**. The code looks like the following:

```
<HTML>
    <HEAD>
    <TITLE>Chapter 1 - Getting Started with Wonder Software</TITLE>
    </HEAD>
```

```
<BODY>

<img src="logo.jpg" width=100 height=100 alt="logo image">
<H2>Getting Started with Wonder Software</h2>
<P>In this section, you'll learn how to add a new user to the
Wonder database.
<h3>To add a new user:</H3>
<OL>
<LI>Open the <B>Admin menu</B> and select <B>Users</B>
<LI>Choose the <B>Add User...</B> button.
<LI>Enter the necessary user information.
</OL>
<P>
Note: Make sure to enter a value in all of the user information
fields. If you skip a field, the Wonder database will reject
the record.
<TABLE WIDTH=100%>
<TR ><TD WIDTH=50%><A HREF="toc.htm">Table Of Contents</A>
</TD><TD ALIGN=RIGHT><A HREF="index.htm">Index</A></TD>
</TR></TABLE>
```

   c. The file contains a number of coding errors that does not make it comply with XHTML standards. Edit the file to correct the coding errors. Add comments to the file that explain each change you make. Refer to the "Adopting XHTML Syntax Rules" section of this chapter for help.

   d. Save the file with the same name.

3. Visit the World Wide Web Consortium Web site (*www.w3.org*). Search for the Cascading Style Sheets specification. List and describe 10 style properties that you can affect with a style rule.

4. Download and install the latest versions of the following browsers onto your computer as necessary:

   ▶ Internet Explorer: *www.microsoft.com/windows/ie/*

   ▶ Netscape: *browser.netscape.com/*

   ▶ Firefox: *www.mozilla.com*

Test the browsers. Write a short paper explaining your likes and dislikes about each browser. Use examples whenever possible to support your opinion. Consider the following:

   a. Give each browser a test drive by using it for a few hours of Web browsing.

   b. Choose a mainstream Web site and test it with all three browsers. What differences can you find in the way the page is displayed?

   c. Which browser offers the best user experience? Why?

   d. Is one browser faster than the others?

5. Describe three common mistakes that Web designers make when building a Web site.

6. Test the HTML conversion capabilities of a standard office application.

    a. Use your favorite word processing, spreadsheet, or presentation graphics program that supports conversion to HTML.

    b. Create a document and export it to HTML.

    c. Examine and evaluate the HTML code. Look for nonstandard coding techniques or tricks that the program uses to render content into HTML. Write a detailed description of your findings.

7. Test cross-browser compatibility.

    a. Make sure you have recent versions of at least two different current browsers installed on your computer. (See "Hands-on Project 4" in this chapter if you need to download and install a browser.)

    b. Browse a variety of Web sites. Make sure to view various pages of the sites in the different browsers.

    c. Write a detailed description of how the various sites appear in the browsers you have chosen. Look for text, layout, and graphic inconsistencies.

8. View source code in a browser.

    In the following steps, you view the source code from a live Web page in your browser. Choose the instructions for Internet Explorer 6.0, Internet Explorer 7.0, Firefox 2.0, or Netscape 8.0.

    To view source code in Internet Explorer 6.0:

    ▶ Click **View** on the menu bar, and then click **Source.** Your system's text editor, such as Notepad, SimpleText, or WordPad, opens and displays the page's source code. You then can save the file to your own hard drive and manipulate the code.

    To view source code in Internet Explorer 7.0:

    ▶ Right-click a blank spot in the browser window, and then choose **View Source** on the shortcut menu. Your system's text editor, such as Notepad, SimpleText, or WordPad, opens and displays the page's source code. You then can save the file to your own hard drive and manipulate the code.

    To view source code in Mozilla Firefox 2.0 or Netscape Navigator 8.0:

    ▶ Click **View** on the menu bar, then click **Page Source.** The page's source code opens in another window of Netscape. You can copy and paste text from this window into your own text or HTML editor, and then manipulate and test the code. You cannot edit directly in the Page Source window.

When you copy code from a Web site, remember to respect the author's copyrights on any original material. Although page layouts are not copyrighted, any original text or graphics they contain are the property of the author and should be properly cited.

Individual Case Project

To complete the ongoing Individual Case Project for this book, you must create a complete stand-alone Web site. The site must have 6–10 pages, displaying at least three levels of information. You can choose your own content. For example, you can do a work-related topic, a personal interest site, or a site for your favorite nonprofit organization. The site will be evaluated for cohesiveness, accessibility, compliance with W3C standards, and visual design. At the end of each chapter, you will complete a different section of the project. For Chapter 1, get started by creating a project proposal, using the following outline. As you progress through the chapters of the book, you will complete different facets of the Web site construction, resulting in a complete Web site.

Project Proposal

Create a one- or two-page HTML document stating the basic elements you will include in your Web site. Create this document using your favorite HTML editor or Notepad. At this stage, your proposal is primarily a draft. At the end of Chapter 2, you will have a chance to modify the proposal and supplement the design details.

Include the following items, if applicable:

- ▶ *Site title*—Specify the working title for the site.
- ▶ *Developer*—Identify yourself and anyone else who will work on the site.
- ▶ *Rationale or focus*—Explain the content and goals of the site, such as billboard, customer support, catalog/e-commerce, informational, or resource. Refer to Chapter 3, "Planning the Site," for help on content types.
- ▶ *Main elements outline*—Describe the main features of the site.
- ▶ *Content*—Estimate the number of individual Web pages.
- ▶ *Target audience*—Describe the typical audience for the site.
- ▶ *Design considerations*—List the design goals for the site.
- ▶ *Limiting factors*—Identify the technical or audience factors that could limit the design goals of the site.

Team Case Project

To complete the ongoing Team Case Project for this book, you and your team must create a complete stand-alone Web site. Your team should ideally consist of 3–4 members assigned by your instructor. The site must contain between 16 and 20 pages, displaying at least three levels of information. You will choose your own topic. For example, you can do a work-related topic, a personal interest site, or a site for a fictional organization. The site will be evaluated for cohesiveness, accessibility, compliance with W3C standards, and visual design. At the end of each chapter, you will complete a different section of the project. For Chapter 1, get started by creating a project proposal, using the following outline. As you progress through the remaining chapters of the book, you will complete different facets of the Web site construction, resulting in a complete Web site.

Project Proposal

Collaborate to create a one- or two-page HTML document stating the basic elements you will include in your Web site. Create this document using your favorite HTML editor or Notepad. At this stage, your proposal is primarily a draft. At the end of Chapter 2, you will have a chance to modify the proposal and supplement the design details.

Include the following items, if applicable:

▶ *Site title*—Specify the working title for the site.

▶ *Development roles*—Identify each team member and individual responsibilities for the project.

▶ *Need*—Describe the need the Web site will satisfy. What is the purpose of the site? Is there an interest group whose needs are not satisfied? Is there a target niche you are trying to fill?

▶ *Rationale or focus*—Explain the content and goals of the site such as billboard, customer support, catalog/e-commerce, informational, or resource. Refer to Chapter 3, "Planning the Site," for help on content types.

▶ *Main elements outline*—Describe the main features of the site.

▶ *Content*—Estimate the number of individual Web pages.

▶ *Target audience*—Describe the typical audience for the site.

▶ *Design considerations*—List the design goals for the site.

▶ *Limiting factors*—Identify the technical or audience factors that could limit the design goals of the site.

▶ *Development schedule, milestones, and deliverables*—Using the dates in your class syllabus as a basis, build a development schedule that indicates milestones and deliverables for each team member.

2

Web Site Design Principles

When you complete this chapter, you will be able to:

- Design for the computer medium
- Create a unified site design
- Design for the user
- Design for accessibility
- Design for the screen

This chapter covers the basic design principles that you will apply to your Web page design as you work through this book. By examining a variety of Web sites, you learn to focus on both the user's needs and the requirements of the content you want to deliver, while planning a site that is easy to navigate and quick to download.

The sample Web pages in this chapter come from a wide range of sites. The Web is so far-reaching in content and design that no collection of pages represents what is typical. Most of the samples illustrate good design principles, although some contain design defects as well. In truth, almost every site has one flaw or another, whether it is confusing accessibility, overambitious design, or poor download time. Judge the samples with a critical eye. Look for elements of design that you can transfer to your own work. As you progress through the book, you will practice and apply these principles to your own Web design efforts.

Design for the Computer Medium

Even though an increasingly wide variety of devices support the Web, your primary goal as a Web page designer is to create Web pages for the computer medium. You must consider how the layout, fonts, and colors will appear on the screen. As an HTML author, you must consider the nonlinear nature of hypertext, weaving the appropriate links and associations into the information. Give users the options to follow the information path they desire by providing appropriate links to related topics. Make them feel comfortable at your site by letting them know where they are and where they can go.

Craft the Look and Feel

The interface that the user must navigate is often called the **look and feel** of a Web site. Users look and feel when they explore the information design of your site. They read text, make associations with links, view graphics, and, depending on the freedom of your design, create their own path through your information. The look and feel is both the way your Web site works and the personality it conveys to the user. Not only should you plan for a deliberate look and feel, but as mentioned in Chapter 1, you must test your design against the variable nature of the Web. You want to ensure that the greatest number of users can navigate your site successfully.

Make Your Design Portable

To be successful, your Web site design must be portable and accessible by users who have different browsers, operating systems, and computer platforms. Many designers make the mistake of testing in only one environment, assuming that their pages look the same to all of their users. No matter how much Web design experience you gain, always remember to test in different environments, even when you feel confident of your results. For example, Figures 2-1 and 2-2 show the same page displayed in Netscape Navigator 8.1 and Netscape Navigator 4.75. The page is created with Cascading Style Sheets (CSS) code that the older version of Netscape cannot interpret. Notice that the page contains a link informing users that they must use an updated browser to view the site. As you can see by comparing the two figures, Netscape 4.75 has significant problems with CSS that render the page unreadable. Although the Netscape 4.x software has almost disappeared from use, it still provides a good example of the problems that can occur when your designs are viewed in different browsers.

Figure 2-1

Netscape 8.1 correctly displays the CSS styles

Figure 2-2

Netscape 4.75 has significant problems with CSS

You can avoid problems such as these by coding to standards and testing for compatibility. Viewing your pages in the browsers your users are likely to have, testing on the popular operating systems, and checking the site on more than one computer platform ensure that your site is accessible to the greatest number of users. Consider analyzing your audience and building a profile of your average user. You will read more about analyzing your audience in Chapter 3.

Design for Low Bandwidth

Plan your pages so that they are accessible at a variety of connection speeds. If your pages download slowly because they contain large, detailed graphics or complicated animations, your users will leave before they ever see your content. The average user clicks away from a site if the page does not download in 10–20 seconds. As you learned in Chapter 1, a greater number of your users have consistent, high-speed connections to the Web, but many users still only have access with lower-bandwidth connections. It is still a good practice to consider these users when you design the look and feel of your site.

The WebMD Web site's main page (*www.webmd.com*), illustrated in Figure 2-3, contains 49 separate images, totaling 205 KB in file size. Although most of these images average only 1 or 2 KB each, the sheer number of images that must be sent to the user's computer means a lengthy download time, especially for first-time visitors.

Figure 2-3

The WebMD site's main page is image intensive

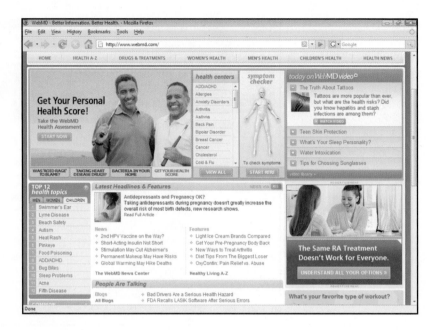

Plan for Easy Access to Your Information

Your information design is the single most important factor in determining the success of your site. It determines how easily users can access your Web content. The goal is to organize your content and present it as a meaningful, navigable set of information. Your navigation options should present a variety of choices to users without detracting from their quests for information.

A visitor to your site may choose to browse randomly or look for specific information. Often users arrive at a page looking for data that is low in the hierarchy of information. Sometimes users arrive at your site seeking a specific piece of information, such as a telephone number or an order form. Anticipate and plan for the actions and paths that users are likely to choose when they traverse your site. Provide direct links to the areas of your site that you feel are most in-demand. Remember that users want to get to your site, retrieve their desired information, and move on.

Plan for Clear Presentation of Your Information

The screen's low resolution makes the computer monitor a poor reading medium. The light source coming from behind the text tires the user's eye. Environmental factors such as glare or physical distance from the screen affect the user as well. To counter this, design your information so it is easier to read. Many Web sites fail this criterion by using too many fonts, colors, and lengthy passages of text. Break text into reasonable segments that make for easier on-screen reading. Think about providing contrasting colors that are easy on the eye, such as dark colors against a light or white background.

Keep in mind that readers have different habits when reading online. Compared to how they read printed text, online visitors scan more and read less, skimming long pages quickly as they scroll through the text. Include plenty of headings so users can find content quickly. Control the width of your text to provide complete, easy-to-read columns. Keep the "seven (plus or minus two)" rule of information design in mind; that is, users cannot comprehend more than seven (plus or minus two) steps or segments of information at one time. For example, a well-written procedure would contain no more than nine steps. Rather than presenting long scrolling pages, break information into smaller chunks and link them with hypertext.

The World Travel Guide Web site (*www.worldtravelguide.net*) offers both clear presentation and easy access to information, as shown in Figure 2-4. The navigation links on the left side of the page are logically organized and offer clear descriptions of their destinations. A navigation "breadcrumb" shows users where they are in the site. (On a Web page, a **breadcrumb** is one or more links near the top of the page that show the current page and any pages above it in the site hierarchy.) A search text box is located at the top of the page for quick and easy access. The text used throughout the site is legible and easy to read online. Groups of featured content links on the page have meaningful headings. Plenty of active white space between the page elements adds to the readability of the page. (You'll learn more about white space later in this chapter.)

Figure 2-4

Clear presentation and easy access

Breadcrumb shows users where they are in the site

Text is legible, designed for online reading

Search feature

Navigation links are clear, easy to read

Active white space separates page elements

Create a Unified Site Design

When designing your site, plan the unifying themes and structure that will hold the pages together. Your choices of colors, fonts, graphics, and page layout should communicate a visual theme to users that orients them to your site's content. The theme should reflect the impression that you or your organization want to convey.

For example, Figure 2-5 shows the main page of the Centers for Disease Control Web site (*www.cdc.gov*). This mainly text-filled page has an open, informational feel. The content is primarily news and information, with links clearly presented. Navigation choices are abundant and separated by meaningful headings. The use of subdued colors, legible fonts, and structured, linear columns emphasize the news and informational theme.

Figure 2-5

Centers for Disease
Control main page

The CDC also maintains a Web site for children (*www.bam.gov*), as illustrated in Figure 2-6.

While the site for adults communicates a serious impression, the site for children combines bright colors, an open, friendly font, a dynamic structure, and eye-catching graphics to present a livelier, more playful theme.

Figure 2-6

Centers for Disease
Control children's page

When you design a site, you must consider more than each individual page. For a well-integrated, unified site, plan smooth transitions, use a grid to provide visual structure, and use active white space. Each of these techniques is explained in the following sections.

Plan Smooth Transitions

Plan to create a unified look among the sections and pages of your site. Reinforce the identifying elements of the site and create smooth transitions from one page to another by repeating colors and fonts and by using a page layout that allows hierarchical levels. Avoid random, jarring changes in your format, unless this is the effect you want to achieve. Consistency creates smooth transitions from one page to the next, reassures viewers that they are traveling within the boundaries of your site, and helps them find information.

Provide grounding for the user by placing navigation elements in the same position on each page. Users orient themselves quickly to your navigation structure. Use the same navigation graphics throughout the site to provide consistency and avoid the need to download a wide variety of graphics.

Think of users turning the pages of a periodical when they browse from Web page to Web page. Although each page should be a complete entity, it also is a part of the whole site. The overall design of a page at any information level should reflect the identity of the site as a whole. For example, Figure 2-7 and Figure 2-8 show the main page and a secondary-level page from the Philadelphia Zoo Web site (*www.philadelphiazoo.org*).

Because these pages share the same color scheme, page banner, and identifying graphics, the Web site offers a smooth transition from the main page to the secondary page and a unified look and feel.

Figure 2-7

Philadelphia Zoo Web site main page

Figure 2-8

Philadelphia Zoo Web site secondary page

Use a Grid to Provide Visual Structure

The structure of a Web page is imposed by the grid or page template you choose for your page design. The **grid** is a conceptual layout device that organizes the page into columns and rows. You can impose a grid to provide visual consistency throughout your site. You can use the grid to enforce structure, but you also can break out of the grid to provide variety and highlight important information.

Web pages that respect the grid and consistently align text and graphic elements have a more polished look than pages that have scattered alignments. The World Health Organization Web site's main page (*www.who.int*) in Figure 2-9 has a strong four-column grid. All of the text and graphic elements on the page align within the grid to create an orderly layout.

Figure 2-9

Grid provides visual structure

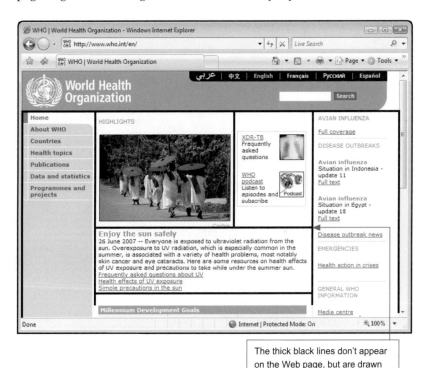

The thick black lines don't appear on the Web page, but are drawn on the figure to emphasize the grid

CHAPTER 2

Most current Web sites use tables in one form or another to give their pages structure and consistency. With table borders turned off, the user cannot tell that the layout is held together by a table; they simply see a coherent, well-structured page. The reliance on tables as a design tool will eventually wane as more users adopt newer browsers that support CSS, which allows columnar positioning without tables. You will read more about CSS positioning in Chapter 10.

Use Active White Space

White spaces are the blank areas of a page, regardless of the color you choose to give them. Use white space deliberately in your design, rather than as an afterthought. Good use of white space guides the reader and defines the areas of your page. White space that is used deliberately is called **active white space** and is an integral part of your design that structures and separates content. Sometimes the strongest part of a design is the active white space. **Passive white space** includes the blank areas that border the screen or are the result of mismatched shapes. Figure 2-10 illustrates active versus passive white space.

Figure 2-10

Areas of active and passive white space

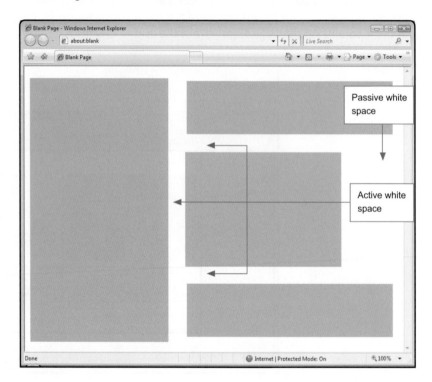

Content presentation can become confused when designers do not use enough active white space to separate and define content. A lack of active white space creates the impression that a page contains too much information and that it will be difficult to find the piece of information you want. The Rough Guides Web site page (*www.roughguides.com*) in Figure 2-11 shows effective use of active white space, making the content very easy to read. Plenty of active white space reduces clutter and clarifies the organization of your ideas.

Figure 2-11

Active white space
enhances legibility

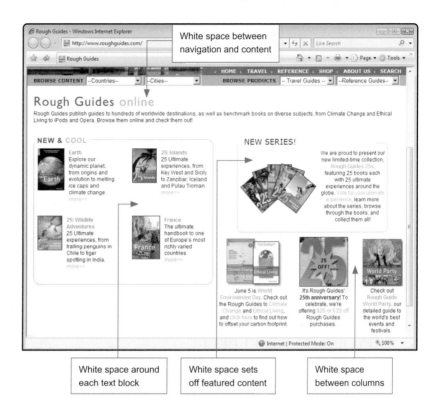

Design for the User

Keep your design efforts centered solely on your user. Knowledge of your audience can help you answer almost all design questions—if it serves the audience, keep it; if it is potentially distracting or annoying, eliminate it. Find out what users expect from your site. If you can, survey them with an online form. Create a profile of your average user by compiling responses to basic questions. What do users want when they get to your site? Are they trying to find customer support and troubleshooting help, or do they want to buy something? Do they want to read articles or search for information? Once you know what your users want from your site, you can evaluate how the design reflects the audience's profile and needs. Consider the main page for Google (*www.google.com*), currently the Web's most popular search engine. The site's main page, shown in Figure 2-12, has no ads, very few links, and is designed for only one purpose—letting users quickly enter a search term.

Compare the main pages from the following sites and consider their target audiences. The E! online Web site (*www.eonline.com*), shown in Figure 2-13, is an entertainment news site. The main page contains competing content that draws the user's eye, such as Flash animations, a Java text scroll, bright colors, and familiar shapes. The overall effect is decidedly similar to television—familiar territory for E! online's audience.

Figure 2-12

Google's simple, task-oriented design

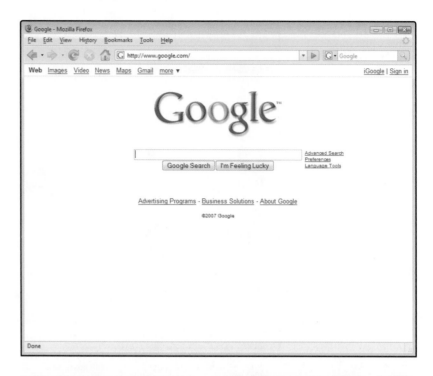

Figure 2-13

A hectic, but appropriate design for E! online's audience

In contrast, the Web site for the *Atlantic Monthly* (*www.theatlantic.com*) in Figure 2-14 projects a strong periodical-like image. The main page components are textual. Even though the page has a lot of content, it is well organized with clear headings and readable text in well-defined columns. The design uses just enough active white space to clearly separate each element on the page. The overall effect evokes the look of a printed page while using the color, linking, and design flexibility that the Web offers.

Figure 2-14

A paper-based design for the *Atlantic*'s audience

These two examples demonstrate how the design suits the audience's visual expectations—the look of the site. However, you also should consider the ways in which users interact with the content—the feel of the site.

Design for Interaction

Think about how the user wants to interact with the information on your Web page. Design for your content type, and decide whether the user is likely to read or scan your pages.

For example, suppose your page is a collection of links, such as a main page or section page. Users want to interact with these types of pages by scanning the content, scrolling if necessary, pointing to graphics to see if they are hyperlinked, and clicking linked text. Design for this type of user interaction by using meaningful column headings, linked text, and short descriptions. Organize links into related topic groups and separate groupings with white space, graphics, or background color.

Suppose the page is an article that contains large blocks of text. Your user is accustomed to interacting with pages of text by scrolling and possibly clicking hyperlinked words of interest. The links may be in the body of the article or contained in a sidebar. Design your pages for this text-oriented content by keeping paragraphs short for online consumption. Make reading easier by using a text column that is narrower than the width of the screen. Keep your text legible by providing enough contrast between foreground and background colors. Provide links that allow the user to jump quickly to related content.

Two screens from the National Public Radio News Web site (*www.npr.org*) illustrate the difference between designing for reading and designing for scanning. Figure 2-15 shows a page designed for scanning. There are three columns of content, presenting a variety of information. Users can look through a variety of links to find a topic of interest, read article abstracts, or choose one of the featured main sections.

Figure 2-15

Page designed for scanning

Once users choose a link, they jump to a page designed for reading, as illustrated in Figure 2-16, which shows a secondary page from the Web site. This page also has a three-column layout, but a more generous middle column that contains main article text. Navigation links along the left side provide related information. Featured main sections are provided in the banner at the top of the page.

Figure 2-16

Page designed for reading

Design for Location

It is difficult to predict the user's exact viewing path. There is, however, general agreement on the relative areas of screen importance. Figure 2-17 depicts the sections of screen "real estate" ranked in order of importance.

Figure 2-17

Relative areas of screen importance

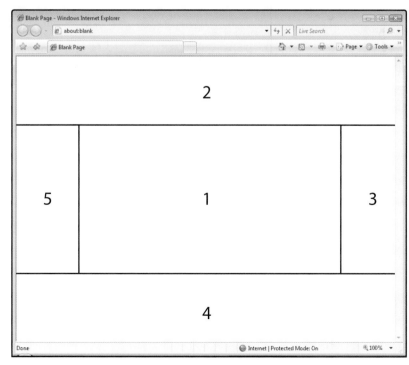

During page design, rank the information you want to display, and then position the most important information in the middle of the window, the next most important across the top, and so on, with the least important or static information in the left margin. For example, Figure 2-18 shows the BBC News main page (*http://news.bbc.co.uk*) with the areas of importance overlaying the content.

Figure 2-18

Areas of screen importance applied to the BBC News Web site

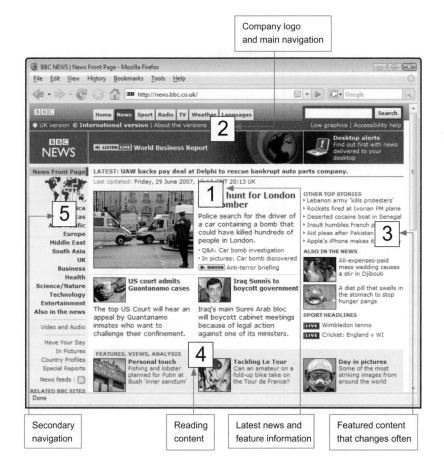

Guide the User's Eye

The user can traverse a page in a variety of ways. Human engineering studies show a wide range of results when tracking a user's eye movements. As you plan your design to guide the user's eye, consider the following two examples of online reading habits.

As a function of normal, paper-based reading habits, the user's eye moves from left to right and back again, as in Figure 2-19.

Figure 2-19

Paper-based reading pattern

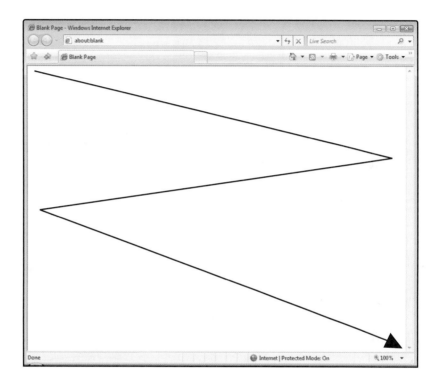

Figure 2-20 shows this viewing pattern applied to the *Atlantic Monthly* Web site. This page's columnar design encourages a paper-based reading pattern, enforcing the appropriate periodical feel for the content.

In contrast, when viewing landscape-based displays, such as televisions, the user may scan information following a clockwise pattern, as shown in Figure 2-21.

Figure 2-20

Paper-based reading pattern applied to *theatlantic.com* Web page

Figure 2-21

Screen-based viewing pattern

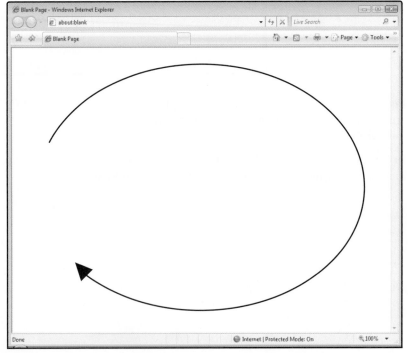

Figure 2-22 shows this viewing style overlaying the United Nations Web site (*www.un.org*). As the user's eyes sweep over the page, they can take in most of the main content areas. This page encourages a screen-based reading pattern.

Figure 2-22

Screen-based reading pattern applied to the UN Web site

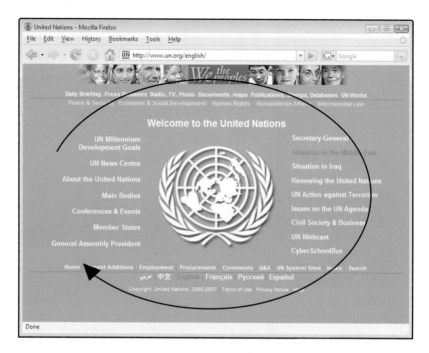

Knowing these common user habits can help you decide where to focus the user's attention by object placement, text weight, and color use. Think about your grid structure and how you want to break out of it to attract attention. Use text weight and size to communicate relative importance of information. Divide content into sections with rules or active white space. Use shapes and color to reinforce location or topic. Get to know your users, and consider the two sample viewing methods, paper-based and screen-based, as you experiment with content placement.

Keep a Flat Hierarchy

Do not make users navigate through too many layers of your Web site to find the information they want. Structuring your Web site to include section- or topic-level navigation pages allows users to find their desired paths quickly. Try to follow the "three clicks rule"; that is, don't make your users click more than three times to get to the content they desire. Provide prominent navigation cues that enable quick access. For example, a standard navigation bar consistently placed on every page reassures users that they will not get lost, and lets them move through the site with flexibility.

Consider providing a site map that graphically displays the organization of your Web site. Figure 2-23 shows a site map from Google (*www.google.com*). This graphical view of the Web site shows all the individual pages and the sections in which they reside. Clear headings organize the content. Users can click to go directly to a page or orient themselves to the site's structure.

Figure 2-23

Google's site map

Use the Power of Hypertext Linking

Unlike paper-based authors, as a hypertext author you have the luxury of adding clickable text and images where necessary to guide users through your information. This powerful ability comes with a measure of responsibility. You make the decisions that determine how users move through your site and process information. Readers browsing through magazines can flip to any page in any order they desire. You can replicate this nonlinear reading method on your Web site with links that let users move from page to page or section to section. With thoughtful hypertext writing, you can engage readers in a whole new way.

Many sites have separate columns of links and topics, but not enough sites provide links within the text. This is a powerful hypertext feature that is not used often enough. Weave links into your prose to offer a variety of paths. Avoid using the meaningless phrase "Click Here" as the hypertext link. Instead provide a helpful textual clue to the destination of the link.

Figure 2-24 shows a page from the Wikipedia Web site (*www.wikipedia.org*). Note how the hypertext links are worked directly into the text. When users click a link, they move to another page of information; from that page they can either go back or move to another page of information, and so on. The abundant hypertext links allow users to create a view of the site's information that is uniquely their own.

Provide plenty of links to let the user get around quickly. Use links to let the user return to the navigation section of your page, to a site map, or to the main page. Do not make the user scroll through lengthy columns. Provide links that let users jump down the page, that allow users to jump back to the top of the page, or that show a clear way back to higher levels of your content.

Provide a hypertext table of contents, as in Figure 2-25, that lets users pick the exact topic they want to view.

Figure 2-24
Good use of textual links

Figure 2-25
Hypertext table of
contents shows all
available topics, and
tracks the user's viewed
pages

The benefit of a hypertext table of contents is the color-coding that shows users which pages they have visited. By default, links are blue when new; they change to purple after they have been visited. A hypertext table of contents instantly shows users where they have been and where they have yet to go.

Glossaries and other densely packed documents become much easier to navigate with the addition of hypertext. Figure 2-26 shows a hypertext glossary that provides plenty of navigation choices for the user.

Figure 2-26

Hypertext glossary with plenty of navigation choices

How Much Content Is Enough?

You can crowd only so much information onto any one Web page. Be conscious of the cognitive load of the user who often thinks that Web pages hold too much information. *Sports Illustrated*'s Web site (*www.si.com*) in Figure 2-27 offers a dizzying array of content choices.

Figure 2-27

A dizzying array of choices

Resist the temptation to overload users with too much information. Provide enough navigation clues to let them find the content they want. Separate content into smaller portions, and use hypertext linking to divide content between pages.

Design for Accessibility

Any large audience for a Web site includes users who want to access your content despite certain physical challenges. Designing for accessibility means developing Web pages that remain accessible despite any physical, sensory, and cognitive disabilities, work constraints, or technological barriers on the part of the user. As Tim Berners-Lee said, "The power of the Web is in its universality. Access by everyone, regardless of disability, is an essential aspect." Most mainstream Web sites are so heavily image- and media-intensive that they are not suitable for adaptive devices such as screen readers, voice browsers, and Braille translators.

Building more accessible content does not mean that you have to forgo more challenging Web designs. Many of the guidelines necessary for developing accessible content naturally lend themselves to creating good design. Two current sets of guidelines are available to Web designers. The W3C's Web Accessibility Initiative publishes the Web Content Accessibility Guidelines (WCAG), and will soon release a second version. The U.S. government has its own set of guidelines, as part of the Rehabilitation Act Amendments of 1998, called Section 508. The law requires federal agencies to provide information technology that is accessible both to federal employees and citizens who have disabilities. Both sets of guidelines help you create more accessible Web content, so which should you use? If you are designing a Web site for the federal government, you must follow the 508 guidelines, but for general public Web sites the W3C guidelines will suffice. Because WCAG 1.0 is already well documented on the Web and in a variety of other sources, the next section examines the WCAG 2.0 guidelines.

NOTE

To find out more about the W3C accessibility initiative, go to *www.w3.org/WAI/*. The site includes many guidelines and standards to build accessible Web content, and explains more about the release of WCAG 2.0. You can learn more about the adaptive devices and assistive technologies for accessible browsing at *www.w3.org/ WAI/References/Browsing*. Finally, you can read the Section 508 guidelines at *www.section508.gov/*.

WCAG 2.0 Guidelines

WCAG 2.0 consists of four main guidelines, which state that Web content must be:

- *Perceivable*—Information and user interface components must be perceivable by users.
- *Operable*—User interface components must be operable by users.
- *Understandable*—Information about the user interface and its operation must be understandable by users.
- *Robust*—Content must be robust enough to be interpreted reliably by a wide variety of user agents, including assistive technologies.

A number of tips, summarized in the following sections, help define the goal of each guideline.

NOTE

To find a quick reference guide to the new WCAG 2.0, see *www.w3.org/WAI/ WCAG20/quickref.*

Perceivable Content

WCAG 2.0 includes the following tips to help you provide perceivable content in your Web pages.

Provide text alternatives for any non-text content so that it can be changed into other forms people need, such as large print, Braille, speech, symbols, or simpler language.

This guideline ensures that all non-text content is available as electronic text. For example, use the alt attribute to describe the function of each visual element. You will learn about this in Chapter 8.

Provide synchronized alternatives for multimedia.

This guideline ensures that users can access multimedia content. For example, provide captioning and transcripts of audio and descriptions of video as alternatives to the multimedia content.

Create content that can be presented in different ways (for example, spoken aloud, simpler layout, and so on) without losing information or structure.

This guideline ensures that information is available in a form that all users can perceive. For example, the best way to meet this guideline is to build well-structured content with separate presentation information (as you learned in Chapter 1). This practice ensures that the structure and relationship of the content does not change, no matter what assistive device or software the user chooses.

Make it easier for people with disabilities to see and hear content, including separating foreground from background.

This guideline ensures that the default presentation is as usable as possible to people with disabilities, making it easier for users to separate foreground information from the background. This basic tenet of Web design, often ignored, is to make sure that information presented on top of a background contrasts sufficiently with the background. You will learn more about this principle in Chapter 8. This guideline also applies to spoken text, so that background sounds do not interfere with understanding the spoken text.

Operable Content

WCAG 2.0 includes the following tips to help you provide operable content in your Web pages.

Make all functionality available from a keyboard.

You should ensure that all actions that can be performed with a mouse or other input device can also be performed with a keyboard.

Provide users who have disabilities enough time to read and use content.

Many users with disabilities take longer to complete tasks than the average user. For example, some text scrolls animate text across the page faster than users with disabilities can read the text. This guideline ensures that these users can complete tasks within their comfort zone.

Do not create content that is known to cause seizures.

Some users with seizure disorders can have a seizure triggered by flashing visual content. The purpose of this guideline is to avoid content that flashes or blinks quickly enough to cause a seizure—for example, the deprecated <blink> element that causes text to flash on and off.

Provide ways to help users with disabilities navigate, find content, and determine where they are.

This guideline ensures that users can find the content they need and keep track of their location, as you read previously in "Plan for Clear Presentation of Your Information" in this chapter. This is a sound and essential design principle when planning for the general public as well as for users who have disabilities.

Understandable Content

WCAG 2.0 includes the following tips to help you provide understandable content in your Web pages.

Make text content readable and understandable.

This guideline ensures the greatest legibility and readability of text. Many characteristics of this guideline are simple, sound design techniques that you will read about in Chapter 7. These techniques include limiting the line length of text, providing appropriate white space, and avoiding large chunks of italic text.

Make Web pages appear and operate in predictable ways.

The purpose of this guideline is to help users with disabilities by presenting content and navigation options in a predictable order from Web page to Web page, as you learned in the "Create a Unified Site Design" section earlier in this chapter. Users who employ screen magnifiers see only part of the screen at any point in time. A consistent page layout makes it easier for them to find navigation bars and other repeated components. Placing page elements in the same relative order within a Web site allows users with reading disabilities to focus on the desired area of the screen, rather than spending additional time looking for what they want.

Help users avoid and correct mistakes that do occur.

This guideline ensures that users can detect when they have made an error—for example, when entering data into a form. Typical error indicators, such as color-coded text or an icon, may not be enough to alert the user. Additional indicators such as sound or highlighted text can aid the user in identifying incorrect entries.

Robust Content

WCAG 2.0 includes the following tips to help you provide robust content in your Web pages.

Maximize compatibility with current and future user agents, including assistive technologies.

This guideline ensures compatibility with current and future browsers, especially assistive technology browsers. To meet this guideline, use standards-compliant markup and validated code, as described in Chapter 1. Present content in standard ways that assistive technology software can recognize and with which it can interact.

Consider providing alternate methods of content presentation to accommodate a variety of users. For users with assistance devices such as screen readers, a text-only alternative is desirable. For example, the BBC News Web site (*http://news.bbc.co.uk*), shown previously in Figure 2-18, offers a text-only alternative to its standard graphics-based Web site, as shown in Figure 2-28.

Figure 2-28

BBC's alternate low-graphics version

NOTE

You can verify that physically challenged people can access your Web pages easily by using WebXACT Watchfire at *http://webxact.watchfire.com/*. This Web-based tool checks your pages by applying the W3C's Web Contents Accessibility Guidelines to your code and recording the number and type of incompatibility problems it finds. Watchfire looks for elements such as consistent use of alt attributes, appropriate color usage, compatibility with screen readers, and ease of navigation.

Design for the Screen

The computer monitor, the destination for your Web pages, is very different from print-based media. You must take the following differences into account when planning your Web site:

- Consider the shape of a computer screen. Although most paper-based media are portrait oriented, the computer screen is landscape oriented—that is, wider than it is tall. Your page design must reflect the space where it is displayed and read.

- While a piece of paper reflects light, a computer screen has light passing through it from behind. This affects your choices of colors and contrasts. Design pages that provide enough contrast for the user to read, but not so much that the colors distract from the content. Avoid light text on a light background and dark text on dark backgrounds.

- Computer screens use a much lower resolution than the printed page. Graphics and text that look fine on a laser printer at 600 dots per inch (dpi) are coarse and grainy at 72 dpi, the typical resolution for a computer monitor. Because of the screen graininess, italic text is especially hard to read in paragraph format. Restrict its use for special emphasis, as in Figure 2-29, which shows a page from the Ohio Historical Society (*www.ohiohistory.org*).

Figure 2-29

Italic text is hard to read online

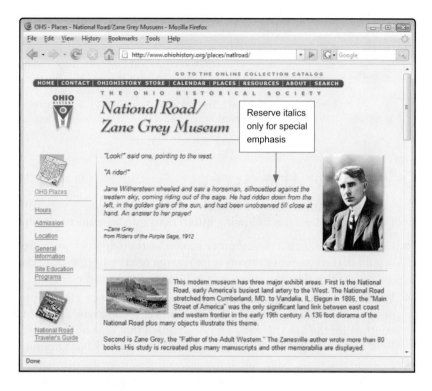

Reformat Content for Online Presentation

Although tempting, it often is a poor choice to take documents that are formatted for print and post them online without considering the destination medium. In most cases, a document that is perfectly legible on paper is hard to negotiate online. The text length, font, and content length do not transfer successfully to the computer screen. Figures 2-30 and 2-31 show the same section of text from Sir Arthur Conan Doyle's *The Red-Headed League.* Figure 2-30 is formatted as if it were a page from a book. The text is dense and fills the screen in large blocks, with no margins to relieve the reader's eye. The Times Roman font, designed for print, is hard to read online.

In contrast, Figure 2-31, from the Sir Conan Doyle Web site, *http://sirconandoyle.com*, shows text that has been designed for online display. The text width is short and easy to read without horizontal scrolling. The font is designed for online reading. The white space on the left side creates a text column that enforces the vertical flow of the page. The differences between these two pages show that text must be prepared thoughtfully for online display.

Figure 2-30

Content formatted for paper

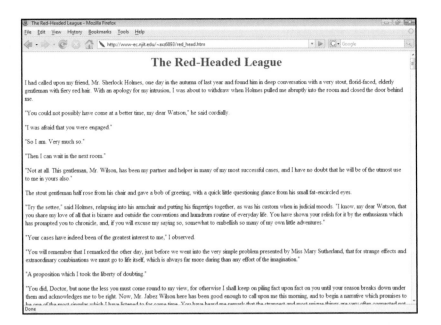

Figure 2-31

Content formatted for the Web

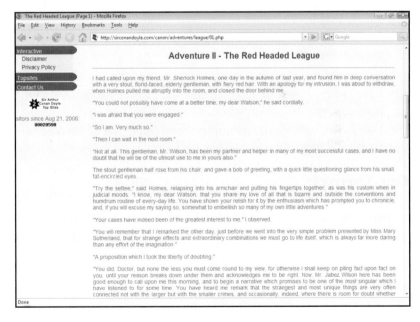

Chapter Summary

Web sites have a wide variety of looks. It is easy to see why so many Web designers get caught up in the medium and forget their message. The lure of technology makes it easy to overlook that you are still trying to communicate with words and pictures, just as humans have for centuries. Adapting those elements to online display for effective communication is the challenge.

Plan a site that stands out and delivers its message. If you stick with the principles you learned in this chapter, you can present information that is both accessible and engaging.

▶ Design specifically for the computer medium, considering how the page layout, fonts, and colors you use appear on the screen.

▶ Craft an appropriate look and feel, and stick with it throughout your site. Test and revise your interface by paying close attention to the demands of online display.

▶ Make your design portable by testing it in a variety of browsers, operating systems, and computing platforms, and use as low a bandwidth as possible.

▶ Plan for easy access to your information. Provide logical navigation tools, and do not make users click through more than two or three pages before they reach the information they are seeking.

▶ Design a unified look for your site. Strive for smooth transitions from one page to the next. Create templates for your grid structure and apply them consistently.

▶ Use active white space as an integral part of your design. Use text, color, and object placement to guide the user's eye.

▶ Know your audience and design pages that suit their needs, interests, and viewing preferences.

▶ Leverage the power of hypertext linking. Provide enough links for users to create their own paths through your information.

▶ Design your text for online display, considering the differences between formatting for the screen and formatting for the printed page.

Key Terms

active white space	look and feel
breadcrumb	passive white space
grid	

Review Questions

1. What is another name for the interface the user must navigate in a Web site?
2. What is a common mistake Web designers make when testing their sites?
3. What is a prime reason users may leave a Web site?
4. What is the single most important factor in determining the success of a Web site?
5. What important factor degrades the legibility of your information?

6. Name three ways to create a unified look for your site.

7. How does a grid layout enhance Web design?

8. What are two coding methods to create a visual grid?

9. Explain active versus passive white space.

10. List three ways to create a smooth transition between pages of a Web site.

11. List two benefits of consistently placing navigation tools.

12. Describe the difference between reading and scanning a page.

13. Name three ways to focus a user's attention.

14. Describe why using "Click Here" as link text is ineffective.

15. Describe the benefits of textual links.

16. Describe the benefits of a hypertext table of contents.

17. Why is the alt attribute so important to navigation?

18. Name three differences between paper-based and screen-based design.

19. Describe a good strategy to format text for online display.

Hands-On Projects

1. Browse the Web for examples of good Web design.

    a. Using a screen-capture program, capture Web pages that show two levels of information from the Web site. For example, capture the main page of a Web site and a secondary page.

    b. Use screen callouts to indicate the unifying characteristics of the pages, such as shared colors, fonts, graphics, and page layout. (A callout is an arrow or line that connects to explanatory text. Many figures in this book have callouts, including Figure 2-1.)

    c. Indicate the areas of active white space and passive white space.

    d. Describe whether the design of the site is appropriate for the content.

2. Browse the Web for examples of poor Web design.

    a. Using a screen-capture program, capture Web pages that show two levels of information from the Web site. For example, capture the main page of a Web site and a secondary page.

    b. Indicate with screen callouts the jarring or distracting inconsistencies of the site, such as abrupt changes in any design elements, including theme and layout.

    c. List detailed recommendations for improving the site design.

3. Write a short essay critiquing a Web site's design. Describe the structural layout of the site and determine whether information is presented clearly and is easily accessible.

4. Browse the Web for sites that use unique navigation methods. Write a short essay describing why the method is or is not successful.

5. Find a Web site that you think needs improvements in its design.

a. Print two pages from the site.

b. Make copies of the originals, and set the originals aside.

c. Using scissors, cut out the main elements of each page. Rearrange the elements and paste them in a design you believe improves the site.

d. Compare and contrast the original with your improved design.

Individual Case Project

Visualize the page design for your site by sketching a number of page layouts for different information levels of the site. For example, sketch the main page, a secondary page, and a content page. You do not have to be concerned with the exact look of the elements, but be prepared to indicate the main components of the pages, such as headings, navigation cues, link sets, text areas, and so on.

Start to organize your site. Create a visual diagram that indicates the main page, section pages, content pages, and so on. Indicate the links between the pages. Indicate whether you will provide alternate navigation choices such as a table of contents and site map.

Team Case Project

Work individually to create your view of the page designs for your site. Sketch a number of page layouts for different information levels of the site. For example, sketch the main page, a secondary page, and a content page. You do not have to be concerned with the exact look of the elements, but be prepared to indicate the main components of the pages, such as headings, navigation cues, link sets, text areas, and so on.

Next, meet and work as a team to create the team's page layouts by combining the best ideas from the individual page designs. Organize your site. Create visual diagrams that indicate the main page, section pages, content pages, and so on. Indicate the links between the pages. Indicate whether you will provide alternate navigation choices such as a table of contents and site map.

3

Planning the Site

When you complete this chapter, you will be able to:

- Create a site specification
- Identify the content goal
- Analyze your audience
- Build a Web site development team
- Create conventions for filenames and URLs
- Set a directory structure
- Create a site storyboard
- Publish your Web site
- Test your Web site
- Refine and update your content
- Attract notice to your Web site

A good Web site design requires a detailed initial planning phase. Before starting to code your site, pick up a pencil and paper and sketch out your site design. Creating the stylistic conventions and conceptual structure of your site beforehand saves time during development. Whether you are creating a single personal Web site or working on a professional Web development team, you save time and improve quality by thoroughly planning the site before you start developing it. This chapter walks you through planning and building a framework for your site, resulting in less recoding when you actually sit down at the computer.

Create a Site Specification

What are your objectives for building a Web site? You may want to increase communication among employees, gain visibility, provide a service, attract new customers, or simply show the world you can code HTML. Because properly maintained Web sites take a lot of work, make sure you have valid and achievable goals for your site.

Start your planning by creating a **site specification**; this is the design document for your site. If you completed the Hands-on Projects and Case Project at the end of Chapter 1, you created a basic draft of a project proposal. You can use some of that information in your site specification. After you read this chapter, you will be able to answer a number of additional questions about your site. You can return to the site specification as you build your site to help maintain your focus.

If you are providing Web site design to a client, the site specification is the first document the client sees that establishes the basic site design. You can visit the Online Companion Web site for this book to look at some sample site specification documents. Answer the following questions in your site specification:

- Why are you building the Web site? Write a two- or three-paragraph mission statement that briefly states the site's goals. What do you or your company or organization hope to gain from creating and maintaining a Web site?

- How will you judge the success of the site? What are the measuring factors you can use to assess the effectiveness of the site?

- Who is the target audience? What are some common characteristics? How can you find out more about your target audience?

- What are the limiting technical factors affecting your site?

- What is the budget? Is there a schedule or target delivery date?

Identify the Content Goal

Consider carefully what type of site you are building. What you want the Web site to accomplish and what your users want from your site may differ. For example, site designers are often concerned with the visual aspects of a Web site, such as the quality of the graphics and the use of animation. Your users probably care more about how quickly they can find information. Adopt your user's perspective. Think about the type of content you are presenting and look to the Web for examples of how best to present it. The following types of Web sites demonstrate ways to focus your content.

- *Billboard*—These sites establish a Web presence for a business or commercial venture. In many cases they are informational and offer no true Web-based content, acting as an online brochure rather than offering Web-based interaction. Many businesses build this type of site first and then slowly add functions such as online ordering and product demonstrations as they become more comfortable with the medium.

- *Publishing*—Most major newspapers and periodicals now publish both to print media and to the Web. These Web sites are some of the most ambitious in breadth and depth of content, often containing multiple levels of information with many page templates. Many publishing sites use special software to create Web pages, drawing content from the same databases that produce their paper-based versions. This allows their authors to write the article once, but have it published to multiple destinations, such as the daily newspaper and the Web site.

- *Portal*—Portals act as gateways to the Web and offer an array of services including searching, e-mail, shopping, news, and organized links to Web resources. Many of the major search engines have been converted into portals to attract more users. These sites are often heavy with advertising content, which is their main source of revenue.

- *Special interest, public interest, and nonprofit organization*—These sites include news and current information for volunteers, devotees, novices, a specific audience, or the general public. Public-service Web sites contain links, information, downloadable files, addresses, and telephone numbers that can help you solve a problem or find more resources. Nonprofit organizations can state their manifestoes, seek volunteers, and foster grassroots virtual communities.

- *Blog*—Short for "Weblog," a blog is a personal Web page that reflects the personality and interests of the author. No matter what your interest, a community of *bloggers* (blog authors) on the Web is devoted to it. Blog Web design varies greatly, reflecting the skills (or lack thereof) of the author. Take the time to visit some blogs and discover the wide range of expression and design. You can easily find blogs by using a blog directory, such as *www.blogcatalog.com* or *www.blogarama.com.*

- *Virtual gallery*—The Web is a great place to show off samples of all types of art and design. Photographers and artists can display samples of their work; musicians can post audio files of their songs; writers can offer sections of text or complete manuscripts. However, keep in mind that any copyrighted material you display on a Web site can be downloaded to a user's machine without your permission. As a solution to this problem, software companies such as Digimarc (*www.digimarc.com*) offer digital watermarking technology that lets artists embed digital copyright information in their electronic files as a deterrent to piracy of proprietary content. This information cannot be seen or altered by the user.

- *E-commerce, catalog, and online shopping*—The Web has become a viable shopping medium that continues to expand as more users improve their Internet access and learn to trust the security of online commerce. Web commerce already has begun to compete successfully with traditional retailing, offering many advantages over mail-order shopping, such as letting the customer know immediately whether an item is in stock. Other types of commerce on the Web include stock trading, airline ticketing, online banking, and auctions. Many software vendors offer turnkey systems that can be integrated with existing databases to speed the development of a commerce site. A good e-commerce site provides users with quick access to the item they want, detailed product descriptions, and easy, secure ordering.

- *Product support*—The Web is a boon to consumers who need help with a product. Manufacturers can disseminate information, upgrades, troubleshooting advice, documentation, and online tutorials through their Web sites. Companies that provide product support information on the Web often find that the volume of telephone-based customer support calls decreases. Software companies especially benefit from the Web; users can download patches and upgrades and use trial versions of software before they buy.

- *Intranet and extranet*—An **intranet** is a smaller, limited version of the Internet on a company's private local area network (LAN), accessible only to those who are authorized to use their network. Many companies have telecommuting employees who need access to company policies, documentation, parts lists, pricing information, and other materials. These employees can be reached via an **extranet**, which is a part of the private intranet extended outside the organization via the Internet. Many organizations mandate a particular browser for employee use, making the Web designer's job a little easier, because they only have to code and test for one browser.

CHAPTER 3

Analyze Your Audience

If possible, analyze your audience and produce an **audience definition**, a profile of your average user. If you are building a new site, work from your market research, look at sites with content similar to yours, and try to characterize your average user. If you have an existing user base, contact your typical users and try to answer the following questions:

- What do users want when they come to your site?
- How can you initially attract them and entice them to return?
- What type of computer and connection speed does your typical visitor have?

Obtaining answers to these questions is especially difficult when your medium is the Web. Though your users may fit no common profile, there are a few ways you can gather information about them. One way is to include an online feedback form in your site. Figure 3-1 shows a sample online survey from the State of Maine Web site (*www.maine.gov/portal/survey.html*).

The survey asks users about their experiences visiting the Web site. It uses both scaled and open-ended questions to elicit a variety of responses from the user concerning the visual and information design of the site.

If you cannot survey your users, or if you feel you are not getting good survey results, try to adopt a typical user's perspective as you define your audience. Here are some questions to consider:

- Who are the typical members of your audience? Are they male or female? Do they have accessibility issues? What is their level of education? What is their reading and vocabulary level? What is their level of technical aptitude?
- Why do people come to your site? Do they want information? Do they want to download files? Are they looking for links to other Web sites?
- Do you have a captive audience, such as a base of loyal customers that want up-to-date information? Are you designing for an intranet, where users are employees of an organization?
- If users are unfamiliar with the site, will they know what you offer?
- How often will users return to your site? Why would they come back?
- What computing platform do your users have? What is their typical connection speed? What type of browser do they use? If you are on an intranet, is there a standard for browsers, connection, and screen resolution?
- Whose skills do you need to build the site? Who will create the graphics, code the pages, and write the text? Do you have the talent and economic resources that you need? Will the results meet the expectations of your users?

Refine your content and presentation even after your site is built and running. Continue soliciting user feedback to keep your site focused and the content fresh.

Figure 3-1

Sample user feedback form

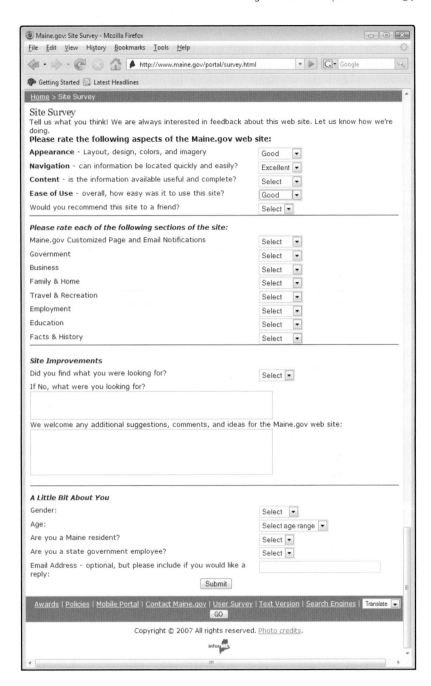

Identify Technology Issues and Constraints

Make your best effort to identify any technological factors—limitations or advantages—that members of your audience share. As you read in Chapter 1, you have to make assumptions about the user's browser, connection speed, operating system, and screen resolution. If you think your user is the average person browsing the Web, you may have to adopt settings that represent the lowest common denominator to satisfy the widest audience. If you feel that you have a primarily high-tech or computer-savvy audience, higher resolution or connection speed may apply. If you are designing an intranet site, you may have the luxury of knowing your users' exact operating systems and browser versions. Whatever the particulars, make sure to design at an appropriate level, or you risk losing visitors.

Identify Software Tools

Determining the software requirements for your Web site is important during the planning process. Try to choose software that matches the complexity and needs of your site so that you do not end up with a tool that is either underequipped or overspecialized. Simple Web sites, including many student sites, can be built with text editors such as Notepad or SimpleText. As your site and skills grow, you might choose to move up to more robust tools such as Adobe Dreamweaver or Adobe GoLive (*www.adobe.com*). These tools offer complete coding, design, and site management capabilities. You may also need graphics tools (discussed in Chapter 8), database software, and online credit and shopping programs, based on the skills and talents of the members of your Web site team, as described in the next section.

One popular type of software is **shareware**, programs that you can download and use for a trial period. After the trial period, users can register the software for a relatively small fee compared to commercially produced software. Because shareware is usually developed by individuals or small software companies, registering it is important to support future development efforts. Some of the most popular and commonly used programs are shareware, such as WinZip, at *www.winzip.com*. WinZip lets you work with .zip archive files, the PC standard for file compression and archiving. If you are sending or receiving files via e-mail, you need WinZip to compress and uncompress them. If you have a Macintosh, you can use Stuffit to compress your files. Stuffit Deluxe and Stuffit Lite, are available in shareware versions at the Aladdin Web site at *www.stuffit.com*. If you are a PC user and someone sends you a Stuffit file, you can expand it with Aladdin's Expander program, which is available free of charge at the Aladdin site. Shareware programs are also available to help you with Web site development. Two great shareware sites that have WinZip as well as hundreds of other programs are Shareware.com (*www.shareware.com)* and Tucows.com (*www.tucows.com).*

NOTE
Although most shareware is created by responsible software developers, it is always best to get shareware from recognized repositories to ensure that you avoid viruses and spyware being transferred to your computer.

Build a Web Site Development Team

Although one person can maintain small Web sites, larger sites require groups of people filling a variety of roles. Of course, the line between these roles can be blurred, and many aspects of site design require collaboration to solve a problem. The following are examples of the types of talent necessary to build a larger, well-conceived site.

- *Server administrators*—Get to know and appreciate the technical people who run your Web server. They take care of the sticky technical issues such as firewalls, ports, internal security, file administration, and backup procedures. Consult with them to determine your Web site's default filename and directory structure. They also can generate reports of how many visitors your site is attracting, where the visitors are coming from, and what pages they like best.

- *HTML coders*—These are the people responsible for creating the HTML code, troubleshooting the site, and testing the site across different operating systems and Web browsers. Most HTML coders are now using editing programs to create code, but it is a valuable skill to know how to open the HTML file in a text editor and code by hand. Knowing how to work directly with the code frees you from dependency on one particular authoring tool and makes you more desirable to companies hiring HTML authors.

- *Designers*—Designers are the graphic artists responsible for the look of the site. They use graphic design software, such as Adobe PhotoShop or Adobe Fireworks. Designers are responsible for the page template design, navigation icons, color scheme, and logos. If your site uses photographic content, the designers are called upon to prepare the photos for online display. They might also create animations and interactive content using Adobe Flash.

- *Writers and information designers*—Writers prepare content for online display, including hypertext information and navigation paths. In addition, many writers are responsible for creating a site style guide and defining typographic conventions, as well as consistency, grammar, spelling, and tone. They also work closely with the designers to develop page templates and interactive content.

- *Software programmers*—Programmers write the programs you need to build interaction into your site. They may write a variety of applications, including Common Gateway Interface (CGI) scripts, Java scripts, and back-end applications that interact with a database. Commerce sites especially need the talents of a programming staff.

- *Database administrators*—The people who are responsible for maintaining the databases play an important role in commercial Web sites. They make sure that your data is accessible and safe.

- *Marketing*—The Marketing Department can generate content and attract visitors to the site.

Create Conventions for Filenames and URLs

Before you sit down at the keyboard, plan the filename conventions for your site. Find out from your system administrator what type of operating system your Web server uses. Typically you develop your Web site locally on a PC or Macintosh and upload the files to the Web server as the last step in the publishing process. If the Web server runs a different operating system from your local development system, any filename or directory structure inconsistencies encountered in transferring your files to the server may break local URL links.

Naming Files

A filename's maximum length, valid characters, punctuation, and sensitivity to uppercase and lowercase letters vary among operating systems, as described in Table 3-1.

Operating System	Filename Conventions
ISO 9660 Standard	Maximum of eight letters followed by a period and a three-letter extension; allowed characters are letters, numbers, and the underscore (_)
DOS and Windows 3.x (FAT file system)	The same as ISO 9660 but with the following additional characters allowed: $ % ' ` - @ ^ ! & [ ] ( ) #
Microsoft Windows/NT, NTFS, and Windows 95 VFAT, Windows 98 FAT32, Windows 2000 NTFS, Windows XP NTFS, Windows Vista	Maximum of 255 letters, all characters allowed except \ / * " < > |
Macintosh	Maximum of 31 letters, all characters allowed except the colon (:)
UNIX	Maximum of 255 letters, all characters allowed except the forward slash (/) and spaces

Table 3-1   Filenaming conventions

Case Sensitivity

If you have an image file named Picture.gif, for example, and you reference that file as <img src="picture.gif" />, the image is displayed properly on a Macintosh or Windows machine. On a UNIX server, however, the image does not load properly because UNIX is case sensitive; "Picture.gif" and "picture.gif" are recognized as two different files. It is best to use lowercase letters for all filenames, including filenames in your HTML code.

Character Exceptions

Like case sensitivity, character use also is incompatible between operating systems. For example, the filename *my stuff.htm* is valid on a Windows PC or Macintosh, but not on a UNIX machine because of the space in the filename. If you transfer a Web site containing *my stuff.htm* to a UNIX server, the links to the file will not work. As another example, the filename *<section2>.htm* is valid on a Macintosh or UNIX machine, but the file would not be recognizable to a Windows NT server because the < > characters are not allowed. It is best when naming your files to leave out special characters such as <, >, /, \, &, *, and blank spaces.

File Extensions

You must use the correct file extensions to identify your file to the browser. HTML text files must end in .htm or .html; whichever you choose, set it as a standard convention for your site. Be careful to add this extension when you are working in your text editor, which may default to saving as .txt. You also must correctly identify image file formats in the file extensions. Joint Photographic Experts Group (JPEG) files must end in .jpg or .jpeg; Graphics Interchange Format (GIF) files must end in .gif; and Portable Network Graphic (PNG) files must end in .png.

Solving the Filename Dilemma

The best way to overcome the restrictions of case sensitivity, character exceptions, and file extensions is to use the convention specified by the International Standards Organization (ISO) for all your files. This convention (often called 8.3, pronounced "eight-dot-three") specifies a maximum of eight characters followed by a period and a three-character extension. Allowed characters are letters, numbers, and the underscore character. Here are some examples of 8.3 filenames:

- mypage.htm
- chap_1.htm
- picture1.jpg
- logo.gif

If you use the 8.3 file-naming convention on your development system, you will have fewer filename problems when you transfer your files to the Web server, regardless of the server's operating system. By sticking with this filename format, you ensure that your files can be transferred across the greatest number of operating systems. Do not forget to use lowercase characters and omit special characters from your filenames to maximize compatibility.

The Default Main Page Name

Every Web site has a default main page that appears when the browser requests the directory of the site rather than a specific file. The URL for such a page always includes a trailing (forward) slash, as in *www.mysite.com/*. In this instance the Web server provides the index file, which usually is named index.htm. Windows NT, however, defaults to an index filename of default.htm, and other servers may be set to other names such as main.htm or home.htm. Before you start coding, check with your system administrator to verify the correct main page filename.

Using Absolute or Relative URLs

Although you may know that URLs are the addresses you type into your browser to access a site, you may not realize that there are two types of URLs: absolute and relative.

Absolute URLs

A **Uniform Resource Locator (URL)** is the unique address of a file's location on the World Wide Web. A **complete** (or **absolute**) **URL** includes the protocol the browser uses, the server or domain name, the path, and the filename. Figure 3-2 shows an example of an absolute URL.

Figure 3-2

Parts of an absolute URL

In this example, *http* is the protocol, and *www.yoursite.com* is the domain name. The path shows that the destination file, *laptop.htm,* resides in the *business/trends* folder. Use complete URLs in your HTML code when linking to another server.

NOTE

When you are browsing the Web, you do not need to enter the protocol because the browser defaults to http://. However, when creating links in your code, you must always include the protocol with a complete URL; otherwise, the browser does not know how to connect to the location you specify.

Relative URLs

Use a relative URL when you are linking to a file that resides on your own computer or server. **Relative URLs** omit the protocol and domain or server name, and specify the path to the file on the same server. Files that reside in the same directory need no path information other than the filename. The following code shows an example of a partial URL.

```
<a href="laptop.htm">link text</a>
```

Set a Directory Structure

When you complete your site, you publish your files on the Web by transferring them to a Web server. A typical Web server has a user area that contains folders for each user; your files are stored in your user area, and files from other Web sites are stored in their user areas. The directory structure of the Web server affects the format of your site's URL.

Figure 3-3 shows a typical Web server directory structure. If you do not register a domain name for your site, you will have a URL that reflects your path in the public area of the Web server. A user enters the following address in the browser to access User2's Web site: *www.webserver.com/user2/*.

Figure 3-3

Typical Web server directory structure

A domain name is an alias that points to your actual location on the Web server, as shown in Figure 3-4. User2 has purchased the domain name *www.mysite.com*. The actual path to User2's content has not changed, but the visitor to the site sees only the domain name. Now User2 can advertise the Web site with a URL that's easy to remember.

Figure 3-4
Domain name hides the
actual path

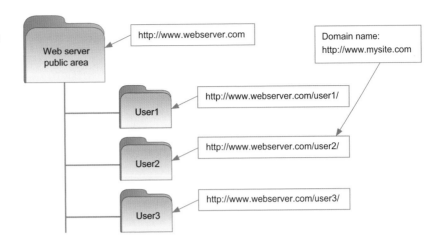

Relative versus Absolute Paths

You will probably build your Web site on a computer that is different from the computer that hosts your site. Keep this in mind when you are designing the directory and file structure. Because your files will be transferred to another computer, any URLs you specify to link to other pages in your site must include paths that are transferable. This is why you should never specify an absolute path in your partial URLs. An absolute path points to the computer's root directory, indicated by a leading (forward) slash in the file path:

```
/graphics/logo.gif
```

If you include the root directory in your partial URLs, you are basing your file structure on your development machine. If the files are moved to another machine, the path to your files will not apply, and your site will include links that do not work because the browser cannot find the files.

To avoid this problem, use relative paths. Relative paths tell the browser where a file is located relative to the document the browser currently is viewing. Because relative paths are not based on the root directory, they are transferable to other computers.

Building a Relative File Structure

The easiest way to ensure that all your path names are correct is to keep all of your HTML and image files in the same directory. Because all files are kept together, the only information you need to put in the src or href attribute is the filename itself. In Figure 3-5, User2 has simplified the directory structure. To reference the file logo.gif, User2 adds the following code in one of the HTML files:

```
<img src="logo.gif" />
```

The simple directory structure shown in the preceding example is fine for a small Web site, but as your site grows you may want to segregate different types of content into separate folders for ease of maintenance. Take a look at the relative file structure for User2's Web site as depicted in Figure 3-6. Notice that User2's Web folder contains three HTML files and one subfolder named images, which contains the graphics and pictures for the Web site.

CHAPTER 3

Figure 3-5

Simplified single folder file structure

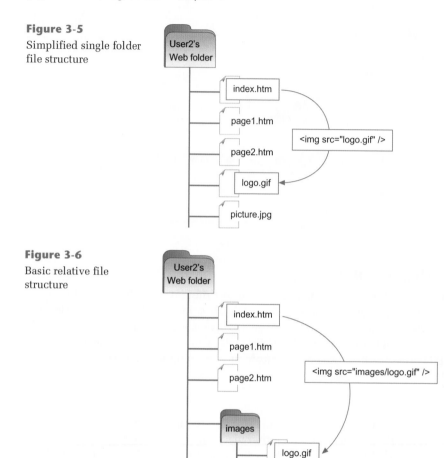

Figure 3-6

Basic relative file structure

To include the image file logo.gif in index.htm, User2 adds the following code to index.htm:

```
<img src="images/logo.gif" />
```

The path in the src value tells the browser to look down one level in the directory structure for the images folder and find the file logo.gif. The path to the file is relative to the file the browser is viewing. This type of relative file structure can be moved to different machines; the relationship between the files does not change, because everything is relative within the Web folder.

User2's Web site may need a more segregated directory structure, as shown in Figure 3-7. In this example, common files such as the index (the home page) and site map reside in the top-level folder. Multiple subfolders contain chapter and image content. Two linking examples are illustrated in this figure:

- *Example 1*—To build a link from page1.htm (in the chapter1 folder) to index.htm, use ../ in the path statement to indicate that the file resides one level higher in the directory structure, as shown in the following code:

```
<a href="../index.htm">Home</a>
```

- *Example 2*—To include the image file logo.gif in page1.htm, use ../ to indicate that the file resides in the images folder, which is one level higher in the directory structure, as shown in the following code:

```
<img src="../images/logo.gif" />
```

Figure 3-7

More segregated relative file structure

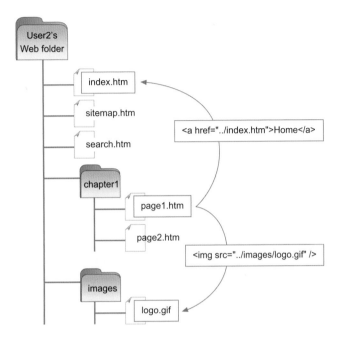

Create a Site Storyboard

Plan your site by creating a storyboard flowchart that shows the structure and logic behind the content presentation and navigation choices you offer. You can sketch your site with paper and pencil or create it using flowcharting software. Sometimes it is helpful to use sticky notes or cards to plan the structure visually. This method lets you easily move pages from one section or level to another. Whichever method you choose, this preliminary planning step is one of the most important in planning your site. You can move pages and whole sections of content freely, plan navigation paths, and visualize the entire site. This is the stage at which to experiment and refine your designs. Once you have started coding the site, it is much more difficult and time consuming to go back and make major changes. Remember to adhere to the filenaming conventions for each of your pages.

Organize the Information Structure

Think about your users' information needs and how they can best access the content of your site. How should your information design map look? Review the sample structures provided in this section and judge how well they fit your information. Your design may incorporate several different structures, or you may have to adapt the structures to your content. Each sample structure is a template; you may have more or fewer pages, sections, topics, or links. You may choose to use bidirectional links where only single-direction links are indicated. Use these examples as starting points and design from there.

Linear Structure

The linear information structure, illustrated in Figure 3-8, guides the user along a straightforward path. This structure lends itself to booklike presentations; once into the content, users can navigate backward or forward. Each page can contain a link back to the main page if desired. Pages may also contain links to a related subtopic. If the users jump to the subtopic page, they only can return to the page that contains the subtopic link. This structured navigation returns them to the same point in the content path.

Figure 3-8

Linear information
structure

Tutorial Structure

The tutorial structure illustrated in Figure 3-9 is perfect for computer-based training content such as lessons, tutorials, or task-oriented procedures. The tutorial structure builds on the simple linear structure in Figure 3-8. The user navigates the concept, lesson, and review pages in order. Because the lessons use hypertext, users can leave the lesson structure and return at any time. They also can choose the order of lessons and start anywhere they want. Notice that the table of contents, index, and site map pages are linked to—and from—all pages in the course. Within each lesson users can navigate as necessary to familiarize themselves with the content before they review. This structure can be adapted to fit content needs; for example, the group of pages in the illustration could be one section of a larger training course.

Figure 3-9

Tutorial structure

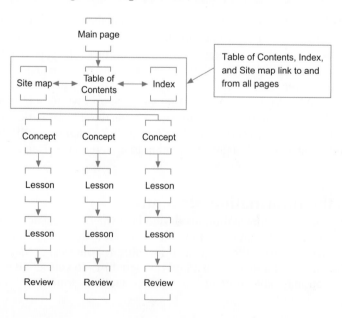

Web Structure

Many smaller Web sites follow the Web-type content structure illustrated in Figure 3-10, which is nonlinear, allowing the user to jump freely to any page from any other page. If you choose to use this type of content structure, make sure that each page includes clear location information and a standardized navigation bar that not only tells users where they are, but where they can go.

Figure 3-10

Web structure

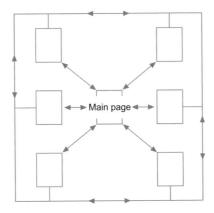

Hierarchical Structure

The hierarchical structure illustrated in Figure 3-11 is probably the most commonly used information design. It lends itself to larger content collections because the section pages break up and organize the content at different levels throughout the site. Navigation is primarily linear within the content sections. Users can scan the content on the section page and then choose the content page of their choice. When they finish reading the content, they can return to the section page. The site map allows users to navigate freely throughout the site. A navigation bar on each page lets the user jump to any section page, the main page, and the site map.

Figure 3-11

Hierarchical structure

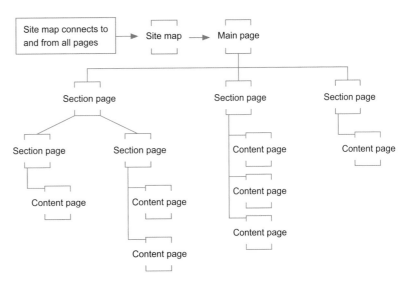

CHAPTER 3

Cluster Structure

The cluster structure illustrated in Figure 3-12 is similar to the hierarchical structure, except that every topic area is an island of information, with all pages in each cluster linked to each other. This structure encourages exploration within a topic area, allowing the user to navigate freely through the content. All pages contain a navigation bar with links to the section pages, main page, and site map.

Figure 3-12

Cluster structure

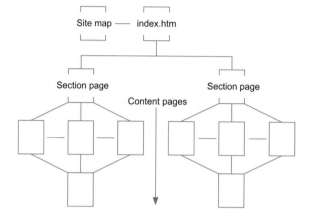

Catalog Structure

The catalog structure illustrated in Figure 3-13 is ideally suited to electronic shopping. The user can browse or search for items and view specific information about each product on the item pages. Users can add items to their shopping cart as they shop. When they are finished, they can review the items in their shopping cart and then proceed to checkout, where they can enter credit card information and finalize the order.

Figure 3-13

Catalog structure

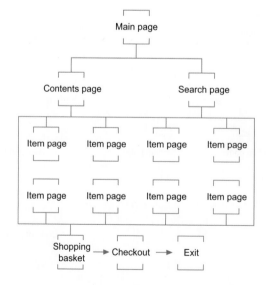

This type of Web site requires back-end data transaction processing to handle the shopping cart tally, process credit card information, and generate an order for the warehouse. Businesses that want to set up an electronic commerce site can purchase ready-made commerce software packages or develop their own from scratch.

Publish Your Web Site

To make your Web site live, you transfer your Web site files to a **Web server**, a computer connected to the Internet and running server software. The software lets the computer use the Hypertext Transfer Protocol (HTTP) to serve HTML files to Web browser clients. Unless your company or organization has a Web server and hosts its own content, you must use the services of a Web hosting provider. After you choose a server to host your files, you need to select file transfer software and upload the Web site files from your development machine to the Web server.

Choose a Web Hosting Service Provider

One of the most important choices you will make is your Web hosting service. This is the company that hosts your Web pages on a Web server, making them available to anyone who knows your URL. Most **Internet service provider (ISP)** companies offer Web hosting services for both personal and business use. The ISP provides you with Internet access, e-mail accounts, and space for a personal or business Web site. If you are building a Web site for business use, your ISP can register a personalized domain name for your Web site.

ISPs provide broadband and dial-up access and most offer Web server space as part of the access package. Small Web sites (around 15–20 pages of content) do not need much more than 1 or 2 MB of server space to hold all of the HTML pages and graphics. Your ISP should provide at least 10 MB of space so your Web page has room to grow. Larger or more complex sites need more server space, especially if you have downloadable files, archives, lots of graphic content, or databases. If you are building a business Web site, seek out larger hosting services that are more appropriate for hosting a complex commercial site.

NOTE
Many ISPs offer proprietary design tools and templates to assist you in building a Web site. It's best to avoid these types of tools as they tend to tie you to the ISP and make it difficult for you switch hosting services and post your Web site elsewhere.

Shopping for an ISP can be a confusing experience, as no two are exactly alike. Do some research and learn about offerings from different vendors. The following sections discuss the features you should seek in an ISP.

DSL and Cable Access

Most Internet users now have access to high-speed, broadband connection services through a Digital Subscriber Line (DSL) or cable modem. To take advantage of DSL or cable access to the Web, you need a network card for your computer and a DSL or cable modem. These providers usually supply a cable modem with the service. Check to make sure that the monthly fee does not include the equipment costs for the modem. Because DSL and cable are "always-on" connections, they introduce an increased security risk that can make your network vulnerable to hackers. If your provider does not offer network security, you must purchase a network security device, known as a gateway router, to protect your computer with a security firewall. The router allows multiple computers in your home or business to share the high-speed Internet connection, while the firewall software blocks intruders from accessing your network.

Dial-Up Access

If you access the Internet using phone lines and a modem, choose an ISP that allows you to connect to its network by placing a local phone call. Make sure that your provider has enough points of presence to make dialing easy. **Points of presence (POPs)** are dial-up access points to your service provider's network. Your service provider should have at least one POP available so you can dial a local number to access the network. Major ISPs, such as AT&T, have POPs throughout the United States. A local ISP covers only the area that includes its subscriber base. Try to match the size of your ISP to the size of your company—a local company does not need the services of a national ISP.

You should not receive a busy signal when you dial up to get Internet access. Unfortunately, you probably will not find out about access problems until after you have become a customer. Do not hesitate to change ISPs if you are not satisfied with ease of access.

Free Utility Software

Your ISP should provide you with a **File Transfer Protocol (FTP)** application for uploading files. (FTP is a standard communications protocol for transferring files over the Internet.) Some ISPs provide HTML editors and other software as well. Some of this software may be shareware, so if you decide to keep it, remember to register with the author.

Accessible Technical Support

Technical support is not a feature, but an absolute necessity. Make sure that your ISP has competent, accessible customer service. When you are checking into ISPs, call and talk with the companies' customer service representatives. Tell them how experienced you are with computers, and let them know what you hope to accomplish (such as set up a Web site or transfer files). Note how long you are on hold when waiting to speak with customer service. Local ISPs may not have a large staff, but they probably have fewer subscribers. National ISPs have so much volume that they may keep you on hold for an unacceptable length of time.

Additional E-mail Addresses

All access accounts come with at least one e-mail address, called a Post Office Protocol 3 (POP3) account. If you are part of a group, you may want an account that has more than one mailbox so that each person can receive his or her own e-mail.

Personal versus Commercial Accounts

Personal ISP accounts generally are less expensive than business accounts. However, you have less disk space, fewer features, and a more complex URL, such as *www.Webserver.com/users/*

yourname/. Once you buy a domain name, your ISP usually upgrades you to a commercial account. Commercial accounts pay more for services, so make sure you do receive more, such as some of the following features.

SQL Database Support

If you are planning on any type of electronic commerce or customized data presentation, you need database support. Databases that understand **Structured Query Language (SQL)**, a programming language that lets you select information from a database, are the most common and powerful type of database.

Secure Socket Layer (SSL) Support

The **Secure Socket Layer (SSL)** is an Internet communications protocol that allows encrypted transmission of data between the user and the server. SSL is necessary if you are planning to set up an electronic commerce site or transmit other sensitive data. Encrypting the data ensures the information cannot be read if the transmission is intercepted.

Register a Domain Name

Domain names are managed by the Internet Corporation for Assigned Names and Numbers (ICANN). ICANN has agreements with a number of vendors to provide domain name registration services. Until recently, Network Solutions was the only vendor of domain names. As more vendors become available, the market for domain names has become more competitive. You can visit Network Solutions to see whether a domain name is available, but you may want to shop around to get the best price. The site (*www.networksolutions.com*) contains a simple form that lets you check to see whether a domain name is already registered. If the domain name is available, you can register online. For an additional fee, your ISP often can register your Web site. If you prefer, you can save the cost of doing this by filling out the online forms yourself, but you still need to contact your ISP to get the IP addresses.

ISP Comparison Checklist

Use the following checklist when you compare ISPs:

- Is the ISP local or national?
- If you are using dial-up Internet access, does the ISP have enough local POPs in your area code?
- Is space available on the ISP's Web server for your Web site?
- Does the ISP offer technical support? When is support staff available?
- How many e-mail addresses do you get with an account?
- Does the ISP provide software, such as an FTP client?
- Does the ISP support the latest connection technologies? (See the "Considering Connection Speed Differences" section in Chapter 1.)
- Does the ISP offer enhanced services, such as SQL database support, Secure Socket Layer (SSL), CGI scripting, and streaming audio and video support?

NOTE
Always keep a backup of your Web site files in case you have any problems during FTP transmissions, or if you accidentally delete or overwrite existing files. Of course, if you ever accidentally delete or overwrite files on your local computer, you can use your Web site files as a backup.

Upload Files with the File Transfer Protocol

To publish your pages on the Web, you must send your HTML code, image, and other files to the Web server. To do this, you need FTP software, often called an FTP client. Some HTML authoring software, such as Microsoft Expression Web and Adobe Dreamweaver, include built-in software packages that let you upload files to your Web server if your ISP supports these features. You also can choose from many shareware FTP programs to upload your files. Visit your favorite shareware site, such as Shareware.com, and search for FTP clients.

NOTE
Wikipedia maintains a list of free ftp clients at http://en.wikipedia.org/wiki/Comparison_of_FTP_clients.

When you have decided which FTP software to use, contact your ISP's customer service department and ask for the correct FTP address for the Web server. You also need your account name and password, which in most cases automatically points your FTP program to the proper directory on the server.

To upload your files, start your FTP program and connect to your Web server using the FTP information provided by your service provider. Your password allows you write access to your directory on the Web server. Once the FTP client has connected to the Web server, you have the option of choosing the files you want to transfer. The FTP client usually displays directories on both the local and remote computers.

Select the files that you want to upload in your local directory listing and transfer them to the Web server. You also can transfer files from the Web server to your computer. The first time you go live with your Web site, you must transfer all the files. Later you will need to upload only the files that you have updated. Once the files have reached the Web server, they are available for access immediately on the Web.

After you find an ISP and publish your Web site to the World Wide Web, it is time to test your Web site in the real-life Internet environment.

NOTE
As discussed earlier in this chapter, make sure that you maintain the exact directory structure on the Web server that you used on your development computer to ensure that all relative file paths are correct.

Test Your Web Site

Even though you performed tests throughout the development of your Web site, you need to continue testing after you post your files live on the Web. If possible, load your files to the Web server and test them before making your URL available for users to access the Web site. If you have enough server space, you may want to establish a testing area on the Web site. You can do this by creating a subdirectory in your public HTML directory. Do not publicize the URL so that your testing area can remain private.

Testing Considerations

Always test in as many different environments as possible. Remember to test for the following Web design variables:

- *Multiple browsers*—Test your site using as many browsers as you can to make sure your work is portable and is displayed consistently.

- *Multiple operating systems*—If you can, test your site from different operating systems. If you have a PC as a development machine, use a Macintosh for testing, and vice versa. You even can run different versions of UNIX on a PC, if necessary. Because computer chip development moves at a lightning pace, machines become outdated quickly. You can find discounted and used machines that often are Internet-capable as long as they have a good Internet connection. Because you won't use these machines to *develop* Web sites (only to *view* them), you do not need the latest or most powerful hardware.

- *Connection speeds*—Do not rely on the same connection speed when testing your Web site, especially if you work in a corporate environment where the connection to the Internet usually is faster than the average user's. Go to a friend's house, library, or Internet café and access your Web site from there. Test for download times at different connection speeds.

- *Display types*—Test at different screen resolutions and color-depth settings to make sure your colors are displayed consistently. Make sure to test different color depths: 8-bit 256 color, 16-bit high color, and 24-bit true color.

In addition, continually test your links. Click through all the links on your Web site, making sure every one takes the user to the intended destination. Any pages that link outside of your Web site need to be tested on a regular basis to make sure that the destination site has not moved, shut down, or posted content different from what you expect.

User Testing

User testing can be as simple as asking a few colleagues to look at your Web site, or as complex as conducting extensive formalized testing. Some companies invest in special user testing labs with videotaping and one-way mirrors to record user behavior, or software that can track users' mouse movements and eye coordination as they look at your Web site. Even if you do not need this level of sophisticated testing, you should perform some type of user assessment of your work. The goal of user testing is to determine whether your Web site is easy to navigate and provides easy access to content. Following are some considerations to take into account when planning for user testing of your site.

Vary Your Subjects

Draw your test subjects from a variety of backgrounds, if possible. Gather test subjects who are representative of your target audience. Find users with varying computing skills and familiarity with the information. Avoid using friends as test users, as they may only compliment your work. You might choose to let users look at the Web site on their own time, but you can learn a lot by watching users interact with your Web site. Make sure to let them navigate and use the Web site without any outside help from you. Just stand back and watch.

Formalize Your Testing

Formalize your testing by creating replicable methods of testing your Web site. Prepare a series of questions that users have to answer after viewing the Web site. Give them a specific task to complete or have them find a particular piece of information. Let them rate the ease of completing such tasks. Compare the results from different users to find any problem areas in navigation. Administer the same testing methods to a variety of users, and watch for trends and consistencies. This lets you compare results or focus on a particular feature of the Web site.

Develop a Feedback Form

Develop a feedback form that users can fill out after they have tested the Web site. Include a set of criteria and let them rate the Web site on a progressive scale, or ask them a series of open-ended questions. You also may want to provide the feedback form online, letting users offer feedback directly from the Web site. Here are some sample questions you might ask:

- Did you find the information you needed?
- Was it easy or difficult to access the information you needed?
- Did you find the Web site visually attractive?
- Did you find the content easy to read?
- Did you find the Web site easy to navigate?
- Did you think the information was presented correctly?
- Did the information have enough depth?
- What area of the Web site did you like the best? Why?
- What area of the Web site did you like the least? Why?
- Would you recommend the Web site to others?

Refine and Update Your Content

Refine your content and presentation based on your user's feedback. When you are evaluating user feedback, look for trends rather than individual aberrations, such as one person's vehement dislike of your color scheme. Pay particular attention to the ease of access to your information. Users should be able to find what they want quickly.

If you have a commercial site, ask your system administrator to set up a program that analyzes your visitors and their preferences when they visit. This type of reporting program, available on most Web servers, reads the communication logs created by the server and extracts information in a report format. These statistical reports vary from program to program, but they can tell you how often users visit, which pages they request the most, and how your Web site traffic varies from month to month.

Plan for ongoing maintenance of your Web site. This is vital to the success of the Web site. Plan to add new links, information, and featured content continually. The Web is a live, immediate medium, and you want your Web site to stay fresh. Test your links to other Web sites regularly to make sure they are active. You annoy your users if you send them to linked content that no longer exists. When you update your pages, inform users on your top-level page or on any page that promises up-to-date information.

Plan for major Web site design changes on a regular basis. Some Web sites reorganize their look on a yearly basis. You can perform ongoing testing and improve your test site while maintaining your live Web site. Pay attention to the trends in the industry by visiting lots of other Web sites. Consider new technologies as they become available and when the bandwidth or browser variables allow you to incorporate them.

Attract Notice to Your Web Site

After you set up your live Web site, it is time to attract visitors. With the millions of pages on the Web, it can be difficult to get your Web site noticed. It is likely that you are trying to attract specific users to your site—people who use your product or who are interested in the same information. Within this narrow audience, publicize your URL as much as possible, in every collateral medium that you can, including business cards, letterhead, catalogs, mailings, and other media. Give users a reason to visit your Web site by offering something they cannot get in any other medium, such as up-to-the-minute pricing or technical information. Give them a reason to come back to your Web site by making your information accessible and useful.

Leveraging Search Engines

Other than knowing your URL, consider how visitors will find your Web site. Many who are interested in a specific topic or information will use a **search engine** Web site to look for sites on a related topic. Search engines are software programs that search out and index Web sites into a catalog format. The way search engines perform searches and arrange their catalogs differs greatly. You can enhance your Web site to take advantage of search engine behavior. Although the following tips can help, there is no guarantee that your Web site will rise to the top of a search engine listing.

For more information on search engine details, visit the Web site *www.searchenginewatch.com*. This site has search engine listings, reviews, ratings, and tests, as well as hints and tips to get your site listed properly with the major search engines.

Use Meaningful Titles

All the pages of your Web site need pertinent information in the <title> element. Some search engines read only the contents of the <title> for Web site information. Also, the contents of the <title> show up in the user's bookmarks or favorites list. Make sure to use meaningful titles that provide information to the user and accurately reflect your site.

Use alt Text with Images

Always add alt information to all of the graphics on your page. Some search engines read the contents of the alt attribute, which is especially useful if you start your page with a graphic. Refer to Chapter 8 for more information on the alt attribute.

Submit URLs to Search Engines

One way to have search engines list your URL is to submit it to each of the popular search engine sites. The site's search engine scans your Web site and indexes the information. Periodically return to the search engine site and search for your Web site name or pertinent search terms. Some search engines are much faster at this process than others, so you may have to resubmit your URL if you do not see your page listed.

Chapter Summary

A successful Web site is the result of careful planning. The steps you take before you actually start coding the site save you time, energy, and expenses in the long run. Remember these guidelines for successful planning:

▶ Start with pencil and paper; your ideas are less restricted and you can easily revise and recast without recoding.

▶ Write a site specification document. You will find it invaluable as a reference while building your site.

▶ Identify the content goal by adopting your users' perspective and learning what they expect from your site.

▶ Analyze your audience and create an audience profile. Focus your site on the users' needs and continue to meet those needs by adapting the site based on user feedback.

▶ An effective site is most commonly the result of a team effort. Leverage different skill sets and experience to build a Web site development team.

▶ Plan for successful implementation of your site by creating portable filename conventions. Build a relative file structure that can be transferred to your Web server without a hitch.

▶ Select a basic information structure for your site and then manually diagram it, customizing it to the needs of your site.

▶ Shop carefully and compare features when you are looking for an ISP or Web host. Consider the future disk space and technology needs of your content.

▶ Download and learn to use an FTP client for use in the often-repeated task of transferring files to your Web site.

▶ After your Web site is live, test it against the basic Web variables of browser, operating system, display resolution, and connection speed.

▶ Test your Web site with a variety of users. Listen carefully to their feedback to identify trouble spots in your information design.

▶ Plan for the maintenance, upkeep, and redesign of your Web site. Keep your content up to date. Let users know when you have made updates to the Web site.

▶ Attract notice to your Web site by taking advantage of search engine technology, using meaningful titles, including alt text with images, and submitting URLs to search engines.

Key Terms

absolute URL	points of presence (POPs)
audience definition	search engine
complete URL	Secure Socket Layer (SSL)
extranet	shareware
File Transfer Protocol (FTP)	site specification
Internet service provider (ISP)	Structured Query Language (SQL)
intranet	Uniform Resource Locator (URL)
partial URL	Web server

Review Questions

1. List three technology constraints that can affect the way a user views your Web site's content.
2. Consult your Web server administrator when you need to determine the _____ and _____ for your site.
3. Name two inconsistencies that can cause broken links when you upload your files to a Web server.
4. List three characteristics of filenames that vary by operating system.
5. The international standard for filenames often is called _____.
6. Which computer operating system is case sensitive?
7. Rename the following files so that they are compatible across all operating systems:
   My file.htm _____
   case:1.htm _____
   #3rdpage.htm _____
8. What is the default main page filename for a Web site?
9. What are the two types of URLs?
10. What are the four parts of a complete URL?
11. What type of URL links to another server?
12. What type of URL links within a server?
13. What affects the format of the URL for your Web site?
14. What is the benefit of purchasing a domain name?
15. Why should you never specify an absolute path in partial URLs?
16. What is the benefit of building a site with relative paths?
17. Files that reside in the same directory need only the _____ to refer to each other.
18. List two benefits of diagramming your site before you start coding.
19. How does a Web site become live?
20. List the four variables to consider when testing your Web site.

Hands-On Projects

1. Browse the Web and find a site you like. Write a brief statement of the Web site's goals.

2. Browse the Web and find Web sites that fit the following content types:

   a. Billboard

   b. Publishing

   c. Special interest

   d. Product support

   Write a short summary of how the content is presented in each Web site and describe how each site focuses on its users' needs.

3. Browse the Web and find a site that does not contain a user survey form. Write a 10- to 15-question user survey that you would use on the site. Tailor the questions to the site's content and goals.

4. Find a billboard-type Web site. Write an analysis of the site that includes functions and features you would add to extend the site's effectiveness for its users.

5. Visit *www.winzip.com* and download the latest version of WinZip. If you have a Mac, visit *www.aladdinsys.com* and download the shareware version of Stuffit. Practice using the software to archive and compress multiple files into a single file.

6. Browse the Web to find examples of the following site structures and describe how the content fits the structure. Think about how the chosen structure adds to or detracts from the effectiveness and ease of navigation of the site. Determine whether the site provides sufficient navigation information. Print examples from the site and indicate where the site structure and navigation information is available to the user.

   a. Linear

   b. Hierarchical

7. Browse the Web to find a site that uses more than one structure type and describe why you think the site's content benefits from multiple structures. Consider the same questions as in Project 3-6.

8. Are there other structure types that are not described in this chapter? Find a site that illustrates a different structure content. Create a flowchart for the site and determine how it benefits from the different structure type.

9. Write a test plan for your Web site.

   a. Create a section for each design variable.

   b. Spell out the exact steps of the test and the different variables to be tested. State explicitly which browsers and version should be used, and on which operating system. Detail the different screen resolutions and connection speeds. List the exact pages that should be tested.

   c. Walk through the test procedure to test its validity.

10. Write a sample user feedback questionnaire.

11. Write a maintenance plan for your Web site.

    a. Include a schedule of content updates for the different sections of the Web site.
    b. Include a schedule of design reviews.
    c. Plan for link maintenance.

Individual Case Project

Write a site specification for the site you defined in Chapters 1 and 2. Include as much information as possible from the project proposal you completed at the end of Chapter 1. Make sure to include a mission statement. Determine how you will measure the site's success in meeting its goals. Include a description of the intended audience. Describe how you will assess user satisfaction with the site. Include technological issues that may influence the site's development or function.

Prepare a detailed flowchart for your site using the preliminary flowchart you created at the end of Chapter 2. Create a filename for each page that matches the ISO 9660 standard. Indicate all links between pages. Write a short summary that describes the flowchart. Describe why you chose the particular structure, how it suits your content, and how it benefits the user.

Team Case Project

Collaborate to write a site specification for the site you defined in Chapters 1 and 2. Include as much information as possible from the project proposal you completed at the end of Chapter 1. Make sure to include a mission statement. Determine how you will measure the site's success in meeting its goals. Include a description of the intended audience. Describe how you will assess user satisfaction with the site. Include technological issues that may influence the site's development or function.

Work individually to determine the information structure you think is optimal for the type of content your site will contain. Then meet and work as a team to determine the information structure using the best pieces of each team member's information structure plan. Prepare a detailed flowchart for your site using the preliminary flowchart you created at the end of Chapter 2. Create a filename for each page that matches the ISO 9660 standard. Indicate all links between pages. Write a short summary that describes the flowchart. Describe why you chose the particular structure, how it suits your content, and how it benefits the user.

4

Planning Site Navigation

When you complete this chapter, you will be able to:

- Create usable navigation
- Build text-based navigation
- Add contextual linking
- Summarize text-based navigation
- Use graphics for navigation and linking

The free-flowing nature of information in a nonlinear hypertext environment can be confusing to navigate. Help your users find content easily rather than making them hunt through a maze of choices. Let your users know where they are at all times and where they can go within your Web site. In this chapter you learn to build user-focused navigation within the hypertext environment to accomplish these goals. Then you can apply these skills in a Hands-on Project.

Creating Usable Navigation

The PC Webopedia defines hypertext as "a system in which objects (text, pictures, music, programs, and so on) can be creatively linked to each other…. You can move from one object to another even though they might have very different forms." Hypertext was envisioned in the 1960s by Ted Nelson, who described it as nonsequential writing in his book *Literary Machines*. Nelson's basic idea of connecting content through hypertext linking influenced the creators of the Web. With hypertext-linked content, users can traverse information in any order or method they choose, creating their own unique views.

Hypertext is a distinctly different environment in which to write and structure information. In traditional paper-based media, users navigate by turning pages or referring to a table of contents or an index separate from the information they are reading. In a hypertext document, users can connect instantly to related information. The hypertext forms of traditional navigation devices, such as tables of contents and cross-references, can be displayed constantly alongside related content. The user can explore at will, jumping from one point of interest to another. Of course, the ease of navigation depends on the number of links and the context in which they were added by the hypertext author.

In HTML, hyperlinks are easy to create and add no extra download time when they are text based. When you are planning your site navigation, do not skimp on navigation cues, options, and contextual links. You can add graphics easily to create attractive navigation elements, as most Web designers do. Remember that every graphic you add to your Web site increases the download time for the user; keep your navigation graphics simple, and reuse the same graphics throughout your Web site. Once the navigation graphics are loaded in the user's cache, the server does not have to download them again. Use an alternate set of text links in the event that the user cannot or will not view your graphics, and to meet accessibility guidelines. You will learn more about text links later in this chapter.

Effective navigation includes providing not only links to other pages in the Web site, but also cues to the user's location. Users should be able to answer the following navigation questions:

- Where am I?
- Where can I go?
- How do I get there?
- How do I get back to where I started?

To allow users to answer these questions, provide the following information:

- The current page and the type of content they are viewing
- Where they are in relation to the rest of the Web site
- Consistent, easy-to-understand links
- Alternatives to the browser's Back button that let users return to their starting point

Locating the User

Figure 4-1 shows a page from the Animal Diversity Web site (*http://animaldiversity.ummz. umich.edu/*) that displays a number of user-orienting features.

Figure 4-1

Providing user location cues

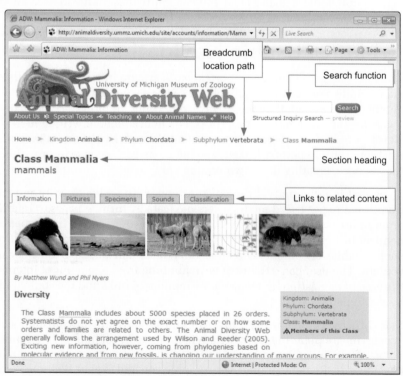

The navigation cues on this page offer many options without disorienting the user. A search option lets the user search the entire site. A linked breadcrumb path at the top of the page shows the user's location within the site hierarchy. Users can click any of the links in the path to move through the content structure. This location device is especially effective in guiding users who may have arrived at this page from somewhere outside this Web site. The section heading identifies the current section, and the links beneath this heading let the user jump to related content pages. Using these navigation devices, users can choose to jump directly to a page, search for information, or move back up through the information hierarchy.

Figure 4-2 shows a section page from The National Arbor Day Foundation Web site (*www.arborday.org*), which also offers the same types of helpful navigation devices as the page from the Animal Diversity Web site.

Figure 4-2
Variety of navigation cues

Limiting Information Overload

Many Web sites tend to present too much information at one time. Lengthy files that require scrolling or have arrays of links and buttons can frustrate and overwhelm the user. You can limit information overload in the following ways:

- *Create manageable information segments*—Break your content into smaller files, and then link them together. Provide logical groupings of choices. Keep a flat hierarchy. A good rule to follow is that users should not have to click more than two or three times to get to the information they desire.

- *Control page length*—Do not make users scroll through never-ending pages. Long files also can mean long downloads. Provide plenty of internal links to help users get around, and keep the pages short. You can judge your page length by pressing the Page Down key; if you have to press it more than two or three times to move from the top to the bottom of your page, break up the file.

- *Use hypertext to connect facts, relationships, and concepts*—Provide contextual linking to related concepts, facts, or definitions, letting the users make the choices they want. Know your material, and try to anticipate the user's information needs.

Building Text-Based Navigation

Text-based linking often is the most effective and accessible way to provide navigation on your site. It can work in both text-only and graphical browsers, and it does not depend on whether your images are displayed properly or not. Although you may want to use linked graphics for navigation, always include a text-based set of links as an alternate means of navigation.

In the following set of steps, you will link a series of sample Web pages using text-based navigation techniques. Figure 4-3 shows the structure of the collection of sample HTML documents that you will use, including the Home page, Table of Contents page, Site Map page, and individual Chapter pages.

Figure 4-3
Sample file structure

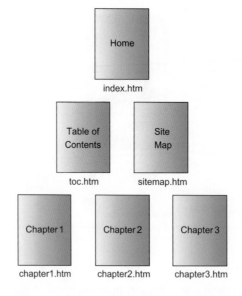

Home	
index.htm	
Table of Contents	Site Map
toc.htm	sitemap.htm
Chapter 1	Chapter 2	Chapter 3
chapter1.htm	chapter2.htm	chapter3.htm

NOTE
This book's Online Companion Web site contains all the HTML files for the sample Web site illustrated in Figure 4-3.

In the hypertext environment, the user should be able to select links in the table of contents to jump to any document in the collection. In the following steps, you will add a variety of linking options that produce different paths through the information. The focus for these steps is the Table of Contents page, toc.htm, and how it relates to the rest of the content in the collection. You will also add navigation options to the individual chapter pages. The Index and Site Map pages are included to complete the sample Web site, and will be target destinations for some of the links you will build.

To complete the steps in this chapter, you need to work on a computer with a browser and an HTML editor or a simple text editor, such as Notepad or SimpleText.

To prepare for linking the Web pages:

1. Copy the following files from the Chapter04 folder provided with your Data Files:

   - index.htm
   - toc.htm
   - sitemap.htm
   - chapter1.htm
   - chapter2.htm
   - chapter3.htm

2. Save the files in a Chapter04 folder in your work folder using the same filenames. (Create the Chapter04 folder, if necessary.) Make sure you save all the files in the same folder.

Linking with a Text Navigation Bar

The Table of Contents page must link to the other main pages of the Web site, allowing users to go directly to the pages they want. You can achieve this by adding a simple text-based navigation bar.

NOTE

In the following set of steps, you use common HTML coding techniques and elements, including <div> and <a>. If necessary, review your basic HTML knowledge before proceeding with these instructions.

To build the navigation bar:

1. From the Chapter04 folder in your work folder, open the file **toc.htm** in your browser. It should look like Figure 4-4.

CHAPTER 4

Figure 4-4

The original HTML file

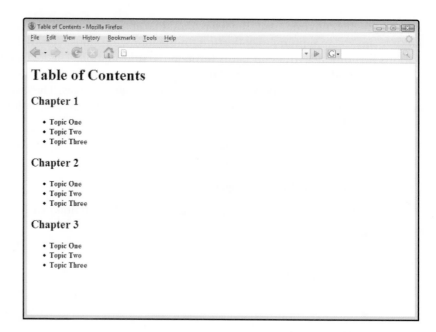

2. Open the file in your HTML editor and examine the code. Notice that this file contains no hypertext links. The complete code for the page follows:

```
<html>
<head>
<title>Table of Contents</title>
</head>
<body>
<h1>Table of Contents</h1>
<h2>Chapter 1</h2>
        <ul>
                <li><strong>Topic One</strong></li>
                <li><strong>Topic Two</strong></li>
                <li><strong>Topic Three</strong></li>
        </ul>
<h2>Chapter 2</h2>
        <ul>
                <li><strong>Topic One</strong></li>
                <li><strong>Topic Two</strong></li>
                <li><strong>Topic Three</strong></li>
        </ul>
<h2>Chapter 3</h2>
        <ul>
                <li><strong>Topic One</strong></li>
                <li><strong>Topic Two</strong></li>
                <li><strong>Topic Three</strong></li>
```

```
          </ul>
     </body>
     </html>
```

NOTE

In this set of steps, you use the id attribute to provide an identifying name for the
<div> element. You can use the id name to apply CSS styles to a section of a Web
page. You will learn more about the id attribute in Chapter 6.

3. Add a <div> element to place the navigation bar immediately following the opening <body>
   tag. Set the **id** attribute to **navbar1** and the **style** attribute to **text-align:center;** as shown in
   the following code. (The new code you should add appears in blue in this step and the
   following steps):

   ```
   <body>
   <div id="navbar1" style="text-align:center;"> </div>
   ```

4. Add text within the new <div> element as shown in the following code.

   ```
   <div id="navbar1" style="text-align:center;">
   Home | Table of Contents | Site Map </div>
   ```

5. Add <a> tags with href attributes that link to the home page and the site map.

   ```
   <div id="navbar1" style="text-align:center;">
   <a href="index.htm">Home</a> | Table of Contents |
   <a href="sitemap.htm">Site Map</a></div>
   ```

6. Add <strong> tags around the Table of Contents text. Because this is the Table of Contents
   page, the text "Table of Contents" is not a hypertext link but is bold to designate the user's
   location. The code looks like this:

   ```
   <div id="navbar1" style="text-align:center;">
   <a href="index.htm">Home</a> | <strong>Table of Contents</strong> |
   <a href="sitemap.htm">Site Map</a></div>
   ```

7. View the finished Table of Contents page in your browser. It should look like Figure 4-5.
   Test your hypertext links to make sure they point to the correct pages.

8. Add this navigation bar to all of the sample pages. Remember to change the links and
   <strong> text to reflect the current page. For example, the Site Map page would have the
   text "Site Map" in bold and list links to the Table of Contents and Home pages. Save
   toc.htm in the Chapter04 folder of your work folder, and leave it open in your HTML editor
   for the next steps.

Figure 4-5

Adding a text-based
navigation bar

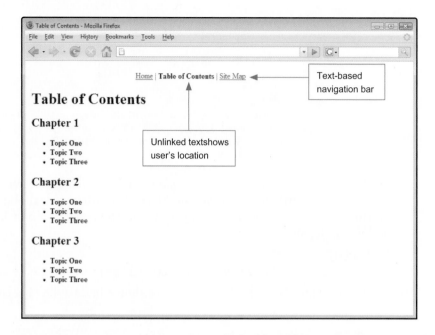

Linking to Individual Files

While the navigation bar lets users access the main pages in the Web site, the table of contents lets users access the exact content they want. The Table of Contents page therefore needs links to the individual chapter files in the Web site. In this set of steps, you will add links to the individual chapter files listed in the table of contents.

To build individual file links:

1. Continue working in the file **toc.htm**. Add the following <a> element around the text "Chapter 1":

   ```
   <h2><a href="chapter1.htm">Chapter 1</a></h2>
   ```

2. Add similar <a> elements around the text "Chapter 2" and "Chapter 3" that point to the files chapter2.htm and chapter3.htm, respectively.

3. Save **toc.htm** and view the finished Table of Contents page in your browser. It should look like Figure 4-6. Test your hypertext links to make sure they point to the correct page.

NOTE

As this example shows, remember always to make <a> the innermost set of tags to avoid extra space in the hypertext link.

This linking method lets the users scroll through the table of contents to scan the chapters and topics and then jump to the chapter they want. The link colors—by default, blue for new and purple for visited—allow users to keep track of which chapters they already have visited.

Figure 4-6
Adding individual file links

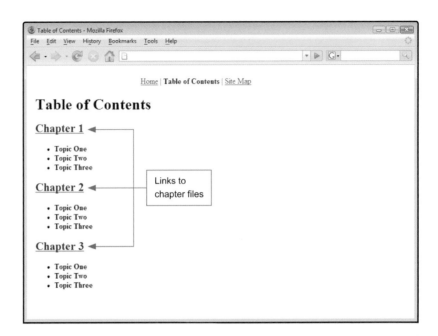

CHAPTER 4

Adding Internal Linking

In addition to linking to external documents, you also can add links for navigating within the table of contents itself. In the Table of Contents page illustrated in Figure 4-6, you will add a "back to top" link that lets users return to the top of the page from many points within the file.

This requires two <a> anchor elements: one uses the name attribute to name a **fragment identifier** in the document; the other targets the fragment name in the href attribute.

To add an internal link:

1. Continue working with the file **toc.htm** in your editor. Add the **name** attribute to the first <a> tag in the text-based navigation bar at the top of the page as shown.

   ```
   <div id="navbar1" style="text-align:center;">
   <a href="index.htm" name="top">
   Home</a> | <strong>Table of Contents</strong> |
   <a href="sitemap.htm">Site Map</a></div>
   ```

   This name attribute identifies the navigation bar text as a fragment of the document named "top." You can then refer to this name as an href target elsewhere in the document. The value of the name attribute can be any combination of alphanumeric characters that you choose.

2. Add an <a> element at the bottom of the page, after the listing for Chapter 3 and just before the closing </body> tag. Reference the target fragment "top" by using the number sign (#) in the href attribute, as shown in the following code.

   ```
   <h2><a href="chapter3.htm">Chapter 3</a></h2>
        <ul>
             <li><strong>Topic One</a><</strong></li>
             <li><strong>Topic Two</a></strong></li>
   ```

```
            <li><strong>Topic Three</a></strong></li>
        </ul>
    <a href="#top">Back to Top</a>
    </body>
```

3. Add a <div> element around the <a> element and set the id attribute to **footer** to identify the division.

```
    <div id="footer"><a href="#top">Back to Top</a></div>
```

4. Save the **toc.htm** file and view the Table of Contents page in your browser. Resize your browser to show only a portion of the page, as shown in Figure 4-7.

Figure 4-7

Adding a Back to Top link

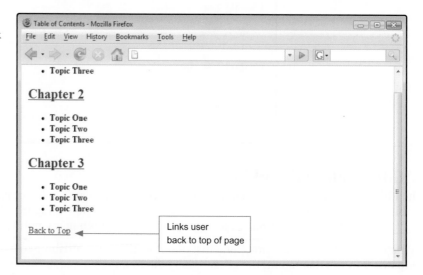

5. Test the link to make sure it opens the browser window at the top of the page, as shown in Figure 4-8.

Figure 4-8

Results of testing the Back to Top link

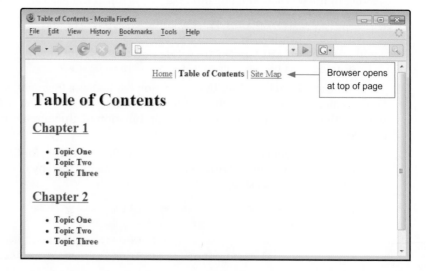

Adding an Internal Navigation Bar

You can use additional fragment identifiers in the table of contents to add more user-focused navigation choices. Figure 4-9 shows the addition of an internal navigation bar.

When users click one of the linked chapter numbers, they jump to the specific chapter information they want to view within the table of contents.

To add an internal navigation bar:

1. Continue working with the file **toc.htm** in your HTML editor. Add a <div> element immediately after the <h1> element as shown. Set the **id** attribute to **navbar2** and the **style** attribute to **text-align:center;** as shown in the following code.

```
<h1>Table of Contents</h1>
<div id="navbar2" style="text-align:center;"> </div>
```

2. Add text to the <div> element as shown in the following code.

```
<div id="navbar2" style=text-align:center;">
Jump down this page to Chapter… 1 | 2 | 3</div>
```

3. Add <a> elements around each chapter number within the <div>. Insert **href** attributes that point to a named fragment for each chapter.

```
<div id="navbar2" style="text-align:center;">Jump down this page
to Chapter…
<a href="#chapter1">1</a> | <a href="#chapter2">2</a> |
<a href="#chapter3">3</a></div>
```

4. Add the **name** attribute to each chapter's <a> element. These are the fragment names you referred to in Step 3. The following code shows the new name attributes in the <a> element for each chapter.

```
<h2><a href="chapter1.htm" name="chapter1">Chapter 1</a>
</h2>
        <ul>
                <li><strong>Topic One</strong></li>
                <li><strong>Topic Two</strong></li>
                <li><strong>Topic Three</strong></li>
        </ul>
<h2><a href="chapter2.htm" name="chapter2">Chapter 2</a>
</h2>
        <ul>
                <li><strong>Topic One</strong></li>
                <li><strong>Topic Two</strong></li>
                <li><strong>Topic Three</strong></li>
        </ul>
<h2><a href="chapter3.htm" name="chapter3">Chapter 3</a>
</h2>
        <ul>
                <li><strong>Topic One</strong></li>
                <li><strong>Topic Two</strong></li>
                <li><strong>Topic Three</strong></li>
        </ul>
```

5. Save the **toc.htm** file in the Chapter04 folder in your work folder, and then close the file. View the Table of Contents page in your browser. Resize your browser to show only a portion of the page, as shown in Figure 4-9.

Figure 4-9

Adding an internal navigation bar

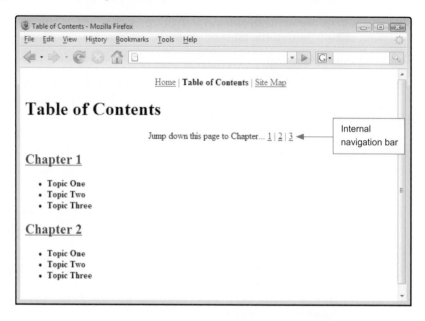

6. Test the navigation bar links by selecting a chapter number and making sure the browser window opens to the correct place in the file. Figure 4-10 shows the result of selecting the Chapter 2 link.

Figure 4-10

Results of testing the internal Chapter 2 link

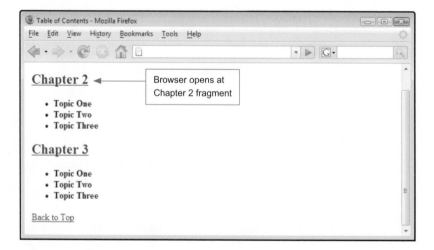

Linking to External Document Fragments

Now that you have completed internal linking in the table of contents, reexamine how the table of contents is linked to each chapter file. Currently, each chapter has one link in the table of contents; users click the chapter link and the browser opens the chapter file at the top. However, each chapter also contains multiple topics, which can be linked as external fragments. You can let users jump from the table of contents to the exact topic they want within each chapter. This requires adding code to both the Table of Contents page and each individual chapter page.

To add links to external fragments:

1. In your HTML editor, open the file **chapter1.htm** from the Chapter04 folder in your work folder.

2. Find the topic headings within the file. For example, the following code produces the topic heading for Topic 1:

   ```
   <h2>Topic 1</h2>
   ```

3. Add an <a> element around the text "Topic1." Set the **name** attribute value to **topic1** for this heading, as shown in the following code.

   ```
   <h2><a name="topic1">Topic 1</a></h2>
   ```

4. Now add the same code to each of the other topic headings in the file, using **topic2** and **topic3** as the name attribute values for the Topic 2 and Topic 3 headings, respectively.

5. Save **chapter1.htm** in the Chapter04 folder of your work folder, and then close the file.

6. In your HTML editor, open the files **chapter2.htm** and **chapter3.htm** from the Chapter04 folder of your work folder. Repeat Steps 2 through 5 for both files, adding appropriate name attribute values for each topic in each file.

7. In your HTML editor, open the file **toc.htm** from the Chapter04 folder of your work folder. (This is the toc.htm file you saved in the last set of steps.)

8. Find the topic links for each chapter within the file. For example, the following code produces three topic links for Chapter 1:

   ```
   <h2><a href="chapter1.htm" name="chapter1">Chapter 1
   </a></h2>
           <ul>
                   <li><strong>Topic One</strong></li>
                   <li><strong>Topic Two</strong></li>
                   <li><strong>Topic Three</strong></li>
           </ul>
   ```

9. Add <a> elements for each topic. The href value is the filename combined with the fragment name. The following code shows the <a> element for the Chapter 1, Topic 1 link.

   ```
   <h2><a href="chapter1.htm" name="chapter1">Chapter 1
   </a></h2>
           <ul>
                   <li><strong><a href="chapter1.htm#topic1">
                   Topic One</a></strong></li>
                   <li><strong>Topic Two</strong></li>
                   <li><strong>Topic Three</strong></li>
           </ul>
   ```

10. Continue to add similar links for each topic listed in the table of contents. When you are finished, your complete page code should look like the following example. (The location of your line breaks might differ.)

```
<html>
<head>
<title>Table of Contents</title>
</head>
<body>
<div id="navbar1" style="text-align:center;">
<a href="index.htm">Home</a> | <strong>Table of Contents
    </strong> | <a href="sitemap.htm">Site Map</a></div>
<h1>Table of Contents</h1>
<div id="navbar2" style="text-align:center;">Jump down this
    page to Chapter...
<a href="#chapter1">1</a> | <a href="#chapter2">2</a> |
<a href="#chapter3">3</a></div>

<h2><a href="chapter1.htm" name="chapter1">Chapter 1</a></h2>
    <ul>
    <li><strong><a href="chapter1.htm#topic1">Topic One
    </a></strong></li>
    <li><strong><a href="chapter1.htm#topic2">Topic Two
    </a></strong></li>
    <li><strong><a href="chapter1.htm#topic3">Topic Three
    </a></strong></li>
    </ul><h2><a href="chapter2.htm" name="chapter2">Chapter 2
    </a></h2>
    <ul>
    <li><strong><a href="chapter2.htm#topic1">Topic One
    </a></strong></li>
    <li><strong><a href="chapter2.htm#topic2">Topic Two
    </a></strong></li>
    <li><strong><a href="chapter2.htm#topic3">Topic Three
    </strong></li>
    </ul><h2><a href="chapter3.htm" name="chapter3">Chapter 3
    </a></h2>
    <ul>
    <li><strong><a href="chapter3.htm#topic1">Topic One
    </a></strong></li>
    <li><strong><a href="chapter3.htm#topic2">Topic Two
    </a></strong></li>
    <li><strong><a href="chapter3.htm#topic3">Topic Three
    </a></strong></li>
    </ul>
<div id="footer"><a href="#top">Back to Top</a></div>
</body>
</html>
```

11. Save the **toc.htm** file in the Chapter04 folder of your work folder, and view it in your browser. Test the topic links by selecting a chapter topic and making sure the browser window opens to the correct place in the correct file. Figure 4-11 shows the result of selecting the Chapter 2, Topic Two link.

When users click the topic links in the table of contents, the browser opens the destination file and displays the fragment. (See Figure 4-11.)

CHAPTER 4

Figure 4-11

Linking to an external fragment

Adding Page Turners

Each chapter file currently contains a navigation bar and fragment identifiers for each topic within the chapter. In this page collection, the user can jump to any file and topic within a file, though some users may want to read the pages sequentially. You can enhance the functions of the navigation bar in the chapter pages by adding page-turner links. Page turners let you move either to the previous or next page in the collection. These work well in a linear structure of pages, as shown in Figure 4-12.

Note that Chapter 1 uses the table of contents as the previous page, while Chapter 3 uses the site map as the next page.

Figure 4-12

Sequential page turning

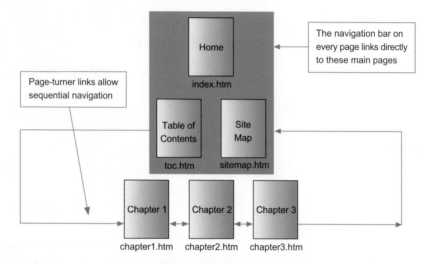

To add page-turner links:

1. In your editor, open the file **chapter1.htm** from the Chapter04 folder of your work folder. If you previously added the text-based navigation bar to the file, it looks like Figure 4-13. (Note that the Latin text is placeholder text, a common design technique that lets you focus on layout instead of content.)

2. If you have not added the text navigation bar, add it now. Insert the following code immediately after the opening <body> tag.

```
<div id="navbar" style="text-align:center;">
<a href="index.htm">Home</a>  |
<a href="index.htm">Table of Contents</a>  |
<a href="sitemap.htm">Site Map</a></div>
```

3. Add the page turner for the previous page. Because this is Chapter 1, make the previous page destination **toc.htm**, as shown in the following code.

```
<div id="navbar" style="text-align:center;">
<a href="index.htm" name="top">Home</a>  |
<a href="toc.htm">Table of Contents</a>  |
<a href="toc.htm">Previous</a>  |
<a href="sitemap.htm">Site Map</a></div>
```

Figure 4-13
Text navigation bar

4. Add the page turner for the next page. Because this is Chapter 1, make the next page destination **chapter2.htm**, as shown in the following code.

```
<div id="navbar" style="text-align:center;">
<a href="index.htm" name="top">Home</a> |
<a href="toc.htm">Table of Contents</a> |
<a href="toc.htm">Previous</a> |
<a href="chapter2.htm">Next</a> |
<a href="sitemap.htm">Site Map</a></div>
```

5. Save the **chapter1.htm** file in the Chapter04 folder of your work folder, and then view it in your browser. Your file should now look like Figure 4-14. Test the page-turner links to make sure they point to the correct files.

6. Add the page-turner links to chapter2.htm and chapter3.htm, changing the Previous and Next links to point to the correct files. Test all your links to make sure they work properly. When you are finished, save and close all the .htm files in the Chapter04 folder of your work folder.

Figure 4-14
Adding page turners in
the navigation bar

Adding Contextual Linking

Many Web sites fail to use one of the most powerful hypertext capabilities—the contextual link. **Contextual links** allow users to jump to related ideas or cross-references by clicking the word or item that interests them. These are links that you can embed directly in the flow of your content by choosing the key terms and concepts you anticipate your users will want to follow. Figure 4-15 shows a page from the Wikipedia Web site (*www.wikipedia.com*) that contains contextual linking.

Note the links within the lines of text, which let the user view related information in context. Including the link within a line of text is more effective than including a list of keywords, because users can see related information within the context of the sentence they are reading. Users also can see that repeated words are linked no matter how many times they appear within the browser window, offering users the opportunity to access additional information at any time.

Figure 4-15
Contextual linking

Text-Based Navigation Summary

You can choose from a variety of navigation options to link a collection of pages. The sample Web pages in this section demonstrate the following text-based linking actions:

- To main pages (Home, Table of Contents, Index)
- To the top of each chapter
- Within the Table of Contents page to chapter descriptions
- From the Table of Contents page to specific topics within each chapter
- Between previous and next chapters
- To related information by using contextual links

Use as many of these options as necessary, but remember to view your content from the user's perspective. Use enough navigation options to allow easy and clear access to your content.

Using Graphics for Navigation and Linking

Like most Web site designers, you probably want to use graphics for some of your navigation cues. The ability to use graphics is one of the most appealing aspects of the Web, but graphics used inconsistently confuse the users. To make sure your navigation graphics help rather than hinder your users, use the same graphics consistently throughout your Web site, for the following reasons:

- *To provide predictable navigation cues for the user*—Once users learn where to find navigation icons and how to use them, they expect them on every page. Consistent placement and design also build users' trust and help them feel confident that they can find the information they want.

- *To minimize download time*—After the graphic is downloaded, the browser retrieves it from the cache for subsequent pages rather than downloading it every time it appears.

NOTE

Remember that linked graphics are the result of placing an <img> element within a set of <a> tags. For example:

```
<a href="index.htm"><img src="home.gif" alt="home page
image" width="50" height="20" /></a>
```

You will read more about this in Chapter 8.

Using Text Images for Navigation

Navigation graphics on the Web come in every imaginable style. Many sites use text images, rather than HTML text, for navigation graphics. Text images are text created as graphics, usually as labels within the graphic. Many Web designers prefer text images because they offer more typeface and design choices.

Figure 4-16 shows the top navigation bar from a page of the Guardian Unlimited Web site (*www.guardian.co.uk*). The navigation bar builds the page name, Web site name, and main section links into a unified graphic that serves as the banner for the top of the page. The banner gives all of the content a consistent look while providing a variety of useful navigation choices. Note that what appears to be a single graphic actually is composed of different graphics held together by a table, a very common technique that you will learn more about in Chapter 7.

Figure 4-16

Using text images in a navigation bar

Using Icons for Navigation

Figure 4-17 shows the navigation icons from the MapQuest Web site (*www.mapquest.com*). The text labeling on the icons points out one of the main problems with icons—not everyone agrees on their meaning. Especially with a worldwide audience, you never can be sure exactly how your audience will interpret your iconic graphics. This is why so many Web sites choose text-based links, even if they are text as graphics.

If you do use navigation icons, be sure to define them. One way is to use a table that lists each icon and describes its meaning. Figure 4-18 shows a page from a student project Web site that clearly explains the Web site's navigation icons.

Figure 4-17

Icons for navigation

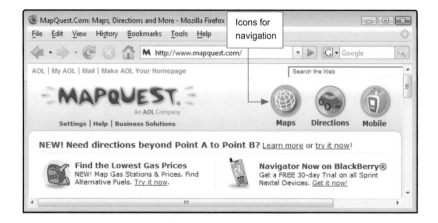

Figure 4-18

Clear definition of navigation icons

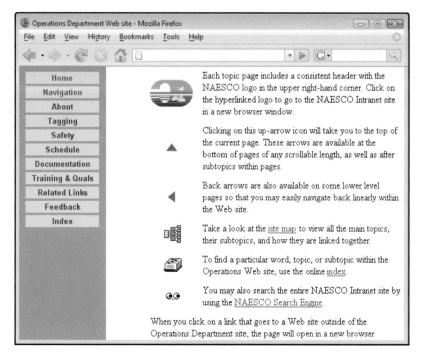

No matter what types of graphics you choose as icons, make sure that your users understand their meaning. Test your navigation graphics on users in your target audience and ask them to interpret the icons and directional graphics you want to use. The most obvious type of graphics to avoid are symbols that are culturally specific, especially hand gestures (such as thumbs up) that may be misinterpreted in other cultures. Other graphics, such as directional arrows, are more likely to be interpreted correctly. Figure 4-19 shows an icon-based navigation bar that includes universally accepted previous, top, and next links.

Figure 4-19

Universal navigation graphics

You also can use navigation graphics to indicate location within a site. For example, you can change the color or shading to indicate which page the user currently is viewing. At the F. A. Cleveland Elementary School Web site, shown in Figure 4-20, the navigation graphic includes an arrow to indicate which section of the site the user currently is viewing.

Figure 4-20

Navigation graphic indicates location

Using the alt Attribute

As you read earlier, you should provide alternate text-based links in addition to graphical links. You can do so by including an alt attribute in the <img> tag of the HTML code for the graphic. Repeating navigation options ensures that you meet the needs of a wide range of users. Some sites choose not to offer a text-based alternative, and this makes it difficult for users who cannot view graphics in their browsers. Figure 4-21 shows the main page of the F. A. Cleveland Elementary School Web site, which consists almost entirely of graphics.

Figure 4-21

Graphics-only navigation

The navigation images in the left column are the only way to navigate the site. Users cannot leave the main page if graphics are turned off or do not download. Figure 4-22 shows the same Web page with images turned off.

Without the graphics, this site offers no navigation information. If you omit alt attributes and make users rely on graphics for navigation, they may be unable to navigate the site effectively.

When you add descriptive alt text, nongraphical browser users can navigate your site. Figure 4-23 shows the F. A. Cleveland Elementary School Web site with the alt attributes added.

With the graphics turned off, users still can navigate the Web site because the alt attribute values appear in the image space. The user finds navigation cues by reading the alt text and pointing to the image areas to find the clickable spots. The inclusion of alt attributes is of prime importance to the accessibility of your Web site.

The code for one of these navigation buttons looks like this:

```
<a href="parent.htm"><img border="0" height="35" src="smparent.gif"
width="113" alt="Parent's Page"></a>
```

Figure 4-22
No alt values in the
<img> tags

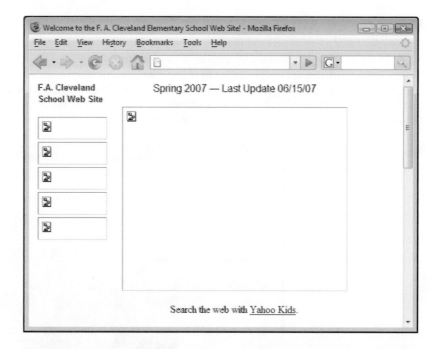

Figure 4-23
alt values in the <img>
tags

Note that you must specify the image width and height in the <img> tag to reserve the image space in the browser.

Chapter Summary

Usable navigation is the result of working with the power of hypertext and designing for your users' needs. Keep the following points in mind:

▶ Work from the user's point of view. Think about where users want to go within your Web site and make it easy for them to get there.

▶ Add plenty of links to make all areas of your Web site quickly accessible to your users. Link to fragments as well as whole pages. Make it easy to get back to your navigation options.

▶ In addition to providing links, make sure you provide plenty of location cues to let users know where they are.

▶ Use text-based navigation bars to link users to other pages in your site. Use other text-based links to help users move through a long page of information or through a table of contents.

▶ Consider text as an alternative to graphical links. Every graphic adds to download time. When using graphics and icons as navigational links, make sure users can interpret these links correctly by including text as part of the images. Also, be sure to use navigation icons consistently throughout your Web site to provide predictable cues for users and to minimize download time.

▶ Include alt values to your <img> tags to provide alternate navigation options for users.

Key Terms

contextual links   fragment identifier

Review Questions

1. List three advantages of linking by using text instead of graphics.
2. What four navigation questions should the user be able to answer?
3. List three types of navigation cues.
4. List three ways to control information overload.
5. Explain why you would include both graphic and text-based links on a Web page.
6. List two navigation cues you can add to a text-based navigation bar.
7. Why is it best to make <a> the innermost element to a piece of text?
8. What <a> tag attribute is associated with fragment identifiers?
9. List two ways to break up lengthy HTML pages.
10. What character entity is useful as an invisible link destination?
11. What attribute do you use to make an <a> tag both a source and destination anchor?
13. How do you link to a fragment in an external file?
14. Page turners work best in what type of structure?
15. What are the benefits of contextual linking?
16. List two reasons for standardizing graphics.

17. What are the benefits of using navigation graphics?

18. What are the drawbacks of using navigation icons?

19. What are the benefits of using the alt attribute?

Hands-On Projects

1. Browse the Web and find a Web site that has a successful navigation design. Write a short summary of why the navigation is effective and how it fits the user's needs. Consider the following criteria:

    a. Are the linking text and images meaningful?

    b. Is it easy to access the site's features?

    c. Can you easily search for content?

    d. Is there a site map or other site-orienting feature?

2. Find an online shopping Web site.

    a. Examine the navigation options and indicate whether you think the navigation adds to or detracts from the online shopping experience.

    b. Describe how to change the navigation to increase its effectiveness.

3. Find an online information resource likely to be used for research. Examine the navigation options and describe how the navigation helps or hinders the user's information-searching process. Consider the following:

    a. How cluttered is the user interface? Does it deter finding information?

    b. Is navigation prominent or secondary to the page design? Does the user always know his or her location in the site? Is the linking text concise and easy to understand? Is the link destination easy to determine from the linking text?

    c. How deep is the structure of the site? How many clicks does it take to get to the desired information?

4. Use your favorite Web search engine to search for navigation icons.

    a. Assemble a set of icons suitable for international audiences.

    b. Assemble a second set of icons that is only understood by a local population.

5. Browse the Web to find examples of Web sites that need better navigation options. Using examples from the Web site, describe how you would improve the navigation choices.

6. Browse the Web to find a Web site that uses more than one navigation method, and describe whether this benefits the Web site and why.

7. Find a site that illustrates a navigation method different from the ones described in this chapter. Describe the navigation method and state whether this benefits the Web site and why.

8. Take an existing paper-based project and turn it into a hypertext document.

a. Use a term paper or report from a previous class that you prepared using a word processor and is available in electronic format. Preferably, the document should contain a table of contents and bibliography.

b. Convert the document to HTML if the program allows, or save the document as ASCII text and paste it into Notepad or an HTML editor.

c. Mark up the document for Web presentation. Include a linked table of contents, topic links, content links, footnote links, and top links. You may find it best to break the single document into a few HTML files and then link them together.

d. Test your document in multiple browsers to ensure its portability.

9. This book's Online Companion Web site contains all the HTML files for the sample Web site illustrated in Figure 4-3. Use these sample HTML files to build an alternate navigation scheme. Refer to the information structure illustrations in Chapter 3 (Figure 3-8 through Figure 3-13) for examples of different navigation models. Choose a structure and code examples of usable navigation for the model.

Individual Case Project

Examine the flowchart you created for your Web site. Consider the requirements of both internal and external navigation. Create a revised flowchart that shows the variety of navigation options you are planning for the Web site.

Using your HTML editor, mark up examples of navigation bars for your content. Make sure your filenames are intact before you start coding. Save the various navigation bars as separate HTML files for later inclusion in your Web pages.

Plan the types of navigation graphics you want to create. Sketch page banners, navigation buttons, and related graphics. Find sources for navigation graphics. For example, you can use public domain (noncopyrighted) clip art collections on the Web for basic navigation arrows and other graphics.

Team Case Project

Work as a team to examine and discuss the flowchart you created for your Web site. Consider the requirements of both internal and external navigation. Collaborating as a team, refine your work to create a revised flowchart that shows the variety of navigation options you are planning for the Web site. Make sure you have standardized your filenames and all team members agree on the naming conventions.

Work individually to create text-based navigation bars for your content. Use your HTML editor to mark up examples of navigation bars for site navigation. Save the various navigation bars as separate HTML files. Have a team meeting where all members can present their navigation schemes. Choose the best scheme or combine features from different schemes to create the navigation for the group's Web site.

Work together to plan the types of navigation graphics you want to create. Assign team members to complete the remaining tasks, which include sketching page banners, navigation buttons, and related graphics, and finding sources for navigation graphics. For example, you can use public domain (noncopyrighted) clip art collections on the Web for basic navigation arrows and other graphics.

5

Working with Tables

When you complete this chapter, you will be able to:

- Understand table basics
- Format tables
- Follow table pointers to create well-designed tables
- Create a page template
- Evaluate examples of page templates

The 3.2 release of HTML in 1997 included table elements for the purpose of organizing tabular data in rows and columns. Web designers quickly realized they could use the table elements to build print-like design structures that allowed them to break away from the left-alignment constraints of basic HTML. With tables, Web designers had the control and the tools to build columnar layouts, align text, add white space, and structure pages. This misuse of the table elements, although well-intentioned, has created problems with Web site accessibility and compatibility that are still influencing Web design today. Although proponents of standards-based Web design (described in Chapter 1) see tables returning to their intended purpose, they currently are still used as the primary design tool throughout the Web.

Cascading Style Sheets (CSS) provides an alternate method of controlling page designs called **positioned layouts** (described in Chapter 10), which are now relatively well supported by the latest releases of the major browsers. CSS positioning offers a rich set of tools for creating complex page designs. The Web design community has been somewhat reluctant to embrace this new approach, because it fears that users with older browsers will not see the page designs as the designer intended. Current Web designers need to be fluent in both uses of tables—as they were originally intended, and also as a page layout tool. In this chapter, you will learn how to use the table elements to create data tables, as well as investigate their use as a page layout tool. In Chapter 10, you will learn how to create table-less positioned layouts using CSS.

Understanding Table Basics

To build effective tables, you must be familiar with table elements and attributes. This section describes the most commonly used table elements and attributes.

When HTML was introduced, tables were used only for tabular data, as shown in Figure 5-1. HTML tables are designed not only to present data properly in the browser window, but to be read sequentially by screen readers and other assistive devices. Some of the table features available to Web designers include the ability to span rows and columns, and to create table header cells that declare the contents of a column of data.

Figure 5-1

The intended use for tables—tabular data

Using Table Elements

The HTML table elements allow the arrangement of data into rows, cells, and columns. Table 5-1 lists the basic table elements and their usage.

Element	Description
table	Establishes the table; contains all other elements that specify caption, rows, content, and formatting
tr	Table row; contains the table cells
td	Table data cell; contains the table data
th	Table header cell; contains header information for a column of data
caption	Provides a short description of the table's contents

Table 5-1   Basic table elements

The HTML **<table> element** contains the table information, which consists of **table row elements <tr>** and individual **table data cells <td>**. These are the three elements used most frequently when you are building tables. See Figure 5-2.

Figure 5-2
Basic data table

The basic table is the result of the following code:

```
<table border="1">
<tr><td>Breed</td><td>Description</td><td>Group</td></tr>
<tr><td>French Bulldog</td><td>Loyal Companion</td>
    <td>Non-Sporting</td></tr>
<tr><td>Wheaten Terrier</td><td>High energy, friendly</td>
    <td>Terrier</td></tr>
<tr><td>English Pointer</td><td>Hunting companion</td>
    <td>Sporting</td></tr>
<tr><td>Australian Cattle Dog</td><td>Guarding, herding</td>
    <td>Working</td></tr>
</table>
```

The <table> element contains the rows and cells that make up the table. The <tr> tag marks the beginning and end of each of the five rows of the table. Notice that the <tr> tag contains the table cells, but no content of its own. The border attribute displays the default border around the table and between each cell.

You may occasionally use the <caption> and <th> elements when creating tables. The **<caption> element** lets you add a caption to the table. By default, captions are displayed at the top of the table. The <caption> element must appear immediately after the opening table tag, as shown in the code sample for Figure 5-3.

The **<th> element** lets you create a table header cell that presents the cell content as bold and centered by default. Figure 5-3 shows the table in Figure 5-2 with a caption and table header cells.

Figure 5-3
Table with caption and
table header row

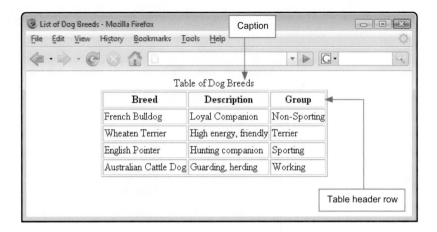

The following code shows the table syntax for Figure 5-3:

```
<table border="1">
<caption>Table of Dog Breeds</caption>
<tr><th>Breed</th><th>Description</th><th>Group</th></tr>
<tr><td>French Bulldog</td><td>Loyal Companion</td>
    <td>Non-Sporting</td></tr>
<tr><td>Wheaten Terrier</td><td>High energy, friendly</td>
    <td>Terrier</td></tr>
<tr><td>English Pointer</td><td>Hunting companion</td>
    <td>Sporting</td></tr>
<tr><td>Australian Cattle Dog</td><td>Guarding, herding</td>
    <td>Working</td></tr>
</table>
```

Table Grouping Elements

An additional set of table elements lets you group rows and columns. These elements are less commonly used than the basic table elements described earlier. The primary use of the grouping elements is to let you apply styles to groups of either rows or columns. Table 5-2 lists the grouping elements.

Element	Description
thead	Signifies table header
tbody	Signifies table body
tfoot	Signifies table footer
col	Specifies column properties
colgroup	Specifies multiple column properties

Table 5-2   Table grouping elements

Rows can be grouped into head, body, and footer sections using the <thead>, <tbody>, and <tfoot> elements, as shown in the following code sample.

```
<table>
<thead>
     <tr><th>Header Cell 1</th><th>Header Cell 2</th></tr>
</thead>
<tfoot>
     <tr><td>Footer Cell 1</td><td> Footer Cell 2</td></tr>
</tfoot>
<tbody>
     <tr><td>Body Cell 1</td><td>Body Cell 2</td></tr>
     <tr><td>Body Cell 3</td><td>Body Cell 4</td></tr>
</tbody>
</table>
```

The <tfoot> group must appear before <tbody> in the table structure to allow the browser to display the table footer before downloading the rows of data contained in the <tbody>.

The <colgroup> and <col> elements allow you to apply style characteristics to groups of columns or individual columns. These elements are an excellent way to specify column widths. The <colgroup> element has a span attribute that lets you set the number of columns specified in the group. Column groups are always applied left to right in the table.

The <col> element lets you specify style characteristics for individual columns. The span attribute specifies the number of columns that are to be styled alike. Both <colgroup> and <col> elements must appear immediately after the opening <table> element, or after the <caption> element if the table contains a caption.

The following code sample shows the use of these elements. In this three-column table, the first two columns are grouped to specify that they both have a width of 80 pixels. Within this group the first column has left-aligned data while the second column has right-aligned data. The third column, which is separate from the group, is center-aligned with a width of 100 pixels. Notice that <col> is an empty element, signified by the closing forward slash.

```
<table border="1">
<caption>Pet Items Order Form</caption>
<colgroup span="2" width="80">
<col align="left" />
<col align="right" />
</colgroup>
<col align="center" width="100" />
<tr><td>Item</td><td>Price</td><td>Quantity</td></tr>
<tr><td>Leash</td><td>32.95</td><td>5</td></tr>
<tr><td>Collar</td><td>12.49</td><td>12</td></tr>
<tr><td>Water Bowl</td><td>6.30</td><td>143</td></tr>
<table>
```

Figure 5-4 shows the result of this code with the alignment and widths as specified in the different columns.

Figure 5-4

Table with colgroup and col settings

Note

The <colgroup> and <col> elements are not supported evenly by all browsers, so test your work carefully.

Defining Table Attributes

Table attributes let you further define a number of table characteristics. You can apply attributes at three levels of table structure: global, row level, or cell level.

Note

Notice that some attributes are marked as **deprecated**, meaning that they are not included in the latest HTML table model. Current Web design trends still heavily favor the use of HTML tables and deprecated attributes for page layout. All of the major browsers will likely continue to support layout tables and deprecated attributes for some time to come.

Using Global Attributes

Global attributes affect the entire table. (See Table 5-3.) Place these attributes in the initial <table> tag.

Attribute	Description
align	Floats the table to the left or right of text. This is a deprecated attribute. The CSS equivalent is the float property, which is described in Chapter 9.
border	Displays a border around the table and each cell within the table; the default value is 1
cellpadding	Inserts spacing within the table cells on all four sides; the value for this attribute is a pixel count
cellspacing	Inserts spacing between the table cells on all four sides; the value for this attribute is a pixel count
width	Adjusts the width of the table; the value can be either a percentage relative to the browser window size or a fixed pixel amount

Table 5-3   Global table attributes

Using Row-level Attributes

Row-level attributes affect an entire row. (See Table 5-4.) Place these attributes in the beginning <tr> tag.

Attribute	Description
align	Horizontally aligns the contents of the cells within the row. Use left, center, or right values. Left is the default.
valign	Vertically aligns the contents of the cells within the row. Use top, middle, or bottom values. Middle is the default.

Table 5-4   Row-level table attributes

Using Cell-level Attributes

Cell-level attributes affect only the contents of one cell. (See Table 5-5.) Place these attributes in the beginning <td> tag.

Attribute	Description
align	Horizontally aligns the contents of the cell. Use left, center, or right values. Left is the default.
colspan	Specifies the number of columns a cell spans
rowspan	Specifies the number of rows a cell spans
valign	Vertically aligns the contents of the cell. Use top, middle, or bottom values. Middle is the default.
width	Adjusts the width of the cell. The value can be either a percentage relative to the table size or a fixed pixel amount. This is a deprecated attribute.

Table 5-5   Cell-level table attributes

CHAPTER 5

Cell-level attributes take precedence over row-level attributes. Even though the following code for a single table row has conflicting align attributes, the align="right" value in the <td> tag overrides the align="center" value in the <tr> tag.

```
<tr align="center"><td>Center-aligned text</td><td
align="right">Right-aligned text </td></tr>
```

Spanning Columns

The colspan attribute lets you create cells that span multiple columns of a table. Column cells always span to the right. Figure 5-5 shows a table with a column span in the first row.

The following code shows the colspan attribute in bold:

```
<table border="1">
<!-- Row 1 contains the column span -->
<tr><th colspan="3">Table of Dog Breeds</th></tr>
<tr><th>Breed</th><th>Description</th><th>Group</th></tr>
<tr><td>French Bulldog</td><td>Loyal Companion</td>
    <td>Non-Sporting</td></tr>
<tr><td>Wheaten Terrier</td><td>High energy, friendly</td>
    <td>Terrier</td></tr>
<tr><td>English Pointer</td><td>Hunting companion</td>
    <td>Sporting</td></tr>
<tr><td>Australian Cattle Dog</td><td>Guarding, herding</td>
    <td>Working</td></tr>
</table>
```

When you build column spans, make sure that all of your columns add up to the correct number of cells. In this code, because each row has three cells, the colspan attribute is set to three to span all columns of the table, as shown in Figure 5-5.

Figure 5-5

Table with a column span

Spanning Rows

The rowspan attribute lets you create cells that span multiple rows of a table. Rows always span down. Figure 5-6 shows the table in Figure 5-5 with a row span added to the right column.

Figure 5-6

Table with row span and new "Organization" column

The following code shows the new cell that contains the rowspan attribute and the extra column cell in the table header row:

```
<table border="1">
<tr><th colspan="4">Table of Dog Breeds</th></tr>
<tr><th>Breed</th><th>Description</th><th>Group</th>
    <th>Organization</th></tr>
<tr><td>French Bulldog</td><td>Loyal Companion</td>
    <td>Non-Sporting</td>
<td rowspan="4">All listed dogs are AKC recognized</td></tr>
<tr><td>Wheaten Terrier</td><td>High energy, friendly</td>
    <td>Terrier</td></tr>
<tr><td>English Pointer</td><td>Hunting companion</td>
    <td>Sporting</td></tr>
<tr><td>Australian Cattle Dog</td><td>Guarding, herding</td>
    <td>Working</td></tr>
</table>
```

The row span cell is the fourth cell in the third row. It spans down through five rows of the table. Notice also that to accommodate the new column, the colspan attribute value in the first row must be changed to four.

Formatting Tables

Now that you understand how to build the basic structure of a table, you can enhance the visual design with a variety of table attributes. In this section you will learn to build fixed or flexible tables, control table width, add white space in a table, and build table-based navigation bars.

Choosing Relative or Fixed Table Widths

Whether you choose to use relative or fixed tables depends on your content, your user's needs, and the amount of control you want over the result. Many Web designers prefer fixed tables because they can ensure that their view of the content is the same as the user's. Although styles have varied over the past few years, the current trend for most mainstream Web sites is to build fixed-width designs.

You can set relative table widths as percentages in the table width attribute. If you choose relative table widths, your tables resize themselves based on the size of the browser window. Figure 5-7 shows a table with the width attribute set to 100 percent at 1024 × 768 resolution.

Figure 5-7

A flexible table at 1024 × 768 resolution

Figure 5-8 shows the same table at 800 × 600 resolution. The browser fits the content into the window, wrapping text as necessary. Notice that the user must scroll to read the remainder of the content. The advantage to using a relative width is that the resulting table is more compatible across different browser window sizes and screen resolutions. The disadvantage is that you have little control over the way the user sees the result, because your content can shift based on browser window size.

You can set absolute table widths as pixel values in the table width attribute. Fixed tables remain constant regardless of the browser window size, giving the designer greater control over what the user sees. The user's browser size and screen resolution have no effect on the display of the page. The disadvantage is that users may not see all of the content on the page without horizontal scrolling. Figure 5-9 shows a table with the width attribute set to a fixed width of 975 pixels. Notice that at 800 × 600 resolution, the table extends beyond the browser window and both horizontal and vertical scroll bars appear.

Figure 5-8

A flexible table at 800 × 600 resolution

Figure 5-9

A table with its width fixed at 975 pixels and viewed at 800 × 600 resolution

Determining the Correct Fixed Width for a Table

If you decide to build fixed tables, you must choose a value for the pixel width. You can determine the value to use based on your user's most common screen resolution size. Currently 1024 × 768 is the screen resolution favored by most users. A small percentage still uses 800 × 600, with the remainder using higher resolutions. The fixed width of your tables must be less than the horizontal measurement of the screen resolution. For example, 975 pixels is the optimum width for a 1024 × 768 screen resolution. Figure 5-10 shows the areas to account for when calculating table width.

Notice the page margin on the left of the screen. The width of this margin is approximately 10 pixels and is built into the browser. The scroll bar on the right of the screen is approximately 20 pixels. Avoid having your table extend into this area, which will cause the horizontal scroll bar to appear. Finally, allow approximately 20 more pixels for a right page margin. Subtracting all of these values from 1024 leaves a table width of 974 pixels. You can round this value to 975 for ease of use. These values vary slightly based on the browser and operating system, so test the results of your work in multiple situations.

Figure 5-10

Areas to account for when calculating table width

Adding White Space in a Table

You can add white space into a table with the cellpadding and cellspacing attributes. These are global attributes (refer to Table 5-3) that affect every cell in the table. The cellpadding and cellspacing attribute values are always pixel amounts. In Figure 5-11 the cellpadding value is set to 10 pixels, which adds 10 pixels of white space on all four sides of the content within each cell.

The cellspacing attribute adds white space between the cells on all four sides rather than within the cells. Figure 5-12 shows the same table with cellspacing set to 10 pixels. Compare Figures 5-11 and 5-10 to see the difference between the two attributes. There is no definite rule to help you determine which of the attributes you should use. You have to experiment with each of your table layouts to decide which attribute works best for the particular situation, then consistently use that attribute throughout your Web site.

Figure 5-11
Cellpadding in a table

Figure 5-12
Cellspacing in a table

Removing Default Table Spacing

Default spacing values are included in the table even when you do not specify values for the table's border, cellpadding, or cellspacing attributes. Without the default spacing values, the table cells would have no built-in white space between them, and the contents of adjoining cells would run together. Depending on the browser, approximately two pixels are reserved for each of these values. You can remove the default spacing by explicitly stating a zero value for each attribute.

The code looks like this:

```
<table border="0" cellpadding="0" cellspacing="0">
```

This very useful technique lets you join the contents of adjacent cells. You can take an image, break it into separate pieces, and then rejoin the pieces in a table by removing the default spacing. Because the image is now composed of separate parts, you can link individual parts of the image to different destinations on your site.

Figure 5-13 shows six images assembled in a table with the default spacing. The background color on this page is set to light blue so you can see the images more clearly. Even though borders are turned off, their default space remains in the table. The default cell padding and cell spacing also add to the white space between the images.

Figure 5-13
Default table spacing

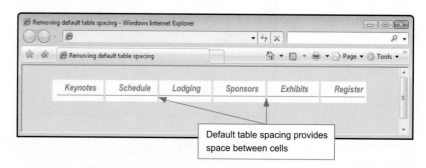

Figure 5-14 shows the same table with border, cellpadding, and cellspacing attributes set to zero.

Figure 5-14
Default table spacing
removed

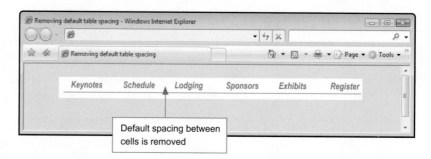

Table Pointers for Well-Designed Tables

To create effective tables, observe the following guidelines:

- Write code that is easy to read.
- Remove extra white spaces.
- Center tables to adapt to different resolutions.
- Stack tables for quicker downloading.
- Avoid nested tables.
- Use Cascading Style Sheets for table styles.

Writing Table Code That Is Easy to Read

The table code can get complicated when you add content to your tables. You have to manage not only the table tags and attributes, but also the text, images, and links in your cells. One small error in your code can cause unpredictable results in the browser.

You can simplify your table creation and maintenance tasks by writing clean, commented code. If you use plenty of white space in the code, you will find your tables easier to access and change. Adding comments helps you quickly find the code you want. The various code samples in this chapter demonstrate the use of comments and white space in table code.

Removing Extra Spaces

Always remove any leading or trailing spaces in your table cell content. These spaces cause problems when you try to join the contents of adjacent cells. In some browsers, the extra spaces create white space or misalignment in the table cells. Figure 5-15 shows code with one extra trailing space in the second cell after the <img> element. This extra trailing white space causes the misalignment of the images shown in Figure 5-16.

Figure 5-15

Extra trailing white space in code

```
                                                            ┌── Extra trailing
                                                            │   space in code
<table border="0" cellpadding="0" cellspacing="0">
<tr>
<td><img width="101" height="40" src="tpkeynt.gif" /></td>
<td><img width="101" height="40" src="tpsched.gif" />  </td>
<td><img width="101" height="40" src="tplodg.gif" /></td>
<td><img width="101" height="40" src="tpspons.gif" /></td>
<td><img width="101" height="40" src="tpexhib.gif" /></td>
<td><img width="88" height="40" src="tpreg.gif" /></td>
</tr>
</table>
```

Figure 5-16

Extra white space causes misalignment

Misalignment caused by extra trailing space

Centering Tables

Centering a fixed table makes it independent of resolution changes, because the table is always centered in the browser window.

Centering tables correctly is a problem because of mixed browser support for CSS. One way to center a table using CSS is to set a style rule that sets the left and right margins of the table to "auto." The following code fragment shows one method of doing this.

```
<table width="750" border style="margin-left: auto; margin-right: auto; ">
```

Browser support for this CSS code is unreliable and you will not achieve consistent results across different browsers.

The most reliable method of centering a table is to use a <div> element with the deprecated align attribute. Figure 5-17 shows a centered table at 1024 × 768 resolution. As the browser size changes, the table always remains centered. The following code shows the use of the <div> element to center the table.

```
<div align="center"
<table width="750" border>
<tr><td colspan="2" height="50">banner</td></tr>
<tr><td height="250" width="20%">column 1</td><td>column 2</td></tr>
</table>
</div>
```

Figure 5-17
Centered table

Note
You can find detailed information on CSS style rules and the <div> element in Chapter 6.

Stacking Tables

Browsers must read the entire table code before displaying the table. Any text outside of a table is displayed first. If you build long tables, they increase the time the user has to wait before the tables appear in the browser. Because of the way browsers display tables, it is better to build several small tables rather than one large one. This technique, called **stacking tables**, also can simplify your table design task, because smaller tables are easier to work with. Figure 5-18 shows a page template built with two stacked tables.

Another benefit of stacking tables is that they are displayed in the same order in which they appear in the code. This means the user can be reading the contents of your first table while the next one downloads. Also, more complex layouts are easier to build if you break them into multiple tables. Notice that the top table in Figure 5-18 has five columns, while the second has three. It would be more difficult to build this layout using a single table.

Figure 5-18

Stacked tables

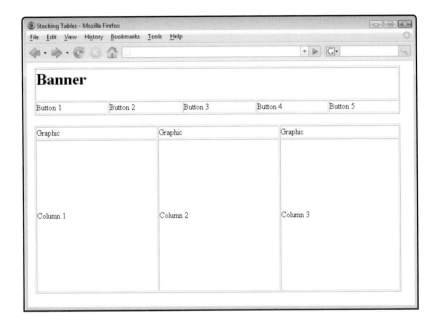

Avoid Nesting Tables

Nesting tables is the practice of placing an entire table within a table cell. This technique gives you the ability to build complex table designs; however, nested tables are not accessible to screen readers and other assistive devices. Although this technique is still widely used, it is being replaced by newer techniques such as CSS positioning (described in Chapter 10). Figure 5-19 shows an example of nested tables, with the outer primary table containing a second table nested in the right column.

The following code sample shows the nested table within a table cell.

```
<td>
<table align="right" width="200" border style="background-color: #cccccc">
<tr><td>Here is some feature info...<br><br>About today's
story...<br><br><br><br></td></tr>
<tr><td>This could be an ad...<br><br><br><br><br></td></tr>
</table>

<p>My father was a St. Bernard, my mother was a collie, but I am a
    Presbyterian. This is what my mother told me, I do not know these
    nice distinctions myself. To me they are only fine large words
    meaning nothing. My mother had a fondness for such;
```

```
... body text...
```

nothing, of course. She had one word which she always kept on hand,
and ready, like a life-preserver, a kind of emergency word to strap
on when she was likely to get washed overboard in a sudden way—
that was the word Synonymous.</p>
```
</td>
```

Figure 5-19
Avoid nesting tables

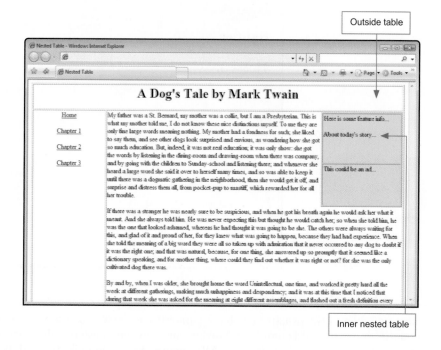

Use Cascading Style Sheets for Table Styling

CSS lets you apply a myriad of colors, spacing, borders, and other styling effects to tables and table content. As you will see in Chapter 9, the variety of style properties lets you create tables that are accessible and simple without giving up design quality. The use of CSS lets you avoid table tricks, such as nesting tables, blank images for spacer cells, and other non-standard practices.

Creating a Page Template

Now that you understand the mechanics of building tables, you can apply your knowledge to creating a page template. This hands-on example demonstrates how to take a design sketch for a Web page and build a template for the page layout. Figure 5-20 shows a sketch of the desired Web page layout. This layout is designed for a base screen resolution of 1024 × 768, so the table will be fixed at a width of 975 pixels.

Notice that the basic structure of the table is three rows by four columns. Each column uses 25% of the total width of the template. Row spans and column spans break across the layout to provide visual interest.

Figure 5-20

Sketch of the visualized layout

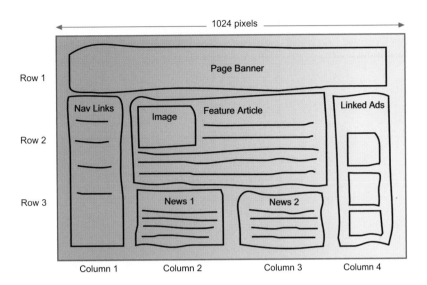

Building the Basic Table Structure

Start by building the basic table structure, including all the cells and rows of the table. As you customize the table, you can remove extraneous cells. The basic structure is a table with three rows and four columns, as shown in Figure 5-21.

To begin building the page template:

1. Copy the **template.htm** file from the Chapter05 folder provided with your Data Files.
2. Save the file to your work folder using the same filename.
3. Open the file in your HTML editor and add the following code to the page between the existing <body> tags:

```
<table border="1">
<tr><td>R1C1</td><td>R1C2</td><td>R1C3</td><td>R1C4</td>
</tr>
<tr><td>R2C1</td><td>R2C2</td><td>R2C3</td><td>R2C4</td>
</tr>
<tr><td>R3C1</td><td>R3C2</td><td>R3C3</td><td>R3C4</td>
</tr>
</table>
```

Notice the use of row and cell placeholders such as R1C1, which stands for Row One, Cell One. These placeholders are visible in the browser and provide helpful reference points as you build a table. Making the borders visible with the border attribute provides another visual reference to the structure of the table. When you complete your design, you can turn borders off by removing the border attribute from the <table> element.

4. Save **template.htm** and leave it open for the next set of steps. Then view the file in the browser. It should look like Figure 5-21.

Figure 5-21

Basic three-row by
four-column table

Setting a Fixed Width

One of the design characteristics of the template is a fixed width that does not depend on the
user's browser size or screen resolution. To create this characteristic, use a pixel value in the table
width attribute.

To set the fixed width:

1. Continue working in the file **template.htm**.

2. Add the width attribute to the opening <table> tag.

3. Add the width attribute value **975** as shown in the following code.

```
<table border="1" width="975">
<tr><td>R1C1</td><td>R1C2</td><td>R1C3</td><td>R1C4</td>
</tr>
<tr><td>R2C1</td><td>R2C2</td><td>R2C3</td><td>R2C4</td>
</tr>
<tr><td>R3C1</td><td>R3C2</td><td>R3C3</td><td>R3C4</td>
</tr>
</table>
```

4. Save **template.htm** and leave it open for the next set of steps. Then view the file in the
browser. It should look like Figure 5-22.

Figure 5-22
Width set to 975 pixels

Creating the Page Banner Cell

The page banner cell is R1C1, which spans the four columns of the table using the colspan attribute. To create the column span successfully, you must remove all but one cell in the first row of the table.

To create the page banner cell:

1. Continue working in the file **template.htm**.

2. Remove the cells shown as blue text in the following code fragment.

   ```
   <tr><td>R1C1</td><td>R1C2</td><td>R1C3</td><td>R1C4</td>
   </tr>
   ```

3. Add the **colspan** attribute to the R1C1 cell and set it to a value of **4**.

4. Add the **align** attribute and set it to **center**.

5. Change the R1C1 text to **Page Banner**. Your complete table code should now look like the following.

   ```
   <table border="1" width="975">
   <tr><td colspan="4" align="center">Page Banner</td></tr>
   <tr><td>R2C1</td><td>R2C2</td><td>R2C3</td><td>R2C4</td>
   </tr>
   <tr><td>R3C1</td><td>R3C2</td><td>R3C3</td><td>R3C4</td>
   </tr>
   </table>
   ```

6. Save **template.htm** and leave it open for the next set of steps. Then view the file in the browser. It should look like Figure 5-23.

Figure 5-23

The Page Banner cell

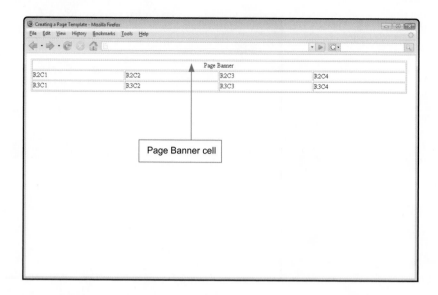

Creating the Feature Article Cell

The Feature Article cell in the layout is cell R2C2, which spans two columns. This column span requires removing one cell in row 2 to make room for the span.

To create the feature article cell:

1. Continue working in the file **template.htm**.

2. Remove the cell shown as blue text in the following code.

```
<table border="1" width="975">
<tr><td colspan="4" align="center">Page Banner</td></tr>
<tr><td>R2C1</td><td>R2C2</td><td>R2C3</td><td>R2C4</td>
</tr>
<tr><td>R3C1</td><td>R3C2</td><td>R3C3</td><td>R3C4</td>
</tr>
</table>
```

3. Add the **colspan** attribute to the R2C2 cell and set it to a value of **2**.

4. Change the R2C2 text to **Feature Article**. Your complete table code should now look like the following. The blue text shows the code you just added.

```
<table border="1" width="975">
<tr><td colspan="4" align="center">Page Banner</td></tr>
<tr><td>R2C1</td><td colspan="2">Feature Article</td>
<td>R2C4</td></tr>
<tr><td>R3C1</td><td>R3C2</td><td>R3C3</td><td>R3C4</td>
</tr>
</table>
```

5. Save **template.htm** and leave it open for the next set of steps. Then view the file in the browser. It should look like Figure 5-24.

Figure 5-24
The Feature Article cell

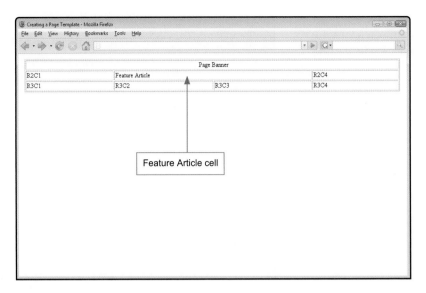

Creating the Link Column Cells

The Nav Links and Linked Ads columns in the layout reside in cells R2C1 and R2C4, respectively. These cells span rows 2 and 3 of the table. The row spans require the removal of cells R3C1 and R3C4, as illustrated in Figure 5-25.

To create the link column cells:

1. Continue working in the file **template.htm**.
2. Remove the cells shown as blue text in the following code fragment.

```
<table border width="975">
<tr><td colspan="4" align="center">Page Banner</td></tr>
<tr><td>R2C1</td><td colspan="2">Feature Article</td>
<td> R2C4</td></tr>
<tr><td>R3C1</td><td>R3C2</td><td>R3C3</td><td>R3C4</td>
</tr>
</table>
```

3. Add the **rowspan** attribute to cells R2C1 and R2C4. Set the value to **2**. The blue text in the following excerpt shows the code you should add.

```
<table border="1" width="975">
<tr><td colspan="4" align="center">Page Banner</td></tr>
<tr><td rowspan="2">R2C1</td><td colspan="2">Feature
Article</td><td rowspan="2">R2C4</td></tr>
<tr><td>R3C2</td><td>R3C3</td></tr>
</table>
```

Figure 5-25

Cells that need to be removed for the row spans

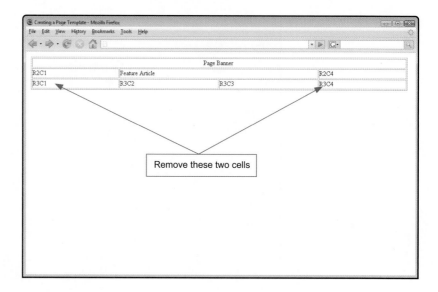

4. Change the R2C1 text to **Nav Links**.
5. Change the R2C4 text to **Linked Ads**.
6. Save **template.htm** and leave it open for the next set of steps. Then view the file in the browser. It should look like Figure 5-26.

Figure 5-26

The Link columns

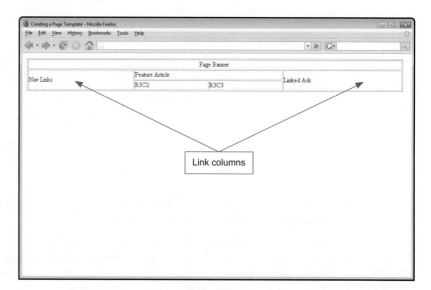

Setting the Column Widths

You can set column widths by using the width attribute at the cell level. Column widths must be set in only one cell per column. Setting the column widths ensures that the text wraps properly without skewing the evenly distributed four-column layout.

To set the column widths:

1. Continue working in the file **template.htm**.

2. Add the **width** attribute and set it to a value of **25%** in both the Nav Links and Linked Ads cells, as shown in the following code.

```
<table border="1" width="975">
<tr><td colspan="4" align="center">Page Banner</td></tr>
<tr><td rowspan="2" width="25%">Nav Links</td>
<td colspan="2">Feature Article</td>
<td rowspan="2" width="25%">Linked Ads</td></tr>
<tr><td>R3C2</td><td>R3C3</td></tr>
</table>
```

3. Change the R3C2 text to **News Column 1**.

4. Change the R3C3 text to **News Column 2**.

5. Add the **width** attribute to the News Column 1 and News Column 2 cells and set it to a value of **25%**, as shown in the following code.

```
<table border="1" width="975">
<tr><td colspan="4" align="center">Page Banner</td></tr>
<tr><td rowspan="2" width="25%">Nav Links</td>
<td colspan="2">Feature Article</td>
<td rowspan="2" width="25%">Linked Ads</td></tr>
<tr><td width="25%">News Column 1</td>
<td width="25%">News Column 2</td></tr>
</table>
```

6. Save **template.htm** and leave it open for the next set of steps. Then view the file in the browser. It should look like Figure 5-27.

Figure 5-27
Column widths
set to 25%

You can set widths at the cell level to either a pixel or percentage amount. Test carefully to make sure that the layout is browser compatible, as column widths can be troublesome.

Note
You can define column widths precisely if you use a graphic within the cell. Because the browser cannot wrap or truncate a graphic, the cell is always at least as wide as the graphic.

Completing and Testing the Template

To prepare the table for content, add the valign attribute to top-align all of the content in the table. To verify that your template works properly, populate it with test content. Finally, remove the borders from the table and test it in different browsers.

Note
The following design samples use Latin text. This is a traditional design technique from the printing layout world, commonly called "greeking." It lets you easily create text areas when you are testing a design. Also, because the text is not understandable to most, the designer's focus is on the content areas rather than on the actual content.

To complete the template:

1. Continue working in the file **template.htm**.
2. Add the **valign** attribute to each of the three <tr> elements in the table. Set the value to **top**. This forces all of the content in the table to align to the top of each row. Refer to the following code to see the changes.

```
<table border="1" width="975">
<tr valign="top">
<td colspan="4" align="center">Page Banner</td></tr>
<tr valign="top">
<td rowspan="2" width="25%">Nav Links</td>
<td colspan="2">Feature Article</td>
<td rowspan="2" width="25%">Linked Ads</td></tr>
<tr valign="top">
<td width="25%">News Column 1</td>
<td width="25%">News Column 2</td></tr>
</table>
```

3. Add test content to the page to verify that it works properly. Start by placing a dummy **<img>** element in the Page Banner cell. The <img> has width, height, and alt attributes but no src value. This allows you to create empty image placeholders, as shown in the following code.

```
<table border="1" width="975">
<tr valign="top">
<td colspan="4" align="center"><img width="965" height="50"
    alt="Page Banner"></td></tr>
<tr valign="top">
<td rowspan="2" width="25%">Nav Links</td>
<td colspan="2">Feature Article</td>
<td rowspan="2" width="25%">Linked Ads</td></tr>
<tr valign="top">
<td width="25%">News Column 1</td>
<td width="25%">News Column 2</td></tr>
</table>
```

4. Add **\<p\>** and **\<strong\>** tags around the Nav Links text to make it bold. Add five **dummy test links** to the Nav Links column. The links look like this:

```
<p><strong>Nav Links</strong></p>
<p><a href="dummy link">link one</a></p>
<p><a href="dummy link">link two</a></p>
<p><a href="dummy link">link three</a></p>
<p><a href="dummy link">link four</a></p>
<p><a href="dummy link">link five</a></p>
```

5. Add the **align** attribute to the opening \<td\> tag in the Nav Links column to center the links within the column. The blue text indicates the code you should add:

```
<table border="1" width="975">
<tr valign="top">
<td colspan="4" align="center"><img width="965" height="50"
    alt="Page Banner"></td></tr>
<tr valign="top">
<td rowspan="2" width="25%" align="center">
<p><strong>Nav Links</strong></p>
<p><a href="dummy link">link one</a></p>
<p><a href="dummy link">link two</a></p>
<p><a href="dummy link">link three</a></p>
<p><a href="dummy link">link four</a></p>
<p><a href="dummy link">link five</a></p>
</td><td colspan="2">Feature Article</td>
<td rowspan="2" width="25%">Linked Ads</td></tr>
<tr valign="top">
<td width="25%">News Column 1</td>
<td width="25%">News Column 2</td></tr>
</table>
```

6. Save **template.htm** and leave it open for the next steps. Then test your work in the browser. The file should look like Figure 5-28.

Figure 5-28

Testing content in the
Nav Links cell

7. Continue to add test content to the remaining cells of the table. In the Feature Article cell, add a dummy **\<img\>** element with the following values:

```
<img width="180" height="140" align="left" alt="Feature Img">
```

8. Add **strong** tags around the Feature Article text, and add some body copy text to the cell as well. The blue text indicates the code you should add along with sample dummy text:

```
<table border="1" width="975">
<tr valign="top">
<td colspan="4" align="center"><img width="965" height="50"
    alt="Page Banner"></td></tr>
<tr valign="top">
<td rowspan="2" width="25%" align="center">
<p><strong>Nav Links</strong></p>
<p><a href="dummy link">link one</a></p>
<p><a href="dummy link">link two</a></p>
<p><a href="dummy link">link three</a></p>
<p><a href="dummy link">link four</a></p>
<p><a href="dummy link">link five</a></p>
</td>
<td colspan="2"><img width="180" height="140" align="left"
    alt="Feature Img"><strong>Feature Article</strong>
<p>Lorem ipsum dolor sit amet, consectetuer
adipiscing elit, sed diem nonummy nibh euismod tincidunt
ut lacreet dolore magna aliguam erat volutpat. Ut wisis
enim ad minim veniam, quis nostrud exerci tution
ullam  corper suscipit lobortis nisl ut aliquip ex ea
commodo consequat. Lorem ipsum dolor sit amet,
consectetuer adipiscing elit, sed diem nonummy nibh
```

```
euismod tincidunt ut lacreet dolore magna aliguam erat
volutpat. Ut wisis enim ad minim veniam, quis nostrud
exerci tution ullamcorper suscipit lobortis nisl ut
aliquip ex ea commodo consequat.</p></td>
<td rowspan="2" width="25%">Linked Ads</td></tr>
<tr valign="top">
<td width="25%">News Column 1</td>
<td width="25%">News Column 2</td></tr>
</table>
```

9. Save **template.htm** and leave it open for the next steps. Then test your work in the browser. When you view the file, it looks like Figure 5-29.

Figure 5-29

Testing content in the Feature Article cell

10. In the Linked Ads cell, add **<strong>** tags around the Linked Ads text. Add 80 pixel × 80 pixel test images. Place each **<img>** element within a set of **<p>** tags to provide white space around each image. Add the **align="center"** attribute to the cell's opening <td> tag to center-align the content. The blue text indicates the code you should add:

```
<table border="1" width="975">
<tr valign="top">
<td colspan="4" align="center"><img width="965" height="50"
    alt="Page Banner"></td></tr>
<tr valign="top">
<td rowspan="2" width="25%" align="center">
<p><strong>Nav Links</strong></p>
<p><a href="dummy link">link one</a></p>
<p><a href="dummy link">link two</a></p>
<p><a href="dummy link">link three</a></p>
<p><a href="dummy link">link four</a></p>
<p><a href="dummy link">link five</a></p>
```

```
</td>
<td colspan="2"><img width="180" height="140" align="left"
    alt="Feature Img"><strong>Feature Article</strong>
<p>Lorem ipsum dolor sit amet, consectetuer adipiscing
elit, sed diem nonummy nibh euismod tincidunt ut lacreet
dolore magna aliguam erat volutpat. Ut wisis enim ad
minim veniam, quis nostrud exerci tution ullamcorper
suscipit lobortis nisl ut aliquip ex ea commodo
consequat. Lorem ipsum dolor sit amet, consectetuer
adipiscing elit, sed diem nonummy nibh euismod
tincidunt ut lacreet dolore magna aliguam erat
volutpat. Ut wisis enim ad minim veniam, quis nostrud
exerci tution ullamcorper suscipit lobortis nisl ut
aliquip ex ea commodo consequat.</p></td>
<td rowspan="2" width="25%" align="center">
<strong>Linked Ads</strong>
<p><img width="80" height="80" alt="ad 1"></p>
<p><img width="80" height="80" alt="ad 2"></p>
<p><img width="80" height="80" alt="ad 3"></p>
</td></tr>
<tr valign="top">
<td width="25%">News Column 1</td>
<td width="25%">News Column 2</td></tr>
</table>
```

11. Save **template.htm** and leave it open for the next steps. Then test your work in the browser. It should look like Figure 5-30.

Figure 5-30

Testing content in the Linked Ads cell

12. Add some test content to the News Column 1 and News Column 2 cells. Use **\<strong\>** tags to bold the heading in each cell.

13. Remove the border attribute from the opening \<table\> element to turn off the table borders. Save **template.htm** and close your HTML editor. Then test your work in the browser. The completed test page template should look like Figure 5-31.

Figure 5-31

The completed page template in Firefox 2

14. Test the page template in multiple browsers. For example, Figure 5-32 shows the page template in Internet Explorer 7.

Figure 5-32

The completed page template in Internet Explorer 7

Here is the complete code for the page:

```
<html>
<head>
<title>Creating a Page Template</title>
</head>

<body>

<table width="975">
<tr valign="top">
<td colspan="4" align="center"><img width="965" height="50"
    alt="Page Banner"></td></tr>
<tr valign="top">
<td rowspan="2" width="25%" align="center">
<p><strong>Nav Links</strong></p>
<p><a href="dummy link">link one</a></p>
<p><a href="dummy link">link two</a></p>
<p><a href="dummy link">link three</a></p>
<p><a href="dummy link">link four</a></p>
<p><a href="dummy link">link five</a></p>
</td>
<td colspan="2"><img width="180" height="140" align="left"
    alt="Feature Img"><strong>Feature Article</strong>
<p>Lorem ipsum dolor sit amet, consectetuer adipiscing elit,
sed diem nonummy nibh euismod tincidunt ut lacreet dolore
magna aliguam erat volutpat. Ut wisis enim ad minim veniam,
quis nostrud exerci tution ullamcorper suscipit lobortis nisl
ut aliquip ex ea commodo consequat. Lorem ipsum dolor sit
amet, consectetuer adipiscing elit, sed diem nonummy nibh
euismod tincidunt ut lacreet dolore magna aliguam erat
volutpat. Ut wisis enim ad minim veniam, quis nostrud exerci
tution ullamcorper suscipit lobortis nisl ut aliquip ex ea
commodo consequat.</p></td>
<td rowspan="2" width="25%" align="center">
<strong>Linked Ads</strong>
<p><img width="80" height="80" alt="ad 1"></p>
<p><img width="80" height="80" alt="ad 2"></p>
<p><img width="80" height="80" alt="ad 3"></p>
</td></tr>

<tr valign="top">
<td width="25%"><strong>News Column 1</strong>
<p>Lorem ipsum dolor sit amet, consectetuer adipiscing elit,
sed diem nonummy nibh euismod tincidunt ut lacreet dolore
magna aliguam erat volutpat. Ut wisis enim ad minim veniam,
quis nostrud exerci tution ullamcorper suscipit lobortis nisl
```

```
ut aliquip ex ea commodo consequat.</p></td>

<td width="25%"><strong>News Column 2</strong>
<p>Lorem ipsum dolor sit amet, consectetuer adipiscing elit,
sed diem nonummy nistrongh euismod tincidunt ut lacreet
dolore magna aliguam erat volutpat. Ut wisis enim ad minim
veniam, quis nostrud exerci tution ullamcorper suscipit
lostrongortis nisl ut aliquip ex ea commodo
consequat.</p></td></tr>
</table>

</body>
</html>
```

Evaluating Examples of Page Templates

The following templates cover a variety of page layout needs. You may choose to stack different templates on top of each other for more complex layouts. Normally you remove this attribute and let the content determine the height of the table.

Note

Note that in these examples, the deprecated height attribute gives the blank tables some vertical height. Also, these tables are designed for 800 × 600 screen resolution, although they can easily be adapted to larger resolutions by changing the table width.

Two-column Template

Figure 5-33 shows a typical two-column template. The left cell is for navigation, the right cell for content. This template is well suited for lengthier text content. You can adjust the width of the table to constrain the text width.

Figure 5-33

Two-column template

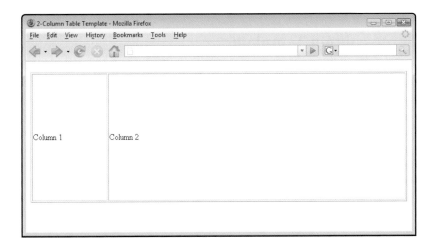

```
<table width="750" height="250" border="1">
<tr>
<td width="20%">Column 1</td>
<td>Column 2</td>
</tr>
</table>
```

Two-column with Banner Template

Figure 5-34 shows a basic two-column template with an additional column span in the first row. You can use the banner row for logos, navigation graphics, or banner ads.

Figure 5-34

Two-column with banner template

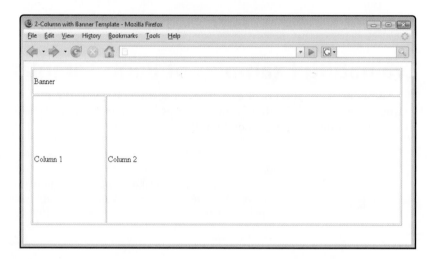

```
<table width="750" border="1">
<tr><td colspan="2" height="50">Banner</td></tr>
<tr><td height="250" width="20%">Column 1</td>
<td>Column 2</td></tr>
</table>
```

Three-column Template

Figure 5-35 shows a three-column template, which can be used to contain plain text or a variety of mixed content. The outer columns can be used for links, advertising, or related content. You can adjust the width of the cells to suit your content.

Figure 5-35

Three-column template

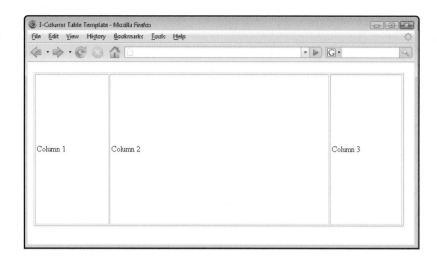

```
<table width="750" height="300" border="1">
<tr>
<td width="20%">Column 1</td>
<td width="60%">Column 2</td>
<td width="20%">Column 3</td>
</tr>
</table>
```

Three-column with Banner Template

Figure 5-36 shows the addition of a banner to the three-column layout. This layout works well as a top-level page of a section or an entire Web site. The columnar structure lends itself to scanning rather than reading.

Figure 5-36

Three-column with banner template

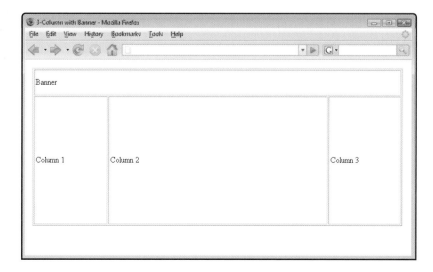

```
<table width="750" border>
<tr><td height="50" colspan="3">Banner</td></tr>
<tr><td height="250" width="20%">Column 1</td>
<td width="60%">Column 2</td>
<td width="20%">Column 3</td>
</tr>
</table>
```

Three-column Sectioned Template

Figure 5-37 shows the right and center columns divided into four content areas. Use this template when you want to provide the user a choice between a variety of topics or sections. You can place navigation information in the left column. You most likely would use this template as a top-level page.

Figure 5-37

Three-column sectioned template

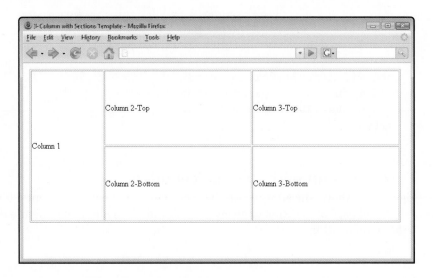

```
<table width="750" height="300" border>
<tr>
<td rowspan="2" width="20%">Column 1</td>
<td>Column 2-Top</td>
<td>Column 3-Top</td>
</tr>
<tr>
<td>Column 2-Bottom</td>
<td>Column 3-Bottom</td>
</tr>
</table>
```

Three-column Main Sectioned Template

Figure 5-38 shows the center column divided into two content areas. Another variety of a top-level page, this one lets you break up the primary area of the screen into two sections. Left and right columns can be used for navigation or associated links.

Figure 5-38

Three-column main sectioned template

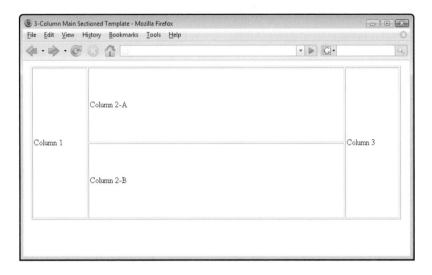

```
<table width="750" height="300" border>
<tr>
<td width="15%" rowspan="2">Column 1</td>
<td width="70%">Column 2-A</td>
<td width="15%" rowspan="2">Column 3</td>
</tr>
<tr>
<td>Column 2-B</td>
</tr>
</table>
```

Chapter Summary

Originally intended for tabular data, tables quickly became the designer's tool of choice for creating page layout templates. Although the current trend is moving away from the use of layout tables, a well-versed Web designer needs to be aware of both standard and non-standard uses of the table elements. Tables can be tricky, so remember the following points:

▶ To build effective page tables, you must be familiar with the HTML table elements and attributes, including the <table>, <caption>, and <th> elements and global, row-level, and cell-level attributes.

▶ Plan your tables by sketching them out on paper first. Numbering the rows and cells can help with your table design tasks.

▶ When designing HTML tables, write table code that is easy to read, remove extra spaces, and choose whether to center or stack tables. Avoid using nested tables and use CSS whenever possible to add presentation style to tables.

▶ Use fixed table widths if you want to determine the size of your page rather than letting the browser determine the width.

▶ Use relative widths if you want to build tables that resize with the browser window, wrapping your content to fit.

▶ Work on your pages with the table borders turned on, which display the cell boundaries. When you are finished with your layout, turn the borders off.

▶ Size your tables based on the page size you want to create. Use 1024 × 768 as your base screen resolution. In most cases you set the width but not the height of your tables, allowing the content to flow down the page.

▶ Test your work. Table settings, especially cell widths and heights, can vary based on the user's browser.

Key Terms

<caption> element	nesting tables
<table> element	positioned layout
<th> element	row-level attribute
cell-level attribute	stacking tables
deprecated	table data cell (<td>)
global attribute	table row element (<tr>)

Review Questions

1. Name three print-based design structures that Web designers can duplicate with tables.
2. What are the three basic table elements?
3. What table element presents its content as bold and centered?
4. What attribute can you use with the <caption> element?

5. What are the three levels of table structure?

6. What attribute would you use to adjust spacing between table cells?

7. What attribute would you use to adjust spacing within table cells?

8. In the following code, which attribute takes precedence?

```
<tr valign="top"><td valign="middle">Cell 1</td>
    <td>Cell 2</td></tr>
```

9. What elements let you apply styles to table columns?

10. What value should colspan equal in the following code?

```
<tr><td>R1C1</td><td>R1C2</td><td>R1C3</td></tr>
<tr><td>R2C1</td><td colspan= >R2C2</td></tr>
```

11. Write the code for a table that fills 75% of the browser window.

12. What is the major disadvantage of relative-width tables?

13. Write the code to remove the default spacing from a table.

14. Why would you want to remove the default spacing from a table?

15. How do extra character spaces affect a table?

16. What is the best way to center a table?

17. What are the benefits of stacking tables?

18. What are two rules for setting column widths in a table?

19. What attribute lets you align content to the top of a cell?

20. What is the difference between removing the border attribute and setting border="0"?

Hands-On Projects

1. Browse the Web and find Web sites that use page templates. You will see the use of templates in Web sites that have a consistent page design across multiple pages of the site.

   a. Create a sketch of a page from the Web site that depicts your idea of the page template.

   b. Examine the code to see how the template was actually built.

   c. Compare and contrast your method with the designer's method of building the template.

2. Practice building test pages.

   a. Using one of the template examples from this chapter, build a mock-up of a finished page using test content.

   b. Test the page in multiple browsers and note any differences in the way the content is displayed.

3. Surf the Web and find examples of Web sites that use fixed tables. Describe why you think the designers chose a fixed layout for the content.

4. Surf the Web and find examples of Web sites that use relative tables. Describe why you think the designers chose a relative layout for the content.

5. Choose an example template from the *Principles of Web Design* Online Companion Web site and fill it with test content.

    a. Set the width to 100%.

    b. Test the results in multiple browsers and at multiple resolutions.

    c. Note any display problems and suggest how you might solve the problems.

6. Create a seamless navigation bar using a table to hold the graphics together. Use the navigation graphics from the *Principles of Web Design* Online Companion Web site, or choose your own graphics.

7. Describe two ways that multiple tables can affect the way your pages download.

8. Build a template that meets the following criteria:

    ▶ Fills the screen at 1024 × 768 resolution without showing a horizontal scroll bar

    ▶ Builds a three-column layout

    ▶ Contains a banner cell that spans the layout

    ▶ Fixes content independent of browser size

Individual Case Project

Design the page templates for the different information levels of your Web site. Create sketches for each template, and describe why the templates fit your content.

You will find all of the page templates shown in this chapter on the *Principles of Web Design* Online Companion Web site. Use these templates as starting points for your Web pages. Adapt the page templates to your own needs or build your page templates from scratch. Test the page templates with content in different browsers to make sure that they are displayed properly.

Once your templates test properly, start to build the files for your Web site by copying the templates to individual files and naming them to match your flowchart from Chapter 3.

Team Case Project

Assign page template design tasks to different team members, and design the page templates for the different information levels of your Web site. Each team member should create multiple designs for the type of page he or she is assigned. For example, one team member should be responsible for the home page designs, one for the section page designs, and one for the article level page designs. Create 2-3 sketches for each template, and meet as a team to determine which template designs are the best for your content. Be prepared to present and defend your page designs to your team members.

You will find all of the page templates shown in this chapter on the *Principles of Web Design* Online Companion Web site. Use these templates as starting points for your Web pages. Adapt the page templates to your own needs or build your page templates from scratch. Test the page templates with content in different browsers to make sure that they are displayed properly.

Once your templates test properly, start to build the files for your Web site by copying the templates to individual files and naming them to match your flowchart from Chapter 3.

6

Introducing Cascading Style Sheets

When you complete this chapter, you will be able to:

- Understand CSS style rules
- Build a basic style sheet
- Understand the cascade and inheritance
- Use basic selection techniques
- Use advanced selection techniques
- Work with the <div> and <span> elements
- Use pseudo-classes and pseudo-selectors

Cascading Style Sheets (CSS) let you control the display characteristics of your Web site. In this chapter, you examine the basic syntax of CSS and learn how to combine CSS rules with your HTML code. You start by examining the CSS style rules, and then apply them to build a basic style sheet. Then you learn how to cascade style sheets, or let multiple style sheets and style rules apply to the same document. You also learn basic selection techniques to apply a particular style declaration to an element in your document. You learn about two elements, <div> and <span>, that were expressly created for use with CSS. Advanced selection techniques include using the class attribute and id attribute to provide customized naming for your elements. Finally you learn about using pseudo-selectors and pseudo-elements to select and apply CSS styles to hyperlinks and other parts of HTML documents.

Understanding CSS Style Rules

In CSS, **style rules** express the style characteristics for an HTML element. A set of style rules is called a **style sheet**. Style rules are easy to write and interpret. The following code shows a simple style rule for the <p> element. Note that the style rules are contained in the <style> element in the document's <head> section. This rule sets all <p> elements in the document to blue 24-point text:

```
<head>
<style type="text/css">
p {color: blue; font-size: 24pt;}
```

```
</style>
</head>
```

A style rule is composed of two parts: a selector and a declaration. The style rule expresses the style information for an element. The **selector** determines the element to which the rule is applied. As you will learn later in this chapter, CSS contains a variety of powerful selection techniques. The **declaration** details the exact property values. Figure 6-1 shows an example of a simple style rule that sets all <h1> headings to red:

Figure 6-1

Style rule syntax

As illustrated in Figure 6-2, the declaration contains a property and a value. The **property** is a quality or characteristic, such as color, font size, or margin, followed by a colon (:). The **value** is the precise specification of the property, such as blue for color, 125% for font size, or 30 px (pixels) for margin, followed by a semicolon (;). CSS contains a wide variety of properties, each with a specific list of values. As you will see later in this chapter, you can combine selectors and property declarations in a variety of ways.

Figure 6-2

Property declaration
syntax

Note

This chapter uses a variety of CSS style rules as examples. Although you have not yet learned about their properties in detail, you will see that the CSS property names express common desktop publishing characteristics such as font-family, margin, text-indent, and so on. The property values sometimes use abbreviations such as "px" for pixel, percentages such as 200%, or keywords such as "bold." You will learn about these properties and values in detail as you progress through this book.

Combining CSS Style Rules with HTML

You can combine CSS rules with HTML code in the following three ways:

- The style attribute
- The <style> element
- An external style sheet

Each method is discussed in detail in the following sections.

Using the Style Attribute

You can define the style for a single element using the style attribute.

```
<h1 style="color: blue">Some Text</h1>
```

You generally use the style attribute to override a style that was set at a higher level in the document, such as when you want a particular heading to be a different color from the rest of the headings on the page. (You'll learn more about overriding a style later in this chapter.) The style attribute is also useful for testing styles during development. You will probably use this method of styling an element the least, because it only affects one instance of an element in a document.

Using the Style Element

The <style> element is always contained in the <head> section of the document. Style rules contained in the <style> element only affect the document in which they reside. The following code shows a <style> element that contains a single style rule:

```
<head>
<title>Sample Document</title>
<style type="text/css">
h1 {color: red;}
</style>
</head>
```

In the previous code, note the type attribute to the <style> element. The value "text/css" defines the style language as Cascading Style Sheets. Although not required, the type attribute should always be included in all of your <style> elements for future compatibility as more style languages become available.

Using External Style Sheets

Placing style sheets in an external document lets you specify rules for multiple Web pages. This is an easy and powerful way to use style sheets because it lets you control the styles for an entire Web site with one style sheet file. An external style sheet is simply a text document that contains the style rules. External style sheets have a .css extension. Here's an example of a simple external style sheet named styles.css:

```
h1 {color: white; background-color: green;}
h2 {color: red;}
```

The style sheet file does not contain any HTML code, just CSS style rules, because the style sheet is not an HTML document. It is not necessary to use the <style> element in an external style sheet.

Linking to an External Style Sheet

The <link> element lets you establish document relationships. It can only be used within the <head> section of a document. To link to an external style sheet, add the **<link> element**, as shown in the following code:

CHAPTER 6

```
<head>
<title>Sample Document</title>
<link href="styles.css" rel="stylesheet" type="text/css">
</head>
```

The <link> element in this code tells the browser to find the specified style sheet. The href attribute states the relative URL of the style sheet. The rel attribute specifies the relationship between the linked and current documents. The browser displays the Web page based on the CSS display information. The advantage of the external style sheet is that you can state the style rules in one document and affect all the pages on a Web site. When you want to update a style, you only have to change the style rule once in the external style sheet.

Adding Comments

CSS allows comments within the <style> element or in an external style sheet. CSS comments begin with the forward slash and asterisk characters (/*) and end with the asterisk and forward slash characters (*/). You can use comments in a variety of ways, as shown in the following code:

```
<style type="text/css">
/* This is the basic style sheet */
h1 {color: gray;} /* The headline color */
h2 {color: red;} /* The subhead color */
</style>
```

Comments provide documentation for your style rules. Because they are embedded directly in the style sheet, they provide immediate information to anyone who needs to understand how the style rules work. Comments are always useful and you should consider using them in all of your code, whether as a simple reminder to yourself, or as an aid to others with whom you work.

Building a Basic Style Sheet

In the following set of steps, you build and test a basic style sheet. Save your file and test your work in the browser as you complete each step. Refer to Figure 6-3 as you progress through the steps to see the results.

To build a basic style sheet:

1. Copy the **basic.htm** file from the Chapter06 folder provided with your Data Files to the Chapter06 folder in your work folder. (Create the Chapter06 folder, if necessary.)

2. In your browser, open **basic.htm**. When you open the file it looks like Figure 6-3.

Figure 6-3

The original HTML
document

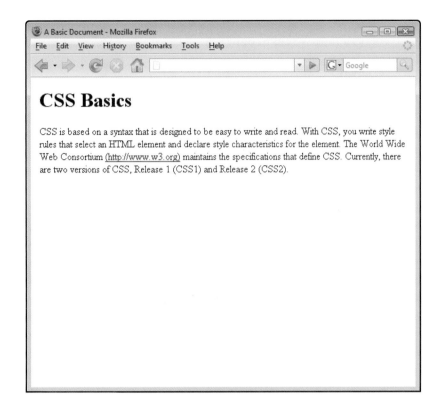

3. Open the **basic.htm** file in your HTML editor and examine the code. Notice that the file
contains basic HTML code with no style information. The complete code for the page
follows:

```
<html>
<head>
<title>A Basic Document</title>
</head>
<body>
<h1>CSS Basics</h1>
<p>CSS is based on a syntax that is designed to be easy to write and
    read. With CSS, you write style rules that select an HTML element
    and declare style characteristics for the element. The World Wide
    Web Consortium <a href="http://www.w3.org">(http://www.w3.org)</a>
    maintains the specifications that define CSS. Currently, there
    are two versions of CSS, Release 1 (CSS1) and Release 2 (CSS2).</p>
</body>
</html>
```

4. Add a **<style> element** in the <head> section to contain your style rules, as shown in the
    following code. Leave a few lines of white space between the <style> tags to contain the
    style rules.

```
<head>
<style type="text/css">

</style>
</head>
```

5. Add a **style rule** for the <h1> element, as shown in blue in the following code. This style rule uses the text-align property to center the heading.

```
<head>
<style type="text/css">
h1 {text-align: center;}
</style>
</head>
```

6. Save the file as **basic.htm** in the Chapter06 folder in your work folder, and then reload the file in the browser. The <h1> element is now centered.

7. Add a **style rule** for the <p> element, as shown in the following code fragment. This style rule uses the font-family property to specify a sans-serif font for the paragraph text. You will learn more about the font-family property in Chapter 7.

```
<head>
<style type="text/css">
h1 {text-align: center;}
p {font-family: sans-serif;}
</style>
</head>
```

8. Save the file as **basic.htm** in the Chapter06 folder and then reload it in the browser. Figure 6-4 shows the finished Web page. Notice that the <p> element is now displayed in a sans-serif typeface.

Figure 6-4

The HTML document styled with CSS

Understanding the Cascade

One of the fundamental features of CSS is that style sheets **cascade**. This means that multiple style sheets and style rules can apply to the same document. HTML authors can attach a preferred style sheet, while the reader might have a personal style sheet to adjust for preferences such as human or technological handicaps. However, only one rule can apply to an element. The CSS cascading mechanism determines which rules are applied to document elements by assigning a weight to each rule based on the following four variables, listed in the order in which they are applied:

- Use of the !important keyword
- Origin of the rule
- Specificity of the selector
- Order of the rule in the style sheet

Determining Rule Weight by Origin

A style rule's weight can be determined by the style sheet in which it resides. CSS allows style sheets to be applied by the author, the user, and the browser. Figure 6-5 shows the style sheet order of precedence.

Figure 6-5

The cascading order of precedence

In the cascading order, rules from the author's style sheet have the greatest weight. This is the page display that most users want to see—the author's intended page design.

The user's style sheet is next in order of importance. Although the designer's rules have more weight, users have the option of turning off the author's styles in the browser, or using the !important keyword to give their rules more weight. If the browser allows, the user can attach his or her style sheet to the document. This allows the user to adjust, for example, the font size or link color to make a page more legible.

The browser's style sheet has the least weight. This is the style sheet that contains the default display information, such as displaying an <h1> heading in Times Bold with a carriage return before and after. The browser's style sheet controls the display of elements that do not have an associated style rule.

Determining Rule Weight by Specificity

Another method of determining style rule weight is the specificity of the rule's element selector. Rules with more specific selectors take precedence over rules with less specific selectors. Examine the following style rules:

```
body {color: black;}
h1 {color: red;}
```

The first rule uses a nonspecific selector, the <body> element. This rule sets the text color for all elements within <body> to black. The second rule has a much more specific selector that sets a rule only for <h1> elements. Because the second rule has a more specific selector, it takes precedence for all <h1> elements within the document.

Determining Rule Weight by Order

CSS applies weight to a rule based on its order within a style sheet. Rules that are included later in the style sheet order take precedence over earlier rules. Examine the following style rules for an example:

```
body {color: black;}
h1 {color: red;}
h1 {color: green;}
```

In this example, <h1> elements in the document appear green because the last style rule specifies green as the color.

Determining Rule Weight with the !important Keyword

A conflict can arise when both the author's and user's style sheets contain a rule for the same element. By default, rules in an author's style sheet override those in a user's style sheet. To balance the bias towards the author's style sheet, CSS has an !important keyword. **!important** lets the user override the author's style setting for a particular element. The following user's style sheet states a rule for <p> elements that sets the font family to arial, regardless of the rule supplied by the author of the document:

```
<style type="text/css">
p {font-family: arial !important;}
</style>
```

This CSS feature improves accessibility of documents by giving users with special requirements control over document presentation, such as increasing font size or changing color contrast.

The !important keyword also allows you to specify that a rule should take precedence no matter what the order in the style sheet. Examine the following style rules for an example:

```
body {color: black;}
h1 {color: red !important; }
h1 {color: green;}
```

In this example, <h1> elements in the document will appear red, even though the rule that sets the color to green would normally take precedence because of its order in the document.

Understanding Inheritance

The elements in an HTML document are structured in a hierarchy of parent and child elements. Figure 6-6 represents the structure of a simple HTML document.

Figure 6-6

HTML document structure

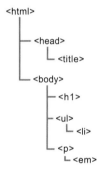

Note the hierarchical structure of the elements. <html> is the parent element of the document. **Parent elements** contain nested elements called **child elements**. Both <head> and <body> are immediate child elements of <html>. Yet, <head> and <body> are parent elements as well, because they contain other nested elements. As you travel further down the document hierarchy, you find additional elements that are both parent and child elements, such as <p> and <ul>.

By default, most CSS properties inherit from parent elements to child elements. The CSS property descriptions in the following chapters and Appendix B list whether a property is inherited. Therefore, if you set a style rule for <ul> elements in the document shown in Figure 6-6, the <li> elements inherit the style rules for <ul>, unless you specifically set a rule for <li>.

You can style multiple document elements with just a few style rules if you let inheritance work for you. For example, consider the following set of style rules for a document.

```
<style type="text/css">
h1 {color: red;}
p {color: red;}
ul {color: red;}
em {color: red;}
li {color: red;}
</style>
```

CHAPTER 6

This style sheet sets the color to red for five different elements in the document. Inheritance lets you write a far simpler rule to accomplish the same results:

```
<style type="text/css">
body {color: red;}
</style>
```

This rule works because all of the elements are children of <body>, and because all the rules are the same. It is much more efficient to write a single rule for the parent element and let the child elements inherit the style. Because <body> is the parent element of the content area of the HTML file, it is the selector to use whenever you want to apply a style across the entire document.

Understanding Basic Selection Techniques

In this section you will review style rule syntax and learn about the following basic selection techniques:

- Using type selectors
- Grouping selectors
- Combining declarations
- Using descendant selectors

Using Type Selectors

As you learned previously, the selector determines the element to which a style declaration is applied. To review, examine the syntax of the style rule shown in Figure 6-7. This rule selects the <h1> element in the document and sets the text color to red.

Figure 6-7

Style rule syntax

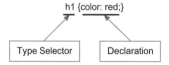

This rule uses a **type selector** to apply the rule to every instance of the element in the document. This is the simplest type of selector, and many style sheets are composed primarily of type selector style rules, as shown in the following code:

```
body {color: gray;}
h2 {color: red;}
p {font-size: 85%;}
```

Grouping Selectors

To make your style rules more concise, you can group selectors to which the same rules apply. For example, the following style rules set the same declaration for two different elements—they set the color of <h1> and <h2> elements to red:

```
h1 {color: red;}
h2 {color: red;}
```

These two style rules can be expressed in a simpler way by separating the selectors with commas:

```
h1, h2 {color: red;}
```

Combining Declarations

In many instances you want to state multiple property declarations for the same selector. The following style rules set the <p> element to 12-point, blue text:

```
p {color: blue;}
p {font-size: 125%;}
```

These two style rules can be expressed in a simpler fashion by combining the declarations in one rule. The declarations are separated by semicolons:

```
p {color: blue; font-size: 125%;}
```

Using Descendant Selectors

A descendant selector (sometimes known as a contextual selector) is based on the hierarchical structure of the elements in the document tree. This selector lets you select elements that are the descendants of other elements. For example, the following rule selects only <b> elements that are contained within <p> elements. All other <b> elements in the document are not affected.

```
p b {color: blue;}
```

Notice that the selector contains multiple elements, separated only by white space. You can use more than two elements if you prefer to choose more specific selection characteristics. For example, the following rule selects <b> elements within <li> elements within <ul> elements only:

```
ul li b {color: blue;}
```

Using the Basic Selection Techniques

In the following set of steps, you will build a style sheet that uses basic selection techniques. Save your file and test your work in the browser as you complete each step. Refer to Figure 6-8 as you progress through the steps to see the results.

To build the style sheet:

1. Copy the **oz.htm** file from the Chapter06 folder provided with your Data Files to the Chapter06 folder in your work folder.
2. Open the file **oz.htm** in your HTML editor and save it as **oz1.htm** in the same location.
3. In your browser, open the file **oz1.htm**. When you open the file, it looks like Figure 6-8.

Figure 6-8

The original oz1.htm
HTML document

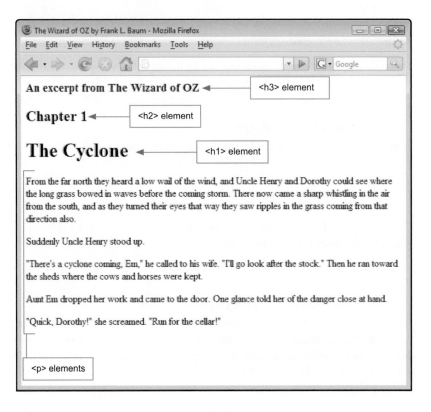

4. Examine the code. Notice that the file contains basic HTML code with no style information.
    The complete code for the page follows:

```
<html>
<head>
<title>The Wizard of OZ by Frank L. Baum</title>
</head>
<body>
<h3>An excerpt from The Wizard of OZ</h3>
<h2>Chapter 1</h2>
<h1>The Cyclone</h1>
<p>From the far north they heard a low wail of the wind, and Uncle
    Henry and Dorothy could see where the long grass bowed in waves
    before the coming storm. There now came a sharp whistling in the
    air from the south, and as they turned their eyes that way they
    saw ripples in the grass coming from that direction also.</p>
<p>Suddenly Uncle Henry stood up.</p>
<p>"There's a cyclone coming, Em," he called to his wife. "I'll go
    look after the stock."  Then he ran toward the sheds where the
    cows and horses were kept.</p>
<p>Aunt Em dropped her work and came to the door. One glance told her
    of the danger close at hand.</p>
```

```
<p>"Quick, Dorothy!" she screamed. "Run for the cellar!"</p>
</body>
</html>
```

5. Add a <style> element in the <head> section to contain your style rules, as shown in the following code. Leave a few lines of white space between the <style> tags to contain the style rules.

```
<head>
<style type="text/css">


</style>
</head>
```

6. Write the style rule for the <h3> element. The requirements for this element are right-aligned gray text. The style rule looks like this:

```
<head>
<style type="text/css">
h3 {text-align: right; color: gray;}
</style>
</head>
```

7. Write the style rules for the <h1> and <h2> elements, which share some common property values. Both elements have a left margin of 20 pixels (abbreviated as px) and a sans-serif font style. Because they share these properties, group the two elements to share the same style rule, as shown in the following code:

```
<head>
<style type="text/css">
h3 {text-align: right; color: gray;}
h1, h2 {margin-left: 20px; font-family: sans-serif;}
</style>
</head>
```

8. Write an additional rule for the <h1> element. The <h1> element has two style properties that it does not share with <h2>, so a separate style rule is necessary to express the border and padding white space within the border. This rule uses the border shortcut property to specify multiple border characteristics—a 1-pixel border weight and solid border style.

```
<head>
<style type="text/css">
h3 {text-align: right; color: gray;}
h1, h2 {margin-left: 20px; font-family: sans-serif;}
h1 {border: 1px solid; padding: 5px;}
</style>
</head>
```

9. Write a style rule for the <p> elements so they have a 20-pixel left margin (to line up with the other elements on the page), a serif font style, and a font size of 120%.

```
<head>
<style type="text/css">
h3 {text-align: right; color: gray;}
h1, h2 {margin-left: 20px; font-family: sans-serif;}
h1 {border: 1px solid; padding: 5px;}
p {margin-left: 20px; font-family: serif; font-size: 120%;}
</style>
</head>
```

Figure 6-9 shows the finished document with the style properties.

Figure 6-9

The oz1.htm HTML document styled with CSS rules

Understanding Advanced Selection Techniques

This section describes the CSS advanced selection techniques that are supported in the newer browsers. These techniques allow more than the basic element-based selection capabilities described in the previous section. You will learn to select elements of an HTML document using the following methods:

- The class attribute
- The id attribute
- The <div> and <span> elements
- The pseudo-class and pseudo-element selectors
- The universal selector

Using the Class Attribute Selector

The class attribute lets you write rules, give them a name, and then apply that name to any elements you choose. You can use class with any HTML element because it is a core attribute. The **core attributes** are id, class, style, and title, and they apply to all HTML elements. To apply a style rule to an element, you can add the class attribute to the element and set it to the name you have specified.

To create a class, declare a style rule. The period (.) flag character indicates that the selector is a class selector. Figure 6-10 shows an example of a rule with a class selector.

Figure 6-10

Class syntax

| Flag character | Class name | Declaration |

After writing the style rule, add it to the document by using the class attribute, as shown in the following code fragment:

```
<p class="quote">This text will be red with a 30 pixel margin.</p>
```

The class attribute lets you select elements with greater precision. For example, read the following style rule:

```
p {font-size: .85%;}
```

This rule sets all <p> elements in the document to a font size of 85 percent. Now suppose that you want one <p> element in your document to have a different style characteristic, such as bold text. You need a way to specifically select that one paragraph. To do this, use a class selector. The following style rule sets the style for the class named special.

```
.special {font-weight: bold; font-family: sans-serif;}
```

The class selector can be any name you choose. In this instance, the class name "special" denotes a special paragraph of the document. Now apply the rule to the <p> element in the document using the class attribute:

```
<p class="special">This is the first paragraph of the document. It has
    a different style based on the "special" class selector.</p>
<p>This is the second paragraph of text in the document. It is a
    standard paragraph without a class attribute.</p>
```

Figure 6-11 shows the result of the style rule.

Figure 6-11

Styling with a class
attribute

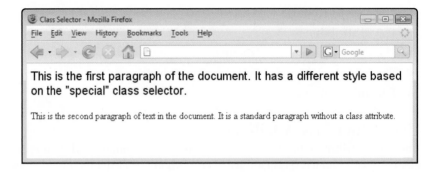

Making Class Selectors More Specific

Using the class attribute is a powerful selection technique, because it allows you to write style
rules with names that are meaningful to your organization or information type. The more specific
your class names become, the greater control you need over the way they are applied. In the
preceding example, you saw a style rule named special that was applied to a <p> element. However, the special style can be applied to any element in the document, not just <p>. To solve this
problem, you can restrict the use of the class attribute to a single element type.

For example, your organization might use a special style for a procedure heading. The style is
based on an <h1> element, with a sans-serif font and left margin of 20 pixels. Everyone in your
organization knows this style is named "procedure." You can use this same style name in your
style sheet, as shown in the following style rule:

```
.procedure {font-family: sans-serif; margin-left: 20px;}
```

To use these rules in the document, you apply the class attribute, as shown in the following code
fragment:

```
<h1 class="procedure">Procedure Heading</h1>
```

This works well, but what happens if someone on your staff neglects to apply the classes properly?
For the style rule to work, it must be applied to an <h1> element. To restrict the use of the
class to <h1> elements, include a prefix for the class selector with the element to which you want
it applied:

```
h1.procedure {font-family: sans-serif; margin-left: 20px;}
```

These style rules restrict the use of the procedure style to <h1>.

Using the id Attribute Selector

The id attribute, like the class attribute, is an HTML core attribute. The difference between id and class is that id refers to only one instance of the id attribute value within a document. This allows you to specify an id value and apply it to one unique element in a document. For example, you might want to specify that only one <p> element can have the id preface and its associated style rule. Figure 6-12 shows a style rule that uses the id preface as a selector:

Figure 6-12

Using the id selector

Notice that the id selector uses a pound sign (#) flag character instead of the period you used with the class selector. You can apply the id value to the appropriate element in the document, in this example a <p> element:

```
<p id="preface">This is a unique paragraph that is the preface of the
    document.</p>
```

The id value uniquely identifies this one <p> element as the preface. No other elements in the document can share this exact id value.

Using the <div> and <span> Elements

The <div> (division) and <span> (span of words) elements are designed to be used with CSS. They let you specify logical divisions within a document that have their own name and style properties. The difference between <div> and <span> is their element display type, which is described in more detail in Chapter 9. <div> is a block-level element, and <span> is its inline equivalent. Used with the class and id attributes, <div> and <span> let you effectively create your own element names for your HTML documents.

Working with <div>

You can use <div> with the class attribute to create customized block-level elements. Like other block-level elements, <div> contains a leading and trailing line break. However, unlike other block-level elements, <div> contains no additional white space around the element. You can set the margin or padding to any value that you want. You will learn more about these properties in Chapter 9.

To create a customized division, declare it with a class or selector in the style rule. The following example specifies a division with a class named column as the selector for the rule:

```
div.column {width: 200px; height: auto; padding: 15px;
    border: thin solid;}
```

To apply this rule, specify the <div> element in the document. Then use the class attribute to specify the exact type of division. In the following example, the code defines the <div> element as the class named column:

```
<div class="column">This division displays as a column of text in the
    browser window. This is one of the uses of the division element as a
    page layout tool with CSS. You will learn more about this in later
    chapters of this book</div>
```

Figure 6-13 shows the result of the style rule.

Figure 6-13

Using the <div> element
to create a column of text

Working with <span>

The <span> element lets you specify inline elements within a document that have their own name and style properties. Inline elements reside within a line of text, such as the <b> or <em> element. You can use <span> with a class or attribute to create customized inline elements.

To create a span, declare it within the <style> element first. The following example specifies a span named logo as the selector for the rule:

```
span.logo {color: white; background-color: black;}
```

Next, specify the <span> element in the document. Then use the class attribute to specify the exact type of span. In the following example, the code defines the <span> element as the class named logo.

```
<p>Welcome to the <span class="logo">Wonder Software</span>
    Web site.</p>
```

Figure 6-14 shows the result of the style rule.

Figure 6-14

Using the <span>
element

Welcome to the Wonder Software Web site.

Using Pseudo-Class and Pseudo-Element Selectors

Pseudo-class and pseudo-element selectors let you express style declarations for characteristics of a document that are not signified with the standard HTML elements. **Pseudo-classes** select elements based on characteristics other than their element name. For example, assume that you want to change the color of a new or visited hypertext link. There is no HTML element that directly lets you express these characteristics of the <a> element. With CSS, you can use the pseudo-class selector to change the link color.

Pseudo-elements let you change other aspects of a document that are not classified by elements, such as applying style rules to the first letter or first line of a paragraph. For example, you might want to create a drop initial or drop capital that extends below the line of type, or make the first line of a paragraph all uppercase text. These are common publishing design techniques that are not possible with standard HTML code. With CSS you can use the :first-letter and :first-line pseudo-elements to add these two style characteristics to your documents.

Using the Link Pseudo-Classes

The :link and :visited pseudo-classes let you change the style characteristics for new, unvisited links (:link) and visited links (:visited). These pseudo-classes only apply to the <a> element with an href attribute, because <a> is the only element in HTML that can be a hypertext link. In other applications, such as Extensible Markup Language (XML), any element can be defined as a hypertext link and have these pseudo-classes applied. In most instances you only want to change the colors of the link from the default blue for new and purple for visited.

The following rules change the colors of the hypertext links:

```
:link {color: red;}
:visited {color: green;}
```

Because these pseudo-classes only affect the <a> element, the following style rules are the same as the preceding ones:

```
a:link {color: red;}
a:visited {color: green;}
```

Some Web sites choose to remove the underlining of their links. You can achieve this effect with the text-decoration property, which is described in more detail in Chapter 7. The following rule removes the default link underline:

```
a:link {text-decoration: none;}
a:visited {text-decoration: none;}
```

These style rules create <a> elements that have the standard blue and purple colors, but no underlining. Whether you choose to use this style for your links depends on the design of your site and the needs of your users. Remember that many Web users are comfortable with the default underlining, and that color alone may not be enough to differentiate links from the rest of your text.

CHAPTER 6

Using the :hover Pseudo-Class

The :hover pseudo-class lets you apply a style that appears when the user points to an element with a pointing device. This is a useful navigation aid to add to the <a> element, with the result that the link appears highlighted when the user points to it with the mouse. The following style rule shows the :hover pseudo-class with the <a> element as the selector.

```
a:hover {background-color: yellow;}
```

This style rule changes the background color of the link to yellow, which is an effective highlight color. Figure 6-15 shows the results of this style rule.

Figure 6-15

The :hover pseudo-class is activated by the mouse pointer

Using the :first-letter Pseudo-Element

Use the :first-letter pseudo-element to apply style rules to the first letter of any element. This lets you create interesting text effects, such as initial capitals and drop capitals which are usually set in a bolder and larger font. Initial capitals share the same baseline as the rest of the text, while drop capitals extend down two or more lines below the text baseline. To apply :first-letter to build an initial capital, specify a style rule like the following:

```
p:first-letter {font-weight: bold; font-size: 200%;}
```

This creates a first letter that is bold and twice the size of the <p> font. For example, if the <p> element has a font size of 12 points, the initial cap will be 24 points. This style rule applies to the first letter of every <p> element in the document without any further additions to the HTML code. However, the problem with this selector is that every <p> element gets the initial capital, where you probably only want the first paragraph in the document to have one. To solve this problem, add a class name, such as initial, to the rule, as shown in Figure 6-16.

Figure 6-16

Using a class selector
with a :first-letter
pseudo-element

This style rule affects only <p> elements with the class value of initial, as shown in the following code:

```
<p class="initial">From the far north they heard a low wail of the wind,
    and Uncle Henry and Dorothy could see where the long grass bowed in
    waves before the coming storm. There now came a sharp whistling in
    the air from the south, and as they turned their eyes that way they
    saw ripples in the grass coming from that direction also.</p>
```

Figure 6-17 shows the result of the style rule:

Figure 6-17

An initial capital styled
with the :first-letter
pseudo-class

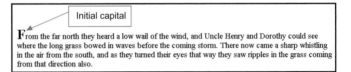

You can make the initial capital a drop capital by adding the float property to the rule, which allows the letter to extend downward. The float property is described in Chapter 9. Here is a :first-letter style rule with the float property added:

```
p.dropcap:first-letter {font-weight: bold; font-size: 200%;
    float: left;}
```

Notice that the class has been changed to signify that this first letter is a drop capital. Remember, you can set the class attribute to any naming value that makes sense to you.

This style rule affects only <p> elements with the class value of dropcap, as shown in the following code:

```
<p class="dropcap">From the far north they heard a low wail of the wind,
    and Uncle Henry and Dorothy could see where the long grass bowed in
    waves before the coming storm. There now came a sharp whistling in
    the air from the south, and as they turned their eyes that way they
    saw ripples in the grass coming from that direction also.</p>
```

Figure 6-18 shows the result of the new style rule.

Figure 6-18

A drop capital
using the :first-letter
pseudo-class

CHAPTER 6

The :first-letter pseudo-element can only be applied to a block-level element. In addition, only the following properties can be applied to the :first-letter selector:

- Font properties
- Color properties
- Background properties
- Margin properties
- Padding properties
- Word-spacing
- Letter-spacing
- Text-decoration
- Vertical-align
- Text-transform
- Line-height
- Text-shadow
- Clear

Using the :first-line Pseudo-Element

The :first-line pseudo-element works in much the same way as :first-letter, except for the obvious difference that it affects the first line of text in an element. For example, the following rule sets the first line of every <p> element to uppercase letters:

```
p:first-line {text-transform: uppercase;}
```

The problem with this code is that it affects every <p> element in the document. As you saw in the preceding :first-letter selector, you can add a class attribute to more narrowly define the application of the :first-line style:

```
p.introduction:first-line {text-transform: uppercase;}
```

This rule transforms to uppercase the first line of the <p> element that contains the following code:

```
<p class="introduction">From the far north they heard a low wail of the
    wind, and Uncle Henry and Dorothy could see where the long grass
    bowed in waves before the coming storm. There now came a sharp
    whistling in the air from the south, and as they turned their eyes
    that way they saw ripples in the grass coming from that direction
    also.</p>
```

Figure 6-19 shows the results of the style rule.

Figure 6-19

First line transformation using the :first-line pseudo-element

FROM THE FAR NORTH THEY HEARD A LOW WAIL OF THE WIND, AND UNCLE
Henry and Dorothy could see where the long grass bowed in waves before the coming storm.
There now came a sharp whistling in the air from the south, and as they turned their eyes that way
they saw ripples in the grass coming from that direction also.

The :first-line pseudo-element can only be applied to a block-level element. In addition, only the following properties can be applied to :first-line. Notice that :first-line does not support padding, margin, or border properties:

- Font properties
- Color properties
- Background properties
- Word-spacing
- Letter-spacing
- Text-decoration
- Text-transform
- Line-height
- Text-shadow
- Clear

Using the Universal Selector

The universal selector lets you quickly select groups of elements and apply a style rule. The symbol for the universal selector is the asterisk (*). For example, to set a default color for all elements within a document, use the following rule:

```
* {color: purple;}
```

You can also use the universal selector to select all children of an element. For example, the following rule sets all elements within a <div> element to a sans-serif typeface:

```
div * {font-family: sans-serif;}
```

Remember that the universal selector is always overridden by more specific selectors. The following style rules show a universal selector along with two other rules that have more specific selectors. In this example, the <h1> and <h2> rules override the universal selector for the <h1> and <h2> elements.

```
* {color: purple;}
h1 {color: red;}
h2 {color: black;}
```

Chapter Summary

This chapter presents the basic syntax of the CSS language. You learned about the different methods of selecting elements and applying style rules in a variety of ways. You saw that the CSS basic selection techniques are often powerful enough to handle most document styling. You learned that the class and id attributes let you create naming conventions for styles that are meaningful to your organization or information type. As you will see in the upcoming chapters, CSS is an easy-to-use style language that lets you gain visual control over the display of your Web content.

▶ CSS rules can be combined with your HTML code in a number of ways. CSS rules are easy to write and read.

▶ CSS uses cascading and inheritance to determine which style rules take precedence. The !important declaration lets users override the author's style rules.

▶ Basic style rules let you apply style rules based on standard element selectors. You can combine the selectors and declarations to create more powerful style expressions. You can also select elements based on the contextual relationship of elements in the document tree.

▶ The advanced selection techniques allow you to use the class and id attribute selectors, which are often paired with the <div> and <span> HTML elements. These elements have no style of their own, but offer a convenient way of expressing style for any section of a document, whether block-level or inline. In addition, class allows you to choose a meaningful naming convention for your style rules.

▶ The pseudo-class and pseudo-element selectors let you change the color and styling of hypertext links and the effect elements of a document, such as first line and first letter, that are not signified with the standard HTML elements.

Key Terms

!important	pseudo-class
cascade	pseudo-element
child element	selector
core attribute	style rule
declaration	style sheet
inheritance	type selector
parent element	universal selector
property	value

Review Questions

1. What are the two parts of a style rule?
2. What are the three ways to combine CSS rules with your HTML code?
3. List two reasons to state a style using the style attribute.

4. What are the advantages of using an external style sheet?

5. What is the inheritance default for CSS rules?

6. What is the benefit of the !important declaration?

7. Write a basic style rule that selects <h1> elements and sets the color property to red.

8. Add the <p> element as an additional selector to the rule you created for question 7.

9. Add a font-size property to the rule and set the size to 14 points.

10. Write a style rule that selects <ul> elements only when they appear within <p> elements and set the color property to red.

11. Write the style rule for a class selector named note. Set the font-weight property to bold.

12. Restrict the rule you developed for question 11 so it can be used only with <p> elements.

13. What is the difference between <div> and <span>?

14. Write a style rule that sets the default document text color to red.

15. What is the advantage of working with the class attribute?

16. What element does this selector choose?

```
p ul li
```

17. What element does this selector choose?

```
div p *
```

What element does this selector choose?

```
p.warning
```

18. What is the advantage of working with the id attribute?

19. Write a style rule that applies a yellow background color to <a> elements when the user points the mouse to a hypertext link.

Hands-On Projects

1. Visit the World Wide Web Consortium Web site and find the CSS Techniques for Web Content Accessibility Guidelines (*www.w3.org/TR/WCAG10-CSS-TECHS/#acss*). Write an essay describing the benefits of using CSS for accessibility and the primary CSS features you would use to ensure accessible content on the Web.

2. By yourself or with a partner, choose a mainstream publishing Web site, such as a newspaper or periodical site. Examine the style characteristics of the site. What common styles can be applied across the site, such as headings, paragraphs, and bylines? Write an analysis of the site's style requirements, and list the styles you would include in the site's style sheet.

3. In this project, you will have a chance to test a few simple style rules on a standard HTML document and view the results in your browser.

   a. Using your HTML editor, create a simple HTML file (or open an existing file) that contains <body>, <h1>, and <p> elements. Save the file as **csstest1.htm** in the Chapter06 folder in your work folder.

b. Add a \<style\> element to the \<head\> section, as shown in the following code.

```
<head>
<title>CSS Test Document</title>
<style type="text/css">

</style>
</head>
```

c. Add a style rule that uses body as a selector and sets the color property to green, as shown in the following code:

```
<style type="text/css">
body {color: green;}
</style>
```

d. Save **csstest1.htm** and view it in the browser. All of the document text should now be green.

e. Now add a style rule that sets \<h1\> elements to be displayed in black:

```
<style type="text/css">
body {color: green;}
h1 {color: black;}
</style>
```

f. Save **csstest1.htm** and view the results in the browser.

g. Finally, add a style rule that sets a margin for \<p\> elements to 30 pixels:

```
<style type="text/css">
body {color: green;}
h1 {color: black;}
p {margin: 30px;}
</style>
```

h. Save **csstest1.htm** and view the results in the browser.

4. In this project, you will have a chance to test a few basic selection techniques on a standard HTML document and view the results in your browser. Save the file and view it in your browser after completing each step.

a. Using your HTML editor, create a simple HTML file (or open an existing file) that contains \<body\>, \<h1\>, \<p\> elements, and so on. Save the file in the Chapter06 folder in your work folder as **csstest2.htm**.

b. Add a \<style\> element to the \<head\> section, as shown in the following code:

```
<head>
<title>CSS Test Document</title>
<style type="text/css">

</style>
</head>
```

    c. Write a style rule that uses body as a selector and sets the color property to the color of your choice.

    d. Find two elements on the page, such as <h1> and <h2>, which can share the same characteristics. Write a single style rule that applies to both elements. Set the color property to red and the margin property to 20px.

    e. Find one element that contains another, such as a <b> or <q> element within a <p> element. Write a descendant selector rule that affects the contained element and sets the color property to green.

5. In this project, you will have a chance to test a few advanced selection techniques on a standard HTML document and view the results in your browser. Save the file and view it in your browser after completing each step.

    a. Using your HTML editor, create a simple HTML file (or open an existing file) that contains the elements: <body>, <h1>, <p>, and so on. Save the file in the Chapter06 folder in your work folder as **csstest3.htm**.

    b. Add a <style> element to the <head> section, as shown in Exercise 4.

    c. Write a rule for a class selector named heading. Set the color property to red and the font-size property to 200%. Apply the heading class to an <h1> or <h2> element in the document.

    d. Write a rule for a class selector named emphasis. Set the color property to yellow. In the document, add a <span> element to a span of words that you want to highlight. Apply the emphasis class to the <span> element.

Individual Case Project

Revisit your project proposal and the page designs you created in Chapter 5. How will you implement Cascading Style Sheets into your project Web site? In the next few chapters, you will learn how to control typography, white space, borders, colors, and backgrounds with CSS. Think about each of these style characteristics and how you will apply them to your page designs. In addition, make a list of possible class names you might use to identify your content. For example, consider using class names for the following page characteristics, as well as creating some of your own:

▶ Body copy

▶ Header (possible different levels)

▶ Footer

Team Case Project

Revisit your project proposal and the page templates you created in Chapter 5. Each team member is responsible for individual templates, such as the home page template, the section page template, and the article level page template.

In the next few chapters, you will learn how to control typography, white space, borders, colors, and backgrounds with CSS. Decide how you will handle these style characteristics in your Web site. Each team member should create a suggested list of styles and naming conventions for use in your site.

For example, you might have top-level, secondary-level, and tertiary-level headings. What names will you use for consistency throughout the site? You might want to name these A-head, B-head, and so on. Also you will need to segregate and name the different copy styles in your site. For example, you might have a different body copy style for the main page than you have on a secondary section or on reading-level pages. Think about the different style properties that you will be able to manipulate (you can look these up in Appendix B) and how you will consistently use, manage, and name these style characteristics for your project Web site. Meet as a team to review each member's ideas and come to an agreement on the proposed styles and naming conventions.

7

Web Typography

When you complete this chapter, you will be able to:

- Understand type design principles
- Understand Cascading Style Sheets (CSS) measurement units
- Use the CSS font properties
- Use the CSS text spacing properties
- Create a font and text properties style sheet

Everyone visiting your Web site is a reader and responds instinctively to words set in type. The consistent use of type provides valuable information cues to the reader, and recent innovations provide powerful tools for working with type. Until recently, Web typography meant having to use too many <font> tags and lots of text as graphics. Today, Cascading Style Sheets offers a potent style language, allowing you to manipulate a variety of text properties to achieve professional, effective results, all without resorting to graphics that add download time.

Understanding Type Design Principles

Type can flexibly express emotion, tone, and structure. Most of the type principles that apply to paper-based design apply to the Web as well. However, it is possible to go overboard by using too many typefaces and sizes, ending up with the "ransom note" look that was characteristic of the early days of page layout programs. Just because you have many typefaces at your disposal does not mean you should use them all. Designing for the Web actually restricts your font choices to those your users have installed on their computers. If you specify a font that is not available, the browser substitutes the default font.

As you work with type, consider the following principles for creating an effective design:

- Choose fewer fonts and sizes.
- Use available fonts.
- Design for legibility.
- Avoid using text as graphics.

NOTE

In strict typography terms, a **typeface** is the name of the type, such as Times New Roman or Futura Condensed. A **font** is the typeface in a particular size, such as Times Roman 24 point. For the most part, on the Web the two terms are interchangeable.

Choose Fewer Fonts and Sizes

Your pages will look cleaner when you choose fewer fonts and sizes of type. Decide on a font for each different level of topic importance, such as page headings, section headings, and body text. Communicate the hierarchy of information with changes in the size, weight, or color of the typeface. For example, a page heading should have a larger, bolder type, while a section heading would appear in the same typeface, only lighter or smaller.

Pick a few sizes and weights in a type family. For example, you might choose three sizes, a large one for headings, a smaller size for subheadings, and your body text size. You can vary these styles by changing the weight; for example, bold type can be used for topic headings within text. Avoid making random changes in your use of type conventions. Consistently apply the same fonts and the same combination of styles throughout your Web site; consistency develops a strong visual identity. The Web Style Guide Web site (*www.webstyleguide.com*) shown in Figure 7-1 is a good example of effective type usage. The site has a strong typographic identity, yet uses only two typefaces. The designers of this site built a visually interesting page simply by varying the weight, size, white space, and color of the text.

Figure 7-1

Effective typographic design

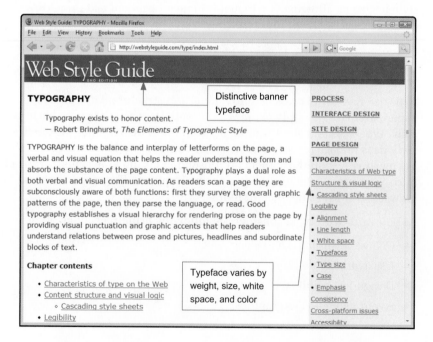

Use Available Fonts

Fonts often are a problem in HTML because font information is client based. The user's browser and operating system determine how a font is displayed, or if it is displayed at all. If you design your pages using a font that your user does not have installed, the browser defaults to Times on a Macintosh or Times New Roman on a PC. To make matters worse, even the most widely available fonts appear in different sizes on different operating systems. Unfortunately, the best you can do about this is to test on multiple platforms to judge the effect on your pages.

To control more effectively how text appears on your pages, think in terms of font families, such as serif and sans-serif typefaces (see Figure 7-2), rather than specific styles. Notice that serif fonts have strokes (or serifs) that finish the top and bottom of the letter. Sans-serif fonts consist of block letters without serifs.

Figure 7-2
Serif and sans-serif type

Because of the variable nature of fonts installed on different computers, you never can be sure the user will see the exact font you have specified. You can, however, specify font substitution attributes (described later in this chapter), which let you specify a variety of fonts within a font family, such as the common sans-serif fonts, Arial or Helvetica.

Table 7-1 lists the most common fonts on the PC, UNIX, and Macintosh systems.

Common PC Fonts	Common UNIX Fonts	Common Macintosh Fonts
Arial	Helvetica	Helvetica
Courier New	Times	Courier
Times New Roman		Palatino
Trebuchet MS		Times
Verdana		Verdana Arial

Table 7-1   Common installed fonts

The table shows that Times (or Times New Roman) is available on all three operating systems; it is the default browser font. Courier is the default monospace font, and Arial or Helvetica is the default sans-serif font. Arial, Trebuchet, and Verdana come with Internet Explorer, so many Macintosh and PC users have these fonts installed. Some Macintosh users only have Helvetica, so it is a good idea to specify this font as an alternate choice when you are using sans-serif fonts.

Design for Legibility

Figure 7-3 shows the same paragraph in Times, Trebuchet, Arial, and Verdana at the default browser size in both Internet Explorer (on the left) and Mozilla Firefox. Notice that subtle variations in the weight, spacing, and rendering of the font families affect the way each is displayed to the user. These variations can be compounded by the operating system and video capabilities of each user's individual computer.

Figure 7-3

Common Web font families in Internet Explorer and Firefox

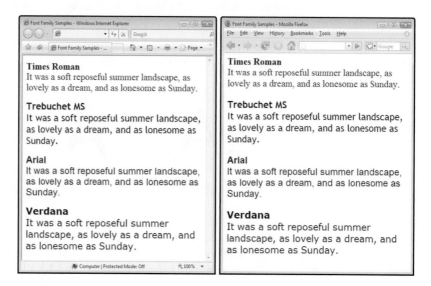

You can see in these examples that where the text wraps at the end of each line depends on the font and the display characteristics of the browser. Because its **x-height** (the height of the letter x in the font) is smaller than that of other fonts, Times can be hard to read, even though it is a serif typeface. This makes it a poor choice for a default font. Trebuchet is a sans-serif face that has a large x-height and rounded letter forms for easy screen legibility. Arial is widely available and is the most commonly used sans-serif font. Verdana is an expanded font—each letter takes up more horizontal space than letters in the other font families. This makes the text easier to read online, but takes much more space on the page.

The size and face of the type you use on your pages determine the legibility of your text. The computer screen has a lower resolution than the printed page, making fonts that are legible on paper more difficult to read on-screen. Keep fonts big enough to be legible, and avoid specialty fonts that degrade when viewed online. To aid the reader, consider adding more white space to the page around your blocks of text and between lines as well. Test your content with both serif and sans-serif body text. Finally, make sure that you provide enough contrast between your text color and the background color; in general, darker text on a light background is easiest to read.

Avoid Using Text as Graphics

If you must use a specific font that you suspect your viewers do not have, you can create text as graphics. Using Adobe Photoshop or another graphics program, create text and save it as either a GIF or JPG file. (See Chapter 8 for more information on these file formats.) This technique allows you to add drop shadows and other effects to your text. However, because you also are adding download overhead with every additional graphic, save text graphics for important purposes, such as the main logo for your page or as reusable navigation graphics. Remember that including text as graphics means users cannot search for that text. Whenever possible, use HTML-styled text on your pages.

Understanding CSS Measurement Units

CSS offers a variety of measurement units, including absolute units, such as points; relative units, such as pixels; and percentages of the base font. The measurement values you choose depend on the destination medium for your content. For example, if you are designing a style sheet for printed media, you can use absolute units of measurement, such as points or centimeters. When you are designing a style sheet for a Web page, you can use relative measurement values that adapt to the user's display type, such as ems or pixels. In this section, you will learn about the following CSS measurement units. These units are detailed in Table 7-2.

- Absolute units
- Relative units
- Percentage

Unit	Unit Abbreviation	Description
Absolute Units		
Centimeter	cm	Standard metric centimeter
Inch	in	Standard U.S. inch
Millimeter	mm	Standard metric millimeter
Pica	pc	Standard publishing unit equal to 12 points
Point	pt	Standard publishing unit, with 72 points in an inch
Relative Units		
Em	em	The width of the capital M in the current font, usually the same as the font size
Ex	ex	The height of the letter x in the current font
Pixel	px	The size of a pixel on the current monitor
Percentage	For example: 150%	Sets a font size relative to the base font size; 150% equals 1.5 times the base font size

Table 7-2 CSS measurement units

Absolute Units

CSS lets you use absolute measurement values that specify a fixed value. The measurement values require a number followed by one of the unit abbreviations listed in Table 7-2. The numeric value can be a positive value, negative value, or fractional value. For example, the following rule sets margins to 1.25 inches:

```
p {margin: 1.25in;}
```

You generally want to avoid using absolute units for Web pages because they cannot be scaled to the individual user display type. They are better used when you know the exact measurements of the destination medium. For example, if you know a document will be printed on 8.5 × 11-inch paper, you can plan your style rules accordingly because you know the physical dimensions of the finished document. Absolute units are better suited to print destinations than Web destinations. Although the point is the standard unit of measurement for type sizes, it is not the best measurement value for the Web. Because computer displays vary widely in size, they lend themselves better to relative units of measurement that can adapt to different monitor sizes and screen resolutions.

Relative Units

The relative units are designed to let you build scalable Web pages that adapt to different display types and sizes. This practice ensures that your type sizes are properly displayed relative to each other or to the default font size set for the browser.

The em Unit

The em is a printing measurement, traditionally equal to the horizontal length of the capital letter M in any given font size. In CSS the **em unit** is equal to the font size of an element. It can be used for both horizontal and vertical measurement. In addition to stating font sizes, em is useful for padding and margins as well. You can read more about this in Chapter 9.

The size of the em is equivalent to the font size of the element. For example, if the default paragraph font size is 12-point text, the em equals 12 points. Stating a text size of 2 em creates 24-point text—two times the default size. This is useful because it means that measurements stated in em are always relative to their environment. For example, assume that you want a larger size heading on your page. If you set the <h1> element to 24 points, it always remains that size. If a user sets his or her default font size to 24 points, the headings are the same size as the text. However, if you use the relative em unit, the size of the heading is always based on the size of the default text. The following rule sets heading divisions to twice the size of the default text:

```
div.heading {font-size: 2em;}
```

The ex Unit

The **ex unit** is equal to the height of the lowercase letter x in any given font. As shown in Figure 7-4, the height of the lowercase letter x varies widely from one typeface to another.

Figure 7-4
Differences in height in the ex unit

Ex is a less reliable unit of measurement than em because the size of the letter x changes in height from one font family to another, and the browser cannot always calculate the difference correctly. Most browsers simply set the ex value to one-half the value of the font's em size.

The px unit

Pixels are the basic picture element of a computer display. The size of the pixel is determined by the display resolution. Resolution is the measure of how many pixels fit on a screen. The standard display resolutions are 640 × 480, 800 × 600, and 1024 × 768. As the resolutions grow in value, the individual pixel size gets smaller, making the pixel relative to the individual display settings. Pixel measurements work well for computer displays, but they are not so well suited to other media, such as printing, because some printers cannot accurately determine the size of the pixel.

Percentages

Percentage values are always relative to another value. For example, the following rule sets the font size for the <body> element to 1.5 times the size of the browser default:

```
body {font-size: 150%;}
```

Child elements inherit the percentage values of their parents. For example, the < b> text in the following example is 125% larger than the <p> that contains it:

```
p {font-size: 12pt;}
p b {font-size: 125%;}
```

The first rule establishes the font size for the <p> element. The second rule selects any <b> elements within <p> elements. Because the <p> element has the font size set to 12 points, the <b> text is displayed at 15 points, or 125% larger than its parent.

How to Read the Property Descriptions

The property descriptions on the following pages and in other chapters are used to provide key information about each CSS property. A property description looks like the following:

border-width property description
Value: thin | medium | thick | <length>
Initial: medium
Applies to: all elements
Inherited: no
Percentages: N/A

Table 7-3 lists the five property description categories.

Category	Definition
Value	The valid keyword or variable values for the property; variable values are set between angle brackets; for example, <length> means enter a length value; (Table 7-4 lists the value notation symbols)
Initial	The initial value of the property
Applies to	The elements to which the property applies
Inherited	Indicates if the property is inherited from its parent element
Percentages	Indicates if percentage values are allowed

Table 7-3   Property description categories

Table 7-4 lists the value category notation.

Notation	Definition
< >	Words between angle brackets specify a variable value; for example, <length>
|	A single vertical bar separates two or more alternatives, one of which must occur; for example, thin | medium | thick
||	Two vertical bars separate options; one or more of the values can occur in any order; for example, underline || overline || line-through
[ ]	Square brackets group parts of the property value together; for example, none | [underline || overline || line-through] means that the value is either none or one of the values within the square brackets
?	A question mark indicates that the preceding value or group of values is optional

Table 7-4   Value category notation

Using the CSS Font Properties

The CSS font properties allow you to control the appearance of your text. These properties describe how the form of each letter looks. The CSS text properties, covered later in this chapter, describe the spacing around the text rather than affecting the actual text itself. In this section, you will learn about the following properties:

- font-family
- font-size
- font-style
- font-variant
- font-weight
- font (shorthand property)

Specifying Font Family

font-family property description
Value: <family-name> | <generic-family>
Initial: depends on user agent
Applies to: all elements
Inherited: yes
Percentages: N/A

The font-family property lets you state a generic font-family name, such as sans-serif, or a specific font-family name, like Helvetica. You can also string together a list of font families, separated by commas, supplying a selection of fonts that the browser can attempt to match.

To make your pages appear more consistent, think in terms of font families, such as serif and sans-serif typefaces, rather than specific styles. Because of the variable nature of fonts installed on different computers, you can never be sure that the user will see the exact font you have specified. You can, however, use font substitution to specify a variety of fonts within a font family, such as Arial or Helvetica, which are both common sans-serif fonts.

Using Generic Font Families

You can use the following generic names for font families:

- **Serif** fonts are the traditional letter form, with strokes (or serifs) that finish off the top and bottom of the letter. The most common serif font is Times.
- **Sans-serif** fonts have no serifs. They are block letters. The most common sans-serif fonts are Helvetica and Arial.
- **Monospace** fonts are fixed-width fonts. Every letter has the same horizontal width. Monospace is commonly used to mimic typewritten text or for programming code. The style rules and HTML code in this book are printed in Courier, a monospace font.

- **Cursive** fonts are designed to resemble handwriting. This is not a well-supported font family.
- **Fantasy** fonts are primarily decorative. Like cursive, fantasy is not a well-supported font family.

The practice of using generic names ensures greater portability across browsers and operating systems, because it does not rely on a specific font being installed on the user's computer. The following rule sets <p> elements to the default sans-serif font:

```
p {font-family: sans-serif;}
```

Of course, if you don't specify any font family, the browser displays the default font, usually some version of Times. Figure 7-5 shows the generic font families in both Internet Explorer (on the left) and Mozilla Firefox. Notice the difference in the display size of the monospace font. Also notice that the cursive font is actually Comic Sans. If a certain font is not available, a different font will be substituted, based on the user's operating system.

Figure 7-5

Generic font families in Internet Explorer and Firefox

Using Specific Font Families

In addition to generic font families, the font-family property lets you declare a specific font family, such as Futura or Garamond. The user must have the font installed on his or her computer; otherwise, the browser uses the default font.

The following rule specifies Arial as the font family for the <p> element:

```
p {font-family: arial;}
```

Specifying Font Substitution

You can specify a list of alternate fonts using commas as a separator. The browser attempts to load each successive font in the list. If no fonts match, the browser uses its default font. The following code tells the browser to use Arial; if Arial is not present, use Helvetica.

```
p {font-family: arial, helvetica;}
```

This rule uses a common font substitution string that produces a sans-serif font on PCs that have Arial installed and Macintosh computers that have Helvetica installed. To further ensure the portability of this rule, add a generic font family name to the list, as shown in the following rule:

```
p {font-family: arial, helvetica, sans-serif;}
```

This rule ensures that the <p> element is displayed in some type of sans-serif font, even if it is not Arial or Helvetica.

Specifying Font Size

font-size property description
Value: <absolute-size> | <relative-size> | <length> | <percentage>
Initial: medium
Applies to: all elements
Inherited: the computed value is inherited
Percentages: refer to parent element's font size

The font-size property gives you control over the specific sizing of your type. You can choose from length units, such as ems or pixels, or a percentage value that is based on the parent element's font size.

The following rule sets the <blockquote> element to 1.5 em Arial:

```
blockquote {font-family: arial; font-size: 1.5em;}
```

To specify a default size for a document, use body as the selector. This rule sets the text to .85 em Arial:

```
body {font-family: arial; font-size: .85em;}
```

You can also choose from a list of absolute size and relative size keywords, described in the following sections.

Absolute Font Size Keywords

These keywords refer to a table of sizes that is determined by the browser. The keywords are:

- xx-small
- x-small
- small
- medium
- large
- x-large
- xx-large

The CSS specification recommends a scaling factor of 1.2 between sizes for the computer display. Therefore, if the medium font is 10 points, the large font would be 12 points (10 × 1.2 = 12).

Solving the Font Size Dilemma

Figure 7-6 shows different font size samples in the browser. With so many different methods of font sizing available, which should you use? The designers of CSS2, Hakon Lie and Bert Bos, recommend always using relative sizes (specifically, the em value) to set font sizes on your Web pages. Here are some reminders about each relative measurement value:

- *Ems*—The best choice, although there are some browser compatibility problems.
- *Percentage*—Works well, but remember that percentages are relative to the value of their parent element.
- *Pixels*—Pixel values are entirely dependent on the user's screen resolution, making it very difficult to ensure consistent presentation.

Figure 7-6

Various font sizes

Specifying Font Style

font-style property description
Value: normal | italic | oblique
Initial: normal
Applies to: all elements
Inherited: yes
Percentages: N/A

The font-style property lets you specify italic or oblique text. The difference between italic and oblique text is subtle. The italic form of a typeface is designed with different letter forms to create the slanted font, while the oblique form is simply normal text slanted to the right. In print-based typography, oblique text is considered inferior to italic. On the Web however, current browsers cannot make the distinction between the two—either value creates slanted text. The following example sets italicized text for the note class attribute.

```
.note {font-style: italic;}
```

Here is the note class applied to a <div> element:

```
<div class="note">A note to the reader:</div>
```

The text contained in the <div> appears italicized in the browser. Remember that italic text is hard to read on a computer display. Use italics for special emphasis, rather than for large blocks of text.

Specifying Font Variant

font-variant property description
Value: normal	small-caps
Initial: normal
Applies to: all elements
Inherited: yes
Percentages: N/A

The font-variant property lets you define small capitals, which are often used for chapter openings, acronyms, and other special purposes. Small capitals are intended to be a different type style from regular capital letters, but this is not supported in all browsers. In fact, some simply downsize the regular capital letters. Figure 7-7 shows an example of small capitals.

Figure 7-7
Small capitals

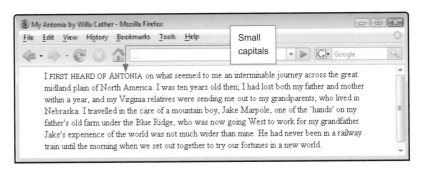

In this example, a <span> element contains the text that is converted to small capitals, as shown in the following code fragment:

```
<span style="font-variant: small-caps;">I first heard of Antonia</span>
    on what seemed to be...
```

CHAPTER 7

This style rule shows the use of the <span> element to affect the style for an inline span of words within a block of text. The style attribute lets you test the style on this one element before adding it to your style sheet.

Specifying Font Weight

font-weight property description
Value: normal | bold | bolder | lighter | 100 | 200 | 300 | 400 | 500 | 600 | 700 | 800 | 900
Initial: normal
Applies to: all elements
Inherited: yes
Percentages: N/A

The font-weight property lets you set the weight of the typeface. The numeric values express nine levels of weight from 100 to 900, although most browsers and fonts do not support such a wide range of weights. The default type weight is equal to 400, with bold text equal to 700. Bolder and lighter are relative weights based on the weight of the parent element. Using the bold value produces the same weight of text as the <b> element. The following style rule sets the warning class to bold:

```
.warning {font-weight: bold;}
```

Using the Font Shortcut Property

font property description
Value: [[<'font-style'> || <'font-variant'> || <'font-weight'>]? <'font-size'> [/ <'line-height'>]? <'font-family'>]
Initial: see individual properties
Applies to: all elements
Inherited: yes
Percentages: allowed on 'font-size' and 'line-height'

The **font property** is a shortcut that lets you specify the most common font properties in a single statement. The syntax of this property is based on a traditional typographical shorthand notation to set multiple properties related to fonts.

As shown in the previous value listing, the font property lets you state the font-style, font-variant, font-weight, font-size, line-height, and font-family in one statement. The only two values that are required are font-size and font-family, which must be in the correct order for the style rule to work. The following rules are examples of the most basic use of the font property:

```
p {font: 12pt arial;}
h1 {font: 2em sans-serif;}
```

The font properties other than font-size and font-family are optional and do not have to be included unless you want to change their default. If you want to include line-height, note that it must always follow a slash after the font-size. The following rule sets 12-point Arial text on 18-point line height:

```
p {font: 12pt/18pt arial;}
```

The font shortcut property lets you abbreviate the more verbose individual property listings. For example, both of the following rules produce the same result:

```
p {font-weight: bold;
     font-size: 18pt;
     line-height: 24pt;
     font-family: arial;}
p {font: bold 18pt/24pt arial;} /* Same rule as above */
```

Although the font shortcut property is a convenience, you may prefer to state explicitly the font properties as shown in the more verbose rule, because they are easier to understand.

Using the CSS Text Spacing Properties

The CSS text properties let you adjust the spacing around and within your text. The properties in this section let you create distinctive text effects that are not possible with standard HTML. In this section, you will learn about the following properties:

- text-indent
- text-align
- text-decoration
- line-height
- vertical-align
- letter-spacing
- word-spacing

Specifying Text Indents

text-indent property description
Value: <length> | <percentage>
Initial: 0
Applies to: block-level elements
Inherited: yes
Percentages: refer to width of containing block

Use the text-indent property to set the amount of indentation for the first line of text in an element, such as a paragraph. You can specify a length or percentage value. The percentage is relative to the width of the containing element. If you specify a value of 15%, the indent will be 15% of the width of the element. Negative values let you create a hanging indent. Figure 7-8 shows two different text-indent effects.

Figure 7-8

Text indents

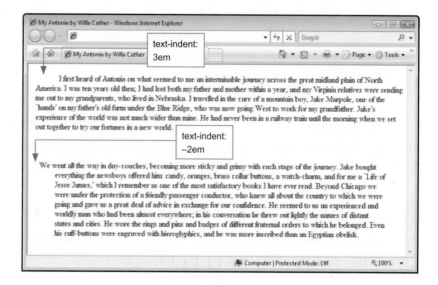

The following rules set an indent of 2 em for the <p> element and -2 em for the <blockquote> element:

```
p {text-indent: 2em;}
blockquote {text-indent: -2em;}
```

Indents are sensitive to the language specification for the document. To determine the default language for a document, the Web server sends a two-letter language code along with the HTML file that is requested by the browser. In left-to-right reading languages (such as English), the indent is added to the left of the first line; in right-to-left reading languages (such as Hebrew), the indent is added to the right of the first line.

Indents are inherited from parent to child elements. For example, the following rule sets a 2-em text indent to a <div> element:

```
div {text-indent: 2em;}
```

Any block-level elements, such as <p>, that are contained within this division have the same 2-em text indent specified in the rule for the parent <div>.

Specifying Text Alignment

text-align property description
Value: left | right | center | justify
Initial: depends on user agent and language
Applies to: block-level elements
Inherited: yes
Percentages: N/A

Use the text-align property to set horizontal alignment for the lines of text in an element. You can specify four alignment values: left, center, right, and justify. The justify value lines up the text on both horizontal margins, adding white space between the words on the line, like a column of text in a newspaper. The following style rule sets the <p> element to justified alignment:

```
p {text-align: justify;}
```

Figure 7-9 shows a sample of all four alignment values.

Figure 7-9
Text alignments

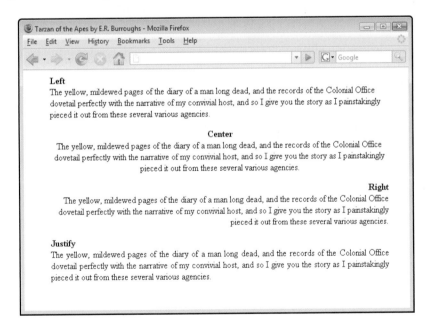

When choosing an alignment value, keep the default settings for the language and the user's preferences in mind. For example, most western languages read from left to right, and the default alignment is left. Unless you are trying to emphasize a particular section of text, use the alignment with which most readers are comfortable. Both right and center alignment are fine for short sections of text, but they make reading difficult for lengthier passages.

Justified text lets you create newspaper-like alignment where the lines of text all have the same length. The browser inserts white space between the words of the text to adjust the alignment so both margins of the text align, as shown in Figure 7-9. Justify is not supported by all browsers, and different browsers might justify the text differently.

Specifying Text Decoration

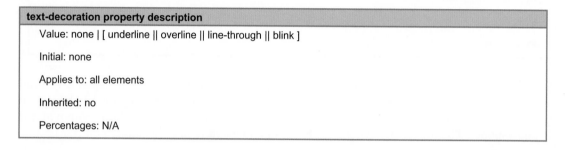

text-decoration property description
Value: none | [underline || overline || line-through || blink]
Initial: none
Applies to: all elements
Inherited: no
Percentages: N/A

Text decoration lets you underline text, an effect that has particular meaning in a hypertext environment. Your users know to look for underlined words as the indicators for hypertext links. Any text you underline appears to be a hypertext link. Except for text links, underlining is an inappropriate text style for a Web page.

Text-decoration also supports the blink value, which creates blinking text. Although you might be tempted to use this effect, most users find the constantly blinking text distracting. The CSS2 specification does not require all browsers to support the blink value. Figure 7-10 shows the different text decorations, except for the blink value.

Figure 7-10
Text decorations

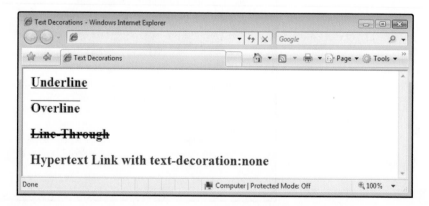

As Figure 7-10 shows, the text-decoration property lets you remove the underlining from the <a> element. As you read earlier, the user commonly relies on the underlining text to indicate a hypertext link. However, some Web sites choose to remove link underlining, indicating links with a color different from the standard text color. You can remove the underlining from your anchor elements with the following rule:

```
a {text-decoration: none;}
```

Users with sight disabilities can have trouble finding the links in your content if you choose to remove the underlining. Alternately, a user can override the author's style rules by setting preferences in his or her browser or applying his or her own style sheet.

Specifying Line Height

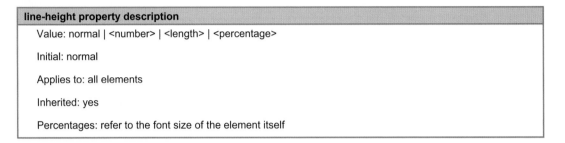

line-height property description
Value: normal | <number> | <length> | <percentage>
Initial: normal
Applies to: all elements
Inherited: yes
Percentages: refer to the font size of the element itself

CSS allows you to specify either a length or percentage value for the line height, which is more commonly called leading, the white space between lines of text. The percentage is based on the font size. Setting the value to 150% with a 12-point font size results in a line height of 18 points. The following rule sets the line height to 150%:

```
p {line-height: 150%;}
```

Figure 7-11 shows the default line height and various adjustments in line height. A gray background color for the Web page and white background color for the text highlight the line box around each line. Notice that the line height is evenly divided between the top and bottom of the element.

Figure 7-11
Line height

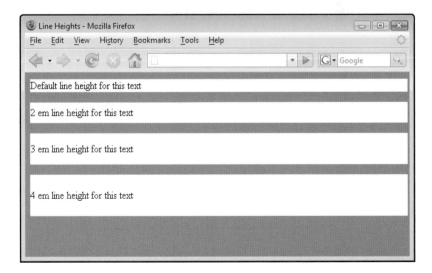

The line-height property can increase the legibility of your text. Adding to the default line height inserts additional white space between the lines of text. On the computer monitor, increasing the white space helps guide the user's eyes along the line of text and provides rest for the eye. Figure 7-12 shows two paragraphs; one with the default line height and one with the line height set to 1.5 em. The increased line height adds to the legibility of the text.

Figure 7-12
Adjusting line height increases legibility

Specifying Vertical Alignment

vertical-align property description
Value: baseline | sub | super | top | text-top | middle | bottom | text-bottom | \<percentage\> | \<length\>
Initial: baseline
Applies to: inline-level and 'table-cell' elements
Inherited: no
Percentages: refer to the 'line-height' of the element itself

The vertical-align property lets you adjust the vertical alignment of text within the line box. Vertical-align works only on inline elements (described in Chapter 9). You can use this property to superscript or subscript characters above or below the line of text and to align images with text. Table 7-5 defines the different vertical-align values. The baseline, sub, and super values are the most evenly supported by the different browsers.

Value	Definition
baseline	Align the baseline of the text with the baseline of the parent element
sub	Lower the baseline of the box to the proper position for subscripts of the parent's box; this value does not automatically create a smaller font size for the subscripted text
middle	The CSS2 specification defines "middle" as "the vertical midpoint of the box with the baseline of the parent box plus half the x-height of the parent"; realistically, this means the middle-aligned text is aligned to half the height of the lowercase letters
super	Raise the baseline of the box to the proper position for superscripts of the parent's box; this value does not automatically create a smaller font size for the superscripted text
text-top	Align the top of the box with the top of the parent element's font
text-bottom	Align the bottom of the box with the bottom of the parent element's font
top	Align the top of the box with the top of the line box
bottom	Align the bottom of the box with the bottom of the line box

Table 7-5   Vertical-align property values

The following rule sets superscripting for the superscript class:

```
.superscript {vertical-align: super;}
```

Figure 7-13 shows different types of vertical alignments.

Figure 7-13
Vertical alignments

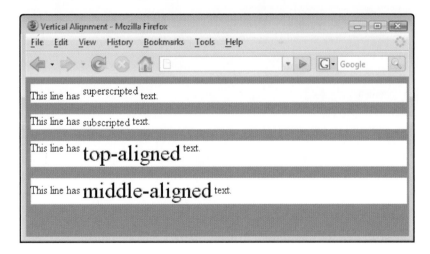

You can also use vertical alignment to align text with graphics. The following rule, added to the <img> element with the style attribute, sets the vertical alignment to top:

```
<img src="image.gif" style="vertical-align: text-top;">
```

Figure 7-14 shows various alignments of images and text. Note that the vertical alignment affects only the one line of text that contains the graphic, because the graphic is an inline element. If you want to wrap a paragraph of text around an image, use the float property, described in Chapter 9.

Figure 7-14
Vertically aligning text
and graphics

Specifying Letter Spacing

letter-spacing property description
Value: normal | <length>
Initial: normal
Applies to: all elements
Inherited: yes
Percentages: N/A

The letter-spacing property lets you adjust the white space between letters. In publishing termi-
nology, this adjustment is called kerning. The length you specify in the style rule is added to the
default letter spacing. The following code sets the letter spacing to 4 points:

```
h1 {letter-spacing: 4pt;}
```

Figure 7-15 shows samples of different letter-spacing values.

Figure 7-15
Adjusting letter spacing

Specifying Word Spacing

word-spacing property description
Value: normal | <length>
Initial: normal
Applies to: all elements
Inherited: yes
Percentages: N/A

The word-spacing property lets you adjust the white space between words in the text. The length you specify in the style rule is added to the default word spacing. The following code sets the word spacing to 2 em:

```
h1 {word-spacing: 2em;}
```

Figure 7-16 shows the result of the word-spacing property.

Figure 7-16
Adjusting word spacing

Creating a Font and Text Properties Style Sheet

In the following set of steps, you will build a style sheet that uses the typographic techniques you learned about in this chapter. Save your file, and test your work in the browser as you complete each step.

To build the style sheet:

1. Copy the **webnews.htm** file from the Chapter07 folder provided with your Data Files to a Chapter07 folder in your work folder. (Create the Chapter07 folder, if necessary.)

2. Open the file **webnews.htm** in your HTML editor, and save it in your Chapter07 folder as **webnews1.htm**.

3. In your browser, open the file **webnews1.htm**. When you open the file, it looks like Figure 7-17.

Figure 7-17
The basic HTML
document

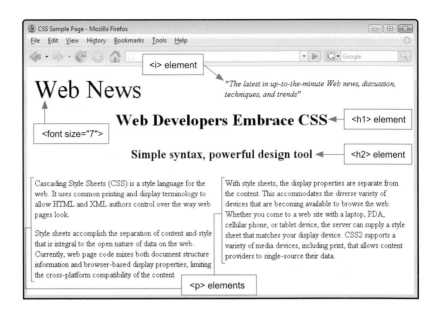

4. Examine the code. Notice that the Web page uses common HTML elements, including the deprecated, but still widely used, <font> element to style the text. HTML table elements build the structure of the layout. For this exercise, the style rules affect only the content within the table, not the table itself. Comments are included to help you locate the various page components. The complete code for the page follows:

```
<html>
<head>
<title>CSS Sample Page</title>
</head>

<body>
<table width="765" cellspacing="10">

<!-- First Row contains banner and tagline -->
<tr>
<td width="50%"><font size="7">Web News</font></td>
<td width="50%"><i>"The latest in up-to-the-minute Web news,
     discussion, techniques, and trends"</i></td>
</tr>

<!-- Second Row contains headline -->
<tr>
<td colspan="2">
<h1 align="center">Web Developers Embrace CSS</h1></td>
</tr>
```

```
<!-- Third Row contains sub-head -->
<tr><td colspan="2">
<h2 align="center">Simple syntax, powerful design tool</h2></td>
</tr>

<!-- Fourth row contains article columns -->
<tr valign="top">
<td>
<p>Cascading Style Sheets (CSS) is a style language for the web.
    It uses common printing and display terminology to allow HTML
    and XML authors control over the way web pages look.</p>
<p>Style sheets accomplish the separation of content and style that
    is integral to the open nature of data on the web. Currently,
    web page code mixes both document structure information and
    browser-based display properties, limiting the cross-
    platform compatibility of the content.</p>
</td>
<td>
<p>With style sheets, the display properties are separate from the
    content. This accommodates the diverse variety of devices
    that are becoming available to browse the web. Whether you
    come to a web site with a laptop, PDA, cellular phone, or
    tablet device, the server can supply a style sheet that
    matches your display device. CSS2 supports a variety of
    media devices, including print, that allow content
    providers to single-source their data.</p>
</td>
</tr>
</table>
</body>
</html>
```

Naming the Style Classes

The first step in building a style sheet for this document is to name the logical document sections to which you can apply styles. You can then use these document section names as class names and apply the style using <div> elements and class attributes. Figure 7-18 shows the basic document with the class names used to apply styles.

Figure 7-18
Logical document
sections

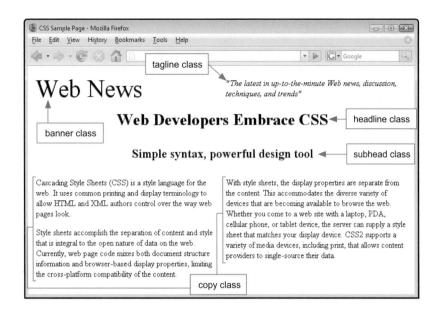

Adding the <style> Section

Because you are working on a single document, you can use a <style> element in the <head>
section to contain your style rules. In the steps throughout the chapter, enter the code shown in
bold and blue.

To add the <style> section:

1. Add a <style> element in the <head> section to contain your style rules as shown in the
   following code. Leave a few lines of white space between the <style> tags to contain the
   style rules.

```
<head>
<title>CSS Sample Page</title>
<style type="text/css">

</style>
</head>
```

Styling the Banner Class

The banner currently uses a <font> element to make the text as large as possible within standard
HTML. <font> is a deprecated element. (Recall that deprecated elements are elements that the
W3C has identified as obsolete.) The <font> element is deprecated specifically in favor of CSS
style rules.

To style the banner class:

1. Write a style rule that selects the banner class. Set the font-size to 4 em and the font-style
   to italic, as shown in the following code:

```
<style type="text/css">
.banner {font-size: 4em; font-style: italic;}
</style>
```

2. Locate the banner text within the file. Remove the <font> elements highlighted in the following code:

```
<!-- First Row contains banner and tagline -->
<tr>
<td width="50%"><font size="7">Web News</font></td>
```

3. Replace the <font> elements with <div> elements. Specify "banner" as the class attribute value as shown below:

```
<!-- First Row contains banner and tagline -->
<tr>
<td width="50%"><div class="banner">Web News</div></td>
```

Figure 7-19 shows the completed banner style.

Figure 7-19
The banner style

Styling the Tagline Class

The tagline element currently uses an <i> element to make the text italicized. Italic text is hard to read on a computer display. You will write a rule that makes the tagline text stand out and easier to read.

To style the tagline class:

1. Write a style rule that selects the tagline class. Set the font-family to monospace and the font-weight to bold, as shown in the following code:

```
<style type="text/css">
.banner {font-size: 4em; font-style: italic;}
.tagline {font-family: monospace; font-weight: bold;}
</style>
```

2. Locate the tagline text within the file. Remove the <i> elements highlighted in the following code:

```
<td width=50%><i>"The latest in up-to-the-minute
Web news, discussion, techniques, and trends"</i></td>
```

3. Replace the <i> elements with <div> elements. Set the class attribute to "tagline," as shown in the following code:

```
<div class="tagline">"The latest in up-to-the-minute
Web news, discussion, techniques, and trends"</div>
```

Figure 7-20 shows the result of the tagline style rules. The monospace text is associated with computers and thus is appropriate for this page.

Figure 7-20

The tagline style

Styling the Headline

The headline currently uses <h1> elements to make the text as large and bold as possible. You will write a style rule that applies five different properties to the headline text.

To style the headline:

1. Write a style rule that selects the headline class. Set the font-family to Arial, and use font substitution to ensure that Arial, Helvetica, or the default sans-serif font applies.

```
<style type="text/css">
.banner {font-size: 4em; font-style: italic;}
.tagline {font-family: monospace; font-weight: bold;}
.headline {font-family: arial, helvetica, sans-serif;}
</style>
```

2. Add more properties to the rule. Set the font-size to 2.5 times the size of the default font, set text-align to center, and set the line-height to 2.5 em. Because this style rule is more complex, you can place the properties on separate lines to make the rule easier to read, as shown in the following code:

```
<style type="text/css">
.banner {font-size: 4em; font-style: italic;}
.tagline {font-family: monospace; font-weight: bold;}
.headline {font-family: arial, helvetica, sans-serif;
          font-size: 2.5em;
          text-align: center;
          line-height: 2.5em;}
</style>
```

3. Finally, set the letter spacing to 5 px to provide extra white space between the headline letters to make the headline more legible.

```
<style type="text/css">
.banner {font-size: 4em; font-style: italic;}
.tagline {font-family: monospace; font-weight: bold;}
.headline {font-family: arial, helvetica, sans-serif;
          font-size: 2.5em;
          text-align: center;
          line-height: 2.5em;
          letter-spacing: 5px;}
</style>
```

4. Locate the headline text within the file. Remove the <h1> elements that are in the following code:

```
<!-- Second Row contains headline -->
<tr>
<td colspan="3">
<h1 align="center">Web Developers Embrace CSS</h1></td>
</tr>
```

5. Replace the <h1> elements with <div> elements. Set the class attribute to headline, as shown in the following code:

```
<div class="headline">Web Developers Embrace CSS</div>
```

Figure 7-21 shows the result of the style rule. The letter spacing adds distinctive white space to the text, setting it off from the rest of the page.

Figure 7-21
The headline style

Styling the Subhead

The subhead mimics the headline style, but on a smaller scale. It also uses Arial as the primary font family, with Helvetica and sans-serif as substitutes.

To style the subhead:

1. Write a style rule that selects the subhead class. Set the font-family to Arial, and use font substitution to ensure that Arial, Helvetica, or the default sans-serif font apply.

```
<style type="text/css">
.banner {font-size: 4em; font-style: italic;}
.tagline {font-family: monospace; font-weight: bold;}
.headline {font-family: arial, helvetica, sans-serif;
           font-size: 2.5em;
           text-align: center;
           line-height: 2.5em;
           letter-spacing: 5px;}
.subhead {font-family: arial, helvetica, sans-serif;}
</style>
```

2. Set font-size to 1.5 times the default font size. Set text-align to center, and set the line-height to 1.75 em, as shown in the following rule:

```
<style type="text/css">
.banner {font-size: 4em; font-style: italic;}
.tagline {font-family: monospace; font-weight: bold;}
.headline {font-family: arial, helvetica, sans-serif;
           font-size: 2.5em;
           text-align: center;
```

```
              line-height: 2.5em;
              letter-spacing: 5px;}
.subhead {font-family: arial, helvetica, sans-serif;
          font-size: 1.5em;
          text-align: center;
          line-height: 1.75em;}
</style>
```

3. Locate the subhead text within the file. Remove the <h2> elements that are bold in the following code:

```
<!-- Third Row contains subhead -->
<tr><td colspan="3">
<h2 align="center">Simple syntax, powerful design tool
</h2></td>
</tr>
```

4. Replace the <h2> elements with <div> elements. Set the class attribute to "subhead," as shown in the following code:

```
<div class="subhead">Simple syntax, powerful design tool</div>
```

Figure 7-22 shows the result of the style rule.

Figure 7-22

The subhead style

Styling the Body Copy

The body copy is the article text in the columns. This text is displayed using the browser's default font. You will write a style rule to enhance the legibility of the text.

To style the body copy:

1. Write a style rule that selects the copy class. Set the line-height property to 1.25 em to aid the legibility of the text.

2. Set the text-indent property to 2 em to set an indent for each paragraph. The style rule follows:

```
.copy {line-height: 1.25em; text-indent: 2em;}
```

3. Locate the <p> elements that contain the body copy.

4. Add class attributes to the <p> elements, and specify "copy" as the attribute value, as shown in the following sample paragraph:

```
<p class="copy">Style sheets accomplish the separation of
content and style that is integral to the open nature of
data on the web. Currently, web page code mixes both
document structure information and browser-based
display properties, limiting the cross-platform
compatibility of the content.</p>
```

Figure 7-23 shows the result of the style rule.

Figure 7-23
The copy style

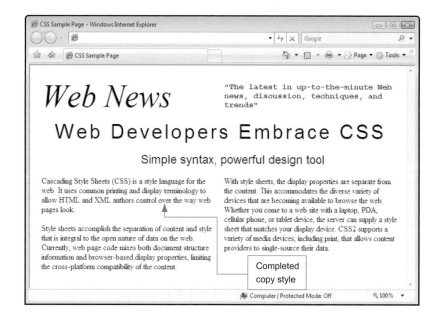

Adding a Small-caps Span

The final style to add is a <span> element that contains the first few words of the article. You will use the font-variant property to set the words in small capitals.

To style the banner class:

1. Locate the first few words in the first paragraph of the article, as shown in the following code:

```
<p class="copy"><strong>Cascading Style Sheets (CSS)</strong> is a style
language for the web. It uses common printing and
display terminology to allow HTML and XML authors
control over the way web pages look.</p>
```

2. Add the <span> element around the selected words, as shown in the following code:

```
<p class="copy"><strong><span></strong>Cascading Style Sheets (CSS)<strong></span></strong> is
a style language for the web. It uses common
printing and display terminology to allow HTML and XML
authors control over the way web pages look.</p>
```

3. Add the style rule in a style attribute to the <span> element. Set the font-variant property to small-caps, as shown in the following code:

```
<p class="copy"><span style="font-variant: small-caps;">
Cascading Style Sheets (CSS)</span> is a style
language for the web. It uses common printing and
display terminology to allow HTML and XML authors
control over the way web pages look.</p>
```

Figure 7-24 shows the result of the font-variant property.

The finished Web page is shown in Figure 7-25.

Figure 7-24
Adding small capitals

Figure 7-25
The finished Web page

Chapter Summary

You can use Cascading Style Sheets to manipulate a variety of text properties and achieve professional-quality typography on your Web site. Keep the following points in mind:

▶ Use type to communicate information structure. Be sparing with your type choices; use fonts consistently and design for legibility.

▶ Remember that HTML text downloads faster than graphics-based text. Use HTML text whenever possible.

▶ Use browser-safe fonts that appear as consistently as possible across operating systems.

▶ Standardize your styles by building external style sheets and linking them to multiple documents.

▶ Test your work. Different browsers and computing platforms render text in different sizes.

▶ Use type effectively by choosing available fonts and sizes. Design for legibility and use text to communicate information about the structure of your material.

▶ Choose the correct measurement unit based on the destination medium. For the computer screen, ems, pixels, or percentage measurements can scale to the user's preferences.

▶ Use font properties to control the look of your letter forms. Specify font-substitution values to ensure that your text is displayed properly across different platforms.

▶ Use the text spacing properties to create more visually interesting and legible text.

Key Terms

cursive font	monospace font
em unit	sans-serif font
ex unit	serif font
fantasy font	text properties
font	typeface
font property	x-height
font shortcut property	

Review Questions

1. What is the default browser font?
2. What does the browser do if you specify a font that is not stored on a user's computer?
3. What are two drawbacks to the use of graphics-based text?
4. What are the three types of CSS measurement units?
5. What is the best destination for absolute units of measurement?
6. Why would you use relative or percentage values for a Web page?
7. What is the size of the em?

8. What determines the size of a pixel?

9. What is the advantage of the generic font families?

10. Write a font-family substitution string that selects Arial, Helvetica, or any sans-serif font for a <p> element.

11. Write a style rule for an <h2> element that specifies bold text that is twice the size of the default font size.

12. Write a rule specifying that <p> elements appear as 14-point text with 20-point leading.

13. Write a rule specifying that <i> elements are displayed in red only when they appear within <p> elements.

14. Write a rule defining a division named "note." Specify 12-point bold Arial text on a yellow background.

15. What three typographic white-space areas can you affect with style rules?

16. Write a style rule to create a white-on-black reverse <h1> heading.

17. Write a style rule for a <p> element with a 24-point hanging indent and a 30-pixel margin on the left and right sides.

18. Rewrite the following rule using the font shortcut property:

```
blockquote {font-style: italic; font-size: 12pt; line-height:
        18pt; font-family: times, serif;}
```

19. What is a benefit of increasing the standard text line height?

20. What is the size of the text indent and line height in the following style rule?

```
p {font-size: 12pt; text-indent: 3em; line-height: 150%;}
```

Hands-On Projects

1. Modify an existing HTML document to use Cascading Style Sheets.

   a. Build styles using the existing standard HTML elements in the file.

   b. Test the work in multiple browsers to verify that all styles are portable.

   c. Remove the files and place them in an external style sheet.

   d. Link the HTML file to the style sheet. Test to make sure the file is displayed properly.

2. Modify an existing HTML document to use Cascading Style Sheets.

   a. Decide on logical divisions for the document.

   b. Give the divisions class names.

   c. Write style rules for the divisions.

   d. Apply the styles to the divisions using <div> or <span>.

   e. Test your work.

3. Browse the Web for examples of good typography. Write a short design critique of why the type works effectively on the Web sites you find.

4. Browse the Web for examples of poor typography. Write a short design critique of why the type is confusing or misleading to the user. Save and print screen shots of the sample Web pages to accompany your critique.

5. In this project you have a chance to test the font and text properties on paragraphs of text. Save and view the file in your browser after completing each step.

   a. Using your HTML editor, create a simple HTML file (or open an existing file) that contains multiple <p> elements and so on. Save the file in your Chapter07 folder as **fonts1.htm**.

   b. Add a <style> element to the <head> section, as shown in the following code:

   ```
   <head>
   <title>CSS Test Document</title>
   <style type="text/css">

   </style>
   </head>
   ```

   c. Write a style rule that uses p as a selector and sets the font-family to a sans-serif font. You can use a generic font family, or choose one of the fonts available on your computer.

   d. Specify a list of alternate fonts to ensure that your font choice is displayed properly across a range of computers.

   e. Specify a text indent for the <p> elements. Use the em value as the measurement unit.

   f. Add the line-height property to the style rule. Experiment with different line heights until you find one that you feel enhances the legibility of the paragraph text.

Individual Case Project

Design the type hierarchy for your Case Project Web site. Create a type specification HTML page that shows examples of the different typefaces and sizes and how they will be used. This can be a mock-up page that uses generic content but demonstrates the overall typographic scheme. Consider the following questions:

▶ What will be the style for the body type?

▶ How many levels of headings are necessary?

▶ What are the different weights and sizes of the headings?

▶ How will text be emphasized?

▶ Will hypertext links be standard or custom colors?

Team Case Project

Revisit your project proposal and the page templates you created in Chapter 5. Each team member has been responsible for individual templates, such as the home page template, the section page template, and the article level page template. Each team member will now hand off the page template that he or she has been working on to another member of the team. This will give you a chance to work with code created by someone else, a situation you will commonly encounter in Web design.

Now that you are reviewing each other's coding work, perform a quality check to ensure your coding is consistent and standards-based. Are you following the correct syntax and file naming conventions? Do all pages contain comments to describe the code?

Working with your new page template, design a few mock-up pages with your ideas for font styles, sizes, and other text conventions. Consider the following questions:

▶ What will be the style for the body type?

▶ How many level of headings are necessary?

▶ What are the different weights and sizes of the headings?

▶ How will text be emphasized?

▶ Will hypertext links be standard or custom colors?

Meet as a group to determine the typographic conventions for your Web site. Create final page mockups that use generic content to demonstrate the overall typographic scheme for the Web site.

8

Graphics and Color

When you complete this chapter, you will be able to:

- Understand graphics file formats
- Choose a graphics tool
- Use the <img> element
- Control image properties with CSS
- Understand computer color basics
- Control color properties with CSS
- Work with images and color
- Control background images with CSS

The ability to freely combine graphics, text, and color into page-type layouts is one feature that makes the Web so attractive and popular, but it also can be the undoing of many Web sites. When you combine these elements wisely, you can produce an attractive and engaging site. Conversely, the use of too many large or complex images, poor color choices, or complicated backgrounds forces users to endure long download times and wade through unreadable text and confusing navigation choices.

Find a good balance between images and text. Use CSS to control image characteristics, such as spacing and text alignment. CSS background images let you enhance page layouts and brand your site.

Use color judiciously to communicate, to guide the reader, or to create branded areas of your site. Test your color choices carefully to make sure they appear properly across different browsers. Also, test at a variety of connection speeds to make sure the time needed to download your graphics does not discourage your readers.

Understanding Graphics File Formats

You currently can use only three image file formats on the Web: GIF, JPG, and PNG. A fourth format, SVG, is a newer standard from the World Wide Web Consortium (W3C) that is not yet in common use. All these formats compress images to create smaller files, but choosing the right file format for an image is important. If you choose the wrong file type, your image will not compress or appear as you expect.

GIF

The **Graphics Interchange Format (GIF)** is designed for online delivery of graphics. GIF uses a "lossless" compression technique, meaning that no color information is discarded when the image is compressed.

The color depth (described in the "Understanding Computer Color Basics" section of this chapter) of GIF is 8-bit, allowing a palette of no more than 256 colors. The fewer colors you use, the greater the compression and the smaller the file size. The GIF file format excels at compressing and displaying flat (unshaded) color areas, making it the logical choice for line art (simple drawings) and color graphics. Because of its limited color depth, however, GIF is not the best file format for photographs or more complex graphics that have gradations of color, such as shadows and feathering.

GIF Transparency

With GIF files you can choose one color in an image to appear as transparent in the browser. The background color or pattern of the page will show through the areas in the image that you have designated as transparent. Using transparent areas allows you to create graphics that appear to have an irregular outside shape, rather than a rectangular shape. Figure 8-1 shows the same shape with and without transparency.

You can create transparent areas using a graphics editor. When you choose the transparent color, all pixels of that color in the image let the background color show through. In Figure 8-1, white is chosen as the transparent color.

Figure 8-1

Transparent and nontransparent GIFs

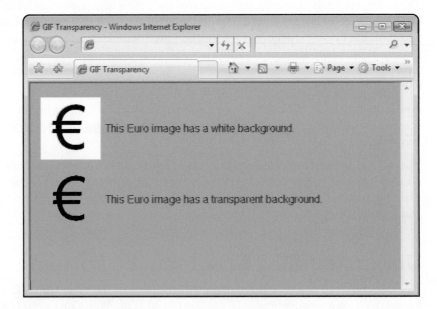

GIF Animation

The GIF format lets you store multiple images and timing information about the images in a single file. This means that you can build animations consisting of multiple static images that change continuously, creating the illusion of motion. This is exactly the same technique used in cell-based animation. You can create animated GIFs by using a variety of shareware and commercial software.

When you create a GIF animation, you can determine the time between frames and the number of times the animation plays. With a little imagination, you can create all types of effects, including text scrolls, color changes, animated icons, and slide shows. Figure 8-2 shows a series of individual GIFs combined to play as one animated GIF. The final GIF animation file is a single file whose name ends in the .gif extension.

Figure 8-2

Individual frames of a GIF animation

GIF animation is somewhat limited when compared with the results of proprietary animation tools such as Adobe Shockwave or Flash, which can play synchronized sounds and allow Web users to interact with the animation. Creating animations with these applications, however, requires browser plug-ins, and viewing the animations demands heavy download times. Unlike most proprietary tools, animated GIFs do not require any special plug-ins for viewing. Also, if you limit color and motion when creating your animations, you can keep your file sizes small for faster downloads.

Use restraint when adding animated GIFs such as blinking icons and scrolling banners to your pages; users may find them annoying because they are repetitive and distract from the page content. Consider choosing to play an animation a limited number of times rather than letting it loop endlessly. Creating animated images with GIF animation software streamlines the process of setting the timing, color palette, and individual frame effects. See Table 8-1 for a list of GIF animation tools.

GIF Construction Set Professional	www.mindworkshop.com/alchemy/gifcon.html
Ulead GIF Animator	www.ulead.com/ga/runme.htm
GIFMation	www.boxtopsoft.com/gifmation.html

Table 8-1   GIF animation tools

JPG

The **Joint Photographic Experts Group** (**JPG**, sometimes called **JPEG**) format is best for photographs or continuous-tone images. JPGs are 24-bit images that allow millions of colors. Unlike GIFs, JPGs do not use a palette to display color.

JPGs use a "lossy" compression routine specially designed for photographic images: when the image is compressed, some color information is discarded, resulting in a loss of quality from the original image. Because the display device is a low-resolution computer monitor, the loss of quality is not usually noticeable. Furthermore, JPG's faster download time compensates for its loss of image quality.

Using Adobe Photoshop or other imaging software, you can translate photographic images into JPG format. When you create the JPG file, you can balance the amount of compression versus the resulting image quality manually. Figure 8-3 shows the Photoshop Save For Web & Devices dialog box.

Figure 8-3

Photoshop Save for Web & Devices dialog box

The Quality list box lets you adjust the quality of the file; the higher the quality, the lower the file compression. You can play with this setting to create good-looking files that are as small as possible. Many photos can sustain quite a bit of compression and still maintain image integrity. The Preview window shows the result of your changes, allowing you to experiment with the image quality before saving the file. Photoshop displays the estimated download time based on the file size.

Note

Whether you are creating GIFs or JPGs, always remember to save an original copy of your artwork or photo. Both file formats permanently degrade the quality of an image as a result of compression. Once you have converted to GIF or JPG, you cannot return to the original image quality.

PNG

The **Portable Network Graphics (PNG)** format is designed specifically for the Web. PNG has been available since 1995 but has been slow to gain popularity because of its lack of browser support.

It is a royalty-free file format that is intended to replace GIF. This lossless format compresses 8-bit images to smaller file sizes than GIF. PNG also is intended to work as an image-printing format, so it supports 8-bit indexed color, 16-bit gray scale, and 24-bit true-color images. Even though PNG supports 24-bit color, its lossless compression routine does not compress as efficiently as JPG, so it is not the best choice for photographic images.

PNG supports transparency and interlacing, but not animation, although the W3C has created a draft specification for a Multiple-image Network Graphics format (MNG) that will support animation. (**Interlacing** is the gradual display of a graphic in a series of passes as the data arrives in the browser.) You can read more about MNG format at *www.libpng.org/pub/mng/*. One useful feature of PNG is its built-in text capabilities for image indexing, allowing you to store a string of identifying text within the file itself. Now that most browsers support PNG, designers can start to use it more often.

SVG

The **Scalable Vector Graphics (SVG)** format is a new standard from the W3C. SVG is not yet supported by all browsers, but it is expected to be widely used on the Web. SVG is a language for describing two-dimensional graphics using XML. SVG files can contain shapes such as lines and curves, images, text, animation, and interactive events. SVG is compatible with common Web technologies such as HTML, XML, JavaScript, and Cascading Style Sheets (CSS). For more information on SVG, visit the W3C's SVG page at *www.w3.org/Graphics/SVG/*.

SVG graphics are scalable to different display resolutions and can be printed on high-resolution printers. An SVG graphic can be reused at different sizes throughout a Web site without downloading multiple files to the user. SVG graphics can be viewed at different sizes based on user needs, allowing magnification of an image to see fine detail or to increase legibility.

SVG is a vector graphics file format. **Vector graphics** represent images as geometrical formulas, as compared with **raster graphics** format, which represents images pixel by pixel for the entire image. GIFs and JPGs are raster formats. The vector graphics format allows SVG graphics to be scalable and cross-platform compatible.

All computer displays, whether desktop or handheld, are raster-type devices. The vector-based SVG files will eventually be displayed on a raster device, so why use SVG? SVG's conversion to pixels is based on the individual display type and settings, resulting in images that reproduce more faithfully for the greatest number of users.

Note
Adobe offers an SVG plug-in for Windows and Macintosh browsers at *www.adobe.com/svg/viewer/install/main.html*.

Using Interlacing and Progressive Display

Most Web-capable graphics editors let you save images in an interlaced (progressive) format. You can choose this display option when creating GIF, PNG, and JPG files. GIF and PNG files use an interlacing format, while JPG files use a progressive format. Interlacing and progressive formats generally are the same thing—the gradual display of a graphic in a series of passes as the data arrives in the browser. Each additional pass of data creates a clearer view of the image until the complete image is displayed. Figure 8-4 shows three rendering passes to display a complete image.

Figure 8-4
Three passes complete this progressive JPG image

The only real advantage to displaying graphics in the interlaced or progressive method is that users immediately see at least a blurred view of the complete image, giving them something to look at while waiting for the entire graphic to download. The disadvantage of choosing this display method is that older browsers may not display the graphic properly, and more processing power is needed on the user's machine to render the image. The use of these methods has declined as increased connection speeds have become more widespread.

Where You Can Find Images

You can acquire images from a variety of sources, including from a graphics professional you hire to create and prepare your images. If your budget does not allow for funding this service, consider one of the following resources:

- *Stock photo collections*—Stock photo collections can cost anywhere from thousands of dollars for a few images to under $20 for thousands of images at your local computer discount store or Web site retailer. These collections contain royalty-free images that you can use for any Web site. You can manipulate the graphics to add or delete text or images, change the color, or make any other modifications. Most stock photo collections include a built-in browsing program that lets you search for a particular image, and some also provide basic image-editing software.

- *Digital camera*—A digital camera lets you take your own photos and use them on the Web. These cameras store photos in JPG format, so you do not have to convert them. Most also provide image-cataloging software, and some include basic image-editing software. The price of digital cameras continues to drop, while the quality of the images gets better and better.

- *Scanner*—Good scanners are available for under $100. You can scan your own photos or images and save them as GIF, JPG, or PNG files for use on your Web site. Remember to set the scanner resolution to 72 dpi to match the computer display resolution.

- *Public domain Web sites*—Many Web sites maintain online catalogs of images that are available for download. Some of these sites charge a small membership fee, so you can download as many images as you want. Other public domain Web sites are completely free.

Note
Wikipedia maintains a list of public-domain stock photo Web sites at http://en.wikipedia.org/wiki/Wikipedia:Public_domain_image_resources.

- *Create your own*—If you need a basic image or if you have graphic design skills, you can download a shareware graphics tool and learn to use it. Keep your custom image simple, such as text on colored backgrounds, and use fundamental shapes and lines. Look at graphics on other Web sites; many are simple but effective and may provide a useful model for your own images.
- *Clip art*—Clip art is a viable alternative for the Web, especially as more polished collections become available for sale on CD-ROM. Price generally corresponds to quality for clip art—if you pay $9.95 for 20,000 images, do not expect excellent quality. You also can use a graphics program to customize clip art to meet your particular needs.

Note
Do not borrow images from other Web sites. Although your browser allows you to copy graphics, you should never use someone else's work unless it is from a public domain Web site and freely available for use. Digital watermarking technology lets artists copyright their work with an invisible signature; if you use someone else's graphics, you may find yourself in a lawsuit.

Choosing the Right Format

The following list summarizes the advantages and disadvantages of each graphic file format for the Web.

- *GIF*—The everyday file format for all types of simple colored graphics and line art. Use GIF sparingly for its animation capabilities to add visual interest to your pages. GIF's transparency feature lets you seamlessly integrate graphics into your Web site.
- *JPG*—Use JPG for all 24-bit full-color photographic images, as well as more complicated graphics that contain color gradients, shadows, and feathering.
- *PNG*—Now that most browsers are supporting it, you can use PNG as a substitute for GIF. Because PNG does not compress your 24-bit images as well as JPG does, do not use it for photos.

Choosing a Graphics Tool

As a Web designer, you may be in the enviable position of having a complete staff of graphic design professionals preparing graphics for your site. Most Web designers, however, do not have this luxury. Whether you want to or not, you eventually must use a graphics tool. Most of your graphics tasks are simple, such as resizing an image or converting an image from one file format to another. More complex tasks often include changing color depth or adding transparency to an image. These are tasks that anyone can learn using any of the popular graphics software currently available.

When it comes to creating images, you may want to enlist professional help. Your Web site will not benefit if you choose to create your own graphics and you are not up to the task. Professional-quality graphics can greatly enhance the look of your Web site. Take an honest look at your skills and remember that the best Web sites usually are the result of collaboration.

You use graphics software to create or manipulate graphics. Most Web designers use Adobe Photoshop, which is an expensive and full-featured product that takes time to master. Adobe Illustrator, a high-end drawing and painting tool, also is available. Other commercial tools you can consider include Ulead PhotoImpact and Adobe Fireworks. Most are available as download-able demos, so you can try before you buy. In general, look for a tool that meets your needs and will not take a long time to learn. Table 8-2 shows a list of Web sites for the graphic tools mentioned in the text.

Graphic tool	URL
Adobe Photoshop and Illustrator	www.adobe.com
Adobe Fireworks	www.adobe.com
Paint Shop Pro	www.jasc.com
Ulead PhotoImpact	www.ulead.com

Table 8-2   Graphic tools Web sites

The list in Table 8-2 is not exhaustive, and you may have to try different tools to find the one that suits your needs.

Of course, you also can choose from a variety of shareware graphics tools. One of the more established tools is Paint Shop Pro. This tool is reasonably priced and contains a full range of image-editing features. Like most other shareware, this tool can be downloaded and used for a trial period.

Using the <img> Element

By definition, <img> is a replaced element in HTML, meaning that the browser replaces the <img> element with the image file referenced in the src attribute. The browser treats the image as it treats a character; normal image alignment is to the baseline of the text. Images that are within a line of text must have spaces on both sides or the text will touch the image.

The <img> element only needs the src attribute for the image to be displayed in the browser. The following is a valid <img> element that displays a GIF file named logo. Note the space and closing slash are needed if you are coding for XHTML.

```
<img src="logo.gif" />
```

Table 8-3 lists the most commonly used attributes.

Attribute	Use
alt	Displays an alternate string of text instead of an image if the user has a text-only browser or has graphics turned off
height	Specifies the height of the image in pixels
src	The only required attribute, src specifies the URL of the graphic file you want to display. As with any URL, the path must be relative to the HTML file.
title	A string of text that provides information about the image. Visual browsers display the contents of the title attribute as a ToolTip or ScreenTip (a pop-up window that appears when the user pauses the pointing device over an object). An audio browser could speak the title information.
width	Specifies the width of the image in pixels

Table 8-3   <img> element attributes

Replacing img Attributes with Style Sheet Properties

Much of the HTML code on the Web does not match XHTML standards. When you visit different Web sites and view their code, you still see a variety of older HTML attributes in use to control image characteristics. Specifically, the align, border, vspace, and hspace attributes have been deprecated in HTML 4.01 in favor of CSS. Table 8-4 shows the equivalent CSS properties that replace these attributes.

Deprecated img Attribute	Equivalent CSS Property
align	The float property allows you to flow text around an image or other object; for example, img {float: left;}
border	The border property lets you set a border on an image or remove the border from a linked image
vspace and hspace	The padding or margin properties set white space around an image. You can control individual sides of the image, or apply white space around the entire image.

Table 8-4   CSS properties that replace img attributes

Specifying alt and title Attribute Text

In Chapter 4, you learned about the benefits of including alt attribute text, which provides a description of the image if the image does not appear. Proper use of the alt attribute improves Web accessibility by describing the function of each image in your Web site. If you use images for navigation, use the alt attribute to provide descriptive navigation information. For example, Figures 8-5 and 8-6 show the same Web page. In one figure, images are visible in the browser; in the other figure, the images are turned off. In Figure 8-6, the navigation bar is still useful because of the descriptive alt text.

Figure 8-5
Image-based navigation

Figure 8-6
Navigation bar with
images turned off

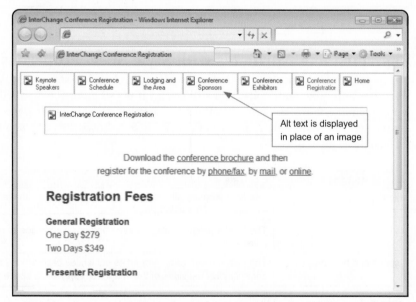

In Netscape 4 and Internet Explorer 5 and 6, the value of the alt attribute appears in a pop-up window when the user uses the mouse to point to an image. This behavior, as defined by the W3C, is actually a function of the title attribute. Netscape 7.0+, Firefox, and Opera 6.0+ will only display the pop-up text if the title attribute is present. Figure 8-7 shows an example of the title attribute used with an <img> element, as shown in the following code:

```
<img src="balloons_sm.jpg" width="200" height="267" alt="Hot Air
    Balloon image" border="0" title="Up, up and away in a hot air
    balloon"/>
```

Figure 8-7
Using the title attribute

Specifying Image Width and Height

Every <img> element on your Web site should contain width and height attributes. These attributes provide important information to the browser by specifying the amount of space to reserve for the image. This information dramatically affects the way your pages download, especially at slower connection speeds. If you have included the width and height, the browser knows how much space the image needs. The browser reserves the space on the page without waiting for the image to download, and displays the rest of your text content. If the browser does not know the width and height values, it must download the image before displaying the rest of the page. This means the user will be looking at a blank page while waiting for the image to download. Figure 8-8 shows the result of including the width and height in the <img> element.

The following code shows the width and height attributes for the image. It indicates that the browser should reserve a 200 × 267-pixel space for the balloons_sm.jpg image and should display the alternate text "Hot Air Balloon image" if it cannot display the image.

```
<img src="balloons_sm.jpg" width="200" height="267" alt="Hot Air
    Balloon image" border="0" title="Up, up and away in a hot air
    balloon" >
```

If you are not using tables, you should set the width and height to preserve the look of your layout, whether the images are displayed or not. In Figure 8-9, the width and height have been omitted. Notice that when the browser does not know the width and height, the text wrapping and appearance of the page change dramatically when the image is not displayed.

Figure 8-8
Image size reserved in
the browser

Figure 8-9
Browser unable to reserve
image size

You may notice that you can manipulate the width and height of the image itself using the width and height attributes in the <img> element. While it is tempting to use these attributes to change a graphic's size without using a graphics program, it is not a good idea. If the original graphic's area is too large and you reduce the size using the width and height attributes, you are not changing the file size of the image—only the area that the browser reserves for the graphic. The user is still downloading the original graphic file; no time is saved. Also, if you do not maintain the ratio of width to height, you distort the image. Figure 8-10 shows an image in its actual size, the size after changing the width and height values in proportion to one another, and the distorted size caused by incorrect width and height values.

Figure 8-10

Manipulating images with width and height attributes

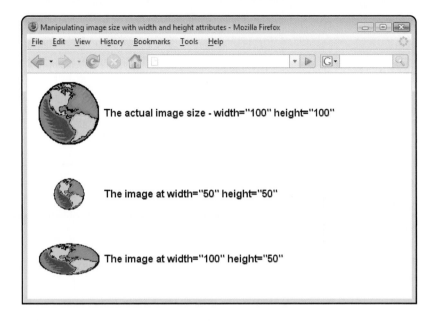

In the following code for the three images, the width and height attributes are bold:

```
<! globe 1 >
<img src="globe1.gif" width="100" height="100" alt="globe" />

<! globe 2 >
<img src="globe1.gif" width="50" height="50" alt="globe" />

<! globe 3 >
<img src="globe1.gif" width="100" height="50" alt="globe" />
```

However, the ability to manipulate image size using the width and height attributes comes in handy in certain circumstances. When creating a layout mock-up, you can test image sizes by manipulating the code.

Sizing Graphics for the Page

One way to keep file sizes small is to size graphics appropriately. Few things are more annoying than opening a Web page you haven't visited before and waiting to download an overly large image. One of the easiest ways to make your graphics download quickly is to keep their dimensions small and appropriate to the size of the page. Figure 8-11 shows a variety of image sizes at 1024 × 768 screen resolution.

Figure 8-11

Sample image sizes at 1024 × 768 screen resolution

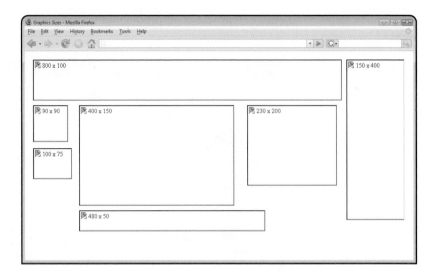

Use these sample image sizes as guidelines when you size your graphics. It is also useful to think of image size in relation to the number of columns in your layout; size your graphics to occupy one, two, or more columns of the page.

Controlling Image Properties with CSS

In this section you will use Cascading Style Sheet properties to control the following image characteristics:

- Removing the hypertext border
- Aligning text and images
- Floating images
- Adding white space around images

Removing the Hypertext Border from an Image

When you create a hypertext image, the browser's default behavior is to display the hypertext border around the image, as shown in Figure 8-12. This border appears blue before—and purple after—you click the image. In a well-designed site, this border is unnecessary because users often use their mouse to point to each image to see whether the hypertext cursor appears. Another reason to abandon the display of hypertext borders is that their color may not complement your graphic.

To remove the hypertext border, add a style attribute with the border property set to "none." Here is the code for the second globe in Figure 8-12, which has the hypertext border turned off:

```
<img src="globe1.gif" width="100" height="100" alt="globe"
style="border: none" />
```

You can read more about the border property in Chapter 9.

Figure 8-12

Removing the hypertext
border from an image

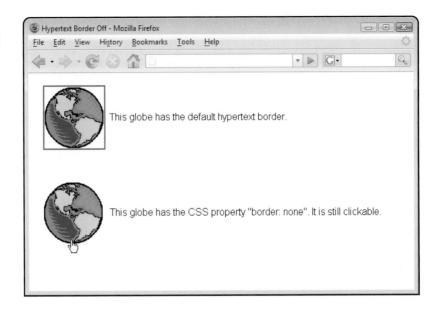

Aligning Text and Images

You can align text along an image border using the vertical-align property. The default alignment
of the text and image is bottom-aligned, which means the bottom of the text aligns with the bottom
edge of the image. You can change the alignment by using either the top or middle values.
Figure 8-13 shows all three alignment values.

Figure 8-13

Text alignment

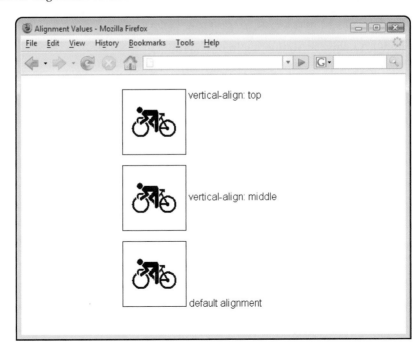

The following code shows the style attributes for each alignment example:

```
<img src="cycle.gif" style="vertical-align: top" border="1" />
<img src="cycle.gif" style="vertical-align: middle" border="1" />
<img src="cycle.gif" border="1" />
```

Floating Images

float property description
Value: left	right	none
Initial: none
Applies to: all elements except positioned elements
Inherited: no
Percentages: N/A

The float property can be used to float an image to the left or right of text.

The following style rules create two classes of <img> elements, one of which floats to the left of text; the other floats to the right:

```
img.left {float: left;}
img.right {float: right;}
```

You can apply these rules to an image using the class attribute within the <img> element, as shown in the following code fragment:

```
<img src="sample.gif" class="left" />
```

Figure 8-14 shows two floating images within a page.

Figure 8-14

Floating images

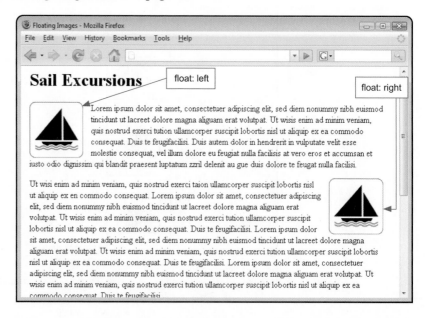

Adding White Space Around Images

Add white space around your images to reduce clutter and improve readability. As shown in Figure 8-15, the default spacing is very close to the image.

Figure 8-15

Image spacing

Use the CSS margin property to increase the white space around an image. You can read more about the margin property in Chapter 9. The following style rule adds 15 pixels of white space on all four sides of an image and floats it to the left of text:

```
<img src="sail.gif" alt="sailboat" border="0" style="margin:
15px; float: left" />
```

You can apply the margin properties to individual sides of an image. The following code shows an image with a 15-pixel margin on the right and bottom sides, floating to the left of text:

```
<img src="sail.gif" alt="sailboat" border="0" style="margin-right:
15px; margin-bottom: 15px; float: left" />
```

You also can add white space into the graphic itself using graphic-editing software.

Understanding Computer Color Basics

Before you create or gather graphics for your Web site, you need a basic understanding of how color works on computer monitors.

Your computer monitor displays color by mixing the three basic colors of light: red, green, and blue, often called RGB colors. Each of these three basic colors is called a color channel. Your monitor can express a range of intensity for each color channel, from 0 (absence of color) to 255 (full intensity of color). Colors vary widely among monitors based on both the user's preferences and brand of equipment.

Color Depth

The amount of data used to create color on a display is called the **color depth**. If your monitor can display 8 bits of data in each of the three color channels, it has a 24-bit color depth (8 × 3 = 24). 24-bit images can contain almost 17 million different colors and are called true-color images. Both JPG and PNG support 24-bit color. If your users have a 24-bit color display, they can appreciate the full color depth of your images. But many monitors cannot display 24-bit images; some have only 16-bit color depth (called high color) and some have only 8-bit color depth. If your monitor does not support the full color depth of an image, the browser must resort to mixing colors in an attempt to match the original colors in the image.

Dithering

The browser must mix its own colors when you display a 24-bit image on an 8-bit monitor, or when you use a file format that does not support 24-bit color. Because the 8-bit monitor has fewer colors to work with (256, to be exact), the browser must try to approximate the missing colors by creating colors from the ones the browser already has. This type of color mixing is called dithering. **Dithering** occurs when the browser encounters a color that it does not support, such as when you try to turn a 24-bit photographic image into an 8-bit, 256-color image. Dithered images often appear grainy and pixelated. The dithering is most apparent in gradations, feathered edges, or shadows. Figure 8-16 shows the same image in both JPG and GIF format at 8-bit, 256 colors.

Figure 8-16

24-bit images on an 8-bit display

The JPG file on the left has a lot of dithering in the sky area of the photo, where the browser was forced to mix colors to approximate the existing colors in the image. The GIF file on the right exhibits a different type of color matching called banding. Unlike dithering, **banding** is an effort to match the closest colors from the GIF's palette to the original colors in the photo. When you create a GIF, you can choose whether or not to use dithering. A nondithered image is smaller than one that uses dithering, but the banding may create an unacceptable image. JPGs, when viewed on an 8-bit or 16-bit display, dither to the closest colors. Photos are best saved as JPGs, even when viewed at a lower color depth, because the dithering creates a more acceptable image.

Using the Web Palette

One way to control dithering is to create images that use nondithering colors. The 216 nondithering colors that are shared by PCs and Macintoshes are called the **Web palette** or **browser-safe**

colors. The nondithering palette only applies to GIF or 8-bit PNG, not to 24-bit JPG. Most Web-capable graphics programs include the Web palette colors. If you do create graphics for the Web, you can avoid trouble by using the Web palette as your color palette for all flat color areas of your graphics. The Web palette, which was once the only color palette acceptable for the majority of monitors, is now becoming less important as higher color depth monitors become the norm. Unless you know specifically that your audience has older monitors, you can forgo using the Web palette.

Note

You can view the Web palette online at *www.lynda.com/hex.asp*. You will find the Web palette organized by both value and hue, with all the hexadecimal codes included.

Using Color Wisely

Because of the variable nature of color on the Web, be sure to test the colors you choose, and use restraint when adding color to your design. Remember that colors do not look the same on different monitor brands and operating systems. When used properly, color can enhance the presentation of your information, providing structural and navigation cues to your user. Conversely, poor use of color distracts from your content and can annoy your users. Dark backgrounds, clashing colors, and unreadable links are just a few examples of the unrestrained use of the HTML color attributes that are common on the Web. Because CSS allows you to easily apply color to any element does not mean that you should apply color haphazardly. Remember that many of your users might have accessibility issues that prevent them from seeing color the way you do. The user's ability to navigate, read, and interact with your content should always determine the choices and use of color in a Web site.

Specifying CSS Color Values

In this section, you will learn about the different ways to express color using CSS properties. CSS lets you specify color values in one of three ways:

- Color names
- RGB color values
- Hexadecimal color values

Which color value method should you use? Hexadecimal color values probably should be your first choice because they are already supported by most browsers. Both hexadecimal and RGB values are more specific and let you express a wider range of color than the color names. Whichever method you choose, make sure to use that method consistently throughout your entire Web site.

Using Color Names

The color name values let you quickly state color using common names. The valid CSS color name values are the 16 basic color names stated in the W3C HTML 4.01 specification, listed in Table 8-5.

Color Name	Hex	Color Name	Hex
Aqua	**00FFFF**	Navy	000080
Black	**000000**	Olive	808000
Blue	**0000FF**	Purple	800080
Fuchsia	**FF00FF**	**Red**	**FF0000**
Gray	808080	Silver	C0C0C0
Green	008000	Teal	008080
Lime	**00FF00**	**White**	**FFFFFF**
Maroon	800000	**Yellow**	**FFFF00**

Table 8-5   Color names recognized by most browsers (colors in boldface are browser-safe)

Although the color names are easy to use, they allow only a small range of color expression. To use a wider variety of available color, you must use a more specific value, such as RGB or hexadecimal.

Using RGB Colors

The RGB color model is used to specify numeric values that express the blending of the red, green, and blue color channels. When you specify RGB values, you are mixing the three basic colors to create a fourth color. Each of the three color channels can be specified in range from 0 to 100%, with 0 representing the absence of the color, and 100% representing the full brilliance of the color. If all three values are set to 0, the resulting color is black, which is the absence of all color. If all three color values are set to 100%, the resulting color is white, which is the inclusion of all colors.

The syntax for specifying RGB is the keyword rgb followed by three numerical values in parentheses—the first for red, the second for green, the third for blue. The following rule states a percentage RGB value:

```
p {color: rgb(0%, 100%, 100%);}
```

RGB color values can be specified as an integer value as well. The integer scale ranges from 0 to 255 with 255 equal to 100%. The following rules specify the same color:

```
p {color: rgb(0%, 100%, 100%);} /* percentages */
p {color: rgb(0, 255, 255);}    /* integers */
```

Using Hexadecimal Colors

HTML uses hexadecimal numbers to express RGB color values, and you can use them in CSS as well. Hexadecimal numbers are a base-16 numbering system, so the numbers run from 0 through 9, and then A through F. When compared to standard base-10 numbers, hexadecimal values look strange because they include letters in the numbering scheme. Hexadecimal color values are six-digit numbers; the first two define the red value, the second two define the green, and the third two define the blue. The hexadecimal scale ranges from 00 to FF with FF equal to 100%. Hexadecimal values are always preceded by a pound sign (#). The following rules specify the same color:

```
p {color: #00ffff;}             /* hexadecimal */
p {color: rgb(0%, 100%, 100%);} /* percentages */
p {color: rgb(0, 255, 255);}    /* integers */
```

Note
Browser-safe hexadecimal colors are always made up of the following two-digit color values: 00, 33, 66, 99, CC, and FF. Therefore, 0066FF is a browser-safe color; 0F66FF is not. You can download a free color picker tool at *www.iconico.com/colorpic/*.

Understanding Element Layers

The color and background properties you will learn about in this chapter let you control three different layers of any element. You can imagine these layers as three individual pieces of tracing paper laid over each other to complete the finished Web page. Each layer is transparent until you add a color or an image. These are the three layers listed in order from back to front:

- *Background color layer*—The back or bottom layer, specified by the background-color property
- *Background image layer*—The middle layer, specified by the background-image property
- *Content layer*—The top layer; this is the color of the text content, specified by the color property

Figure 8-17 shows the three layers applied to the <body> element. Using body as the selector applies these effects to the entire content area of the Web page. The background color layer is cyan. It lies behind all of the other layers. The background image layer has an image tiled vertically along the left side of the browser. It overlays the background color. The top layer contains the content. Notice that the content layer overlays both the background image and background color layers.

Figure 8-17
Element layers

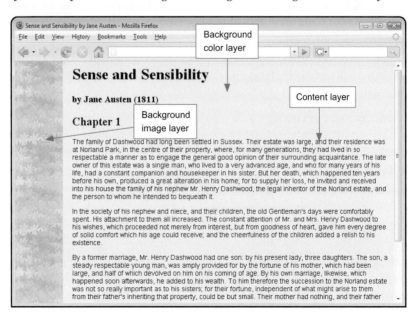

Controlling Color Properties with CSS

In this section you will use Cascading Style Sheet properties to control the following color characteristics:

- Specifying color values
- Setting default text color
- Changing link colors
- Specifying background color
- Setting the page background color
- Creating a text reverse
- Using background color in tables

Specifying Color Values

Color property description
Value: <color>
Initial: depends on browser
Applies to: all elements
Inherited: yes
Percentages: N/A

The color property lets you specify the foreground color of any element on a Web page. This property sets the color for both the text and the border of the element unless you have specifically stated a border color with one of the border properties (see Chapter 9).

The value for the color property is a valid color keyword or numerical representation, either hexadecimal or RGB (described earlier in the "Using RGB Colors" section). The following style rules show the different methods of specifying a color:

```
p {color: blue;}              /* color name */
p {color: #0000ff;}           /* hexadecimal value */
p {color: rgb(0,0,255);}      /* RGB numbers */
p {color: rgb(0%,0%,100%);}   /* RGB percentages */
```

Figure 8-18 shows a <p> element with the color set to blue. By default, the element's border is the same color as the element content.

Figure 8-18

The element border defaults to the text color

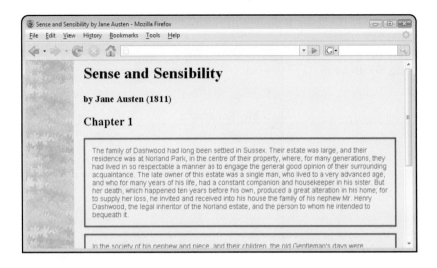

Here is the style rule for the paragraph. Notice that the border color is not specified, so the element's border is the same color as the content.

```
p {font-family: sans-serif; color: #3333cc; font-size: .85em;
line-height: 1.25 em; border: solid; padding: 1em;}
```

Setting the Default Text Color

Color is inherited from parent to child elements. If you set the color for <body>, all elements on the page inherit their color from the <body> element, effectively setting the default text color for the entire Web page. The following rule sets the color for the <body> element:

```
body {color: #006633;}
```

Changing Link Colors

You can change the colors of hypertext links by using the following special CSS classes:

- *link*—The unvisited link color; the default is blue.
- *active*—The active link color. This is the color displayed when the user points to a link and holds down the mouse button. The default is red.
- *visited*—The visited link color; the default is purple.

You can use these special classes only with the <a> tag. The syntax uses a colon (:) flag character, as shown in the following examples:

```
a:link {color: #cc0033;}      /* new links are red */
a:active {color: #ff0000;}    /* active links are black */
a:visited {color: #cccccc;}   /* visited links are green */
```

The result of this code is shown in Figure 8-19.

Figure 8-19
Changing link colors

The familiar blue (for new links) and purple (for visited links) colors are one of the most recognizable navigation cues for users visiting your site. Keep in mind that some users might have sight disabilities, such as color blindness, that could prevent them from seeing your Web pages in the way you intend. However, many sites do change their links to match their design color scheme. Changing link colors is acceptable as long as you maintain color consistency and preserve the contrast between the new and visited link colors to provide a recognizable difference to the user.

Specifying Background Color

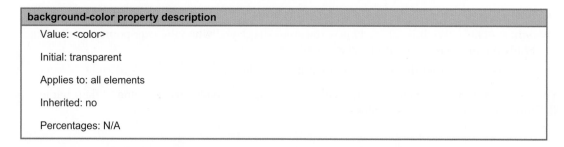

background-color property description
Value: <color>
Initial: transparent
Applies to: all elements
Inherited: no
Percentages: N/A

The background-color property lets you set the background color of any element on a Web page.

The background color includes any padding area (explained in Chapter 9) that you have defined for the element. Figure 8-20 shows <p> elements with background color and different padding values.

Figure 8-20

Background color and padding

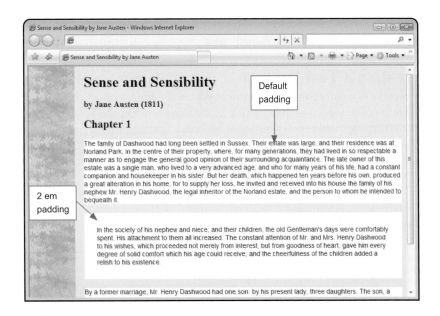

The background-color property can be applied to both block-level and inline elements. The following style rule selects a span element to apply a background color:

```
span {background-color: #ffffff;}
```

This rule is then applied to the span element that surrounds the author's name in the code:

```
<span>Jane Austen</span>
```

The result is shown in Figure 8-21

Figure 8-21

An inline element with a background color

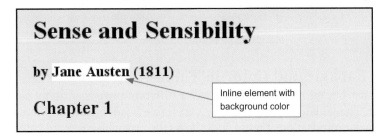

Setting the Page Background Color

To set the page background color, use body as the selector. This sets the background color for the content area of the Web page. By default, the background color of any element is transparent. Therefore, all elements show the page background color unless the background-color property is specifically stated. The following rule sets a background color for the <body> element:

```
body {background-color: #cccccc;}
```

It is always a good practice to include a page background color because some users might have a default background color that is different from the color you chose in your design. Even if you plan on a white page background, you can never be sure that all users have their default set to white, so include the background-color property rather than relying on the user's settings.

Creating a Text Reverse

A reverse is a common printing effect where the background color, which is normally white, and the text color, which is usually black, are reversed. On the Web you can do this in your choice of color. Reverses are usually reserved for headings rather than the regular body text. You can easily create a reverse with a style rule. The following rule sets the background color of the <h1> element to blue, and the text color to white:

```
h1 {color: #ffffff; background-color: blue; padding:.25em;}
```

The element padding is set to.25 em to increase the background color area. Figure 8-22 shows the result of the style rule.

Figure 8-22

Reverse text in a heading

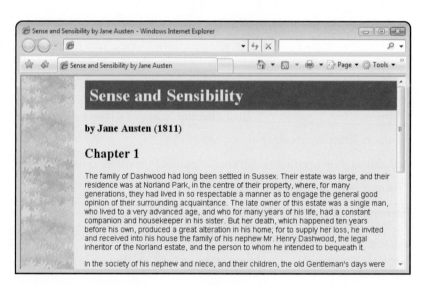

Using Background Color in Tables

You can use background color in tables for different purposes, all by using the background-color property. The table <table>, table row <tr>, table header <th>, and table data <td> elements all accept background colors. Figure 8-23 shows the use of background color to highlight information in a table.

Use the table elements as selectors when you use the background-color property. You may also need to use class identifiers to uniquely identify which cells or rows have background colors applied, as in the following style rules:

```
table {background-color: #ffffff;}   /* Sets table background to white */
tr.hilite {background-color: yellow;}   /* Sets "hilite" class row
      background to yellow */
th.header {background-color: #cc9966;}  /* Sets "header" class cell
      background to lt. brown */
```

Figure 8-23
Background color in tables

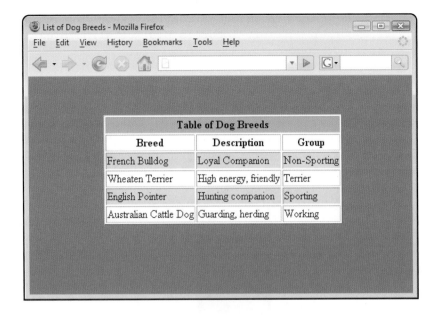

Working with Images and Color

In this set of steps you will add an image and color information to a Web page. The code you will add to the file appears in blue.

To add the image to the Web page:

1. Copy the **wildflowers.htm** file and the **daisy.jpg** file from the Chapter 08 folder provided with your Data Files to the Chapter08 folder in your work folder. (Create the Chapter 08 folder, if necessary.)

2. Start Notepad or another text editor and open the file **wildflowers.htm**.

3. Add an <img> element to the page immediately after the opening <p> tag, as shown in the following code in blue text:

```
<html>
<head>
<title>Growing Wildflowers</title>
</head>
<body>
<h1>Growing Wildflowers</h1>
<p><img src="daisy.jpg"> Lorem ipsum dolor sit amet,
consectetuer adipiscing elit, sed diem nonummy nibh
euis mod tincidunt ut lacreet dolore magna aliguam erat
volutpat.
```

   ... body text...

```
adipiscing elit, sed diem nonummy nibh euismod tincidunt ut lacreet
dolore magna aliguam erat volutpat. Ut wisis
```

```
enim ad minim veniam, quis nostrud exerci tution
ullamcorper suscipit lobortis nisl ut aliquip ex
eacommodo consequat.
</p>
</body>
</html>
```

4. Save the file and view it in the browser. It should look like Figure 8-24.

Figure 8-24

Adding an image to a
Web page

5. Add attributes to the image to provide size and alternate text information. The image width and height are both 100 pixels. The alt and title attributes can contain any text you choose to describe the image, such as "daisy image." The following code fragment shows the attribute additions.

```
<img src="daisy.jpg" width="140" height="187"
alt="daisy image" border="0" title="The Wild Daisy" />
```

6. Wrap the text around the image by adding a CSS style rule to the image. Use the style attribute with the float property set to "left" as shown in the following code fragment:

```
<img src="daisy.jpg" width="140" height="187"
alt="daisy image" border="0" title="The Wild Daisy"
style="float: left;" />
```

7. Save the file and view it in the browser. When you view the file it looks like Figure 8-25.

Figure 8-25

Floating the image to the left of text

8. Adjust the right margin of the image by adding a margin-right property to the style attribute. Set the measurement value to 20 px, as shown in the following code:

```
<img src="daisy.jpg" width="140" height="187"
    alt="daisy image" border="0" title="The Wild Daisy"
    style="float: left; margin-right: 20px;" />
```

9. Save the file and view it in the browser. It should look like Figure 8-26.

Figure 8-26

Adding a right margin to the image

10. Add a style attribute to the <h1> element to change the color to a forest green. The hexadecimal code is 006633. The following code fragment shows the <h1> element with the style attribute.

```
<h1 style="color: #006633">Growing Wildflowers</h1>
```

11. Finish the page by setting the background color to a light green. Add a style attribute to the body element and set the background color to light green, hexadecimal value 99cc99, as shown in the following code fragment:

```
<body style="background-color: #99cc99">
```

12. Save the file and close the editor. Then view the finished page in the browser. It should look like Figure 8-27, with a deep green heading and light green page background. The complete code for the page follows.

Figure 8-27

The finished Web page

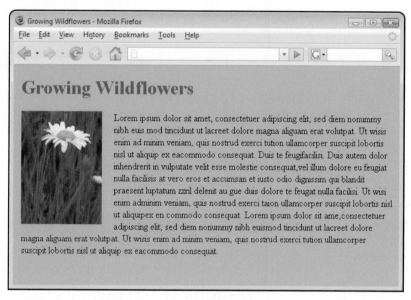

```
<html>
<head>
<title>Growing Wildflowers</title>
</head>
<body style="background-color: #99cc99">
<h1 style="color: #006633">Growing Wildflowers</h1>
<p><img src="daisy.jpg" width="140" height="187" alt="daisy image"
     border="0" title="The Wild Daisy" style="float: left;
     margin-right: 20px; "> Lorem ipsum dolor sit amet,
consectetuer adipiscing elit, sed diem nonummy nibh
euis mod tincidunt ut lacreet dolore magna aliguam erat
volutpat.
```

... body text...

```
adipiscing elit, sed diem nonummy nibh euismod tincidunt ut
lacreet dolore magna aliguam erat volutpat. Ut wisis
enim ad minim veniam, quis nostrud exerci tution
ullamcorper suscipit lobortis nisl ut aliquip ex
eacommodo consequat.
</p>
</body>
</html>
```

Controlling Background Images with CSS

In this section you will use Cascading Style Sheet properties to control the following background characteristics:

- Specifying a background image
- Creating a page background
- Creating an element background
- Specifying background repeat
- Creating a vertical repeat
- Specifying background position
- Creating a centered background image
- Positioning vertical and horizontal background images

Specifying a Background Image

background-image property description
Value: <url>
Initial: none
Applies to: all elements
Inherited: no
Percentages: N/A

The background-image property lets you specify which image to display. Other CSS background properties control how the image is displayed.

With standard HTML, the only behavior of background images is to tile completely across the browser background. This is also the default behavior with the CSS background-image property. Figure 8-28 shows a document with an image tiled across the background.

Figure 8-28

Default background
image behavior

The background image from this example is shown in Figure 8-29. It is tiled repeatedly both
vertically and horizontally.

Figure 8-29

The individual
background image

In Figure 8-28, the text that is displayed over this busy background is illegible. When choosing
page backgrounds, keep the legibility of your text in mind. Avoid overly busy and distracting
backgrounds that make your content difficult to read.

Specifying the Background Image URL

To specify a page background image, use the <body> element as the selector, because <body> is
the parent element of the content area. To use an image in the background, you must specify the
relative location of the image file in the style rule. CSS has a special notation for specifying a URL,
as shown in Figure 8-30.

Figure 8-30

URL value syntax

Creating a Page Background

To tile an image across the entire background of the Web page, use body as the selector, as shown in the following rule. This is the style rule that was used to create Figure 8-28.

```
body {background-image: url(ivy.jpg);}
```

Creating an Element Background

You can also use the background-image property to apply an image to the background of any element. The following rule sets a background image for the <h1> element:

```
h1 {background-image: url(bluetex.jpg); padding: .25em;}
```

The padding property adds extra space around the <h1> element to show an additional area of the background image. Figure 8-31 shows the result of the style rule.

Figure 8-31

Background image applied to an element

Specifying Background Repeat

background-repeat property description
Value: repeat	repeat-x	repeat-y	no-repeat	inherit
Initial: repeat
Applies to: all elements
Inherited: no
Percentages: N/A

The background-repeat property lets you control the tiling of background images across the document or element background.

A background image must be specified for this property to work, so you always use the background-image property with the background-repeat property. Table 8-6 lists the background-repeat values.

Value	Background Image Behavior
repeat	The image is repeated across the entire background of the element; this is the default behavior.
repeat-x	The image is repeated across the horizontal (x) axis of the document only.
repeat-y	The image is repeated across the vertical (y) axis of the document only.
no-repeat	The image is not repeated; only one instance of the image is shown in the background.

Table 8-6   Background-repeat property values

Creating a Vertical Repeat

The repeat-y value of the background-repeat property lets you create a vertical repeating background graphic. Figure 8-32 shows an example of this effect.

The style rules for this Web page follow. Notice the use of the margin-left property to align the heading and paragraph elements properly with the background image.

```
body {background-image: url(ivy.jpg); background-repeat: repeat-y;}
h1, h2, h3, p {margin-left: 70px;}
```

Figure 8-32

Vertical repeating background image

Creating a Horizontal Repeat

The repeat-x value of the background-repeat property lets you create a horizontal repeating background graphic. Figure 8-33 shows an example of this effect.

Figure 8-33

Horizontal repeating background image

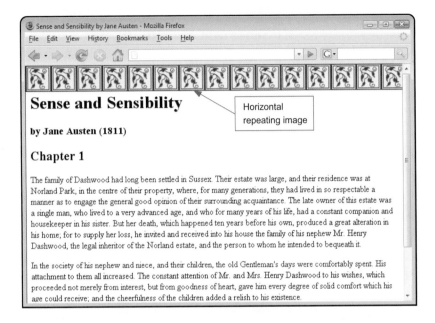

The style rules for this Web page follow. Notice the use of the margin-top property to align the <h1> element properly with the background image.

```
body {background-image: url(ivy.jpg); background-repeat: repeat-x;}
h1 {margin-top: 50px;}
```

Creating a Nonrepeating Background Image

The no-repeat value of the background-repeat property lets you create a single instance of an image in the background. This is useful if you want to apply a watermark effect on your page. As you will see, the no-repeat value can be enhanced by using it in combination with the background-position property, described in the next section.

Figure 8-34 shows an example of a nonrepeating background image.

The following style rule shows the use of the no-repeat value:

```
body {background-image: url(ivy.jpg);
      background-repeat: no-repeat;}
h1 {margin-top: 50px;}
```

In this style sheet, the margin-top property is set to 50 px to properly align the <h1> element beneath the single background image. To position this single background image elsewhere on the page, you can use the background-position property.

Figure 8-34

Nonrepeating
background image

Specifying Background Position

background-position property description
Value: [[<percentage> | <length>]{1,2} | [[top | center | bottom] || [left | center | right]]
Initial: 0% 0%
Applies to: block-level and replaced elements
Inherited: no
Percentages: refer to the size of the box itself

The background-position property lets you use three types of values: percentage, length, or keywords. Table 8-7 lists the values and their meanings. Figure 8-35 shows the keyword positions in the element box and their equivalent percentage values.

You can use the keywords in Table 8-7 alone ("left") or in combination ("left top") to position the background image. Figure 8-35 shows the nine keyword positions and their percentage equivalents. The keywords can be used interchangeably, so the values "left top" and "top left" are the same.

Figure 8-35

Keyword and percentage
background positions

left top 0% 0%	center top 50% 0%	right top 100% 0%
left center 0% 50%	center 50% 50%	right center 100% 50%
left bottom 0% 100%	center bottom 50% 100%	right bottom 100% 100%

Value	Background Image Behavior
percentage	The percentage values are based on the starting point of the upper-left corner of the containing element's box. The first percentage value is horizontal; the second is vertical. For example, the value "45% 30%" places the background image 45% from the left edge and 30% from the top edge of the containing box.
length	Length values work in much the same way as percentages, starting from the upper-left corner of the element's containing box. The first length value is horizontal; the second is vertical. For example, the value "100px 200px" places the background image 100 pixels from the left edge and 200 pixels from the top edge of the containing box.
keywords	The keywords are: ♦ left ♦ right ♦ center ♦ top ♦ bottom

Table 8-7   Background-position property values

Creating a Centered Background Image

You can use the background-position property to place vertical, horizontal, or nonrepeating images. Probably one of the most popular uses of the background-position property is to combine it with the background-repeat property to create a centered background image, which mimics a printed watermark on the Web page. Figure 8-36 shows this effect.

CHAPTER 8

Figure 8-36

A centered nonrepeating
background image

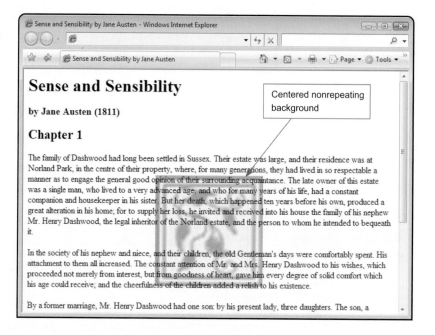

The image in Figure 8-36 has been altered in a graphics program for use in the background by
reducing the color intensity until the image is faintly visible. It is larger and lighter than the
original shown in Figure 8-29. The following style rule centers the nonrepeating background
image:

```
body {background-image: url(lgivy.jpg);
      background-repeat: no-repeat;
      background-position: center;}
```

Positioning Vertical and Horizontal Background Images

You can also position images that repeat on either the horizontal or vertical axis of the Web page.
The following style rule positions the vertical repeating background image along the right side of
the browser window:

```
body   {background-image: url(ivy.jpg);
        background-repeat: repeat-y;
        background-position: right;}
p      {margin-right: 70px;}
```

As in previous examples, the <p> element that sets the right margin must be adjusted to keep the
text from running over the background. Figure 8-37 shows the result of the style rule.

Figure 8-37

Positioning a vertical
repeating background
image

You can also position a horizontal repeating image. The following rule positions a horizontal repeating background image along the bottom of the browser window:

```
body {background-image: url(ivy.jpg);
      background-repeat: repeat-x;
      background-position: bottom;}
```

Figure 8-38 shows the result of the style rule.

Figure 8-38

Positioning a horizontal
repeating background
image

Applying the Background Properties

In this set of steps, you have a chance to apply some of the background properties you learned about in this chapter. As you work through the steps, refer to Figure 8-40 to see the results you will achieve. Save your file and test your work in the browser as you complete each step.

To build the style sheet:

1. Copy the **mars.htm** and **pattern1.jpg** files from the Chapter08 folder provided with your Data Files to the Chapter08 folder in your work folder. Then open **mars.htm** in your HTML editor.

2. In your browser, open **mars.htm**. When you open the file, it looks like Figure 8-39.

Figure 8-39

The beginning Web page

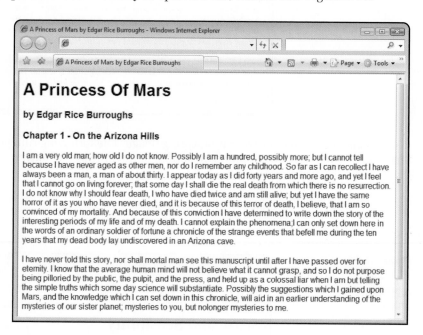

3. Examine the code. Notice the <style> section of the file. It currently contains a style rule that sets the font family and line height for the text. The complete code for the page follows:

```
<html>
<head>
<title>A Princess of Mars by Edgar Rice Burroughs</title>
<style type="text/css">
body    {font-family: sans-serif;
         line-height: 1.25em;}
</style>
</head>
<body>
<h1>A Princess Of Mars</h1>
```

```
<h3>by Edgar Rice Burroughs</h3>
<h3>Chapter 1 - On the Arizona Hills</h3>
<p>I am a very old man; how old I do not know. Possibly I am a hundred,
    possibly more; but I cannot tell because I have never aged as
    other men, nor do I remember any childhood. So far as I can
    recollect I have always been a man, a man of about thirty.
    I appear today as I did forty years and more ago, and yet I feel
    that I cannot go on living forever; that some day I shall die the
    real death from which there is no resurrection.  I do not know
    why I should fear death, I who have died twice and am still
    alive; but yet I have the same horror of it as you who have
```

... body text...

```
    Possibly the suggestions which I gained upon Mars, and the knowledge
    which I can set down in this chronicle, will aid in an earlier
    understanding of the mysteries of our sister planet; mysteries to
    you, but no longer mysteries to me.</p>
</body>
</html>
```

4. In your HTML editor, start by setting the background color for the Web page. The finished design uses a brown background. Write a style rule that uses body as the selector and sets the background-color property to #cc6633 (brown):

```
<style type="text/css">
body    {font-family: sans-serif;
         line-height: 1.25em;
         background-color: #cc6633;}
</style>
```

5. Next, build the style for the <h1> element, which is a text reverse. Use h1 as the selector, specify a background color of #663300 (dark brown) and a text color of #ffffff (white). Add padding of .25 em:

```
h1    {color: #ffffff; background-color: #663300;
       padding: .25em}
```

6. Add a background image for the Web page (**pattern1.jpg**).Add the background-image property to the existing style rule for the <body> element, because you want to apply the background image to the entire Web page.

```
body    {font-family: sans-serif;
         line-height: 1.25em;
         background-color: #cc6633;
         background-image: url(pattern1.jpg);}
```

7. When you test the new style rule you added in Step 6, you see that the background image tiles across the entire background of the Web page. You want to restrict the tiling of the background graphic to the left margin of the browser. To accomplish this, use the background-repeat property set to repeat-y. Add this property to the existing style rule:

```
body    {font-family: sans-serif;
         line-height: 1.25em;
         background-color: #cc6633;
         background-image: url(pattern1.jpg);
         background-repeat: repeat-y;}
```

8. The background now repeats correctly on the left side of the browser window, but the content text is illegible against it. To fix this problem, add a margin-left property for all of the elements that contain text: <h1>, <h2>, <h3>, and <p>. Specify a value of 125 px, as shown in the following rule:

```
h1, h2, h3, p {margin-left: 125px;}
```

10. The finished code for the style sheet follows. Figure 8-40 shows the completed Web page.

```
<html>
<head>
<title>A Princess of Mars by Edgar Rice Burroughs</title>
<style type="text/css">
body    {font-family: sans-serif;
         line-height: 1.25em;
         background-color: #cc6633;
         background-image: url(pattern1.jpg);
         background-repeat: repeat-y;}
h1      {color: #ffffff;
         background-color: #663300;
         padding: .25em}
h1, h2, h3, p {margin-left: 125px;}
</style>
</head>
```

Figure 8-40

The finished Web page

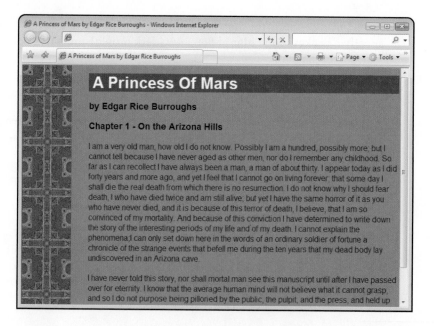

Chapter Summary

To create an engaging, accessible, and informative Web site, you must use graphics wisely. Keep the following points in mind:

▶ You currently can use only three image file formats on the Web: GIF, JPG, and PNG. These formats all compress images to create smaller files. Unless you choose the appropriate file format, your image will not compress and appear as you expect. SVG is a new file format from the W3C that offers vector-based graphics for the Web.

▶ Your computer monitor displays color by mixing the three basic colors of light: red, green, and blue (RGB). Colors vary widely from one monitor to another, based on both the user's preferences and the exact brand of equipment.

▶ Reduce image size to the appropriate dimensions for a Web page. If you must use a larger image, let the user view a thumbnail first, and provide the file size information.

▶ Test your colors carefully to make sure that the widest variety of users can access your content. Consider restricting your color palette to the colors available in the browser-safe palette to ensure the greatest portability of your Web pages.

▶ Color names are not always the best way to specify color values because of their variable nature. Consider using RGB or the more common hexadecimal values instead.

▶ Use the color property to set foreground colors for elements. Remember that the element border defaults to the element color unless you specifically state a border color.

▶ Background colors affect any padding areas in the element. They can be applied to both block-level and inline elements.

▶ Choose background images that do not detract from the legibility of your content. Use the background-repeat and background-position properties to control the appearance of images in the background.

▶ Test your work on different browsers and computing platforms, because they render colors differently. Test at different color depths as well.

CHAPTER 8

Key Terms

banding

browser-safe colors

color depth

dithering

Graphics Interchange Format (GIF)

interlacing

Joint Photographic Experts Group (JPG or JPEG)

Portable Network Graphics (PNG)

raster graphics

Scalable Vector Graphics (SVG)

vector graphics

Web palette

Review Questions

1. What are the three image file formats you can use on a Web site?
2. Which file formats support 24-bit color?
3. Explain a file's color depth control.
4. How many colors does GIF support?
5. What is the browser-safe palette?
6. What is lossless file compression?
7. Which file formats support transparency?
8. What are the drawbacks of using animated GIFs?
9. Explain lossy image compression.
10. What image characteristics can you control using the JPG format?
11. What are some options for acquiring images for your site?
12. Which image format should you use for a two-color company logo?
13. Which image format should you use for a photograph?
14. What three attributes should you always include in the image tag? Why?
15. How many layers can you work with when designing pages?
16. What are the three different ways to express color values in CSS?
17. How is the default border color of an element determined?
18. What are the three special selectors that let you change link colors?
19. To what type of elements can you apply a background color?
20. What is the default background image behavior?

Hands-On Projects

1. Practice using the CSS float property:
   a. Download an image from the Online Companion Web site or find an image of your own.
   b. Add text around the image. Experiment with the float property and its values to view the way text wraps.
   c. Test the work in multiple browsers to verify that the text wraps consistently.
2. Practice using the CSS margin property attributes:
   a. Download an image from the Online Companion Web site or find an image of your own.
   b. Add text around the image. Experiment with the margin property to add white space around the image.
   c. Test the work in multiple browsers to verify that the text spacing is consistent.

3. Practice using width and height image attributes:

   a. Download an image from the Online Companion Web site or find an image of your own.

   b. Build a simple page that contains text and multiple images. Do not include the width and height attributes in the <img> tag.

   c. With the images turned off in your browser, view the page.

   d. Add the appropriate width and height information to the <img> tag for each image.

   e. Again, turn the images off in your browser and view the page. Note the differences between the two results and the way your layout is affected.

4. Experiment with background color in tables. Use the CSS background-color property and different table element selectors to add color. Test the result in multiple browsers. Note the differences and similarities in the ways that the browsers handle table color.

5. Browse the Web and choose a site that you feel exhibits positive use of color, both in content and backgrounds. Write a short design critique that describes how the use of color enhances the legibility of the site and improves user access to information.

6. Browse the Web and choose a mainstream (not amateur) site that can benefit from a change in color scheme. Look for problems with legibility of text over background colors, use of nonstandard linking colors, and so on. Write a short essay that describes the changes you would implement to improve the use of color on the site.

Individual Case Project

Gather or create the boilerplate graphics to use on the different pages of your site. These include any banner, navigation, section, or identifying graphics. Add these graphics to the test pages of your site. Test the images in multiple browsers to make sure they are displayed properly.

Think about the different color requirements for your content, and decide how the legibility can be enhanced. Can color communicate information about the structure of your information?

Determine the color choices for your Web site. Pick the colors for text, the background color in tables, and page backgrounds.

Establish graphics standards for your Web site, including but not limited to the following:

▶ Decide whether you will use a standard amount of white space around each graphic.

▶ Determine exactly which img attributes should be included in all <img> tags.

▶ Formulate a standard for all alt and title attributes.

▶ Formulate a basic set of image standards for your site. Use this as the display standard for testing your graphics.

Write a short standards document that can be provided to anyone contributing to the site.

Team Case Project

Work with your team to decide on the graphics and color choices for your project Web site. These include any banner, navigation, section, or identifying graphics, and the colors for text, the background color in tables, and page backgrounds.

You may need to bring sample graphics or mock-up HTML pages to present your ideas on these characteristics to your team members.

Establish graphics standards for your Web site, including but not limited to the following:

▶ Decide whether you will use a standard amount of white space around each graphic.

▶ Determine exactly which img attributes should be included in all <img> tags.

▶ Formulate a standard for all alt and title attributes.

▶ Formulate a basic set of image standards for your site. Use this as the display standard for testing your graphics.

Write a short standards document that can be submitted to the instructor and provided to the team members.

After you have reached a general consensus, go back to work on the page template you adopted in Chapter 7. Create more finished mock-ups of your page design. Trade the page layout examples with your team members. Look for unifying characteristics that give your site a unique identity. Make sure the colors and graphics flow though the different page levels on the site. Work towards smooth transitions between your pages. You want all the pages to exhibit a graphic identity that connects them together.

9

Using the Box Properties

When you complete this chapter, you will be able to:

- Understand the CSS visual formatting model
- Use the CSS box model
- Use the margin, padding, and border properties
- Use the special box properties
- Apply the box properties
- Customize list-item elements

In this chapter, you will explore the CSS box properties. These properties let you control the margin, padding, and border characteristics of block-level elements. To understand how these properties work, you will first learn about the CSS visual formatting model and box model. These models control the way content is displayed on a Web page. Then you will learn about the margin, padding, and border properties and how you can use them to enhance the display of content in the browser. Finally, you will see how the special box properties—width, height, float, and clear—let you create floating text boxes.

The CSS Visual Formatting Model

The **CSS visual formatting model** describes how the element content boxes should be displayed by the browser. The visual formatting model is based on the hierarchical structure of the HTML document and the element display type. In HTML, elements fall into three display type categories:

- *Block*—Block-level elements appear as blocks such as paragraphs. Block elements contain inline boxes that contain the element content.
- *Inline*—Inline-level elements contain the content within the block-level elements. They do not form new blocks of content.
- *List-item*—List-item elements create a principal box around list-item inline boxes. List-item elements appear as bulleted or numbered lists.

Figure 9-1 shows three different block-level elements: <body>, <h1>, and <p>. The <h1> and <p> elements contain inline content boxes.

Figure 9-1

The CSS visual
formatting model

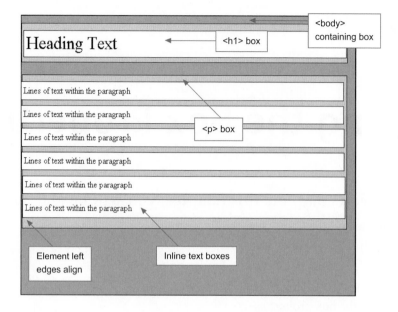

Figure 9-1 also shows that parent elements contain child elements. The parent element is called the **containing box**. You can see that <body> is the containing box for the elements of a Web page. All other elements' boxes reside within <body>. In Figure 9-1, the <body> element is the containing box for the <h1> and <p> elements. The <p> element is the containing box for the inline text that comprises the paragraph text.

CSS lets you specify margin, border, and padding values for all block-level elements. In some instances, the values you specify depend on the containing box that is the parent of the element you want to affect. For example, if you choose a percentage value for a margin, the percentage value is based on the containing box. In Figure 9-1, a 10% margin value for the <p> element would create margins that are 10% of the width of the containing box, in this case, the <body> element.

Specifying Element Display Type

display property description
Value: block | inline | list-item | none
Initial: inline
Applies to: all elements
Inherited: no
Percentages: N/A

The CSS display property determines the display type of an element. When you are working with HTML, you will probably not use the display property very often because the browser contains default element display information for each HTML element. For example: <h1>, <p>, and <blockquote> elements are block-level elements; <b> and <i> are inline elements. In most cases, you want the browser to display each element using the default element type. However, there may be times when you want to manipulate this property. The following style rule changes the default display type for an <h1> element from block to inline.

```
h1 {display: inline;}
```

The result of this style rule is an <h1> element that behaves like an inline element, as shown in Figure 9-2.

Figure 9-2

Manipulating the display property

Note

The display property "none" value lets you hide an element so that it is not displayed in the browser. This can be useful in a Web page where you want to display only some of the information on a page.

Using the CSS Box Model

The **CSS box model** describes the rectangular boxes that contain content on a Web page. Each block-level element you create is displayed in the browser window as a box containing content. Each content box can have margins, borders, and padding, as shown in Figure 9-3.

Figure 9-3

The CSS box model

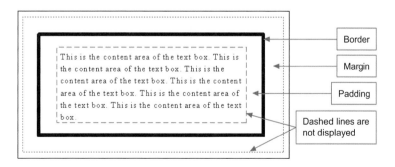

As Figure 9-3 illustrates, the content box is the innermost box, surrounded by the padding, border, and margin areas. The padding area has the same background color as the content element, but the margin area is always transparent. The border separates the padding and margin areas.

Figure 9-4 shows the box model areas in a paragraph element. This paragraph has 2-em padding, a thin black border, and 2-em margins. Notice that the margin area is transparent.

Figure 9-4

The CSS box model areas in a <p> element

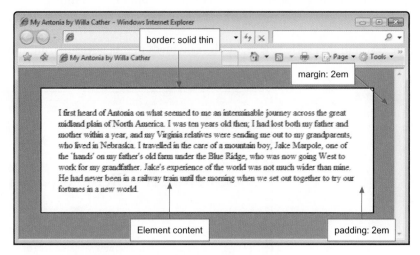

The following code shows the style rule for the paragraph in Figure 9-4:

```
p {margin: 2em;
    padding: 2em;
    border: solid thin black;
    background-color: white;}
```

The margin and padding properties set the length to 2 em for all four sides of the box. The border property is a shorthand property that sets the border-style property to solid, the border-weight property to thin, and the border-color property to black. The background-color property sets the paragraph background color to white.

CSS lets you specify margin, padding, and border properties individually for each side of the box. Figure 9-5 shows that each area has a left, right, top, and bottom side. Each one of the sides can be referred to individually. If the browser supports the individual properties, you can select, for example, the padding-bottom, border-top, or margin-left properties if you prefer.

Figure 9-5

The CSS box model individual sides

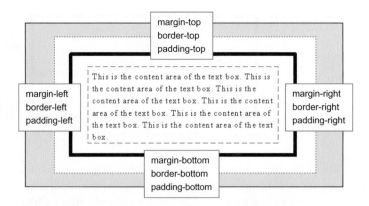

Figure 9-6 shows a paragraph with a variety of different box property settings. The style rule for the paragraph is:

```
p {margin-left: 50px;
    margin-right: 20px;
    padding-left: 10px;
    padding-right: 20px;
    border-left: solid thick black;
    border-right: solid thick double;
    background: white;}
```

Figure 9-6

The CSS box model individual sides in a <p> element

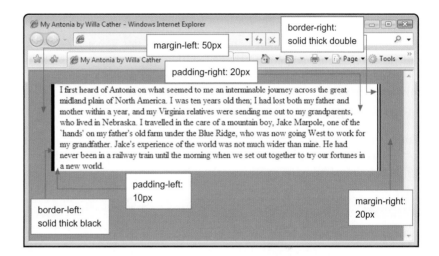

Measurement Values

The margin, border, and padding properties let you state two types of measurement values—either a length or a percentage. (For a full discussion of measurement values, see Chapter 7.) If you use a percentage value, the percentage is based on the width of the containing box, as described earlier. If you choose a length, you have to decide whether to use an absolute or relative value. As with font sizes, you are better off using relative units such as ems or pixels when you are stating margin, border, or padding sizes. The relative measurement values let you build scalable Web pages. In some instances, it's preferable to use the absolute values, such as the point, but these are generally more useful when you know the exact measurements of the output device.

Using the Margin Properties

The margin properties let you control the margin area of the box model. Margins are always transparent, showing the background of their containing element. You can use margins to enhance the legibility of text, create indented elements, and add white space around images.

CHAPTER 9

Specifying Margins

margin property description
Value: <length>	<percentage>
Initial: 0
Applies to: all elements
Inherited: no
Percentages: refer to width of containing block

The margin property is a shorthand property that lets you set all four individual margins with one property. You can specify either a length or percentage value. The most commonly supported usage of the margin property is to state one value for all four margin sides, as shown in the following style rule:

```
p {margin: 2em;}
```

You also can choose to state individual margin settings within this same rule. This can be confusing, because the individual margin settings change based on the order within the rule. Table 9-1 shows how the syntax works.

Number of Values	Example	Description
1 value	p {margin: 1em;}	All four margins are 1 em
2 values	p {margin: 1em 2em;}	Top and bottom margins are 1 em Left and right margins are 2 em
3 values	p {margin: 1em 2em 3em;}	Top margin is 1 em Right and left margins are 2 em Bottom margin is 3 em
4 values	p {margin: 1em 2em 3em 4em;}	Top margin is 1 em Right margin is 2 em Bottom margin is 3 em Left margin is 4 em

Table 9-1   Shorthand notation for the margin property

To make your style rules more specific and easy to read, you can use the individual margin properties, such as margin-left, rather than the shorthand notation. The individual margin properties are described in the next section.

Figure 9-7 shows two paragraph elements. The first paragraph has the margin set to 2 em; the second has the default margin setting.

Notice that the increased margins enhance the legibility of the text. However, only the horizontal margins on the left and right side of the paragraph are beneficial. The extra vertical margin between the paragraphs is too large and breaks up the flow of the text. To solve this problem, you can use the individual margin properties, described next.

Figure 9-7

Using the margin
property

Specifying the Individual Margin Properties

margin-left, margin-right, margin-top, margin-bottom individual property descriptions
Value: <length> | <percentage>
Initial: 0
Applies to: all elements
Inherited: no
Percentages: refer to width of containing block

The individual margin properties let you control each of the individual margins: margin-left, margin-right, margin-top, and margin-bottom. The following style rules set the left and right margins for two different paragraph elements:

```
p.margin1 {margin-left: 50px; margin-right: 30px}
p.margin2 {margin-left: 100px; margin-right: 100px}
```

As Figure 9-8 shows, both paragraphs now have their specified margins.

Figure 9-8

Using the individual margin properties

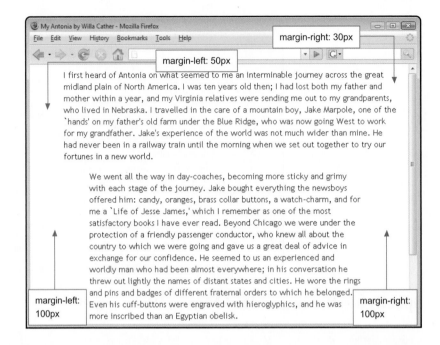

Negative Margins

You can set negative margin values to achieve special effects. For example, to achieve a hanging indent you can override the default browser margin by setting a negative value. Although it varies by browser, the default left margin is approximately 10 pixels. The following rule sets a negative value of -10 pixels:

```
p {margin-left: -10px;}
```

Figure 9-9 shows two paragraphs, one with the default margin and one with a negative margin.

Figure 9-9

A <p> element with negative left margin

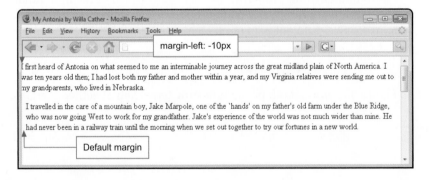

You can also use negative margins to remove the default margins from other elements. Figure 9-10 shows two <h1> elements, one with the default margins, and one with the bottom margin set to a negative value. The following rule sets a negative value of 24 pixels:

```
h1 {margin-bottom:-24px;}
```

Figure 9-10

An <h1> element with
negative bottom margin

Although neither of the preceding negative margin results really enhances the legibility of the text, you might someday encounter a design problem that requires a negative margin solution; it's helpful to know that CSS allows you to do this.

Collapsing Margins

To ensure that the spacing between block-level elements is consistent, the browser collapses the vertical margins between elements. The vertical margins are the top and bottom element margins. The browser does not add the value of the two, but picks the greater value and applies it to the space between the adjoining elements. To illustrate this, consider the following rule:

```
p {margin-top: 15px; margin-bottom: 25px;}
```

If the browser did not collapse the vertical margins, the paragraphs would have 40 pixels of space between each paragraph. Instead, the browser collapses the margin. Following the CSS convention, the browser sets the vertical margin between paragraphs to 25 pixels, the greater of the two values. Figure 9-11 shows the results of collapsing the margins with the preceding style rule.

Figure 9-11

The browser collapses
vertical margins

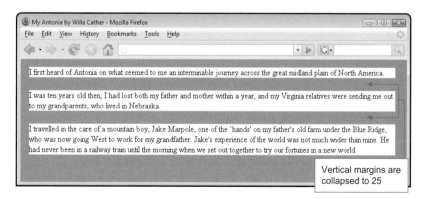

Using the Padding Properties

The CSS padding properties let you control the padding area in the box model. The padding area is between the element content and the border. The padding area inherits the background color of the element, so if a <p> element has a white background, the padding area will be white as well. If you add a border to an element, you will almost always want to use padding to increase the white space between the content and the border, as shown in Figure 9-12.

Figure 9-12

Default padding and 2em padding

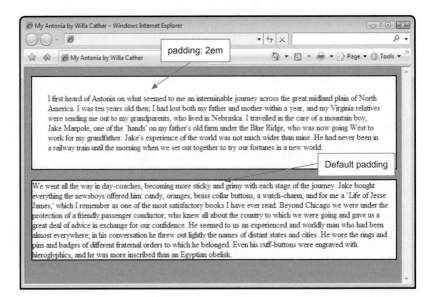

Specifying Padding

padding property description
Value: <length> | <percentage>
Initial: 0
Applies to: all elements
Inherited: no
Percentages: refer to width of containing block

The padding property is a shorthand property that lets you set all four individual padding values with one rule. You can specify either a length or a percentage value. Unlike margins, you cannot collapse the padding area or set negative padding values.

The most common usage of the padding property is to state one value for all four padding sides, as shown in the following style rule:

```
p {padding: 2em;}
```

You can also choose to state individual padding settings in the padding property. Like the margin shorthand property described earlier, the individual padding settings change based on the order within the rule. Table 9-2 shows how the syntax works.

Number of Values	Example	Description
1 value	p {padding: 1em;}	Top, bottom, left, and right padding are 1 em
2 values	p {padding: 1em 2em;}	Top and bottom padding are 1 em Left and right padding are 2 em
3 values	p {padding: 1em 2em 3em;}	Top padding is 1 em Right and left padding are 2 em Bottom padding is 3 em
4 values	p {padding: 1em 2em 3em 4em;}	Top padding is 1 em Right padding is 2 em Bottom padding is 3 em Left padding is 4 em

Table 9-2   Shorthand notation for the padding property

Specifying the Individual Padding Properties

padding-left, padding-right, padding-top, padding-bottom individual property descriptions
Value: <length>	<percentage>
Initial: 0
Applies to: all elements
Inherited: no
Percentages: refer to width of containing block

The individual padding properties let you control the individual padding areas: padding-left, padding-right, padding-top, and padding-bottom. The following style sets the top and bottom padding areas for the paragraph, along with complementing borders and a white background:

```
p {padding-top: 2em;
   padding-bottom: 2em;
   border-top: solid thin black;
   border-bottom: solid thin black;
   background-color: #ffffff;}
```

As Figure 9-13 shows, the paragraph now has the default left and right padding with 2-em top and bottom padding.

Figure 9-13

Using the individual padding properties

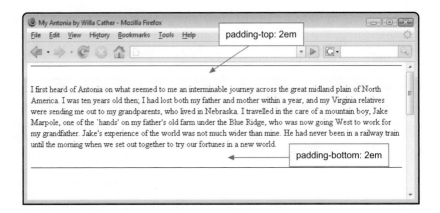

Using the Border Properties

The border properties let you control the appearance of borders around elements. The border area resides between the margin and padding. You can set 20 border properties, many of which are too specific for common use. You will most likely use the five border shorthand properties, which include:

- border
- border-left
- border-right
- border-top
- border-bottom

These shorthand properties let you state border-style, border-color, and border-width for all four borders or for any of the individual sides of the box. However, you can also state much more specific borders by using the border properties separately. Table 9-3 lists the entire range of 20 border properties.

Description	Property Name		
Overall shorthand property	border		
Individual side shorthand properties	border-left, border-top, border-right, border-bottom		
Specific shorthand property	border-style	border-width	border-color
Individual properties	border-left-style border-right-style border-top-style border-bottom-style	border-left-width border-right-width border-top-width border-bottom-width	border-left-color border-right-color border-top-color border-bottom-color

Table 9-3   Border properties

To use the shorthand properties, you must first understand the three border characteristics—border-style, border-color, and border-width. Then you will learn how to use the border shorthand properties.

Specifying Border Style

border-style property description
Value: <border-style>
Initial: none
Applies to: all elements
Inherited: no
Percentages: N/A

The border-style is the most important border property because it must be stated to make a border appear. The border-style property lets you choose from one of the following border style keywords:

- *none*—No border on the element; this is the default setting
- *dotted*—Dotted border
- *dashed*—Dashed border
- *solid*—Solid line border
- *double*—Double line border
- *groove*—Three-dimensional border that appears to be engraved into the page
- *ridge*—Three-dimensional border that appears to embossed (or extend outward from the page)
- *inset*—Three-dimensional border that appears to set the entire box into the page
- *outset*—Three-dimensional border that appears to extend the entire box outward from the page

The following code shows an example of the border-style property in use:

```
p {border-style: solid;}
```

Figure 9-14 shows examples of the borders. The purple background for this page enhances the display of the three-dimensional styles, which do not look the same on a white background. Not all borders are supported by all browsers, so test your work carefully. If you specify a border style that is not supported, the border defaults to solid.

You can also choose to state border styles for individual sides using the border-style property. The individual border style settings change based on the order within the rule. Table 9-4 shows how the syntax works.

Figure 9-14

Different border styles

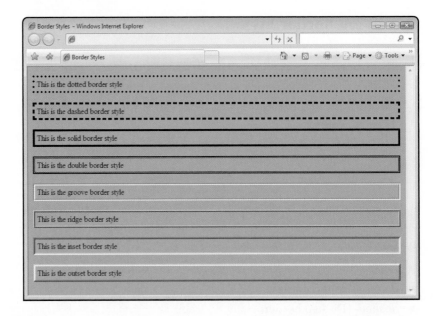

Number of Values	Example	Description
1 value	p {border-style: solid;}	All four borders are solid.
2 values	p {border-style: solid double;}	Top and bottom borders are solid Left and right borders are double
3 values	p {border-style: solid double dashed;}	Top border is solid Right and left borders are double Bottom border is dashed
4 values	p {border-style: solid double dashed dotted;}	Top border is solid Right border is double Bottom border is dashed Left border is dotted

Table 9-4   Shorthand notation for the border-style property

Of course, if you examine the rules in Table 9-4, you can see they will create odd effects. For example, a paragraph with a different border style for each side is not a common design technique. Remember to use restraint and keep the user in mind when working with border styles.

Individual Border Styles

You can also specify individual borders styles with the following border-style properties:

- border-left-style
- border-right-style
- border-top-style
- border-bottom-style

These properties let you single out one border and apply a style. The following rule applies only to the left border of the element:

```
p {border-left-style: double;}
```

Specifying Border Width

border-width property description
Value: thin | medium | thick | <length>
Initial: medium
Applies to: all elements
Inherited: no
Percentages: N/A

The border-width property lets you state the width of the border with either a keyword or a length value. You can use the following keywords to express width:

- thin
- medium (default)
- thick

The width of the rule when you use these keywords is based on the browser. The length values let you state an absolute or relative value for the border; percentages are not allowed. Using a length value lets you create anything from a hairline to a very thick border. The following code shows an example of the border-width property in use:

```
p {border-width: 1px; border-style: solid;}
```

Remember that the border is not displayed unless the border-style property is stated. Figure 9-15 shows examples of different border widths.

You can also choose to state individual border widths in the border-width property. The individual border width settings change based on the order within the rule. Table 9-5 shows how the syntax works.

Figure 9-15

Different border widths

Number of Values	Example	Description
1 value	p {border-width: 1px;}	All four borders are 1 pixel wide
2 values	p {border-width: 1px 2px;}	Top and bottom borders are 1 pixel wide Left and right borders are 2 pixels wide
3 values	p {border-width: 1px 2px 3px;}	Top border is 1 pixel wide Right and left borders are 2 pixels wide Bottom border is 3 pixels wide
4 values	p {border-width: 1px 2px 3px 4px;}	Top border is 1 pixel wide Right border is 2 pixels wide Bottom border is 3 pixels wide Left border is 4 pixels wide

Table 9-5   Shorthand notation for the border-width property

Individual Border Widths

You can also specify individual borders widths with the following border-width properties:

- border-left-width
- border-right-width
- border-top-width
- border-bottom-width

These properties let you single out one border and apply a width. The following rule applies only to the left border of the element:

```
p {border-left-width: thin;}
```

Specifying Border Color

border-color property description
Value: <color>
Applies to: all elements
Inherited: no
Percentages: N/A

The border-color property lets you set the color of the element border. The value can be either a hexadecimal value, RGB value, or one of the 16 predefined color names listed in Table 9-6.

Aqua	Navy
Black	Olive
Blue	Purple
Fuchsia	Red
Gray	Silver
Green	Teal
Lime	White
Maroon	Yellow

Table 9-6   Predefined color names

To set a border color, use the property as shown in the following rule:

```
p {border-color: red; border-width: 1px; border-style: solid;}
```

The default border color is the color of the element content. For example, the following style rule sets the element color to red. The border is also red because a border color is not specified.

```
p {color: red; font: 12pt arial; border: solid;}
```

You can also choose to state individual border colors in the border-color property. The individual border color settings change based on the order within the rule. Table 9-7 shows how the syntax works.

Number of Values	Example	Description
1 value	p {border-color: black;}	All four borders are black
2 values	p {border-color: black red;}	Top and bottom borders are black Left and right borders are red
3 values	p {border-color: black red green;}	Top border is black Right and left borders are red Bottom border is green
4 values	p {border-color: black red green blue;}	Top border is black Right border is red Bottom border is green Left border is blue

Table 9-7   Shorthand notation for the border-color property

Individual Border Colors

You can also specify individual border colors with the following border-color properties:

- border-left-color
- border-right-color
- border-top-color
- border-bottom-color

These properties let you single out one border and apply a color. The following rule applies only to the left border of the element:

```
p {border-left-color: red; border-style: solid;}
```

Using the Border Shorthand Properties

The shorthand properties are the most common and easiest way to express border characteristics. When you use these shorthand properties, you are stating the style, color, and width of the border in one concise rule.

Specifying Borders

border		
Value: <border-width> | <border-style> | <color>		
Initial: see individual properties		
Applies to: all elements		
Inherited: no		
Percentages: N/A		

The border property lets you state the properties for all four borders of the element. You can state the border-width, border-style, and border-color in any order. Border-style must be included for the border to appear. If you do not include border-width, the width defaults to medium. If you do not include border-color, the border appears in the same color as the element. The following example rules show different uses of the border property.

The following rule sets the border-style to solid. The border-weight defaults to medium. The border-color is the same as the color of the <p> element; because no color is stated, the border color is black.

```
p {border: solid;}
```

The following rule sets the border-style to solid. The border-weight is 1 pixel. The border-color is red.

```
p {border: solid 1px red;}
```

The following rule sets the border-style to double. The border-weight is thin. The border-color is blue. Notice that the order of the values does not matter.

```
p {border: double blue thin;}
```

Specifying Individual Borders

border-top, border-right, border-bottom, border-left
Value: <border-top-width> || <border-style> || <color>
Initial: see individual properties
Applies to: all elements
Inherited: no
Percentages: N/A

You can set individual border properties using the individual border shorthand properties. These let you state border-style, border-width, and border-color in one statement that selects a single element border. For example, the following rule sets border-style to solid and border-weight to thin for both the left and right borders. Because no color is stated, the borders default to the element color.

```
p {border-left: solid thin; border-right: solid thin;}
```

The following rule sets border-style to double and border-color to red for the top border. Because no border-weight is stated, the weight defaults to medium.

```
p {border-top: double red;}
```

Using the Special Box Properties

The special box properties are used primarily with objects such as images. In most instances you will not set these properties for normal block-level elements. However, you can use them to create floating text boxes, as shown in Figure 9-16.

CHAPTER 9

Figure 9-16

A floating text box

In this section, you will learn about the following special box properties:

- width
- height
- float
- clear

After you have learned about the four properties, you will see how they are used to create a floating text box like the one shown in Figure 9-16.

Width

width property description
Value: <length> | <percentage>
Initial: auto
Applies to: all elements but text inline elements, table rows, and row groups
Inherited: no
Percentages: refer to width of containing block

The width property lets you set the horizontal width of an element. Width is not intended for normal block-level elements, but you can use it to create floating text boxes or to manipulate images. In most cases, you set the padding or margins of the elements rather than explicitly stating a width.

The width property accepts either a length value or a percentage. The percentage value is based on the width of the containing element box. By default, the value of width is set to auto, which is based on the content of the element minus the padding, border, and margins, if applicable. The following is an example of width property usage:

```
div {width: 200px;}
```

Use percentages or relative measurement values, such as pixels (px), to ensure that your widths are portable across different screen resolutions.

Height

height property description
Value: <length> | <percentage>
Initial: auto
Applies to: all elements but text inline elements, table columns, and column groups
Inherited: no
Percentages: N/A

The height property lets you set the vertical height of an element. Like width, height is not intended for normal block-level elements, but you can use it to create floating text boxes or to manipulate images. In most cases you set the padding or margins of the elements rather than explicitly stating a height.

The height property accepts either a length value or a percentage. The percentage value is based on the height of the containing element box. By default, the value of height is set to auto, which is based on the content of the element minus the padding, border, and margins, if applicable. The following is an example of height property usage:

```
div {height: 150px;}
```

Float

float property description
Value: left | right | none
Initial: none
Applies to: all elements except positioned elements and generated content (See Appendix B.)
Inherited: no
Percentages: N/A

The float property lets you position an element to the left or right edge of its parent element. Float is most commonly used for <img> elements, allowing alignment of an image to the left or right of text. You can also use the float property to align a text box to the left or right edge of its parent.

Floating Text Boxes

The float property can also be used to float a text box to the left or right of text. Used with the width and height properties, you can create a text box of the type shown earlier in Figure 9-16.

CHAPTER 9

The advantage to this type of layout is that no HTML tables are used to create the design; rather, a simple CSS rule is all that is necessary.

The rule for the left-floating text box looks like this:

```
.floatbox   {width: 125px;
             height: 200px;
             float: left;
             background-color: #ffff66; /* yellow */}
```

This rule states a class named floatbox. The rule sets the width, height, and float properties of the element, and sets the background color to a hexadecimal color value that is a shade of yellow.

The class floatbox can then be applied to an element in the document. The code from the document follows. The <p> is the element to which the class is applied.

```
<body>
<p class="floatbox">"No romantic novel ever written in America is one
half so beautiful as My Antonia"<br><br>H.L. Mencken </p>
I first heard of Antonia on what seemed to me an interminable journey
across the great midland plain of North America. I was ten years
old then; I had lost both my father and mother within a year,
and my Virginia relatives were sending me out to my grandparents,
who lived in Nebraska.<p>

<p>I travelled in the care of a mountain boy, Jake Marpole,
one of the 'hands' on my father's old farm under the Blue Ridge,
who was now going West to work for my grandfather.
Jake's experience of the world was not much wider than mine. He had
never been in a railway train until the morning when we set out
together to try our fortunes in a new world.</p>
</body>
```

The float box can be enhanced by adding some of the other properties you learned about in this chapter. The following rule adds 1-em padding for the entire element, a 2-em right margin, and a 1-pixel solid black rule:

```
.floatbox   {width: 125px;
             height: 200px;
             float: left;
             background-color: #ffff66; /* yellow */
             padding: 1em;
             margin-right: 2em;
             border: solid black 1px;}
```

The enhanced float box is much more legible and improves the page layout. Figure 9-17 shows the result of the new properties added to the rule.

Float is supported by the most recent versions of Internet Explorer, Firefox, Opera, and Netscape.

Figure 9-17

The enhanced floating text box

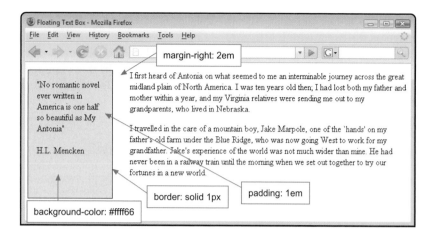

Clear

clear property description
Value: none | left | right | both
Applies to: block-level elements
Inherited: no
Percentages: N/A

The clear property lets you control the flow of text around floated elements. You only use the clear property when you are using the float property. Clear lets you force text to appear beneath a floated element, rather than next to it. Figure 9-18 shows an example of normal text flow around an element.

Figure 9-18

Normal text flow around a floating image

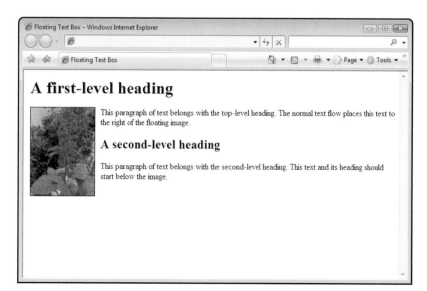

This figure shows an image with the float property set to "left." The text flows down around the image on the right, which is the correct behavior. The second-level heading and paragraph, however, are not appearing in the correct position. They should be positioned beneath the floating image. To correct this problem, use the clear property. In this instance, the <h2> should be displayed clear of any left-floating images. Add this style rule directly to the <h2> element with the style attribute as follows:

```
<h2 style="clear: left;">
```

Figure 9-19 shows the result of adding the clear property.

Figure 9-19

Using the clear property

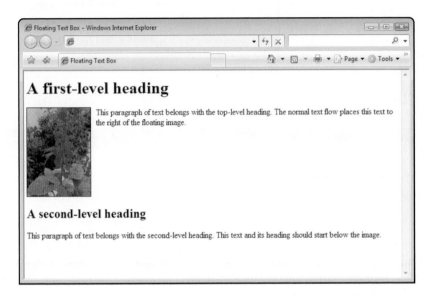

The code for this page follows:

```
<html>
<head>
<title>Floating Text Box</title>
<style type="text/css">
img.left {float: left; margin-right: 10px;}
</style>
</head>
<body>
<h1>A first-level heading</h1>
<p><img src="salvia.jpg" width="125" height="167" alt="Salvia"
class="left" border="1">This paragraph of text belongs with the
top-level heading. The normal text flow places this text to the
right of the floating image.</p>

<h2 style="clear: left;">A second-level heading</h2>
```

```
<p>This paragraph of text belongs with the second-level heading. This
text and its heading should start below the image.</p>
</body>
</html>
```

Notice that the clear property lets you clear from either left- or right-floating images using the "left" and "right" values. The "both" value lets you control text flow in the event you have floating images on both the left and right sides of the text.

Applying the Box Properties

In the following steps, you have a chance to apply some of the properties you learned about in this chapter. As you work through the steps, refer to Figure 9-21 to see the results you will achieve. Save your file and test your work in the browser as you complete each step.

To apply the box properties:

1. Copy the **boxtest.htm** file from the Chapter09 folder provided with your Data Files to a Chapter09 folder in your work folder. (Create the Chapter09 folder, if necessary.)

2. Open the file **boxtest.htm** in your HTML editor and save it in your work folder as **boxtest1.htm**.

3. In your browser, open the file **boxtest1.htm**. When you open the file it looks like Figure 9-20.

Figure 9-20

The original HTML document

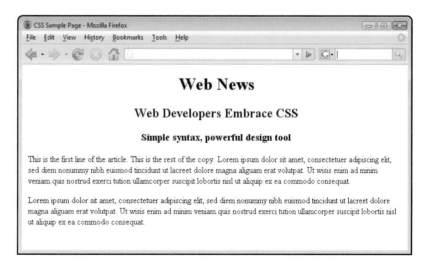

4. Examine the code. Notice the <style> section of the file. It contains three basic style rules that center the <h1>, <h2>, and <h3> elements. The complete code for the page follows:

```
<html>
<head>
<title>CSS Sample Page</title>
<style type="text/css">
```

```
h1 {text-align: center;}
h2 {text-align: center;}
h3 {text-align: center;}
</style>
</head>
<body>
<h1>Web News</h1>
<h2>Web Developers Embrace CSS</h2>
<h3>Simple syntax, powerful design tool</h3>
<p>This is the first line of the article. This is the rest of the
copy. Lorem ipsum dolor sit amet, consectetuer adipiscing elit,
sed diem nonummy nibh euismod tincidunt ut lacreet dolore magna
aliguam erat volutpat.  Ut wisis enim ad minim veniam.quis
nostrud exerci tution ullamcorper suscipit lobortis nisl ut
aliquip ex ea commodo consequat.
</p>
<p>Lorem ipsum dolor sit amet, consectetuer adipiscing elit, sed diem
nonummy nibh euismod tincidunt ut lacreet dolore magna aliguam
erat volutpat.  Ut wisis enim ad minim veniam.quis nostrud
exerci tution ullamcorper suscipit lobortis nisl ut aliquip
ex ea commodo consequat.</p>
</body>
</html>
```

5. Start by styling the <h1> element with a 1-em margin. Add the margin property to the existing <h1> style rule:

```
h1 {text-align: center; margin: 1em;}
```

6. The <h2> element has a margin-bottom property of 1 em. Add this property to the existing style rule:

```
h2 {text-align: center; margin-bottom: 1em;}
```

7. The <h3> has the most complex style effects, so break the style rule into separate lines. Start by adding .5 em of padding to the top and bottom of the element. Add the properties to the existing style rule:

```
h3 {text-align: center;
    padding-top: .5em;
    padding-bottom: .5em;}
```

8. Now add top and bottom borders to the <h3>. Set the style to solid and the weight to thin. Because the default rules are black, you do not have to state a color.

```
h3 {text-align: center;
    padding-top: .5em;
    padding-bottom: .5em;
    border-top: solid thin;
    border-bottom: solid thin;}
```

9. Finish the <h3> by setting the left and right margins to 40 pixels:

```
h3 {text-align: center;
    padding-top: .5em;
    padding-bottom: .5em;
    border-top: solid thin;
    border-bottom: solid thin;
    margin-left: 40px;
    margin-right: 40px;}
```

10. Finish styling the document by setting the <p> left and right margins to 40 pixels, to line up with the borders of the <h3>:

```
h3 {text-align: center;
    padding-top: .5em;
    padding-bottom: .5em;
    border-top: solid thin;
    border-bottom: solid thin;
    margin-left: 40px;
    margin-right: 40px;}
p {margin-left: 40px; margin-right: 40px;}
```

Figure 9-21 shows the results of the style rules.

Figure 9-21

The finished Web page

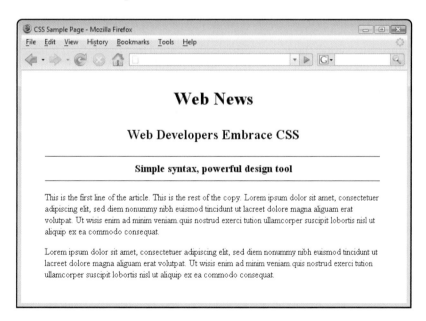

Customizing Lists

The list-style properties let you control the visual characteristics of elements that have a display property value of "list-item." These properties let you set the appearance of the marker that indicates each item within the list. With CSS, the marker can be a symbol, number, or image. You can also determine the position of the marker next to the list content.

The two common elements that have a default display value of "list-item" are <ul> and <ol>, which generate a bulleted (unordered) and ordered list, respectively. The following code shows a sample of each type of list:

```
<!-- Bulleted List -->
<h3>Things to do...</h3>
<ul>
<li>Buy dog food</li>
<li>Clean up the house</li>
<li>Take a rest</li>
</ul>
<!-- Ordered List -->
<h3>Places to go...</h3>
<ol>
<li>Paris</li>
<li>Sydney</li>
<li>Cairo</li>
</ol>
```

Figure 9-22 shows the result of this code. Notice that the default markers are a solid bullet, called a "disc" for the <ul> list, and an Arabic numeral called "decimal" for the <ol> list. You can change these marker values with the CSS list-style properties.

Figure 9-22

The unordered and ordered list elements

Specifying the list-style-type Property

The list-style-type property lets you customize the list marker to a variety of different values.

list-style-type
Value: disc | circle | square | decimal | decimal-leading-zero | lower-roman | upper-roman | lower-greek | lower-alpha | lower-latin | upper-alpha | upper-latin | hebrew | armenian | georgian | cjk-ideographic | hiragana | katakana | hiragana-iroha | katakana-iroha | none Initial: disc Applies to: elements with 'display: list-item' Inherited: yes Percentages: N/A

The list-style-type property lets you specify one of three types of markers for a list. You can choose either a symbol, a numbering system, or an alphabetical system. CSS allows a wide variety of marker values. Remember to test support for these markers in different browsers. Tables 9-8, 9-9, and 9-10 list the different values and their descriptions.

Value	Description
disc	A filled circle (see Figure 9-23)
circle	A hollow circle (see Figure 9-23)
square	A filled square (see Figure 9-23)

Table 9-8   Bulleted list values

Value	Description
decimal	Decimal numbers, beginning with 1; this is the default numbering
decimal-leading-zero	Decimal numbers padded by initial zeros (01, 02, 03…)
lower-roman	Lowercase roman numerals (i, ii, iii…)
upper-roman	Uppercase roman numerals (I, II, III…)
hebrew	Traditional Hebrew numbering
georgian	Traditional Georgian numbering
armenian	Traditional Armenian numbering
cjk-ideographic	Plain ideographic numbers
hiragana	Japanese hiragana language characters
katakana	Japanese katakana language characters
hiragana-iroha	Japanese hiragana-iroha language characters
katakana-iroha	Japanese katakana-iroha language characters

Table 9-9   Numerical list values

CHAPTER 9

Value	Description
lower-alpha	Lowercase ASCII letters (a, b, c, ... z)
upper-alpha	Uppercase ASCII letters (A, B, C, ... Z)
lower-greek	Lowercase classical Greek

Table 9-10   Alphabetical list values

Figure 9-23 shows the different supported list types.

Figure 9-23

Different list types in Firefox

To specify a list-style type, select the list container element, either ul or ol, and specify the value as shown in the following style rules:

```
ol {list-style-type: decimal-leading-zero;}
ul {list-style-type: circle;}
```

There may be times when you want to specify a list-style-type within an individual list. You can do this by using the style attribute within the <ul> or <ol> element as shown in the following:

```
<ol style="list-style-type: lower-alpha;">
<li>Item One</li>
<li>Item Two</li>
<li>Item Three</li>
</ol>
```

This style rule affects only this one instance of the list.

Specifying the list-style-image Property

The list-style-image property lets you easily attach an image to a list and have it repeated as the marker symbol.

list-style-image
Value: <url>	none	inherit
Initial: none
Applies to: elements with 'display: list-item'
Inherited: yes
Percentages: N/A
Media: visual

The list-style-image property lets you replace the standard symbol with an image of your choice. The following code shows the style rule that attaches an image to a bulleted list:

```
ul {list-style-image: url(pawprint.gif);}
```

Figure 9-24 shows the result of the style rule. The image is repeated whenever a list element is used.

Figure 9-24

Attaching an image as a list marker

Specifying the list-style-position Property

The list-style-position property lets you determine the placement of the list marker, either inside or outside the list-item content box.

list-style-position
Value: inside | outside | inherit
Initial: outside
Applies to: elements with 'display: list-item'
Inherited: yes
Percentages: N/A
Media: visual

The default value is outside. Figure 9-25 shows the two types of list position values.

Figure 9-25

Positioning the list marker

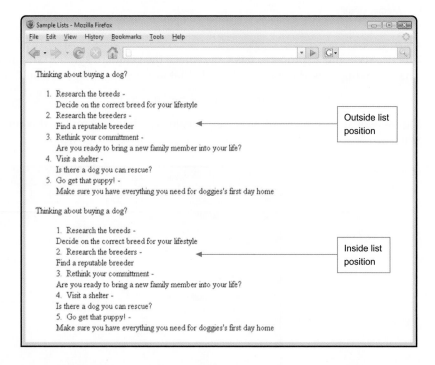

This figure shows two <ol> lists. The style rules for this page use a class selector to differentiate between the two:

```
ol.outside {list-style-position: outside;}
ol.inside {list-style-position: inside;}
```

The class is then applied to each <ol> element, as shown in the following code fragment for the first list:

```
<ol class="outside">
```

The class is applied to the second list in the same way:

```
<ol class="inside">
```

Using the list-style Shorthand Property

Like the other shorthand properties, the list-style property lets you write a single rule to specify all of the list-item properties.

list-style shorthand property description
Value: [<list-style-type> || <list-style-position> || <list-style-image>] | inherit
Initial: not defined for shorthand properties
Applies to: elements with 'display: list-item'
Inherited: yes
Percentages: N/A
Media: visual

The list-style shortcut property lets you state the following list-style properties in one concise style rule:

- List-style-type
- List-style-image
- List-style-position

You can specify values in any order. In the following style rule, the list is set to lower alphabetical letters that are inside the list box:

```
ol {list-style: lower-alpha inside;}
```

Applying the List Style Properties

In the following set of steps, you will learn how to style list-item elements with the list-style properties. As you work through the exercise, refer to Figure 9-27 to see the results you will achieve. Save your file and test your work in the browser as you complete each step.

To apply the list-style properties:

1. Open the file **lists.htm** in your HTML editor and save it in your work folder as **lists1.htm**.
2. Copy the image file **diamond.gif** into your work folder.
3. In your browser, open the file **lists1.htm**. When you open the file it looks like Figure 9-26. Notice that the file contains three lists. You will apply a different list-style to each list.
4. The first list on the page is a bulleted list that currently displays the default disc (bullet) style. Write a style rule that uses a class selector "circle" to uniquely select the list. Set the list-style-type property to change the bullet style to circle.

```
ul.circle {list-style-type: circle;}
```

Figure 9-26

The beginning Web page

5. Now apply the style to the first list by adding the class attribute to the <ul> element.

```
<!-- Bulleted List -->
<ul class="circle">
<li>Bread</li>
<li>Milk</li>
<li>Cheese</li>
<li>Eggs</li>
</ul>
```

6. The second list on the page is an ordered list that currently displays the default decimal style. Write a style rule that uses a class selector alpha to uniquely select the list. Set the list-style-type property to change the style to upper-alpha.

```
ol.alpha {list-style-type: upper-alpha;}
```

7. Now apply the style to the first list by adding the class attribute to the <ol> element.

```
<!-- Alphabetical List -->
<ol class="alpha">
<li>Spring</li>
<li>Summer</li>
<li>Fall</li>
<li>Winter</li>
</ol>
```

8. The third list on the page is an unordered list that currently displays the default bullet style. Write a style rule that uses a class selector image to uniquely select the list. Set the list-style-image property to a URL value, using the image file diamond.gif.

```
ul.image {list-style-image: url(diamond.gif);}
```

9. Now apply the style to the first list by adding the class attribute to the <ol> element. Figure 9-27 shows the finished document.

```
<!-- List Image -->
<ul class="image">
<li>Spruce</li>
<li>Pine</li>
<li>Elm</li>
<li>Birch</li>
</ul>
```

Figure 9-27

The completed Web page in Firefox

Chapter Summary

In this chapter you learned about the concepts of the CSS box and visual formatting models. You saw how the margin, padding, and border properties let you control the space around block-level elements on a Web page. You learned to customize lists with the CSS list-style properties. By using these properties judiciously, you can enhance the legibility of your content. You also learned how the special box properties let you create interesting text effects such as floating text boxes without the use of HTML table elements.

▶ The CSS box model lets you control spacing around the element content.

▶ You can state values of margin, border, and padding for all four sides of the box or individual sides.

▶ To build scalable Web pages, choose relative length units such as ems or pixels.

▶ The browser collapses vertical margins to ensure even spacing between elements.

▶ Margins are transparent, showing the color of the containing element's background color. Padding takes on the color of the element to which it belongs.

▶ The border properties let you add borders to all individual sides or all four sides of an element. The three border characteristics are style, color, and width. Style must be stated to make the border appear.

▶ The special box properties let you create floating images or text boxes.

▶ Remember to use margin, border, and padding properties judiciously to enhance the legibility of your content, rather than just for novelty effects.

▶ The list-style properties let you manipulate list characteristics.

Key Terms

box model	CSS visual formatting model
containing box	

Review Questions

1. What are the three space areas in the box model?
2. Which space area is transparent?
3. What does the visual formatting model describe?
4. What is the visual formatting model based on?
5. What are percentage measurement values based on?
6. What are the preferred length units for margins and padding?
7. In the following rule, what is the size of the vertical margins between paragraphs?

```
p {margin-top: 15px; margin-bottom: 10px;}
```

8. Where is the padding area located?

9. What are the five most common border properties?

10. What is the default border style?

11. What is the default border weight?

12. What is the default border color?

13. What are the two types of color values?

14. What does the float property let you do?

15. What does the clear element let you do?

16. Write a style rule for a <p> element that sets margins to 2 em, padding to 1 em, and a black, solid 1 pixel border.

17. Write a style rule for an <h1> element that sets top and bottom padding to .5 em with a dashed thin red border on the bottom.

18. Write a style rule for a <p> element that creates left and right padding of 1 em, a left margin of 30 pixels, and a left black medium double border.

19. Which two elements are used to create lists in HTML?

20. What are the three types of list styles markers you can specify?

Hands-On Projects

1. Browse the Web and choose a site that you feel exhibits good handling of white space to increase the legibility of the content. Write a short design critique of why the white space works effectively.

2. Browse the Web and choose a site that can benefit from the box properties available in CSS. Print a copy of the page and indicate where you would change the spacing and border properties. Write a short essay that describes the changes you want to achieve and how they increase the legibility of the page content.

3. In this project, you will create a floating text box.

   a. Copy the **float.htm** file from the Chapter09 folder provided with your Data Files to a Chapter09 folder in your work folder. (Create the Chapter09 folder, if necessary.)

   b. Open the file **float.htm** in your HTML editor and save it in your work folder as **float1.htm**.

   c. In your browser, open the file **float1.htm**. When you open the file it looks like Figure 9-28.

Figure 9-28

The original HTML file for Project 3

d. Examine the page code. Notice that there is an existing style rule that sets a background-color for a floatbox class, as shown in the following code fragment:

```
.floatbox {background-color: #ccc; }
```

e. This class is applied to the first <p> element in the document, as shown in Figure 9-28. Your goal is to use a variety of box properties to create a finished page that looks like Figure 9-29.

Figure 9-29

The finished HTML file for Project 3

Use the following properties to create the finished floating text box:

▶ width

▶ height

▶ float

▶ padding

> ► margin-right
> ► border

Experiment with the different properties until you achieve results that look as close to the finished page as possible.

4. In this project, you will have a chance to test the border properties. Save and view the file in your browser after completing each step.

a. Using your HTML editor, create a simple HTML file (or open an existing file) that contains heading and paragraph elements. Save the file in your Chapter09 folder as **borders.htm**.

b. Add a <style> element to the <head> section as shown in the following code:

```
<head>
<title>CSS Test Document</title>
<style type="text/css">


</style>
</head>
```

c. Experiment with the different border styles. Start by applying any of the following style rules to your document's elements:

```
h1 {border: solid 1px black;}
h2 {border-top: solid 1px; border-bottom: solid 3px;}
p {border-left: double red; border-right: solid 1px;}
```

d. Experiment with adding padding properties to your style rules to offset the borders from the text. The following style rules have sample padding properties to try:

```
h1 {border: solid 1px black; padding: 20px;}
h2 {border-top: solid 1px; border-bottom: solid 3px;
    padding-top: 15px; padding-bottom: 30px;}
p {border-left: double red; border-right: solid 1px;
    padding-left: 30px; padding-right: 20px;}
```

e. Continue to experiment with the border and padding properties. Try adding color and margin properties to see how the elements are displayed.

Individual Case Project

Create the box model conventions for your Web site. Build on the typographic classes you created in Chapter 7. Think about the different spacing requirements for your content and decide how the legibility can be enhanced using the box properties. Add this information to the type specification HTML page that shows examples of the different typefaces and sizes and how they will be used. Decide on margins, padding, and borders and which elements will benefit from their use. Create before and after sample HTML pages that reflect the enhanced design.

Team Case Project

Work with your team to decide on the box model conventions for your project Web site. These include any spacing specifications for your content that will increase legibility and clarity.

You may need to create sample mock-up HTML pages to present your ideas on these characteristics to your team members. Decide on margins, borders, and padding and how you will use these in your Web site. Think about creating floating boxes within sections for text highlights, how to standardize the look of different sections of your site with increased white space, and how borders can help to emphasize headings and columns.

After you have reached a general consensus, go back to work on the page template on which you are currently working. Create more finished mock-ups of your page design. Trade the page layout examples with your team members to reach consensus.

10

Creating Positioned Layouts

When you complete this chapter, you will be able to:

- Understand basic positioning concepts
- Apply CSS positioning properties
- Build a page layout with positioned elements

In a standard HTML document, the default positioning of elements is generally top to bottom and left to right. This basic display scheme frustrated designers who wanted to build more complex layouts, resulting in the use of tables as a page layout tool. The CSS positioning properties were introduced with CSS, level 2 (CSS2). They let you build Web pages without using cumbersome tables to control page layout. With positioning you can choose the exact placement of elements within the browser window. The new generation of browsers offers more robust support for positioning, as you will see in the examples throughout the chapter.

Positioning Elements

The CSS positioning properties give you control over the way element boxes are laid out in a Web page. As you will see, these properties let you specify four different types of positioning. They let you control the positioning of the elements and remove them from the normal flow of elements on the page. The CSS positioning properties also let you build pages that have elements positioned at different places in a Web page without using tables as containers, making content more accessible and reserving the use of tables for tabular data.

You also can use the CSS positioning properties with scripts to provide more interactive content to the user. **Scripts** are small pieces of programming that are written with a scripting language such as JavaScript. When scripting languages are combined with the CSS positioning properties, Web pages can offer more user interaction than simple hypertext links. Scripts can change the content of a Web page after it has been displayed in the browser, build interactive forms and games, and simulate animation effects.

Note

For more information on scripting, see books such as *JavaScript (Fourth Edition)* by Don Gosselin and *HTML, JavaScript, and Advanced Internet Technologies* by Karl Barksdale and E. Turner, both published by Cengage Learning.

Understanding the Normal Flow of Elements

By default, the browser normally displays elements on the page one after the other, depending on whether the elements are block-level or inline elements. Some elements float to the left or right of other elements on the page, as you saw in Chapter 9, Using the Box Properties. Element position can be affected by margin or padding properties, but generally the browser lays out element boxes from top to bottom and left to right until all elements that comprise the Web page have been displayed.

In the normal flow for block-level elements, boxes are laid out vertically one after the other, beginning at the top of the containing block. Each box's left edge touches the left edge of the containing element unless the box is floated or the layout model is right to left, as in a right-aligned language such as Hebrew. The space between boxes is determined by the margin settings. The normal flow determines the sequence of element display with which you are familiar in standard HTML. For an example of normal flow, examine the following HTML code fragment and the resulting normal flow diagram in Figure 10-1:

```
<body>
        <h1>The document heading</h1>
        <p>A paragraph of some text</p>
        <p>Another paragraph of text</p>
</body>
```

Figure 10-1

Block-level element normal flow

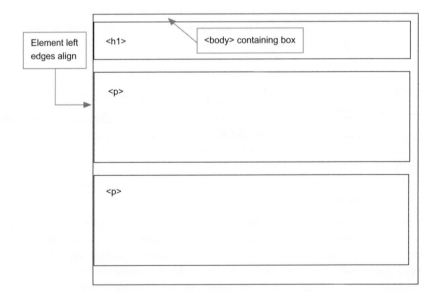

The <body> element is the containing element for the content section of the Web page. The elements within the <body> element are displayed exactly in the order they appear in the code from top to bottom; in this example, an <h1> followed by two <p> elements. Elements do not appear next to each other unless they are floated (see Chapter 9) or have a display type of "inline."

In the normal flow for inline elements, boxes are laid out horizontally, beginning at the top of the containing block. The inline boxes comprise the lines of text within, for example, a <paragraph>

element. The browser flows the text into the inline boxes, wrapping the text to the next line box as determined by the constraints of the containing box or the browser window size.

Specifying Box Position Type

The position property lets you specify the type of positioning for an element if it will be something other than the default positioning type, which is static.

position property description
Value: static | relative | absolute | fixed
Initial: static
Applies to: all elements, excluding generated content
Inherited: no
Percentages: N/A

Table 10-1 lists the different positioning values and their meanings.

Value	Description
Static	This is the default value. The element box is a normal box, laid out according to the normal document flow.
Absolute	The element box's position is specified with the position offset properties, described later in this section. These properties specify offsets with respect to the element box's containing box. Absolutely positioned boxes are removed from the normal flow. They have no impact on the layout of other elements on the page.
Fixed	The element box's position is calculated according to the "absolute" model, but in addition, the box is fixed with respect to the browser window. When the user scrolls the document, fixed elements do not move, but appear in the same position.
Relative	The element box's position is calculated relative to its normal position in the document flow.

Table 10-1   Position property value descriptions

The following style rule uses the position property to set a <div> element's position type to absolute:

```
div {position: absolute;}
```

Specifying Box Position Offsets

The box offset properties let you specify the exact positioning values for any element that has a position property set to absolute, fixed, or relative.

Box offset properties: top, right, bottom, left
Value: <length> | <percentage> | auto
Initial: auto
Applies to: positioned elements
Inherited: no
Percentages: refer to width of containing block

The offset properties determine the position of an element based on its containing box. The values refer to the distance from the edges of the containing block. For example, the following HTML code and style rule create an absolutely positioned <div> element that is offset in its containing box by 130 pixels from the left edge and 100 pixels from the top edge.

```
<html>
<head>
<title>Absolute Positioning</title>
<style type="text/css">
div {position: absolute;
     left: 130px;
     top: 100px;
     background-color: #ffcc33;}
</style>
</head>
<body>
<div>This is an absolutely positioned division element.</div>
</body>
</html>
```

The containing box in this example is the <body> element. The division is offset 130 pixels from the left side of the containing block and 100 pixels from the top side. In addition, a background color has been specified to make the division easier to see in the browser. The result of this code is shown in Figure 10-2.

Figure 10-2

Offset box positioning

Note

Pixels are the most convenient measurement unit when you are specifying absolute or fixed offset values. To avoid guessing screen measurements, use a shareware tool such as Screen Ruler, available from *www.microfox.com* to easily measure pixels on your computer monitor.

In Figure 10-2, the width of the <div> element is determined by the content it contains. You can use the width property, described in Chapter 9, to specify a width for the positioned division. You can also use the height property if the height of the element needs to be controlled. The following style rule shows the addition of the width property to further define the appearance of the element:

```
div {position: absolute;
left: 130px;
top: 100px;
width: 100px;
background-color: #ffcc33;}
```

Figure 10-3 shows the result of adding the width property to the style rule.

Figure 10-3

Specifying element width

Absolute Positioning

When you specify absolute positioning, an element's position is explicitly stated with respect to its containing box, as you saw in Figure 10-2. An absolutely positioned element is removed from the normal document flow and has no impact on other elements, but it does establish a new containing box for child elements. The child elements of an absolutely positioned element can follow the normal flow or have positioning types of their own. Absolute elements also can overlap the contents of another box, depending on their z-index property (described later in the chapter).

The following HTML code and style rules create two nested <div> elements. The outside <div> element is positioned within its containing <body> element. The inside <div> element is positioned within its containing outside <div> element.

```
<html>
<head>
<title>Absolute Positioning</title>
<style type="text/css">
div.outside {position: absolute;
     left: 130px;
     top: 100px;
     width: 200px;
     height: 200px;
     background-color: #ffcc33;}

div.inside {position: absolute;
     top: 150px;
     left: 150px;
     width: 50px;
     height: 50px;
```

```
        border: solid thin black;
        background-color: #ffffff;}
</style>
</head>
<body>
<div class="outside">Outside
<div class="inside">Inside</div>
</div>
</body>
</html>
```

Figure 10-4 shows the result of this code.

CHAPTER 10

Figure 10-4

Nested positioned elements

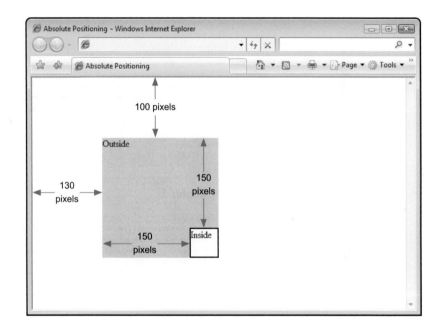

Fixed Positioning

Fixed positioning is a subcategory of absolute positioning, except that the containing box for a fixed element is always the browser window. Fixed elements stay in the same place at all times, regardless of how the user scrolls the document. Fixing an element lets you create a frame-type layout, where a content element can be scrolled independently of an adjoining navigation element, as shown in Figure 10-5.

Figure 10-5

Fixed positioning

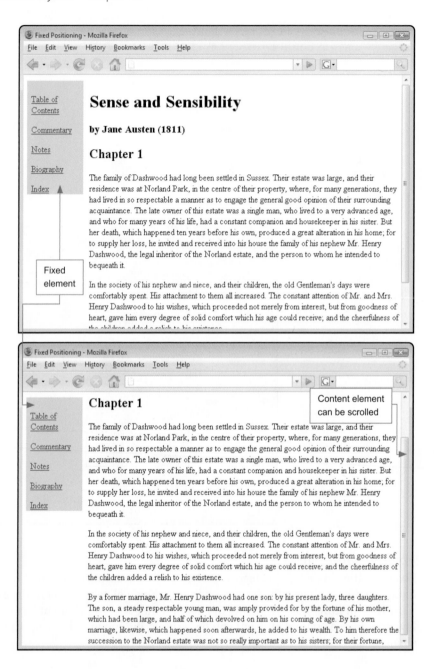

The following code shows the style rules for both elements in Figure 10-5:

```
div.fixed {position: fixed;
    left: 10px;
    top: 10px;
    background-color: #cccccc;
    width: 100px;
```

```
        height: 200px;
        padding-top: .5em;
        padding-left: .5em;}
div.content {position: absolute; left: 130;}
```

Notice that the fixed element has a specific width and height that sets the size of the element in the browser window. The left and top offset properties specify the fixed position of the element. The content element, which contains the page content, has no specific width or height properties, allowing the element size to be flexible based on the browser window size. The left offset property positions the element so it will not overlap the fixed element.

As you can see from the previous example, the ability to fix an element is a powerful design feature that will be very useful when it is fully supported. At the time of this writing, the fixed value is supported by Firefox and Opera, but not by Internet Explorer.

Relative Positioning

The relative position value lets you shift an element from its default position in the normal flow to a new position within the browser window. The new position is relative to the element's default position. The offset properties let you adjust the position of the element. Relative positioning is sometimes useful when building columnar layouts with CSS, but for the most part it is a relatively unused positioning value.

When you position an element with relative positioning, the space it previously occupied in the normal flow is reserved. This is different from absolute positioning, where the element is entirely removed from the normal flow. Figure 10-6 illustrates this difference. In the far-left browser, the three divisions are in the normal flow. In the middle browser, the blue element has its position property set to absolute. Notice that the space it occupied in the normal flow has been removed and the red element moves up. In the right browser, the blue element has its position property set to relative. The space it occupied in the normal flow has been reserved.

Figure 10-6

Absolute versus relative positioning

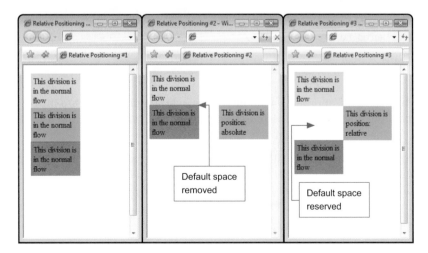

Specifying Visibility

The visibility property specifies whether an element is displayed in the browser.

Visibility property description
Value: visible | hidden | inherit
Initial: inherit
Applies to: all elements
Inherited: no
Percentages: N/A

Setting an element's visibility to hidden is different from setting the display property to none, because elements that are set to hidden still take up space in the normal flow. Elements that have their display property set to none are removed from the normal flow. The visibility property will normally be used with scripts to add or remove elements based on user interactions.

Specifying Stacking Level

The z-index property lets you specify an element's stacking level. In CSS2, each element can be positioned horizontally on the x-axis, vertically on the y-axis, and from front to back on the z-axis as the user faces the computer screen. The **stacking level** is the ordering of elements on the z-axis.

z-index property description
Value: auto | <integer> | inherit
Initial: auto
Applies to: positioned elements
Inherited: no
Percentages: N/A

The z-axis is important if element boxes overlap, or if boxes are moved using a script. With scripting, the stacking level can be changed for an element as the user interacts, allowing content to change layers based on user input.

You can use an integer, either positive or negative, to specify the stacking level. Levels are always based on the root element, usually <body>, which has a stacking level of 0. Therefore, positive numbers stack in front of the body, while negative numbers stack behind it. Figure 10-7 shows a conceptual illustration of stacking levels.

Figure 10-7

The order of stacking levels

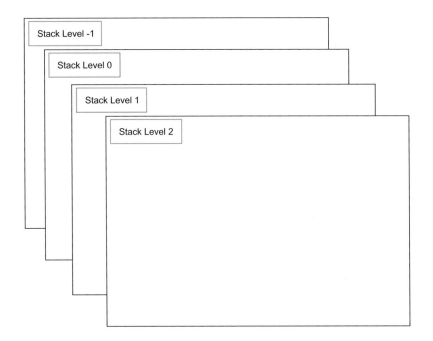

Because every element can be a container of other elements, each element establishes its own stacking level context. Therefore, an element that is at stack level 1 sets its own stacking context, starting with level 0, for any contained elements.

The following code shows style rules for four <div> elements, each with a different stacking level:

```
div.behind {position: absolute;
     top: 10px;
     left: 10px;
     z-index: -1;
     width: 100px;
     height: 200px;
     border: solid thin black;
     background: #ffffff;}
div {position: absolute;
     top: 40px;
     left: 40px;
     width: 400px;
     height: 200px;
     border: solid thin black;
     background: #ffffff;}
div.level1 {position: absolute;
     top: 80px;
     left: 80px;
     z-index: 1;
     width: 100px;
     height: 200px;
```

```
        border: solid thin black;
        background: #ffffff;}

div.level2 {position: absolute;
        top: 120px;
        left: 120px;
        z-index: 2;
        width: 100px;
        height: 200px;
        border: solid thin black;
        background: #ffffff;}
```

These style rules set the stacking levels for the four <div> elements shown in Figure 10-8.

Figure 10-8

Stacking levels in the browser

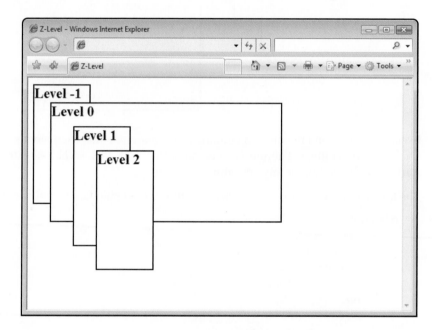

Building a Page Layout with Positioned Elements

In the following set of steps, you will see how you can use the CSS positioning and offset properties to build a page layout without the use of any tables. The source file for these steps, dogpark.htm, contains four <div> elements that are already completely styled with font effects, background images, and so on. You will position the styled elements to complete the page design. For the purposes of this activity, you will build the positioned layout to fit within an 800 × 600 browser, demonstrating the ability to constrain elements to a set width. As you work through the steps, refer to Figure 10-13 to see the results you will achieve. Save your file and test your work in the browser as you complete each step.

Note
You can add borders to each element, making it easier to see the dimensions of the page objects as you develop this page layout. Add the following border property for each element:

```
border: solid thin black;
```

You can remove this border property from each element when you have completed the layout.

To position the styled elements for your page design:

1. Copy the **dogpark.htm**, **doghowl.gif**, and **pawback.gif** files from the Chapter10 folder provided with your Data Files to the Chapter10 folder in your work folder. (Create the Chapter10 folder, if necessary.)

2. Open the file **dogpark.htm** in your HTML editor and save it in your work folder as **dogpark1.htm**.

3. In your browser, open the file **dogpark1.htm**. It should look like the file illustrated in Figure 10-9. The four <div> elements are laid out according to the normal flow; that is, they are laid out in the order in which they appear in the code.

Figure 10-9
The beginning Web page

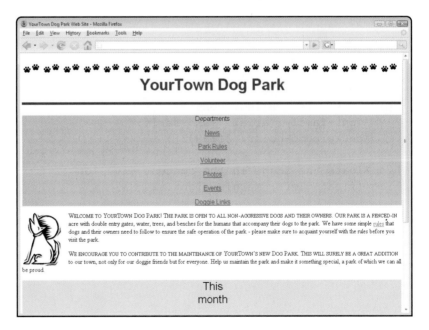

4. Examine the code in the file. The style section contains comments that explain the style rules. The body section of the document contains the following <div> elements:

   ■ Banner element
   ■ Links element

- ■ Content element
- ■ Quote element

The complete code for the page follows:

```
<html>
<head>
<title>YourTown Dog Park Web Site</title>
<style type="text/css">

/* Sets page background to white */
body {background-color: #ffffff;}

/* Styles the h1 within the banner element */
h1 {text-align: center;
    color: #000066;
    font-family: arial;
    font-size: 2.5em;
    padding-top: 30px;
    padding-bottom: 20px;
    border-bottom: solid 6px;}

/* The banner element */
div.banner {background-image: url(pawback.gif);
    background-repeat: repeat-x;}

/* The links element */
div.links {text-align: center;
    font-family: arial, sans-serif;
    background-color: #ff9933;}

/* Floats the image in the content division */
img {float: left; margin-right: 20px;}

/* Styles the content element paragraph first line */
p.article:first-line {font-variant: small-caps;}

/* The content element */
div.content { }

/* The quote element */
div.quote {font-family: arial;
    font-size: 1.75em;
    text-align: center;
    background-color: #99ffff;}
</style>
</head>
```

```
<body>

<!-- The Banner Element -->
<div class="banner"><h1>YourTown Dog Park</h1></div>

<!-- The Links Element -->
<div class="links">
Departments
<p><a href="news.htm">News</a></p>
<p><a href="views.htm">Park Rules</a></p>
<p><a href="scents.htm">Volunteer</a></p>
<p><a href="treats.htm">Photos</a></p>
<p><a href="hydrant.htm">Events</a></p>
<p><a href="links.htm">Doggie Links</a></p>
</div>


<!-- The Content Element -->
<div class="content"><p class="article"><img src="doghowl.gif">
Welcome to YourTown Dog Park! The park is open to all non-aggressive
dogs and their owners. Our park is a fenced-in acre with double
entry gates, water, trees, and benches for the humans that
accompany their dogs to the park. We have some simple
<a href=" ">rules</a> that dogs and their owners need to follow
to ensure the safe operation of the park - please make sure to
acquaint yourself with the rules before you visit the park.</p>
<p class="article">
We encourage you to contribute to the maintenance of YourTown's new Dog
Park. This will surely be a great addition to our town, not only
for our doggie friends but for everyone. Help us maintain the
park and make it something special, a park of which we can all
be proud.</p>
</div>

<!-- The Quote Element -->
<div class="quote">This<br>month<br>-
<br>Annual<br>Halloween<br>Costume<br>Contest!</div>
</body>
</html>
```

Positioning the Banner Element

The banner element is the first object in the page layout. The normal flow of the document controls the position of this element, so no explicit positioning is necessary. However, because no tables contain the element, you must specify a width and height for the element.

To position the banner element:

1. Find the rule for the banner element in the document's style section. Specify a width of 750 pixels and a height of 100 pixels by adding the following blue code:

```
/* The banner element */
div.banner {background-image: url(pawback.gif);
        background-repeat: repeat-x;
        width: 750px;
        height: 100px;}
```

2. Set the bottom margin for the banner element to 10 pixels, as in the following blue code. Figure 10-10 shows the completed banner element.

```
/* The banner element */
div.banner {background-image: url(pawback.gif);
        background-repeat: repeat-x;
        width: 750px;
        height: 100px;
        margin-bottom: 10px}
```

Figure 10-10

The completed banner element

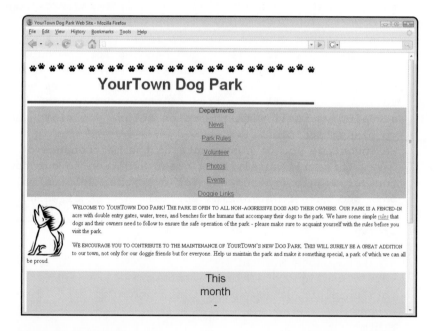

Positioning the Links Element

The links element fills the left column of the lower-half section of the layout (see Figure 10-11). You will need to specify width and height properties as you did with the banner element earlier. Although this element would align to the left side of the page in the normal flow, you will specify absolute positioning and offset properties to make sure that this element is placed exactly where you want it to appear on the page.

To size the links element:

1. Find the rule for the links element in the document's style section. Specify a width of 150 pixels and a height of 360 pixels by adding the code that appears in blue.

```
/* The links element */
div.links {text-align: center;
    font-family: arial, sans-serif;
    background-color: #ff9933;
    font-weight: bold;
    padding-left: 20px;
    padding-right: 20px;
    width: 150px;
    height: 360px;}
```

2. Set the links element's position property to absolute, and offset it from the top of the page by 140 pixels by adding the code that appears in blue.

```
/* The links element */
div.links {text-align: center;
    font-family: arial, sans-serif;
    background-color: #ff9933;
    font-weight: bold;
    padding-left: 20px;
    padding-right: 20px;
    width: 150px;
    height: 360px;
    position: absolute;
    top: 140px;}
```

Figure 10-11 shows the completed links element. Notice that the content element has moved and now appears behind the links element. This is because you have removed the links element from the normal flow by specifying absolute positioning. The content and quote elements are still following the normal flow, and move into place as if the links element was not there. As you continue through these steps, you will adjust the content and quote elements to correct this behavior.

CHAPTER 10

Figure 10-11

The completed links
element

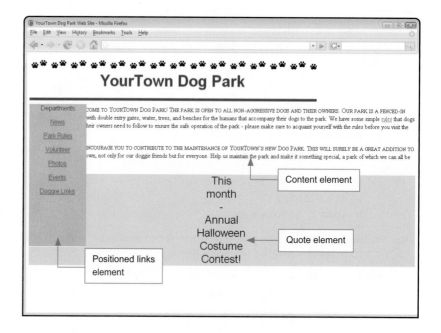

Positioning the Content Element

The content <div> element fills the middle of the browser window. Currently, the style rule for
this element contains no style properties. You will set this element's width and height, and position it in the middle of the page with the offset properties.

1. Find the rule for the content element in the document's style section. Specify a width of
    400 pixels and a height of 300 pixels by adding the code that appears in blue.

```
/* The content element */
div.content {width: 400px;
    height: 300px;}
```

2. Set the content element's position property to absolute. Offset it from the top of the page
    by 140 pixels, and from the left side of the page by 180 pixels by adding the code that appears
    in blue.

```
/* The content element */
div.content {width: 400px;
    height: 300px;
    position: absolute;
    left: 180px;
    top: 140px;}
```

Figure 10-12 shows the completed content element. Notice that the quote element has moved and
now appears behind the content element. As with the previous links element, the content element
is now removed from the normal flow because of absolute positioning. The next set of steps will
move the quote element into its correct position.

Figure 10-12

The completed content element

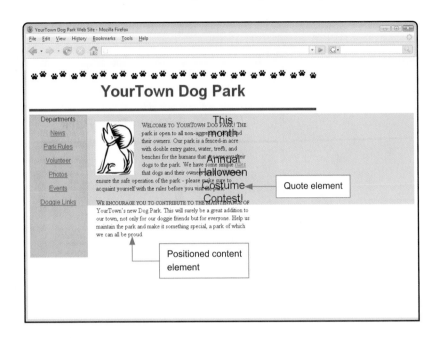

Positioning the Quote Element

The quote <div> element fills the right lower half of the browser window. As with the other page elements, you will specify the element's width, height, and position.

To size the quote element:

1. Find the rule for the quote element in the document's style section. Specify a width of 150 pixels and a height of 360 pixels by adding the code that appears in blue.

```
/* The quote element */
div.quote {font-family: arial;
    font-size: 1.75em;
    text-align: center;
    background-color: #99ffff;
    width: 150px;
    height: 360px;}
```

2. Set the quote element's position property to absolute. Offset the element's position from the top of the page by 140 pixels to align it with the other elements on the page, and add an offset from the left side of the page of 610 pixels by adding the code that appears in blue.

```
/* The quote element */
div.quote {font-family: arial;
    font-size: 1.75em;
    text-align: center;
    width: 150px;
    height: 360px;
    position: absolute;
    left: 610px;
    top: 140px;}
```

Figure 10-13 shows the completed Web page with the positioned quote element.

Figure 10-13

The completed page layout in Firefox 2

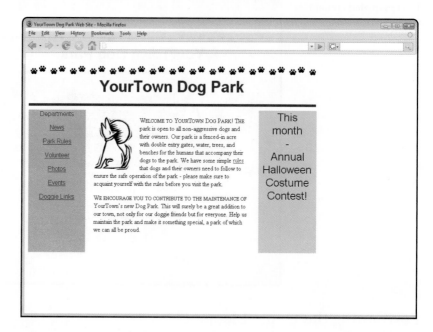

Testing the Page Layout

Now that you have completed the style rules for the document, it is time to test it in different browsers. To test the finished layout, view it in different browsers and look for any discrepancies. Figure 10-13 shows the Web page in Firefox 2. Figures 10-14 and 10-15 show the finished page layout in Internet Explorer 7 and Opera 9, respectively. As you can see, the page layout is displayed consistently in all three browsers.

Figure 10-14

The completed page layout in Internet Explorer 7

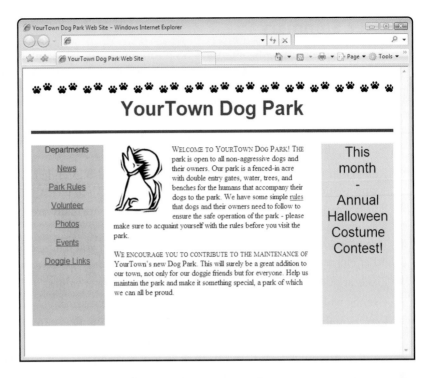

Figure 10-15

The completed page layout in Opera 9

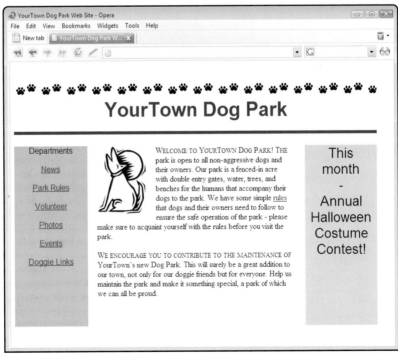

Chapter Summary

In this chapter you learned about the CSS positioning properties and how to apply them to Web page design. You learned about the normal flow of elements in the document and how the positioning properties let you remove elements from the normal flow. You examined the positioning properties and saw how the different positioning values affected an element's behavior. You also learned how to position elements using offsets for horizontal and vertical positioning, and stacking levels for z-axis overlapping. Finally, you applied what you learned by building a complete page layout using the positioning properties.

▶ Remember that the CSS positioning properties are also intended for use with programming scripts that can build interaction and animation into Web pages.

▶ The normal flow dictates the way in which elements normally are displayed in the browser window.

▶ When you remove an element from the normal flow, you may see unexpected behavior from other elements that are following the normal flow.

▶ Pixels are the most convenient measuring unit for offset values.

▶ Use the width and height properties to specify element sizes.

▶ Each containing box sets its own context for positioning. For example, an absolutely positioned box can contain elements that follow the normal flow.

▶ Fixed positioning "pastes" the element to one position, regardless of how the user scrolls.

▶ Relative positioning, stacking levels, and visibility are normally used with scripting languages to create dynamic effects.

Key Terms

script	stacking level

Review Questions

1. What is the normal flow for block-level elements?
2. What are the four types of positioning?
3. What determines space between boxes in the normal flow?
4. What is the default horizontal positioning for block-level elements?
5. What is the default positioning type?
6. How is the position for an absolute element determined?
7. What is the containing element for the content section of a Web page?
8. In the normal flow, which property lets you position elements next to each other?
9. What is the difference between absolute and fixed positioning?
10. What standard HTML layout type can you create using fixed positioning?
11. What is relative positioning used for?

12. What does the z-index property determine?

13. What is the most convenient measurement value when you are specifying absolute or fixed offset values?

14. What determines the default width of a positioned element?

Hands-On Projects

1. Explain why using CSS positioning is preferable to using tables to control page layout.

2. Download Screen Ruler from the Web at *http://microfox.com*. Install the software on your computer and learn to use it to measure pixel distances in your page layouts.

3. In this exercise, you will experiment with absolute positioning.

   a. Open the file **position.htm** in your HTML editor and save it in your work folder as **position1.htm**.

   b. In your browser, open the file **position1.htm**. When you open the file, it looks like Figure 10-16.

Figure 10-16

The original position.htm file

   c. Examine the code. Notice that there is an existing style section with a style rule for the `<div>` element that sets the basic characteristics shown in Figure 10-16. The style section code for the document follows:

```
<style type="text/css">
div {background-color: #66ff99;
     width: 100px;
     height: 200px;
```

```
        padding: 1em;
        border: solid 1px;}
</style>
```

   d. Add a position property to the style rule and set the value to "absolute."

   e. Add a left property to the style rule and experiment with different measurement values to offset the <div> element from the left side of the browser window.

   f. Add a top property to the style rule and experiment with different measurement values to offset the <div> element from the top of the browser window.

4. In this exercise, you will experiment with flexible positioning.

   a. Open the file **flexible.htm** in your HTML editor and save it in your work folder as **flexible.htm**.

   b. In your browser, open the file **flexible.htm**. When you open the file, it looks like Figure 10-17.

Figure 10-17

The original flexible.htm file

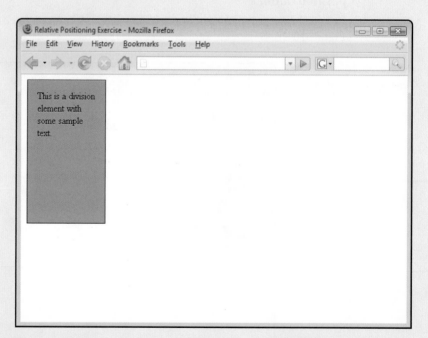

   c. Add a position property to the style rule and set the value to "flexible."

   d. Add a left property to the style rule and experiment with different percentage measurement values to offset the <div> element from the left side of the browser window.

   e. Resize your browser to test the flexible positioning. Notice that the <div> element moves to accommodate the different browser sizes.

   f. Add a top property to the style rule and experiment with different relative measurement values to offset the <div> element from the top of the browser window.

g. Resize your browser to test the flexible positioning. Notice that the <div> element moves to accommodate the different browser sizes.

5. Create an HTML document that has three <div> elements. Build a three-column layout with absolute positioning where each <div> element fills one-third of the browser window at 1024 × 768 resolution.

Individual Case Project

Choose a page from your project Web site that uses tables to control the page layout and rebuild it using positioning. You will have to remove the table elements entirely from the page and rebuild each cell's content as a unique element that can be selected and positioned on the page. Submit two sample pages: one controlled with tables and the other controlled with positioning properties.

Team Case Project

Each team member is responsible for different page templates for the different information levels of your Web site. For example, one team member is responsible for the home page design, one for the section page design, and one for the article-level page design. Rebuild your page template using the CSS positioning properties described in this chapter. You can choose to try to rebuild the exact layout you achieved with the table, or build an entirely different view of the page layout. You will have to remove the table elements entirely from the page and rebuild each cell's content as a unique element that can be selected and positioned on the page. Submit two sample pages: one controlled with tables and the other controlled with positioning properties.

11

Creating Framed Layouts

When you complete this chapter, you will be able to:

- Understand the benefits and drawbacks of frames
- Understand and use frame syntax
- Customize frame characteristics including scroll bars, borders, and margins
- Understand and use frame targeting and special targeting names
- Design content to fit framesets properly
- Design framesets that accommodate different screen resolutions

The HTML frame elements let you partition the canvas area of the browser into multiple windows called **frames**. Each frame can display a separate, independent HTML document. The use of frames has become a subject of controversy on the Web. In many cases, framed Web sites are poorly designed. They detract from the user's experience with heavy download times and confusing navigation. The judicious use of frames, however, can enhance your Web site, allowing you to consistently display navigation information and content concurrently. Frames can be the right solution for solving specific information problems or for providing large collections of content. This chapter explains how to work with frames to display your information effectively.

Understanding Frames

HTML frames were introduced by Netscape for the 2.0 release of its browser. Frames now are supported in all browsers. Controversial since their inception, frames can polarize Web designers, some lauding the benefits, others characterizing them as unnecessary. As you will see, frames can work well if you use them correctly.

Frames allow you to divide the browser window into independent windows, each displaying a separate HTML document. Figure 11-1 shows an example of a framed set of pages that contains three independent frames.

Figure 11-1

Typical frameset

Each of these frames displays a separate HTML file. To create this frameset, you would first create the individual HTML files, and then create the HTML file containing the frame code that holds the three documents together.

Frame Benefits

Frames offer a number of benefits, including allowing users to scroll independently in one frame without affecting the contents of an adjoining frame. This is an ideal way to present large collections of information that are hard to navigate using the traditional single-page browser display. For example, Figure 11-2 shows a frameset that displays a table of contents in one frame, search tools in another, and content in a third.

Because the frames can be scrolled independently, the table of contents and search tool are always visible to the user. This may be exactly the type of additional function you need to solve an information design problem.

Frames work best when you keep them simple. Two or three frames per frameset should be enough to accommodate your information needs. More frames will clutter the screen, making it difficult for your reader to find information.

Figure 11-2

Frames can aid
navigation

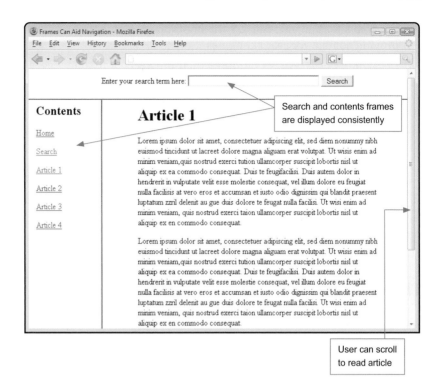

Frame Drawbacks

Frames present a variety of drawbacks that you need to consider before committing your content to a frame-based organization.

- *Bookmarks*—Although the newer browsers solve this problem, many browsers do not let the user bookmark individual pages from a Web site. Because the pages are all referenced from a single HTML frame file, the user cannot return to an exact page within a site, only to the main framed page.

- *Download overhead*—Because the browser is loading more than one document, the initial download time can be higher for a framed set of documents than for a single HTML document.

- *Confusing navigation*—Users can become confused if you build complicated framed document sets without enough navigation choices to let users jump to the page of their choice. The Back button in the browser only lets the user load the previous page displayed within the frame, which may not be what the user expects.

- *Visual confusion*—Too many frames within the browser window, each with its own scroll bars, can confuse the user and provide a poor use of the available screen. Limit the number of frames to avoid breaking the browser window into too many sections.

- *Frames and search engines*—Frameset code contains no actual content. The content is contained in the HTML files displayed in the frames. Search engines that read the content of a page for indexing will find no information on a framed page. For this reason it is a good idea to avoid using a framed document as the top-level page for your Web site. Provide a standard HTML page as your top-level page, and use the framed content at a lower level of the Web site. You also can use the <noframes> element (described later in this chapter) to provide content for search engines.

- *User preferences*—Users can force their browsers to display pages outside of your frameset. Make sure that your pages can stand alone if a user chooses to display a page on its own. You may want to add a simple text-based navigation bar on each page that is not viewable within the framed document, but can be used to navigate your Web site if a user breaks out of the frameset. You also may want to give the user a choice to navigate your Web site either with or without frames by adding links on the main page to framed and unframed versions of your Web site.

Frame Syntax

HTML frameset documents contain the code that assembles the frames and their contents. Frameset documents themselves have no actual content; therefore, they have no <body> element.

The <frameset> Element

The <frameset> element is the container for the frameset code. The cols and rows attributes let you specify the characteristics of the frameset. You can specify a frameset as either cols or rows, but not both. The width (specific to columns) and height (specific to rows) can be expressed as either a percentage value or pixel count in the cols and rows attributes. As with tables, percentage widths build frames that are relative to the browser window size. Absolute pixel widths are fixed regardless of the browser size. The following code is an example of a simple frameset document that divides the browser canvas into two rows:

```
<html>
<head>
<title>Frame Rows</title>
</head>
<frameset rows="20%,80%">
<frame src="top.htm" />
<frame src="bottom.htm" />
</frameset>
</html>
```

Figure 11-3 shows the result of this code.

Figure 11-3

Two-row frameset

The <frame> Element

Re-examine the code for Figure 11-3. The <frame> element determines the contents of each frame. Row framesets fill top to bottom. The first <frame> element tells the browser the file to display in the top row, and the second <frame> element points to the file for the bottom row.

The <frame> element is an empty element. The **src attribute** provides the location of the file that is displayed within the frame. Other attributes to the <frame> tag let you name the frame for targeting, specify if frames have a scroll bar, and indicate whether the user can resize the frame. These attributes are described later in this chapter.

In Figure 11-4, the frameset is divided into two column frames.

In this frameset the left column is 150 pixels wide. The right column defaults to the remainder of the browser window size. In the following code, note the syntax in the opening <frameset> tag. The cols attribute determines the width of the columns. The first value sets the left column to 150 pixels. The asterisk (*) character tells the browser to fill the right column to the remainder of the browser window.

```
<html>
<head>
<title>Frame Columns</title>
</head>
<frameset cols="150,*">
<frame src="left.htm" />
<frame src="right.htm" />
</frameset>
</html>
```

Figure 11-4

Two-column frameset

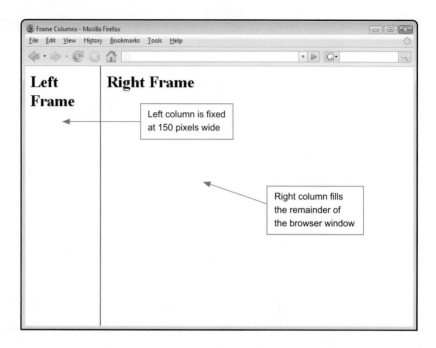

Because the left column is set to a fixed width, it will remain unchanged regardless of the user's browser size or screen resolution. Also note that in column framesets, the frames fill left to right. The first <frame> element fills the left column, the second fills the right column.

The <noframes> Tag

The <noframes> tag lets you provide an alternate page for users who do not have a frames-compliant browser. You can enclose the contents of a standard Web page, contained in a set of <body> tags, within the <noframes> element. This alternate page code follows the frameset code in the HTML file:

```
<html>
<head>
<title>frames</title>
</head>
<frameset cols="75%, 25%">
     <frame name="index" src="index.htm" />
     <frame name="title" src="title.htm" />
<noframes>
<body>
(alternate page html code)
</body>
</noframes>
</frameset>
</html>
```

Note

Although most browsers can display frames, it still is a good idea to add <noframes> content to help search engines index your framed content. When encountering a framed set of pages, some search engines look for the <noframes> element for content information.

Nesting Frames

Nesting allows you to break the screen into both row and column frames. Figure 11-5 shows a rows frameset that contains a nested columns frameset in the second row.

Figure 11-5

Nested frameset

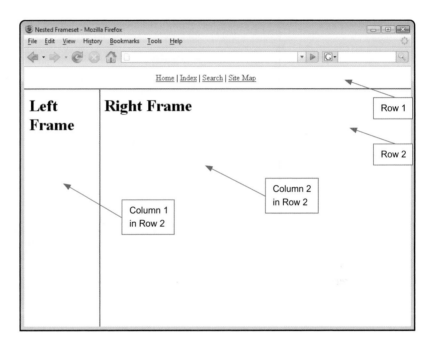

The following commented code shows the nesting of the framesets:

```html
<html>
<head>
<title>Nested Frameset</title>
</head>
<frameset rows="40,*">
<frame src="topnav.htm" /> <!-- this is row 1 -->
<frameset cols="20%,80%"> <!-- nested frameset fills row 2 -->
<frame src="left.htm" /> <!-- this is column 1 -->
<frame src="right.htm" /> <!-- this is column 2 -->
</frameset>
</frameset>
</html>
```

Notice in the preceding code that two closing </frameset> tags are necessary to close both framesets.

Restricting Resizing

By default, the user has the option of resizing your frames by clicking and dragging the frame border. In most situations you probably want to restrict resizing, so the user sees the frameset the way you intended. Figure 11-6 shows a frameset that the user has resized by clicking and dragging the frame border.

Figure 11-6

Default allows the user to resize the frame

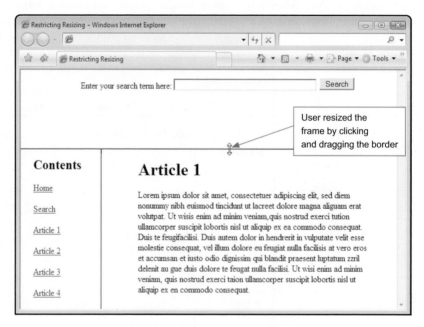

Unless you have a specific reason, you probably want to restrict the user's ability to resize your frames. To restrict resizing, add the noresize attribute to the <frame src> elements in your frameset, as shown in the following code:

```
<html>
<head>
<title>Restricting Resizing</title>
</head>
<frameset rows="50,*">
<frame src="search.htm" noresize />
    <frameset cols="135,*">
    <frame src="contents.htm" noresize />
    <frame src="article1.htm" noresize />
    </frameset>
</frameset>
</html>
```

Customizing Frame Characteristics

Besides setting frame features such as nesting and resizing, you can control characteristics such as scroll bars, frame borders, and frame margins.

Controlling Scroll Bars

By default, scroll bars in frames are set to appear automatically if the content is not accessible within the frame window. In most cases this is the best setting for scroll bars, because you will not need to worry about them. No matter the user's browser size or screen resolution, if scroll bars are necessary they will appear. Sometimes, however, you may want to control whether scroll bars are displayed. Use the scrolling attribute in the <frame src> element to control scroll bars. The valid values are "yes," "no," or "auto," which is the default setting.

Figure 11-7 shows a three-frame frameset. Notice that the top frame displays a scroll bar even though no additional content follows the search text box.

The browser displays a scroll bar because the height of the top frame is slightly smaller than the browser finds necessary to display the content. One way to solve this problem is to change the height of the frame. Because this frame looks good at this height, however, you can remove the scroll bar by adding the scrolling="no" attribute to the <frame src> element. Figure 11-8 shows the result of the attribute addition.

Figure 11-7

Unnecessary default scroll bar

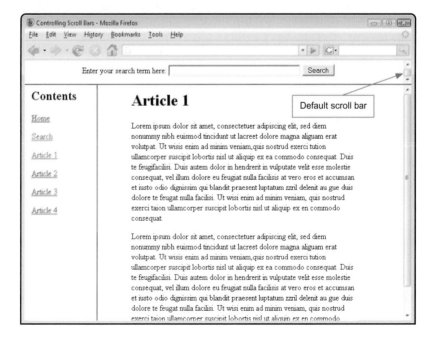

Figure 11-8

Top frame scroll bar
turned off

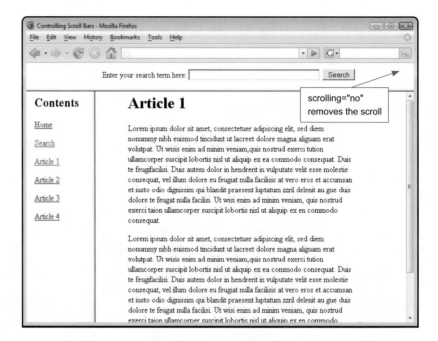

The scroll bar no longer is displayed, which enhances the look of the frameset. Also, because a scroll bar indicates additional information, omitting the scroll bar reflects the content of this page more accurately. The code for the complete frameset follows:

```
<html>
<head>
<title>Controlling Scroll Bars</title>
</head>
<frameset rows="50,*">
<frame src="search.htm" scrolling="no" />
    <frameset cols="135,*">
    <frame src="contents.htm" />
    <frame src="article1.htm" />
    </frameset>
</frameset>
</html>
```

Controlling Frame Borders

As with tables, you can choose not to display frame borders, or to remove the default border spacing between frames entirely. This technique lets you create seamless frames with no visible dividing line, unless a scroll bar pops up. Figure 11-9 shows an example of a two-frame frameset with the frame borders turned off.

Figure 11-9
Frame borders turned off

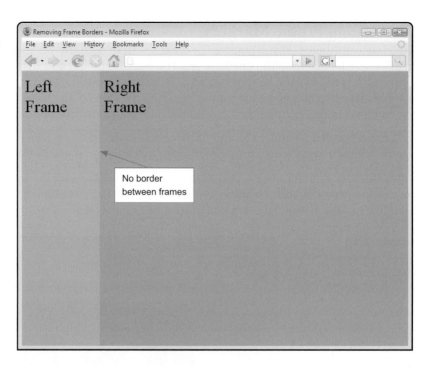

To make sure that the frame border and spacing are turned off for all browsers, use the border attribute set to "0" as shown in the following code:

```
<html>
<head>
<title>Removing Frame Borders</title>
</head>
<frameset cols="150,*" border="0">
<frame src="leftframe.htm" />
<frame src="rightframe.htm" name="content" />
</frameset>
</html>
```

Note
Older browsers do not agree on the attributes you should use to turn off frame borders. Netscape Navigator 4.0 requires frameborder="no" and border="0" attributes. Internet Explorer 5.0 can interpret frameborder="no" correctly, but you need to set framespacing="0" to remove the default border spacing between frames. All of these attributes reside in the opening <frameset> tag. If you have trouble with frame borders, then test these attributes in your code.

CHAPTER 11

Controlling Frame Margins

Two frame attributes let you control the pixel width of both the vertical and horizontal margins in a frame. The marginwidth attribute lets you control the left and right margins, while marginheight affects the top and bottom margins. Setting these attributes to zero (0) lets you remove the margins entirely, allowing your content to touch the sides of the frame. You most likely would use these attributes in combination with the frame border attributes described earlier.

Add the marginheight and marginwidth attributes to the <frame> element for the frame you want to affect. Figure 11-10 shows a frameset with two different margin settings.

The left frame has both margin attributes set to zero (0). Even so, the top margin still includes some space, due to built-in leading in the line of text. The left margin, however, has been completely removed. In the right column both margins have been set to 30 pixels.

Figure 11-10

Frame borders and margins removed

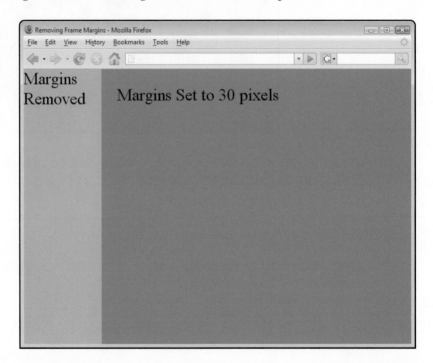

Targeting in Framesets

The power of frames comes from the ability to have one frame display information consistently while the contents of a second frame might change based on the user's choice. By default, a link loads into the same frame from which it was selected. You can change this default behavior and target the destination of a link to another frame in the frameset. In this section you will learn how to target within the simple frameset shown in Figure 11-11.

Figure 11-11

Targeting from one frame to another

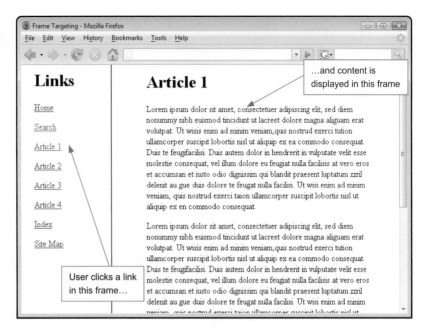

To target from one frame to another, you must perform two tasks:

1. Name your frames using the name attribute in the <frame> element.
2. Target links to display their content in the named frame.

Naming Frames

To name a frame, add the name attribute to the <frame> element. You do not have to name all of the frames within a frameset, only the frames you want to target. Figure 11-12 shows a frameset with two frames. The right frame is named "main."

Here is the HTML code for the frameset illustrated in Figure 11-12.

```
<html>
<head>
<title>Frame Targeting</title>
</head>
<frameset cols="150,*">
<frame src="navcol.htm" />
<frame src="article1.htm" name="main" />
</frameset>
</html>
```

The name attribute in the second <frame> element names the right frame window "main." You now can target this window to display linked content.

Figure 11-12

Naming a frame for targeting

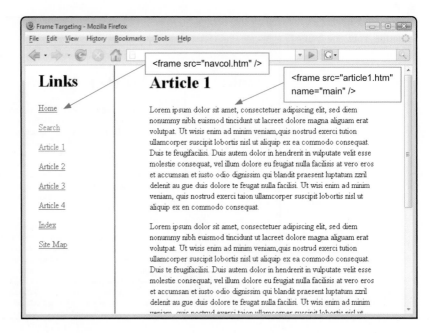

Targeting Named Frames

To target the named frame, you must edit the HTML document that contains the <a> elements and provide target attributes that tell the browser which frame displays the content. You can use the target attribute in either the <base> or <a> elements.

Targeting in the <base> Element

In this example, the HTML document that occupies the left frame window is named "navcol.htm." Adding the <base> element lets you set the default target frame for all of the links in the document. The <base> tag is an empty tag that resides in the <head> section of the document. The code in navcol.htm shows the <base> element.

```
<html>
<head>
<title>Frame Links</title>
<base target="main">
</head>
<body>
<h1>links</h1>
<p><a href="index.htm">home</a></p>
<p><a href="search.htm">search</a></p>
<p><a href="article1.htm">article 1</a></p>
<p><a href="article2.htm">article 2</a></p>
<p><a href="article3.htm">article 3</a></p>
<p><a href="article4.htm">article 4</a></p>
```

```
<p><a href="contindx.htm">index</a></p>
<p><a href="sitemap.htm">site map</a></p>
</body>
</html>
```

Notice the <base> element contains the target attribute set to "main." This establishes the default window target name for all of the links contained in the file. Any link that the user selects will be displayed in the frame window named "main."

Targeting in the <a> Element

You can override a default base target by using the target attribute in the <a> element. This allows you to target a specific link to a destination different from the base target. You can target a different window within the frameset, or can use one of the special targeting values in the next section. The following <a> element targets article1.htm to the frame named "frame2."

```
<a href="article1.htm" target="frame2">Article 1</a>
```

Note

Make sure that you match the case of both the target and name attributes, or the browser will not be able to resolve the target name.

Using Special Target Names

There are four special target names that you can use with the target attribute in either the <base> or <a> elements. Table 11-1 lists the special names.

Name	Description
_self	This is the default behavior for links in a frameset. The linked content is loaded into the same window as the <a> element. You most likely would use this in the <a> element to override a base target.
_blank	This name opens a new browser window to display the linked content. This result can cause navigation confusion for the users who may not realize that they are looking at a new instance of the browser.
_parent	This name lets you break out of a child frameset and display the link in the parent frameset one level up in the frameset hierarchy. This name is useful only when you have a link in a frameset that displays an embedded frameset. In most cases using embedded framesets is poor navigation design that will confuse your user.
_top	The most useful of all the special names, _top lets you remove frames and display the linked content in a fresh browser window.

Table 11-1   Special target names

Notice that all of these special names begin with an underscore. Any other target name that begins with an underscore will be ignored by the browser.

Special target names can help you in a variety of situations. For example, you can use special target names when you link to other sites from within a frameset. Figure 11-13 shows the Harvard University Art Museum Web site shown within a framed site.

Figure 11-13

Harvard University Art Museum Web site shown within a framed site

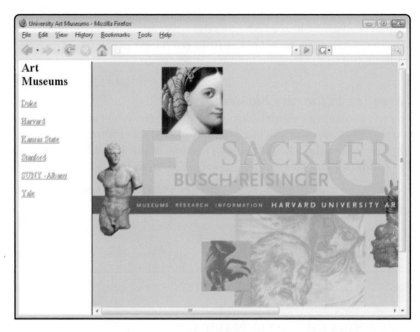

As you can see, loading the framed Harvard University Art Museum Web site within a frameset does not work well. The size of the frame is too small to display the Web site properly, causing multiple horizontal and vertical scroll bars. You can solve this problem by using special target names to break out of the frameset. There are two ways to handle this problem:

- Use _blank to load the Web page in a new browser window
- Use _top to load the Web page to the top of the existing window

Using _blank

The _blank special target name lets you load the linked content into a new instance of the browser. Figure 11-14 shows the results, with the newly launched browser window overlapping the window that contains the link.

Figure 11-14

Using _blank launches a second browser window

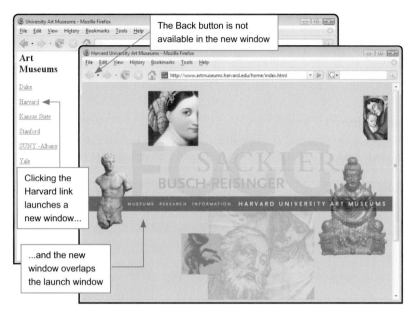

Notice that the Back button is not available in the new browser window because this is the first page in the new window. Not being able to use Back can be disorienting to users who rely on it for navigation.

Remember that the targeting information is in the file that contains the links, not the frameset file. In this example, the _blank target name resides in the <base> element, setting the default target for all of the links within the file. The following code shows the use of _blank in the left navigation column in Figure 11-14:

```
<html>
<head>
<title>Art Museums</title>
</head>
<base target="_blank" />
<body>
<h2>Art Museums</h2>
<p><a href="http://www.duke.edu/web/duma/">Duke</a></p>
<p><a href="http://www.artmuseums.harvard.edu/">Harvard</a></p>
<p><a href="http://www.ksu.edu/bma/">Kansas State</a></p>
<p><a href="http://www.stanford.edu/dept/SUMA/">Stanford</a></p>
<p><a href="http://www.albany.edu/museum/">SUNY - Albany</a></p>
<p><a href="http://www.yale.edu/yuag/">Yale</a></p>
</body>
</html>
```

This code contains one flaw. Using _blank as the default target name means that every link in this window will launch a new browser window. Before long, the user's screen will become cluttered by overlapping windows. For this reason, limit the use of _blank for special purposes, or do not use it at all.

CHAPTER 11

Note

If you decide to use _blank, you can help the users by letting them know that clicking the link will open a new browser window.

Using _top

Using _top as a special target name displays the linked content in a non-framed window using the same instance of the browser. Figure 11-15 shows the results.

Figure 11-15

Using _top loads content at the top level of the same window

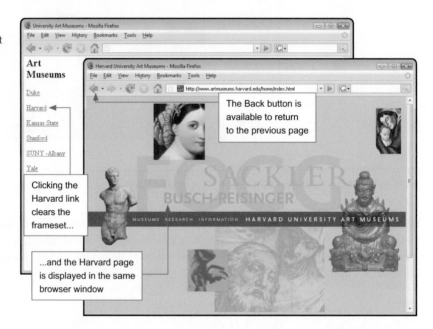

The browser clears the frameset and loads the Harvard link in the same window. The Back button is available if the user wants to return to the previous page. Because the browser maintains only one open window, there is no additional memory overhead or confusion for the user. This effect is hard to reproduce on paper, so use the sample files on the Online Companion Web Site to see an example.

Designing Effective Frames

You must build your pages to fit within the frames in which they will be displayed. You also will need to accommodate different screen resolutions that can affect the size of the frame within the frameset. As with tables, decide whether you will use fixed or relative framesets. You also can choose to mix these two measurement types within a single frameset, which can be the best way to handle multiple screen resolutions.

Mixing Fixed and Variable Frames

Examine the following sample frameset that mixes a fixed frame and a variable frame to accommodate different resolutions.

Here is the code for a sample frameset:

```
<html>
<head>
<title>Designing Frame Content</title>
</head>
<frameset cols="125,*">
<frame src="leftfxd.htm" />
<frame src="article1.htm" name="main" />
</frameset>
</html>
```

Notice that the code for the left column is fixed at 125 pixels. The asterisk (*) wildcard character sets the right column to a variable width that changes, based on the browser size. Figure 11-16 shows the result of this frameset code.

Figure 11-16

Mixing fixed and variable frames

Division elements in each HTML file keep the content aligned within the frameset. The division borders are turned on so you can see them. The division element in the left frame has a fixed width of 150 pixels. This frame and content will be displayed consistently regardless of the screen resolution. The code for the table in the left frame content, leftfxd.htm, follows:

```
<html>
<head>
<title>Left Fixed Column</title>
<base target="main">
<style type="text/css">
div {width: 125px; border: solid thin; text-align: center;}
</style>
</head>
<body>
<div>
<h1>Links</h1>
<p><a href="index.htm">Home</a></p>
<p><a href="search.htm">Search</a></p>
<p><a href="article1.htm">Article 1</a></p>
<p><a href="article2.htm">Article 2</a></p>
<p><a href="article3.htm">Article 3</a></p>
<p><a href="article4.htm">Article 4</a></p>
<p><a href="article5.htm">Article 5</a></p>
<p><a href="article6.htm">Article 6</a></p>
<p><a href="index.htm">Index</a></p>
<p><a href="sitemap.htm">Site Map</a></p>
</div>
</body>
</html>
```

The right frame is a variable width; therefore, the content within the right frame is contained in a centered division element set to an 80 percent width. The 80 percent width allows for white space on both sides of the text. The code for the right frame content, article1.htm, follows:

```
<html>
<head>
<title>Right Variable Column</title>
</head>
<style type="text/css">
div {width: 80%; border: solid thin; margin-left: 10%;
     margin-right: 10%; padding: 10px;}
</style>
<body>
<div>
<h1>Article 1</h1>
<p>lorem ipsum dolor sit amet, consectetuer adipiscing elit,
sed diem nonummy nibh euismod ti . . .(content abbreviated)</p>
</div>
</body>
</html>
```

If you are building a row frameset, you can use this same fixed and variable coding method. Set one row to a fixed width, and let the second row default to the remainder of the browser canvas, as shown in the following code:

```
<html>
<head>
<title>Fixed/Variable Rows</title>
</head>
<frameset rows="50,*">
<frame src="search.htm" scrolling="no" />
<frame src="article1.htm" />
</frameset>
</html>
```

This code creates the page shown in Figure 11-17.

Figure 11-17

Fixed top row, variable second row

The top row is 80 pixels high. The second row fills the browser window regardless of screen resolution.

A final example of the fixed/variable method is a common three-row frameset. In this set the top and bottom rows contain navigation, while the middle row contains content. The top and bottom rows are fixed, and the middle row is variable. Here is the code:

```
<html>
<head>
<title>Fixed/Variable Rows</title>
</head>
<frameset rows="50,*,35">
<frame src="search.htm" scrolling="no" />
<frame src="article1.htm" name="main" />
```

```
<frame src="botmnav.htm" scrolling="no" />
</frameset>
</html>
```

Figure 11-18 shows this frameset.

Figure 11-18

Three-row frameset with variable middle row

Working with Framesets

In this set of steps you will build a frameset that contains links to a small web of pages. The frameset will include navigation and content frames, with the links targeted from one window to another within the frameset.

To build the frameset:

1. Copy the following files from the Chapter11 folder provided with your Data Files to the Chapter11 folder in your work folder:

   - frame.htm
   - hot.htm
   - new.htm
   - navigate.htm
   - info.htm
   - order.htm
   - welcome.htm

2. Start Notepad or another text editor and open the file **frame.htm**. It contains the following code:

```
<html>
<head>
<title>Frameset Practice</title>
</head>
</html>
```

3. Add the< frameset> element, defining a frameset with two columns. Set the left column to 140 pixels and the right column to 80%, as shown in the following code:

```
<html>
<head>
<title>Frameset Practice</title>
</head>
<frameset cols="140, 80%">
</frameset>
</html>
```

4. Add the first <frame> element with a src attribute that selects the file navigate.htm.

```
<html>
<head>
<title>Frameset Practice</title>
</head>
<frameset cols="140, 80%">
<frame src="navigate.htm" />
</frameset>
</html>
```

5. Add the second <frame> element with a src attribute that selects the file welcome.htm.

```
<html>
<head>
<title>Frameset Practice</title>
</head>
<frameset cols="140, 80%">
<frame src="navigate.htm" />
<frame src="welcome.htm" />
</frameset>
</html>
```

6. Save the file and view it in the browser. It should look like Figure 11-19.

7. Test the links in the navigation frame. When you click a link, the page opens in the default frame rather than the content frame, as shown in Figure 11-20.

CHAPTER 11

Figure 11-19
The practice frameset

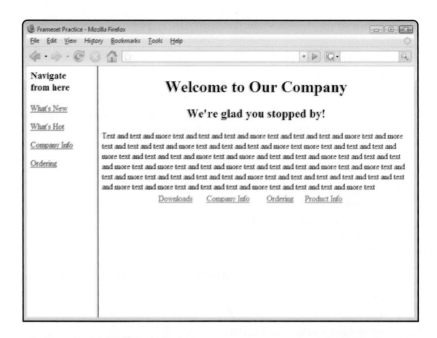

Figure 11-20
Default linking behavior

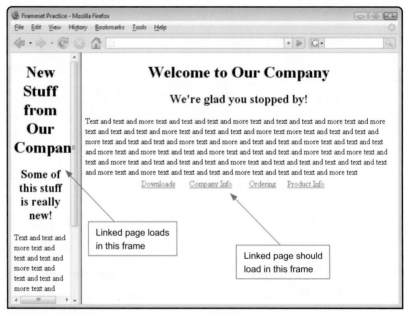

8. Correct the linking behavior by adding targeting. In the file frame.htm, add names to the frames, as shown in the following code, and then save the file.

```
<html>
<head>
<title>Frameset Practice</title>
</head>
```

```
<frameset cols="140, 80%">
<frame src="navigate.htm" name="navigate" />
<frame src="welcome.htm" name="content" />
</frameset>
</html>
```

9. In Notepad or your text editor, open the file **navigate.htm** from your work folder. In the head section of the file, add the <base> element with a target attribute that selects the content frame, as shown in the following code:

```
<html>
<head>
<title>Navigator</title>
<base target="content" />
</head>
<body>
<h3>Navigate<br>from here</h3>
<p><a href="new.htm">What's New</a></p>
<p><a href="hot.htm">What's Hot</a></p>
<p><a href="info.htm">Company Info</a></p>
<p><a href="order.htm">Ordering</a></p>
</body>
</html>
```

10. Save the file **navigate.htm**.

11. Open the file **frame.htm** in your browser. When you test the links in the navigation frame, the linked pages should be displayed in the content frame, as shown in Figure 11-21.

Figure 11-21

The completed frameset

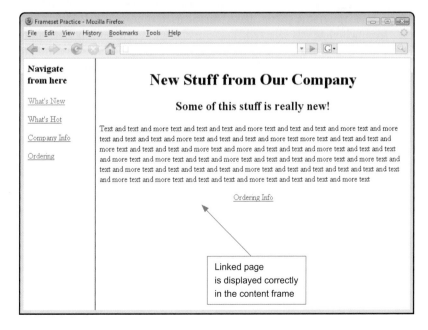

Chapter Summary

▶ Frames allow you to divide the browser window into independent windows, each displaying a separate HTML document. Frames allow users to scroll in one frame without affecting the contents of an adjoining frame. This is an ideal way to present large collections of information that are hard to navigate using the traditional single-page browser display.

▶ Although frames offer a number of benefits, you should use them judiciously. Make sure that your content benefits from the use of frames, and build simple framesets with no more than two or three frames.

▶ Frames present drawbacks that you need to consider before committing your content to a frame-based organization. These drawbacks include the inability to bookmark pages, increased download times, potential navigation and visual confusion, and the inability of search engines to find framed documents.

▶ Because frameset documents contain no content, they are not the best choice for the top-level page of your Web site. Consider using a standard HTML page for the top-level, and then link to your framed content.

▶ HTML frameset documents contain the code that assembles the frames and their contents. The <frameset> element is the container for the frameset code. Frameset documents themselves have no actual content; therefore, they have no <body> element.

▶ The <frame> element is an empty element that determines the contents of each frame. The src attribute provides the location of the file that is displayed within the frame. Other attributes to the <frame> tag let you name the frame for targeting, specify whether frames have a scroll bar, and indicate whether the user can resize the frame.

▶ Use the <noframes> element to contain alternate information about your Web site for users with browsers that cannot display frames.

▶ You can design frames where one frame displays unchanging information while the contents of a second frame change based on the user's choice. By default, a link loads into the same frame from which it was selected. You can change this default behavior and target the destination of a link to another frame in the frameset. To target from one frame to another, you first must name your frames using the name attribute in the <frame> element, and then target links to display their content in the named frame.

▶ Use special target names to solve unique design problems, favoring _top over _blank whenever possible.

▶ Frameset display is affected by the base screen resolution you use to code your framed pages. Decide on the lowest common denominator screen resolution that will display the frameset effectively. You also can build framesets using a combination of fixed and variable frame widths to accommodate different screen resolutions.

▶ Test your work. Different browsers and screen resolutions may affect the look of your framesets.

Key Terms

frame	src attribute
nesting	

Review Questions

1. What is the main benefit of frames?
2. Why do framesets add to initial download time?
3. Name two ways frames potentially may confuse users.
4. Why do search engines have problems with framesets?
5. What are the two attributes you use to structure the look of a frameset?
6. How does the order of the <frame> element within the <frameset> element affect the display of the frameset?
7. What is the purpose of the <noframes> element?
8. What is the benefit of the noresize attribute?
9. What is the default setting for the scrolling attribute?
10. List the correct attributes to the <frameset> element that will remove the frame borders in browsers.
11. What are the two tasks you must perform to add targeting to a frameset?
12. Which element lets you set a default target for all links in a document?
13. List the four special target names.
14. Are target names case-sensitive?
15. Which special target name is the default behavior for links in a frameset?
16. What is the major drawback of the _blank special target name?
17. How can you control the display of content within a frameset?
18. What additional browser elements can affect the display of your frameset?
19. How can you accommodate frameset display at varying screen resolutions?

Hands-On Projects

1. Visit the Online Companion Web Site and download some of the sample frame content files.

    a. Build a two-column frameset that contains a fixed left navigation frame and a variable right content frame.

    b. Target all of the links in the left frame to the right content frame.

    c. Restrict the user's ability to resize the frames.

    d. Test your work in different browsers and at different resolutions.

2. Visit the Online Companion Web Site and download some of the sample frame content files.

    a. Build a two-row frameset that contains a fixed top navigation frame and a variable bottom content frame.

    b. Target all of the links in the top frame to the bottom content frame.

    c. Completely remove the frame borders.

    d. Test your work in different browsers and at different resolutions.

3. Visit the Online Companion Web Site and download some of the sample frame content files.

    a. Build a simple two-row or two-column frameset, or use one of the framesets from Exercise 1 or 2. Add links to your navigation frame that point to live Web sites.

    b. Add a special target name that will load the linked Web sites into a new browser window.

    c. Test the links and view the browser's behavior.

    d. Test the results in different browsers.

4. Visit the Online Companion Web Site and download some of the sample frame content files.

    a. Build a simple two-row or two-column frameset, or use one of the framesets from Exercise 1 or 2. Add links to your navigation frame that point to live Web sites.

    b. Add a special target name that will load the linked Web sites at the top-level of the existing browser window.

    c. Test the links and view the browser's behavior.

    d. Test the results in different browsers.

Individual Case Project

Build a test frameset that you would consider using if you were required to adopt frames for your project Web site. Use some sample content pages from your project Web site. Test your frameset at different resolutions and in different browsers. Code your frameset to work at both 800 × 600 and 1024 × 768 resolutions. Write a short description of how you would have to change your existing design and content to adapt to a frameset.

Team Case Project

Work as a group to determine whether frames will enhance the effectiveness of your Web site and presentation of your content. Write a design summary that states how your Web site would benefit from the use of frames, and include a sketch of the structure and navigation of your proposed framed Web site. Discuss targeting behavior and how you would handle links to sites outside your own. Discuss whether you would have a framed page or standard HTML page for the top-level page of your Web site.

Build a test frameset to demonstrate the design ideas in your written summary. Include some sample content pages. Test your frameset at different resolutions and in different browsers. Code your frameset to work at both 800 × 600 and 1024 × 768 resolutions. If the testing shows positive results, consider adopting the frameset for your completed Web site.

12

Working with Forms

When you complete this chapter, you will be able to:

- Understand how forms work
- Understand form syntax
- Create input objects
- Build forms within tables
- Build and test a sample form

This chapter covers the HTML form elements. Forms let you build interactive Web pages that collect information from a user and process it on the Web server. You can use forms to gather information and create databases or to send customized responses to your users. Forms collect—but do not process—data. The data processing must be performed on the Web server that hosts the form. Forms are the basis for online commerce; without them users would not be able to enter customer address, credit card, and ordering information on the Web.

Understanding How Forms Work

Figure 12-1 shows a typical form. You can use a variety of input elements for the form based on the type of information you want to gather from your user. Forms usually contain basic HTML formatting tags such as <p> and <br>. Forms can also be built within tables, which helps control their visual layout. Well-designed forms include active white space, aligned form elements, and clear labels. Use the design principles you have learned throughout this book to create forms that are legible and easy to use.

The HTML form itself is the interface for the user to enter data, but all of the actual data processing is performed on the server using applications that usually reside in the Common Gateway Interface (CGI). The **Common Gateway Interface** is the communications bridge between the Internet and the server. Using programs called "scripts," CGI can collect data sent by a user via the Hypertext Transfer Protocol (HTTP) and transfer it to a variety of data processing programs, including spreadsheets, databases, or other software running on the server. The data processing software then can work with the data and send a response back to CGI, and then on to the user, as shown in Figure 12-2.

CHAPTER 12

Figure 12-1

A sample HTML form

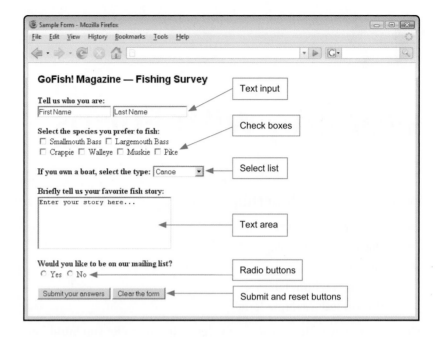

Figure 12-2

Common Gateway
Interface architecture

The programs that transfer the data are called **CGI scripts**, which can be written in a variety of programming languages. If you are not already familiar with writing CGI scripts, enlist the assistance of a programmer, unless you want to master programming skills in addition to your HTML skills. You can also download CGI scripts from the Web that are in the public domain and use them on your site. These freely available software programs usually come with instructions.

NOTE

A good source for CGI scripts is Matt's Script Archive at *www.scriptarchive.com* and the CGI Directory at *www.cgidir.com*.

Another scripting language used with HTML forms is **JavaScript**, which was originally created for the Netscape browser in 1995. JavaScript is a client-side scripting language, which means that it runs on the user's computer, rather than on the server like the CGI scripts. JavaScripts are the source of many annoying Web site interactions such as multiple pop-up windows, disabling the user's Back button, or creating tracking cookies on the user's computer. However, when used correctly, JavaScript can enhance your Web site with beneficial programming functions, including form validation that checks a user's form entries for errors before the result is sent to the CGI script. A complete JavaScript tutorial is out of the scope of this book, though there are many good references available on the Web or in print. For more information on scripting, see books such as *JavaScript, Fourth Edition* by Don Gosselin and *HTML, JavaScript, and Advanced Internet Technologies* by Karl Barksdale and E. Turner, both published by Course Technology Cengage Learning.

NOTE
Good sources for JavaScript information on the Web include the following:
www.yourhtmlsource.com/javascript/
www.w3schools.com/js/default.asp

Understanding Form Syntax

Five basic form elements are commonly used and supported by the major browsers. These are <form>, <input>, <select>, <option>, and <textarea>. HTML 4.01 introduced five new form elements: <button>, <fieldset>, <label>, <legend>, and <optgroup>. In this section you will learn how to use all of these elements.

Using the <form> Element

The **<form> element** is the container for creating a form, as the <table> element is the container for the elements that create a table. A form has a number of attributes that describe how the form data is handled, as described in Table 12-1.

Attribute	Description
action	The URL of the application that processes the form data; this URL usually points to a CGI script file
enctype	The content type used to submit the form to the server (when the value of the method is "post"); most forms do not need this attribute
method	Specifies the HTTP method used to submit the form data; the default value is "get" • Get—The form data is appended to the URL specified in the action attribute • Post—The form data is sent to the server as a separate message
accept	A comma-separated list of content types that a server processing this form can handle correctly; most forms do not need this attribute
accept-charset	A list of allowed character sets for input data that is accepted by the server processing this form; most forms do not need this attribute

Table 12-1   Form attributes

CHAPTER 12

The <form> element by itself does not create a form. It must contain **form controls** (such as <input> elements) and possibly some formatting elements as well to control the look of the form. A variety of form controls are available for collection information, as described in the following sections. The following code shows a typical <form> element with some of the attributes listed in Table 12-1. This code specifies that the form data the user enters is being sent to a program named script.cgi that resides on a Web server.

```
<form action="http://www.website.com/cgi_bin/script.cgi"
method="post">
```

Creating Input Objects

The <input> element defines many of the form input object types. Table 12-2 lists the available object types. You use the type attribute to specify the object type.

Type Attribute Value	Description
text	Creates a text entry field that lets the user enter a single word or a line of text; this is the default object type
password	Creates the same type of text entry field created by the value "text," but the user entry is masked by asterisks
checkbox	Provides on/off toggles that the user selects. Check boxes are best used with multiple-answer questions. Multiple check boxes can contain the same name, letting you group them together so that users can select multiple values for the same property.
radio	Lets a user choose one value from a range of values; when radio buttons are grouped together with the same name, only one choice can be selected
submit	Sends the form data to the server using the transmission method specified in the <form> element; every form needs a submit button
reset	Clears the form of any user-entered data and returns it to its original state
hidden	Adds a control that is not displayed in the browser; the hidden type is useful for sending additional information with the form data that may be needed for processing
image	Adds a graphic button to the form, rather than the default button
button	Creates a button that has no default behavior. The button's function is usually defined by a script. When the user pushes the button, the script function is triggered.
file	Lets the user select a file that is submitted with the form

Table 12-2   <input> element types

Creating Text Boxes

The text entry box is the most commonly used <form> element. The default text box is 20 characters long, although you can change this value using the size attribute. The user can enter an unlimited number of characters in the text box even though they exceed the visible length. You can constrain the user's entry of text with the maxlength attribute and supply a default value for the text with the value attribute. The following code shows a simple form with two text boxes.

```
<form action="http://someserver/cgi_bin/script.cgi"
method="post">

<b>Tell us who you are:</b><br>

<input type="text" name="firstname" size="20"
maxlength="35" value="First Name" />

<input type="text" name="lastname" size="20"
maxlength="35" value="Last Name" />

</form>
```

This code creates the two text box inputs shown in Figure 12-3.

Figure 12-3
Text box inputs

Creating Check Boxes

Check boxes are on/off toggles that the user can select. You can use the name attribute to group check boxes, allowing the user to select multiple values for the same property.

In the following code, the various fish species check boxes are grouped together with the name attribute set to "species." Notice that the check boxes are grouped within a <p> element. This code creates the form shown in Figure 12-4.

```
<form action="http://someserver/cgi_bin/script.cgi" method="post">
<b>Tell us who you are:</b><br>

<input type="text" name="firstname" size="20" maxlength= "35"
value="First Name" />

<input type="text" name="lastname" size="20" maxlength= "35"
value="Last Name" /><br>

<p><b>Select the species you prefer to fish:</b><br>

<input type="checkbox" name="species" value="smbass" />
Smallmouth Bass

<input type="checkbox" name="species" value="lgbass" />
Largemouth Bass <br>
```

```
<input type="checkbox" name="species" value="crappie" />
Crappie

<input type="checkbox" name="species" value="walleye" />
Walleye

<input type="checkbox" name="species" value="muskie" />
Muskie

<input type="checkbox" name="species" value="pike" /> Pike
</p>

</form>
```

Figure 12-4
Check box inputs

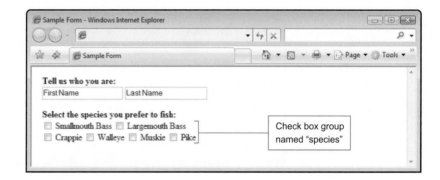

To check a check box by default, you can use the checked attribute. The following code fragment shows the syntax for this attribute. Here, the Pike check box is checked by default.

```
<input type="checkbox" name="species" value="pike" checked />
Pike
```

Creating Radio Buttons

Radio buttons are like check boxes, but only one selection is allowed. When radio buttons are grouped with the name attribute, only one value can be selected to be "on," while all other values must be "off." To preselect one of the radio buttons, you use the checked attribute.

In the following code, the "Yes" and "No" radio buttons are grouped together with the name attribute set to "list." The user can choose only one of the two values. The "Yes" value is pre-selected with the checked attribute. This code creates the form shown in Figure 12-5.

```
<form action="http://someserver/cgi_bin/script.cgi"
method="post">
<b>Tell us who you are:</b><br>
<input type="text" name="firstname" size="20" maxlength= "35"
value="First Name" />

<input type="text" name="lastname" size="20" maxlength= "35"
value="Last Name" /><br>
```

```
<p><b>Select the species you prefer to fish:</b><br>

<input type="checkbox" name="species" value="smbass" />
Smallmouth Bass

<input type="checkbox" name="species" value="lgbass" />
Largemouth Bass <br>

<input type="checkbox" name="species" value="crappie" />
Crappie

<input type="checkbox" name="species" value="walleye" />
Walleye

<input type="checkbox" name="species" value="muskie" />
Muskie

<input type="checkbox" name="species" value="pike" />
Pike </p>

<p><b>Would you like to be on our mailing list?</b><br>
<input type="radio" name="list" value="yes" checked /> Yes
<input type="radio" name="list" value="no" /> No
</p>

</form>
```

Figure 12-5
Radio button inputs

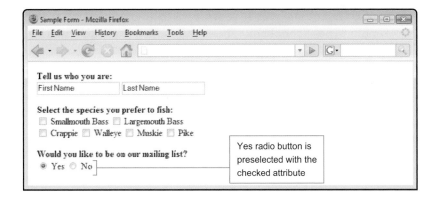

NOTE

Use check boxes when you want to create a question to which multiple answers are allowed. Use radio buttons when you want users to choose only one answer.

Creating Submit and Reset Buttons

The submit and reset button input types let the user either send the form data to be processed or clear the form and start over. These are predefined functions that are activated by the button type. Set the input type to either "submit" or "reset." The default button text values are "Submit Query" and "Reset." You can use the value attribute to customize the button text.

The following code shows the addition of submit and reset buttons with customized button text. Figure 12-6 shows the result of the code.

```
<form action="http://someserver/cgi_bin/script.cgi"
method="post">
<b>Tell us who you are:</b><br>
<input type="text" name="firstname" size="20" maxlength= "35"
value="First Name" />

<input type="text" name="lastname" size="20" maxlength= "35"
value="Last Name" /><br>

<p><b>Select the species you prefer to fish:</b><br>

<input type="checkbox" name="species" value="smbass" />
Smallmouth Bass

<input type="checkbox" name="species" value="lgbass" />
Largemouth Bass <br>

<input type="checkbox" name="species" value="crappie" />
Crappie

<input type="checkbox" name="species" value="walleye" />
Walleye

<input type="checkbox" name="species" value="muskie" />
Muskie

<input type="checkbox" name="species" value="pike" /> Pike
</p>

<p><b>Would you like to be on our mailing list?</b><br>
<input type="radio" name="list" value="yes" checked /> Yes
<input type="radio" name="list" value="no" /> No
</p>

<input type="submit" value="Submit your answers" /> <input
type="reset" value="Clear the form" />

</form>
```

Figure 12-6

Submit and reset input buttons

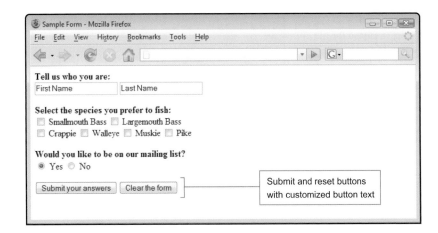

Submit and reset buttons with customized button text

Creating a Custom Event Button

You can create customized buttons that you can use with programming languages such as JavaScript. This type of button differs from the reset and submit buttons because it does not have a predefined function. When a user clicks the button, the event activates a function contained in an associated program. In the following code fragment, the button has a customized value of "Calculate." Figure 12-7 shows the button in the browser.

```
Click the calculate button to total your order:
<input type="button" value="Calculate" />
```

Figure 12-7

A customized button

Creating an Image for the Submit Button

You can choose an image file and use it instead of the default button image for the submit button. The image type works only for the submit function. Make sure that the image you choose is an acceptable Web file format (GIF, PNG, or JPG). The src attribute contains the location of the image file. Remember to include an alt attribute as you would with any other image.

The following code shows the use of an image (submit.gif) for the submit button. Figure 12-8 shows the result.

```
<h3>Click the button to find out more:</h3>
<input type="image" src="submit.gif" alt="submit button" />
```

CHAPTER 12

Figure 12-8

Using an image for the submit button

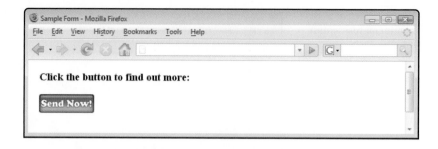

Letting the User Submit a File

The file type input object lets users select a file on their own computers and send it to the server. This type lets you create a text input area for the user to enter a filename. The length of the text input is specified with the size attribute. The file type automatically includes a browse button that lets users browse for a file in their computers' directory systems.

The following code shows the file input type. In this case, the text box accepts up to 30 characters. The result is shown in Figure 12-9.

```
Use the Browse button to select your file:<br>
<input type="file" size="30" />
```

Figure 12-9

File type input

Creating a Password Entry Field

The password type input object works like a text input box, with the additional feature that the entered text is hidden by asterisks rather than shown on the screen. This is a very low level of password protection, as the password is only protected from unauthorized users looking at the screen. The password itself is sent to the server as plain text, and anyone with network access could read the password information. If you use passwords, check with your system administrator to see whether you can send passwords over a secure Internet connection.

The following code shows the use of the password type input. Both the user name and password text boxes accept up to 30 characters. Figure 12-10 shows the result.

```
Enter your user name and password:<br>
user name: <input type="text" size="30" /><br>
password: <input type="password" size="30" />
```

Figure 12-10

Password type input

Enter your user name and password:
user name:
password:

Using the <select> Element

The <select> element lets you create a list box or scrollable list of selectable options. The <select> element is a container for the <option> element. Each <option> element contains a list value.

The following code shows the standard type of list box; the user can choose one value from the list. Figure 12-11 shows the result of the code. Notice that the first option in the list is the value that appears in the list box text area.

```
<b>If you own a boat, select the type:</b>
<select name="boats">
<option>Canoe</option>
<option>Jon Boat</option>
<option>Kayak</option>
<option>Bass Boat</option>
<option>Family Boat</option>
</select>
```

You can select the default value in a list by adding the selected attribute to an <option> element. In the following list, "Bass Boat" is the default value.

```
<b>If you own a boat, select the type:</b>
<select name="boats">
<option>Canoe</option>
<option>Jon Boat</option>
<option>Kayak</option>
<option selected>Bass Boat</option>
<option>Family Boat</option>
</select>
```

Figure 12-11

A select list box

If you own a boat, select the type: Canoe
Canoe
Jon Boat
Kayak
Bass Boat
Family Boat

You can also choose to let the user pick multiple values from the list by adding the multiple attribute to the <select> element. This results in a scrollable list rather than a list box. The following code and Figure 12-12 show the use of the multiple attribute. The size attribute specifies how many of the list options are visible at a time. The following list shows six options at once.

```
<p align="center"><b>Select your favorite kinds of snacks:
</b><br>
<select name="snacks" multiple size="6">
<option>Potato Chips</option>
<option>Popcorn</option>
<option>Peanuts</option>
<option>Pretzels</option>
<option>Nachos</option>
<option>Pizza</option>
<option>Fries</option>
</select>
</p>
```

Figure 12-12

A scrollable select list

Grouping List Options

You can group and label sets of list options with the <optgroup> element and label attribute. The result is a heading for a series of options within a list. Figure 12-13 shows the result of using the <optgroup> element. The browser determines the format of the labels, but they are usually bold italic. In the following code, the snack list is divided into two groups: salty snacks and hot snacks.

```
<p align="center"><b>Select your favorite kinds of snacks:
</b><br>
<select name="snacks" multiple size="6">
<optgroup label="Salty Snacks">
<option>Potato Chips</option>
<option>Popcorn</option>
<option>Peanuts</option>
<option>Pretzels</option>
</optgroup>
<optgroup label="Hot Snacks">
<option>Nachos</option>
```

```
<option>Pizza</option>
<option>Fries</option>
</optgroup>
</select>
</p>
```

Figure 12-13
Grouping list options

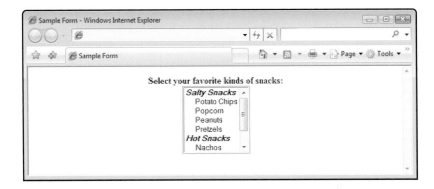

Using the <textarea> Element

The <textarea> element lets you create a text area for user input larger than the <input> text type object described previously. You can specify the width and height of the text area with the cols and rows attributes. Because of browser differences, text entered in a text area does not wrap automatically; the user must press the Enter key at the end of each line of text. You can set the wrap attribute to "virtual" to force the text to wrap automatically in the user's browser window. Any text you enter in the <textarea> element appears as the default text in the user's browser.

The following code shows a text area set to 30 columns wide by 5 rows high. Figure 12-14 shows the result of the code.

```
<p><b>Briefly tell us your favorite fish story:</b><br>
<textarea name="fishstory" rows="5" cols="30">
Enter your story here...
</textarea>
</p>
```

Figure 12-14
<textarea> element

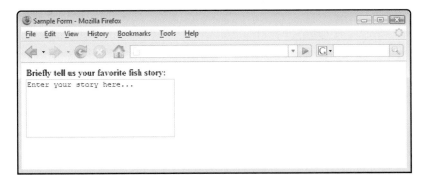

Creating Input Groupings

You can use the <fieldset> and <legend> elements to create groupings of different types of <input> elements. The <fieldset> element contains the <input> elements, and the <legend> element contains a label for the grouping. These two elements help make your forms more readable and increase their accessibility to various browsers. Figure 12-15 shows the use of the <fieldset> and <legend> elements. The code for the page follows.

```
<form action="http://someserver/cgi_bin/script.cgi" method
="post">
<fieldset>
<legend><b>Select the species you prefer to fish:</b>
</legend>
<input type="checkbox" name="species" value="smbass" />
Smallmouth Bass
<input type="checkbox" name="species" value="lgbass" />
Largemouth Bass <br>
<input type="checkbox" name="species" value="crappie" />
Crappie
<input type="checkbox" name="species" value="walleye" />
Walleye
<input type="checkbox" name="species" value="muskie" />
Muskie
<input type="checkbox" name="species" value="pike" /> Pike
</fieldset>

<br>

<fieldset>
<legend><b>Select the rod type you prefer to use:</b>
</legend>
<input type="checkbox" name="species" value="ltspin" /> Light
Spinning
<input type="checkbox" name="species" value="mdspin" />
Medium Spinning <br>
<input type="checkbox" name="species" value="hvspin" /> Heavy
Spinning
<input type="checkbox" name="species" value="fly" /> Fly
<input type="checkbox" name="species" value="btcas" /> Bait
Casting
</fieldset>
</form>
```

Figure 12-15

Grouping and labeling
<input> elements

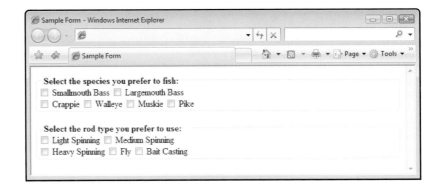

Building Forms within Tables

Most forms need some type of formatting to increase their legibility. As you have seen in the form samples in this chapter, forms need at least basic formatting elements, such as <br> and <p>, to place form elements on separate lines and add white space. Even with these basic formatting elements, the look of your form may not be acceptable. Figure 12-16 shows a typical form. Notice how the left justification of the form elements gives a ragged look to the form.

Figure 12-16

Typical form layout

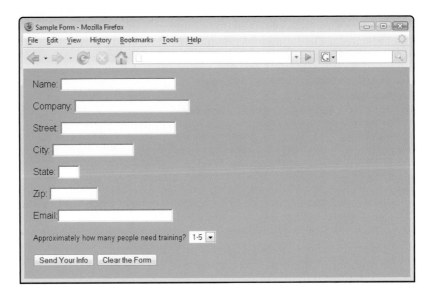

In contrast to Figure 12-16, the form in Figure 12-17 has been placed within a table, producing a more visually appealing form that is easier for the user to follow when entering data.

Figure 12-17

Form layout enhanced with a table

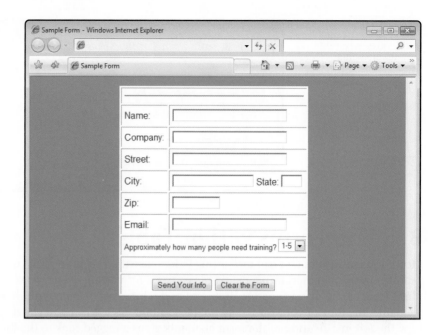

Placing a form within a table is no different from placing standard HTML content within a table. Usually the <form> element contains a table, which in turn contains each of the individual form input elements. The following code builds the form in Figure 12-17:

```
<div align="center">
<form method="post" action="http://someserver/cgi_bin/
script.cgi">
<table cellpadding="5" border>
<tr><td colspan="2"><hr></td></tr>

<tr><td>Name:</td><td><input type="text" size="30"
maxlength="256" name="name" /></td></tr>

<tr><td>Company:</td><td><input type="text" size="30"
maxlength="256" name="company" /></td></tr>

<tr><td>Street:</td><td><input type="text" size="30"
maxlength="256" name="street" /></td></tr>

<tr><td>City:</td><td><input type="text" size="20"
maxlength="256" name="city" />State:<input type="text" size= "2"
maxlength="2" name="state" /></td></tr>

<tr><td>Zip:</td><td><input type="text" size="10"
maxlength="256" name="zip" /></td></tr>

<tr><td>Email:</td><td><input type="text" size="30"
maxlength="256" name="email" /></td></tr>
```

```
<tr><td colspan="2"><font size="2">Approximately how many
people need training?</font>
<select name="numstudent" size= "1">
<option selected>1-5
<option>10</option>
<option>20</option>
<option>30</option>
<option>40</option>
<option>50</option>
</select></td></tr>

<tr><td colspan="2"><hr></td></tr>

<tr><td align="center" colspan="2">
<input type="submit" value="Send Your Info" />
<input type="reset" value="Clear the Form" />
</td></tr>

</table>
</form>
</div>
```

Building and Testing a Sample Form

In the following set of steps, you will build a form for an online job search service. Users of the service will enter address and personal information into the form, and may attach a copy of their resume. To complete the steps, you must enter the URL posted on the Online Companion Web site so that the form works properly.

To begin building a sample form:

1. Copy the file **form.htm** from the Chapter12 folder provided with your Data Files to the Chapter12 folder in your work folder. (Create the Chapter12 work folder, if necessary.)

2. Open **form.htm** in your HTML editor, save it as **wonderform.htm**, and then examine the code. You will have to fill in the value for the action attribute in the <form> element. You will find this URL value on the Online Companion Web site.

```
<html>
<head>
<title>Wonder Software Online Job Search Form</title>
</head>
<body>
<h1>Wonder Software Online Job Search</h1>
<form action="Enter URL here" method="post">
</form>
</body>
</html>
```

3. Begin building the form by adding three text <input> elements, one each for the user's name, e-mail address, and telephone number. Set the size and name attribute values as shown in the following code. Use <br> to format the text <input> elements and labels.

```
Name:<br><input size="30" name="name" /><br>
Email:<br><input size="30" name="email" /><br>
Phone:<br><input size="30" name="phone" />
```

4. Group this set of fields with a <fieldset> and accompanying <legend> element, as shown in the following code.

```
<fieldset>
<legend>Contact Information</legend>
Name:<br><input size="30" name="name" /><br>
Email:<br><input size="30" name="email" /><br>
Phone:<br><input size="30" name="phone" />
</fieldset>
```

5. Save wonderform.htm and leave it open for the next set of steps. Then view the file in the browser; it should now look like Figure 12-18.

Figure 12-18

Form with three text <input> elements

Adding Check Boxes

Continue to build the form by adding check box <input> elements to collect information from the user. You will add a list box of job title types. The user can make only one selection from the list.

To continue building the form:

1. Continue working in the file **wonderform.htm**.

2. Add an <h3> element with text to identify the check box inputs.

```
<h3>
Select Your Target Job Title (choose one):</h3>
```

3. Add the check box inputs as shown. The name attribute groups the check boxes together under the category "jobtitle." Each check box is identified with a unique value.

```
<input type="checkbox" name="jobtitle" value="ae" />
Account Executive<br>

<input type="checkbox" name="jobtitle" value="bd" />
Business Development<br>

<input type="checkbox" name="jobtitle" value="is" /> Inside
Sales<br>

<input type="checkbox" name="jobtitle" value="sm" /> Sales
Manager<br>

<input type="checkbox" name="jobtitle" value="vp" /> VP
Sales
```

4. Save sample form.htm and leave it open for the next set of steps. Then view the file in the browser; it should now look like Figure 12-19.

Figure 12-19

Form with check box <input> elements

Adding a List Box and Radio Buttons

Continue to build the form by adding two more <input> elements to collect information from the user. You will add a list box of job position options and a question with a yes or no answer.

To continue building the form:

1. Continue working in the file **wonderform.htm**.
2. Add a <select> element with four blank <option> tags, as shown in the following code. Place this code after the closing <fieldset> tag from the previous procedure.

```
<p>
Select the type of position you desire:
<select name="position">
<option> </option>
<option> </option>
<option> </option>
<option> </option>
</select>
</p>
```

3. Fill in a value for each option, as shown in the following code:

```
<p>
Select the type of position you desire:
<select name="position">
<option>Part-time contract</option>
<option>Full-time contract</option>
<option>Part-time permanent</option>
<option>Full-time permanent</option>
</select>
</p>
```

4. Beneath the select list, add the following question:

```
<p>
Are you willing to relocate?
</p>
```

5. Add two <input> elements with the type set to "radio" to create radio buttons. Use a <br> element to place the radio buttons under the question text.

```
<p>
Are you willing to relocate?<br>
Yes <input type="radio" />
No <input type="radio" />
</p>
```

6. Add a value attribute for each element. Set the value for the Yes button to "yes." Set the No button to "no." Also, add a name attribute that groups the radio buttons together with a value of "relocate."

```
<p>
Are you willing to relocate?<br>
Yes <input type="radio" value="yes" name="relocate" />
No <input type="radio" value="no" name="relocate" />
</p>
```

7. Save wonderform.htm and leave it open for the next set of steps. Then view the file in the browser; it should now look like Figure 12-20.

Figure 12-20

Adding a select list and radio buttons

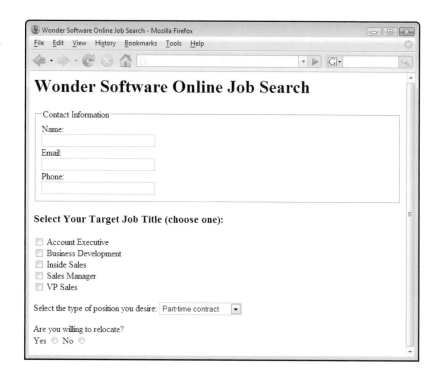

Adding Submit and Reset Buttons

You will finish the form by adding the submit and reset buttons.

To continue building the form:

1. Continue working in the file **wonderform.htm**.

2. Finish the form by adding submit and reset button element types and setting values for each button, as shown in the following code.

```
<br>
<input type="submit" value="Send your info" />
<input type="reset" value="Clear the form" />
```

3. Save wonderform.htm, close it, and then view the file in the browser. The complete form should now look like Figure 12-21.

Figure 12-21

The completed form

The complete code for the page follows:

```
<html>
<head>
<title>Wonder Software Online Job Search Form</title>
</head>
<body>

<h1>Wonder Software Online Job Search</h1>

<form action="Enter URL here" method="post">

<fieldset>
<legend>Contact Information</legend>
Name:<br><input size="30" name="name" /><br>
Email:<br><input size="30" name="email" /><br>
Phone:<br><input size="30" name="phone" />
</fieldset>
```

```
<h3>
Select Your Target Job Title (choose one):</h3>

<input type="checkbox" name="jobtitle" value="ae" /> Account
Executive<br>
<input type="checkbox" name="jobtitle" value="bd" /> Business
Development<br>
<input type="checkbox" name="jobtitle" value="is" /> Inside
Sales<br>
<input type="checkbox" name="jobtitle" value="sm" /> Sales
Manager<br>
<input type="checkbox" name="jobtitle" value="vp" /> VP Sales

<p>
Select the type of position you desire:

<select name="position">
<option>Part-time contract</option>
<option>Full-time contract</option>
<option>Part-time permanent</option>
<option>Full-time permanent</option>
</select>
</p>

<p>
Are you willing to relocate?<br>
Yes <input type="radio" value="yes" name="relocate" />
No <input type="radio" value="no" name="relocate" />

</p>
<br>
<input type="submit" value="Send your info" />
<input type="reset" value="Clear the form" />
</form>
</body>
</html>
```

Testing the Form

Test the form by connecting to the Internet, adding sample data, and submitting the form information. This form is processed using a CGI script that is stored on the Online Companion Web site server. The script is a program that processes the user-submitted data and returns a response in the form of an HTML page.

The script validates the information sent by the user and returns an error message if the data is not correct. For example, the script checks the following conditions:

- All of the form fields must have data.
- All of the text fields are limited to 255 characters. The script strips out anything that is not a letter, number, or special character needed for an e-mail or phone number.
- The values for job title and position must match the values from the example exactly.
- If the user fails to select any job titles, the script returns an error.

To test the form:

1. Make sure you are connected to the Internet.
2. Open the file **wonderform.htm** in your browser.
3. Enter test data into the form fields, as shown in Figure 12-22.

Figure 12-22

The HTML form with sample data

4. Click the submit button to send the test data to the Web server. If you have completed the form correctly, the Web server should return your results in an HTML page, as shown in Figure 12-23. (Note that none of the data you submit is being collected.)

Figure 12-23

The HTML return page compiled from the form data

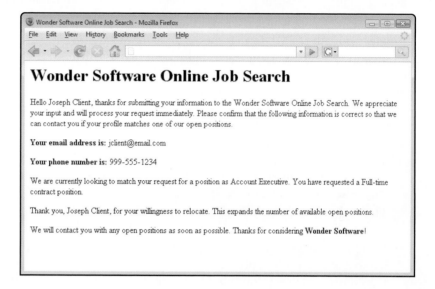

5. Retest the form by entering different data and making different choices, such as changing your relocation choice or leaving a field blank. Test the form to see the different responses.

Chapter Summary

A usable form interface is the result of choosing the correct form elements for the type of data you are requesting and designing a clear and readable form. Keep the following points in mind:

▶ You need to work with some type of server-based software program to process the data from your form. An HTML form is the interface for the user to enter data, and the data processing is performed on the server using applications that usually reside in the Common Gateway Interface (CGI).

▶ The <form> element is the container for creating a form. A form has a number of attributes that describe how the form data is handled, such as action, which often specifies the URL of a CGI script file to process the form data.

▶ You have a variety of form elements to choose from when building a form. The <input> element defines many of the form input object types. Use the correct type of input object for the type of data you are gathering. For example, use check boxes for multiple-choice questions. For a long list of choices, use a select list.

▶ The <fieldset> and <legend> elements let you create more visually appealing forms that have logical groupings of <input> elements with a title.

▶ Most forms should be formatted to improve their legibility. The most basic formatting elements are <br> and <p>, which place form elements on separate lines and add white space. You can avoid the ragged look of forms by placing them within tables to control the alignment of <input> elements.

Key Terms

<form> element	form control
CGI script	JavaScript
Common Gateway Interface (CGI)	

Review Questions

1. Where does the form processing software usually reside?
2. What are the five commonly supported form elements?
3. What does the action attribute in the <form> element contain?
4. What are the two possible values of the form method attribute?
5. How can you group multiple check boxes together?
6. How are radio buttons different from check boxes?
7. How do you control the length of a user's entry in a text <input> element?
8. How do you enter default text in a text <input> element?
9. How do you force a check box to be selected by default?
10. What button must be included with every form?

11. How do you change the default button image for the submit button?

12. What input type lets the user attach a file to the form data?

13. What is the security problem with the password input type?

14. What are the two types of select lists?

15. What attributes let you specify the width and height of the <textarea> element?

Hands-On Projects

1. In this project, you will build text box form elements.

   a. In your HTML editor, open the file **blankform.htm** in the Chapter12 folder in your work folder.

   b. Save the file as **textbox.htm** in the same location.

   c. Examine the code. The file contains only the default HTML elements and an empty <form> element.

   d. Build the form shown in Figure 12-24. Refer to the following table for each form element's attribute values.

Name	Size	Maxlength
Street	20	35
City	20	35
State	2	35
Zip	10	35

Figure 12-24
Form with text boxes

2. In this project, you will build check box form elements.

   a. In your HTML editor, open the file **blankform.htm** in the Chapter12 folder in your work folder.

   b. Save the file as **checkbox.htm** in the same location.

    c. Examine the code. The file contains only the default HTML elements and an empty <form> element.

    d. Build the form shown in Figure 12-25.

    e. Group the check boxes with a name attribute set to "flavor."

Figure 12-25
Form with check boxes

3. In this project, you build radio button form elements.

    a. In your HTML editor, open the file **blankform.htm** in the Chapter12 folder in your work folder.

    b. Save the file as **radio.htm** in the same location.

    c. Examine the code. The file contains only the default HTML elements and an empty <form> element.

    d. Build the form shown in Figure 12-26.

    e. Make sure that "Yes" is the selected option.

    f. Group the radio buttons with a name attribute set to "offer."

Figure 12-26
Form with radio buttons

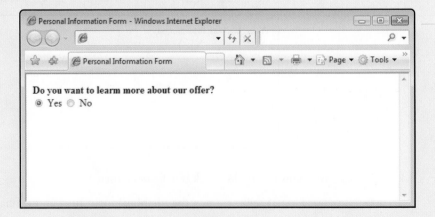

4. In this project, you will build a text area form element.

   a. In your HTML editor, open the file **blankform.htm** in the Chapter12 folder in your work folder.

   b. Save the file as **textarea.htm** in the same location.

   c. Examine the code. The file contains only the default HTML elements and an empty <form> element.

   d. Build the form shown in Figure 12-27. The text area is 6 rows by 35 columns.

Figure 12-27
Form with text area

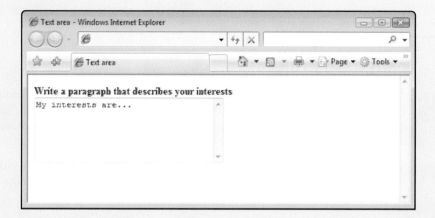

5. In this project, you will build a select form element.

   a. In your HTML editor, open the file **blankform.htm** in the Chapter12 folder in your work folder.

   b. Save the file as **select.htm** in the same location.

   c. Examine the code. The file contains only the default HTML elements and an empty <form> element.

   d. Build the form shown in Figure 12-28.

Figure 12-28
Form with list box

Individual Case Project

Build a user feedback form for your project Web site. You can refer to the sample feedback form in Chapter 3 for ideas. Customize the types of questions you ask to match the content of your site. Create both scaled questions and open-ended questions for your users. For example, ask users to rate the navigation of your site on a scale of 1 to 5, and also include a text area input where they write about their experience of navigating your Web site. Although you will not be able to activate the form (because you don't have an appropriate script to process the data), you can demonstrate the types of questions you would ask users to find out more about their habits when they visit your site.

Team Case Project

Each team member creates and submits to the instructor his or her own feedback form, as described in the preceding Individual Case Project. You are free to design the form any way you choose, but it must include the navigation characteristics, typographic specifications, and design conventions of your project Web site.

Then meet as a team and choose the best features, questions, and design characteristics from each member's submitted form. Create a new form that combines these features and add it to your project Web site.

13

Web Page Design Studio

When you complete this chapter, you will be able to:

- Apply the design, layout, and CSS skills you learned throughout this book by building a home page for a fictional Web site
- Describe the design process and decisions a Web designer must make in a standards-based development process
- Test your work in multiple browsers for consistency as you progress
- Troubleshoot compatibility issues as they arise

In this chapter, you have a chance to apply a variety of skills building a mock-up layout design for a fictional Web site. Your "clients" want a home page design for their Web site named DogWorld. The site presents an online periodical of information for dog owners. The content types include feature articles, regular columnists, editorials, advertising, and a search function. The clients have employed a graphic designer to create page graphics for the site. The designer has worked from preliminary sketches provided by the clients to provide a conceptual main page design in two different color schemes. As the Web site designer, you will work with the graphic artist, testing content and browser compatibility, to implement a completed HTML version of the conceptual site.

The Initial Design Process

The clients sketched out a basic idea for the site, shown in Figure 13-1. They also submitted a Web site specification document to the graphic designer providing background information about the audience, content, and design of the Web site.

Figure 13-1

The original design
sketch

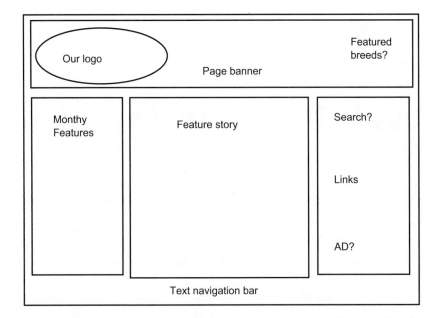

Original Design Specification

- **Site Title:** DogWorld

- **Content Focus:** DogWorld is a special interest Web site for dog owners and fanciers. The site presents periodical-type information for dog owners in an online format. The variety of content includes feature articles, regular columnists, editorials, advertising, and a searchable archive.

- **Mission Statement:** The goal of DogWorld is to inform people of the latest in news, information, trends, and products in the world of dogs. The site will have an open, accessible design that will allow ease of navigation and access to content. A search feature will let users access articles and content from the publication's entire history, using DogWorld's archive database.

- **Main Elements Outline:**

  - **Home page**
    A portal to the site's content, containing article descriptions, links to regular columns and external Web sites, advertising, and a search feature

  - **Editorial**
    Our editor's column for sounding off on the latest dog-related issues

  - **Dog Advice**
    A Q & A between DogWorld readers and guest personalities, including trainers, vets, and breeders

- **Your Email**
  A place for user correspondence and editorial answers
- **Training Tips**
  Basic dog training tips and techniques
- **Breed List**
  Breed resources including links to DogWorld articles, external Web sites, a list of breeders, and breed-specific rescue shelters

- **Target Audience:** The target audience for this Web site is anyone who owns or loves dogs. This is a broad audience, and the Web site must be accessible to users with a wide variety of computers, connection speeds, and computing skills.

- **Design Considerations:** The Web site must be accessible in all popular browsers. Based on the latest research, our average prospective visitor uses a Windows-based PC with Internet Explorer, Netscape, or Firefox.

Based on discussions with the clients and the basic information provided in the sketch, the artist created an initial design and sent it back to the clients for approval. The designer created this initial design mockup using Photoshop, so it is not an actual Web page, but a picture of what the finished Web site will look like.

Figure 13-2 shows the designer's first draft of the Web site. The clients reviewed and critiqued the design. Although they liked the basic layout, they did have some specific complaints. They thought the logo area was too plain and there were too many pictures of dogs in the page banner. The text overall was too small, and the section boxes in the left column needed more white space and seemed cluttered. The clients also wanted the dog bone image to look like a dog tag and decided to remove the highlighting on the link text in the right column.

In addition, the clients suggested a dog-related shape in the background of the page banner to make it more interesting, and wanted to see the entire page in a different color scheme. The clients also noted that the brown text in the feature image was hard to read.

The designer went back to the drawing board and returned with two new versions of the site, shown in Figures 13-3 and 13-4. This new page design incorporated many of the changes the clients requested. The red version of the color scheme gave the clients a chance to explore something other than the aqua and brown scheme the designer suggested. After reviewing both of the new versions, the clients decided to move forward with the aqua and brown design shown in Figure 13-3.

CHAPTER 13

Figure 13-2

Designer's first draft of the page design

Figure 13-3

The second draft of the site in aqua and brown

Figure 13-4
The second draft of the
site in red and brown

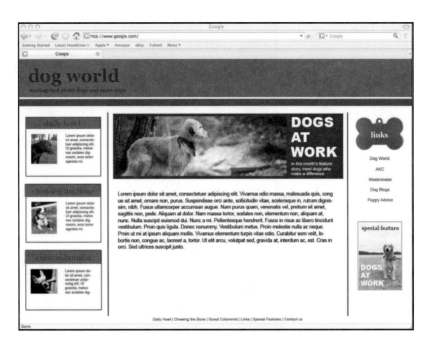

The clients knew they wanted to make other changes, including adding a search form and a space to advertise upcoming articles. They were happy enough with the basic design to hand it over to the HTML coder, who will build some mock-up pages for further testing and refinement. This is your project for the chapter.

Creating the Mock-up Web Page

In the following set of steps, you build a table-based version of the design that the clients approved. Using simple tables combined with CSS is a sound transitional Web design technique. The tables hold the layout together, while CSS controls the fonts, colors, spacing, and alignment. The designer provided you with the images and color information you need to re-create the design using HTML.

Figure 13-5 shows the results you need to achieve and the table structure that creates the layout for the page. The page is a fixed design based on a 1024 × 768 screen resolution. Notice that the design uses two simple tables stacked on top of each other to hold the content together. The table borders are highlighted with heavy black lines that will not appear in the finished Web page.

Figure 13-5

The home page
design showing
table structure
and approximate
column measurements

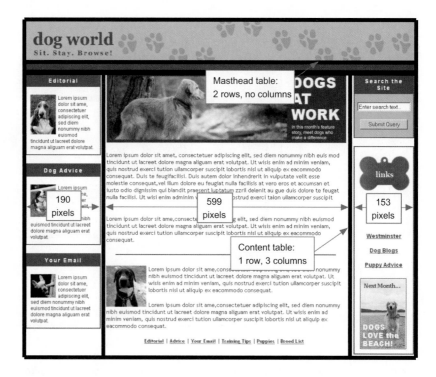

Figure 13-5 also shows the approximate measurements you will use in creating the mock-up layout.

You need to determine the approximate widths of the columns in the content table so you know the pixel measurements to use in the design. The graphic designer provided the Dogs at Work image as 599 pixels wide. If the content table width is 975 pixels, deducting the width of the Dogs at Work image leaves 376 pixels (975 − 599 = 376).

Divide this remainder by 2 to find how many pixels remain for the two outer columns; the answer is 188 (376 / 2 = 188). You also have to factor white space between the columns into the design. As you build and test the layout, you can adjust these widths to find the best balance between the content columns. Figure 13-5 shows that the left column will be wider than the right column.

The graphic designer provided you with a variety of images from the initial design. You can use these when you create the mock-up of the layout. Figure 13-6 shows the images and their filenames.

Figure 13-6

Image files used in the home page design

To start working on the file:

1. Open the file **dogworld.htm** in your HTML editor and save it in your work folder as **dogworld1.htm**.

2. Copy the following image files into your work folder.

   - bottomdog.jpg
   - brown_bar.jpg
   - brown_rule.jpg
   - dogs_at_work.jpg
   - leftdog1.jpg
   - leftdog2.jpg
   - leftdog3.jpg
   - links_img.jpg
   - masthead_green.jpg
   - next_month.jpg

3. Open the file **dogworld1.htm** in your browser. When you open the file, it looks like Figure 13-7.

Figure 13-7

Basic table layout

4. View the source code in your browser or text editor. The file contains the standard HTML elements including an empty <style> element in the head section where you will add the style rules. A comment in the head section lists the hexadecimal color codes that the graphic designer provided. The body section contains the basic table structure you will use to create the page layout. The table contains comments to identify each table and placeholder text such as "masthead" to identify each table cell. The complete code for the page follows:

```
<html>
<head>
    <title>Welcome to Dog World!</title>
<!--
Hex Color Codes
Brown: #613838
Red: #e32026
Green: #93d4cd
-->
<style type="text/css">

</style>
</head>
<body>
<!-- Masthead Table -->
<table width="975" border>
<tr>
<td>Masthead</td>
</tr>
<tr>
<td>Brown bar</td>
</tr>
</table>
<!-- Content Table -->
<table width="975" border>
<tr valign="top">
<td>Column 1</td>
<td>Column 2</td>
<td>Column 3</td>
</tr>
</table>
</body>
</html>
```

Note

The finished code for the completed page design is included for your reference at the end of the chapter.

Building the Masthead

The masthead at the top of the DogWorld Web page contains the DogWorld banner graphic and brown horizontal bar in two separate rows of the opening table.

To build the masthead section:

1. In the masthead table code, locate the first row and cell containing the word "Masthead" as shown.

   ```
   <td>Masthead</td>
   ```

2. Remove the word "Masthead" and add an <img> tag that specifies the image masthead_green.jpg. The image is 975 pixels wide by 95 pixels high. Add an appropriate alt attribute value. The blue text shows the changes to the code.

   ```
   <td><img src="masthead_green.jpg" width="975" height="95"
   alt="DogWorld masthead image" /></td>
   ```

Note

Remember, always use width, height, and alt attributes in every <img> element to ensure quick download and accessibility.

3. Continue working in the opening table. Locate the second row and cell containing the words "Brown bar" as shown.

   ```
   <td>Brown bar</td>
   ```

4. Remove the words "Brown bar" and add an <img> tag that specifies the image brown_bar.jpg. The image is 975 pixels wide by 20 pixels high. Add an appropriate alt attribute value as well. The blue text shows the changes to the code.

   ```
   <td><img src="brown_bar.jpg" width="975" height="20" alt="brown
   bar image" /></td>
   ```

5. Finally, locate the masthead <table> tag and remove the existing width and border attributes in the following blue code. These are no longer necessary because the images will set the width of the table, and the borders detract from the finished look of the design.

   ```
   <table width="975" border>
   ```

6. Save your file and view the results in the browser. To simulate a real Web design environment, you should test in at least two browsers to ensure compatibility of the design. Figures 13-8 and 13-9 show the masthead design in Internet Explorer and Firefox, respectively.

Figure 13-8
The masthead design in
Internet Explorer

Figure 13-9
The masthead design in
Firefox

Building the Small Feature Boxes

The left column of the DogWorld Web page contains three small feature boxes that highlight the content of the monthly columns, as shown in Figure 13-10. Each feature box contains a text-reverse heading, a photo, and some copy. Three feature boxes are stacked in the left column. Before CSS became popular, these feature boxes would have been constructed with nested tables stacked in the table's left column. With CSS you can create a more modern design that uses <div> elements to create the feature boxes.

To build the small feature boxes:

1. Locate the opening <table> tag in the content table and remove the existing width and border attributes in the following blue code:

   ```
   <table width="975" border>
   ```

2. Locate the first row and cell and remove the text "Column 1" as shown.

   ```
   <td>Column 1</td>
   ```

3. Add a <div> element within the first column as shown. Include an <h4> element with the heading text, "Editorial."

   ```
   <td>
   <div class="smfeature">
   <h4>Editorial</h4>
   </div>
   </td>
   ```

Figure 13-10

Small feature boxes in left column

Small feature boxes

Note

Remember to write your style rules in the empty <style> element in the document's head section.

---

4. Write a style rule with "smfeature" as the class selector. Set the width to 190 pixels and the height to auto. Add a thin solid border and use the brown hexadecimal code specified by the graphic designer.

```
.smfeature {
   width: 190px;
   height: auto;
   border: thin solid #613838;}
```

Note

The 190 pixel width of the smfeature division, plus any added margin measurements, sets the column width of the table.

---

5. Save the file and view it in the browser. Figure 13-11 shows the result of the style rule. The smfeature division is 190 pixels wide, with the specified brown border. You will style the <h4> heading text next.

Figure 13-11

The basic smfeature division—190 pixels wide, brown border

6. Build the new style rule for the smfeature h4 class. Use descendant selection to make sure this style rule applies only to <h4> elements when they appear within a smfeature division as shown.

```
.smfeature h4 { }
```

7. Write the style rules for the <h4> heading text. Set the font-family to arial, the font-size to 85%, the text color to white, and the background color to the brown hexadecimal value.

```
.smfeature h4 {
    font-family: arial;
    font-size: 85%;
    color: #fff;
    background: #613838;}
```

Note

Remember that it is always good coding practice to include comments throughout your code. For example, you may want to add comments in the style sheet that identify each style rule and what effect it has on the Web page. View the finished code at the end of the chapter for comment examples.

8. Save your work and view it in the browser. Figure 13-12 shows the result of the style rule. The <h4> heading text is now white text reversed against the brown background.

Figure 13-12
Heading text

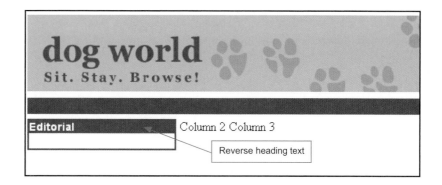

9. Finish styling the <h4> heading text. Align the text to center, and add 2 pixels of letter spacing and .5 em of padding.

```
.smfeature h4 {
    font-family: arial;
    font-size: 85%;
    color: #fff;
    background: #613838;
    text-align: center;
    letter-spacing: 2px;
    padding: .5em;}
```

10. Save your work and view it in the browser. Figure 13-13 shows the result of adding the final three properties to the h4 heading text style rule.

Figure 13-13
The completed h4
heading text

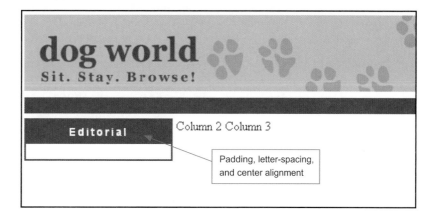

Adding Content to the Small Feature Box

Now that you have created the basic structure of the small feature box, you can add some text and an image to test the box for content presentation.

To add content to the small feature box:

1. Locate the smfeature division in the left column of the table.

```
<div class="smfeature">
<h4>Editorial</h4>
</div>
```

2. Add a <p> element and some text. You can open the file **greeking.txt** and copy some of the text to use within the <p> element as shown.

Note

Remember that designers use greeking text to simulate areas of text in a test layout.

```
<div class="smfeature">
<h4>Editorial</h4>
<p>
Lorem ipsum dolor sit ame, consectetuer adipiscing elit, sed diem
nonummy nibh euismod tincidunt ut lacreet dolore magna aliguam
erat volutpat.</p>
</div>
```

3. Add an <img> element within the paragraph. Specify the file leftdog1.jpg for the source. The image is 64 pixels wide and 96 pixels high. Add an appropriate alt attribute as well. Make sure to place the <img> element immediately following the opening <p> element as shown.

```
<div class="smfeature">
<h4>Editorial</h4>
<p>
<img src="leftdog1.jpg" width="64" height="96" alt="Editorial dog
photo" /> Lorem ipsum dolor sit ame, consectetuer adipiscing elit, sed
diem nonummy nibh euismod tincidunt ut lacreet dolore magna aliguam
erat volutpat.</p>
</div>
```

4. Save the file and test your work in the browser. It should look similar to Figure 13-14.

Figure 13-14

The partially styled smfeature content

5. Write a new style rule to set style properties for the <p> and <img> elements that reside within the small feature box. Use a descendant selector to apply the style only to the <p> elements that are children of the smfeature division.

```
.smfeature p { }
```

6. Set the font-family to arial and the font-size to 75%. Set the text color to black, and add a margin of 10 pixels to add some white space between the paragraph text and the border of the smfeature box that contains it.

```
.smfeature p {
    font-family: arial;
    font-size: 75%;
    color: 000;
    margin: 10px; }
```

Note

Remember that it's easy to test different font sizes. If you're not happy with the font size, change the value in the style rule, save, and reload the page in the browser.

7. Add a new descendant selector that selects the <img> within the smfeature division. Use the float property to float the image to the left of the paragraph text. Add a 5 pixel right margin to add white space between the image and the text.

```
.smfeature img {float: left; margin-right: 5px;}
```

8. Save the file and view the results in the browser. Figures 13-15 and 13-16 show the completed smfeature division in Firefox and Internet Explorer, respectively. The two browsers interpret the box model differently, resulting in inconsistent layouts.

Figure 13-15
Results in Firefox

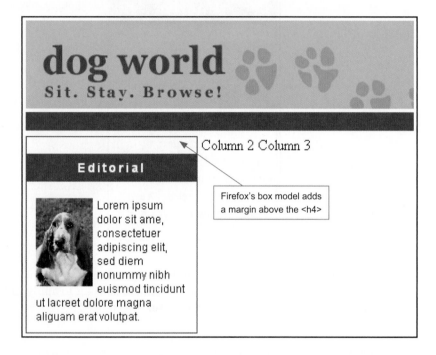

9. To solve this problem, add a margin-top property to the <h4> style rule and set it to 0 pixels. This removes the top margin in Firefox, but has no effect on the display in Internet Explorer.

```
.smfeature h4 {
    font-family: arial;
    font-size: 85%;
    color: #fff;
    background: #613838;
    text-align: center;
    letter-spacing: 2px;
    padding: .5em;
    margin-top: 0px;}
```

10. Test your results in both browsers again to make sure the smfeature boxes look the same.

Figure 13-16
Results in Internet
Explorer

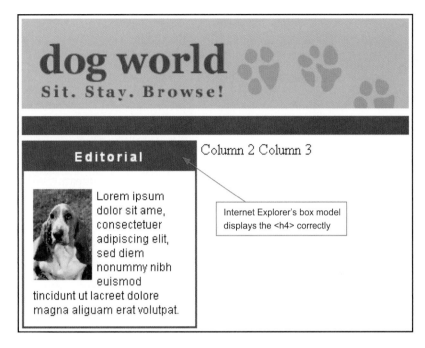

Completing the Left Column Layout

Now that you have created a single small feature box, you can copy it and add two more smfeature boxes to the left column.

1. Locate the existing smfeature division you just completed, copy it, and paste two more divisions into the table's left column.

2. Change the heading, dog image, and alt text in the two new small feature boxes as shown in the following code:

```
<td>
<div class="smfeature">
<h4>Editorial</h4>
<p>
<img src="leftdog1.jpg" width="64" height="96" alt="Editorial
dog photo" /> Lorem ipsum dolor sit ame, consectetuer adipiscing elit,
sed diem nonummy nibh euismod tincidunt ut lacreet dolore magna
aliguam erat volutpat.</p>
</div>

<div class="smfeature">
<h4>Dog Advice</h4>
<p>
<img src="leftdog2.jpg" width="64"  height="79"
alt="Dog Advice dog photo" /> Lorem ipsum dolor sit ame, consectetuer
adipiscing elit, sed diem nonummy nibh euismod tincidunt ut lacreet
dolore magna aliguam erat volutpat.</p>
</div>
```

```
<div class="smfeature">
<h4>Your Email</h4>
<p>
<img src="leftdog3.jpg" width="64" height="57"
alt=" Your Email dog photo" /> Lorem ipsum dolor sit ame, consectetuer
adipiscing elit, sed diem nonummy nibh euismod tincidunt ut lacreet
dolore magna aliguam erat volutpat.</p>
</div>
</td>
```

3. Finally, add two margin properties to the smfeature style rule to add white space to the right and below each small feature box. Locate the smfeature rule in the style sheet and add the properties as shown.

```
.smfeature {
   width: 190;
   height: auto;
   border: thin solid #613838;
   margin-bottom: 20px;
   margin-right: 10px;}
```

4. Save the file and view the results in the browser. Figure 13-17 shows the result of adding feature boxes and margin properties to the left column.

Figure 13-17

The completed left column with small feature boxes

Note
Remember to test your layout in multiple browsers as you progress through the design process.

Building the Feature Article Section

The middle column of the content table contains the feature story image, two sections of text separated by a dividing rule, a secondary image, and a text navigation bar, as shown in Figure 13-18.

Figure 13-18

The feature article section

To build the feature article section:

1. Locate the second cell in the content layout table. Remove the text "Column 2" in the following blue code.

    ```
    <td>Column 2</td>
    ```

2. Add an <img> tag that specifies the image file dogs_at_work.jpg. The image is 599 pixels wide by 163 pixels high. Add an appropriate alt attribute value as well. The blue text shows the changes to the code.

    ```
    <td><img src="dogs_at_work.jpg" width="599" height="163"
    alt="dogs at work feature image" /></td>
    ```

3. Add two <p> elements of greeking following the <img> element. Specify "bodycopy" as the class attribute as shown.

```
<td><img src="dogs_at_work.jpg" width="599" height="163"
alt="dogs at work feature image" />
<p class="bodycopy">Lorem ipsum dolor sit amet, consectetuer
adipiscing elit, sed diem nonummy nibh euis mod tincidunt ut
lacreet dolore magna aliguam erat volutpat.</p>
<p class="bodycopy">Ut wisi enim adminim veniam, quis nostrud
exerci taion ullamcorper suscipit lobortis nisl ut aliquipex en
commodo consequat. </p>
</td>
```

4. Write the bodycopy class style rule. This applies to all of the paragraphs in the feature article section. Set the font-size to 85%. Specify a font-family of arial or sans-serif with a line-height of 1.25 em. Finally, add a right margin of 10 pixels to the paragraphs to provide some white space at the end of the text lines.

```
.bodycopy {font-size: 85%;
            font-family: arial, sans-serif;
            line-height: 1.25em;
            margin-right: 10px; }
```

5. Save the file and view the results in the browser. Figure 13-19 shows the page in Firefox. The feature article text extends beyond the image because the width of the right column (Column 3) is not constrained by any content. You will fix this problem later by adding the search and links features to the right column.

Figure 13-19

Partially completed feature article section

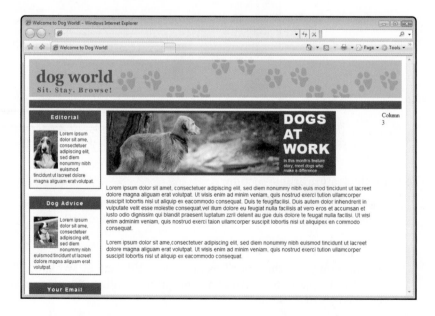

6. Continue working on the feature article section. Add an <img> element that specifies the image file brown_rule.jpg. This is the brown divider rule that separates the feature article from the secondary article. The image is 550 pixels wide by 4 pixels high. Add an appropriate alt attribute value as well. The blue text shows the changes to the code.

```
<img src="brown_rule.jpg" width="550" height="4" alt="brown
divider line" />
```

Note
You can test different sizes of an image by manipulating the width and height attributes. Once you decide on a size, create a graphic that is the actual size you need for the finished page.

7. Place the <img> element within a set of <div> tags. Use the align attribute to align the brown divider rule to the center of the column.

```
<div align="center"><img src="brown_rule.jpg" width="550"
height="4" alt="brown divider line" /></div>
```

8. After the brown separator image, add two more <p> elements containing greeking text. Add more greeking text than shown in the code sample to simulate a complete paragraph. Set the class attribute to "bodycopy".

```
<div align="center">
<img src="brown_rule.jpg" width="550" height="4" alt="brown
divider line" /></div>
<p class="bodycopy">Lorem ipsum dolor sit ame, consectetuer
adipiscing elit</p>
<p class="bodycopy">Lorem ipsum dolor sit ame, consectetuer
adipiscing elit</p>
```

9. Save the file and view the results in the browser. Figure 13-20 shows the page in Internet Explorer.

10. Within the first <p> element you just inserted, add an image tag that specifies the file "bottomdog.jpg." The image is 100 pixels wide by 100 pixels high. Add a class attribute that specifies a class named "feature2".

```
<div align="center">
<img src="brown_rule.jpg">
</div>
<p class="bodycopy"><img src="bottomdog.jpg" width="100"
height="100" alt="Feature 2 dog image" class="feature2" /> Lorem
ipsum dolor sit ame, consectetuer adipiscing elit, sed diem
nonummy nibh euismod tincidunt ut lacreet dolore magna aliguam
erat volutpat. Ut wisis enim ad minim veniam, quis nostrud exerci
tution ullamcorper suscipit lobortis nisl ut aliquip ex eacommodo
consequat.</p>
```

Figure 13-20

Adding the divider rule and secondary article paragraphs

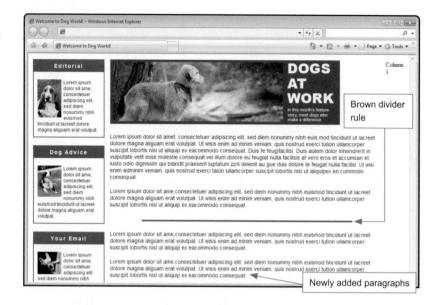

11. Add a style rule to the style sheet for the class "feature2" that controls the image you just added. Set the float property to left and add a right margin of 5 pixels to offset the image from the surrounding text.

```
feature2 {float: left; margin-right: 5px;}
```

12. Save the file and view the results in the browser. Figure 13-21 shows the newly added divider bar, secondary article text, and floating image.

Figure 13-21

Adding the divider bar, secondary article text, and floating image

Adding a Text Navigation Bar

The middle column of the content table contains a text navigation bar. This set of links is centered in the middle column.

Note

Remember that a text navigation bar is the most effective and accessible way to provide navigation on your site. Always include a text-based set of links as an alternate means of navigation.

To build the text navigation bar:

1. Add a new style rule to the style sheet for the class "footer." The style rule sets the text alignment of the navigation to the center of the column.

   ```
   .footer {text-align: center;}
   ```

2. Add a <p> element and the text navigation bar at the bottom of the feature column, after the secondary article paragraphs. Because you are creating a mock-up of the Web page, the <a> elements do not have to link to any actual pages. For now, specify index.htm as the value for the href attribute in all of the links in the navigation bar, as shown in the following code:

   ```
   <p class="footer">
   <a href="index.htm">Editorial</a> |
   <a href="index.htm">Advice</a> |
   <a href="index.htm">Your Email</a> |
   <a href="index.htm">Training Tips</a> |
   <a href="index.htm">Puppies</a> |
   <a href="index.htm">Breed List</a>
   </p>
   ```

3. Save the file and view the results in the browser. Figure 13-22 shows the navigation bar added to the bottom of the feature article column. You will change the font and color later when you add more hypertext links to the right column of the layout.

Figure 13-22

Text navigation bar added to the main feature column

Building the Search Section

The right column of the content table contains the search form, links section, and two images: the links dog tag and the "Next Month" feature graphic, as shown in Figure 13-23. The search form lets users search the articles archive for specific content. You will build this section first.

Figure 13-23

The search and links section

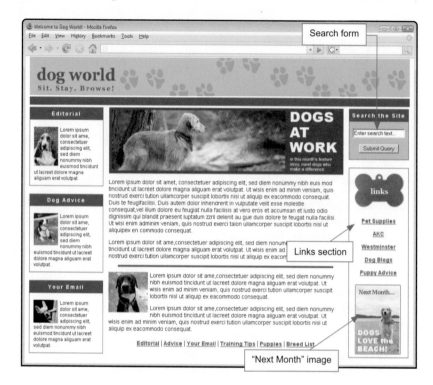

To build the search section:

1. Locate the third cell in the content layout table. Remove the text "Column 3" as shown.

   ```
   <td>Column 3</td>
   ```

2. Add an align attribute to the opening <td> tag and set the value to "center" to center the content in the column.

   ```
   <td align="center"></td>
   ```

3. Add a <div> element and searchbox class within the column as shown. Include an <h4> element with the heading text "Search the Site."

   ```
   <td align="center">
   <div class="searchbox">
   <h4>Search the Site</h4>
   </div>
   </td>
   ```

4. Build a style rule for the searchbox class. The search box is exactly the same as the small feature boxes you created earlier in the Web site layout. Copy the existing smfeature and smfeature h4 style rules from the small feature box section and paste them in the style sheet where shown in the following code. Rename the styles searchbox and searchbox h4 as shown.

```
.searchbox {
    width: 152;
    height: auto;
    border: thin solid #613838;
    margin-bottom: 20px;
    margin-left: 15px;}

.searchbox h4 {
    font-family: arial;
    font-size: 85%;
    color: #fff;
    background: #613838;
    text-align: center;
    letter-spacing: 2px;
    padding: .5em;
    margin-top: 0px;}
```

5. The search box has a different background color, as shown in Figure 13-22. Add the background-color property to the searchbox style rule and set the hexadecimal value to #93d4cd. Also, center the contents of the searchbox using the text-align property.

```
.searchbox {
    width: 152;
    height: auto;
    border: thin solid #613838;
    margin-bottom: 20px;
    margin-left: 15px;
    background-color: #93d4cd;
    text-align: center;}
```

6. Because the search box is in the right column of the layout, you will add white space in the form of a margin property to the left of the searchbox. Change the existing margin-right property to margin-left and set the value to 10 pixels as shown. Figure 13-24 shows the partially completed search box.

```
.searchbox {
    width: 152;
    height: auto;
    border: thin solid #613838;
    margin-bottom: 20px;
    margin-left: 10px;
    background-color: #93d4cd;
    text-align: center;}
```

Figure 13-24
Partially completed
search box

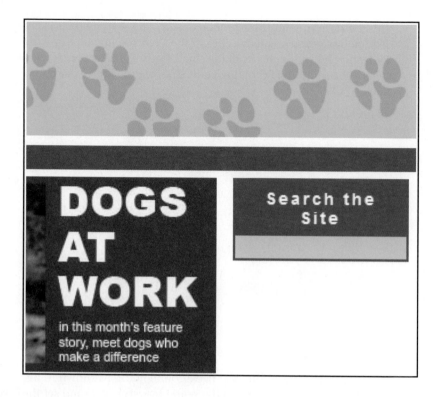

Adding the Search Form

Because this is a mock-up layout, you need to add only enough form code to simulate how the user form interface will appear.

Note
Remember that forms work with software programs on the server to process data supplied by the user. The action attribute specifies the URL of the program that will process the data.

To add the search form:

1. Locate the new searchbox division in the right column and add the form code as shown. This form code is not complete; it is missing both method and action attributes that determine how the form data is processed.

```
<td align="center">
<div class="searchbox">
<h4>Search the Site</h4>
<form>
<input type="text" value="Enter search text..."
maxlength="25" size="18">
<p><input type="submit"></p>
```

```
</form>
</div>
</td>
```

2. Save the file and view the results in the browser. Figure 13-25 shows the completed search box.

Figure 13-25

The completed search box

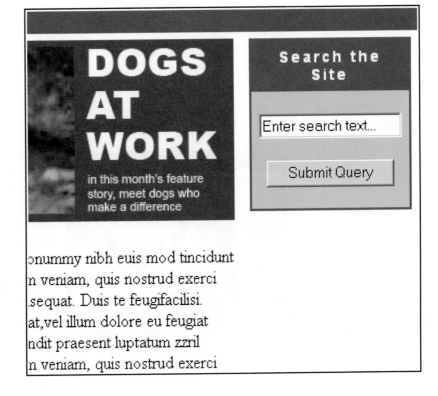

Building the Links Section

The links section contains two images and some hypertext links contained within a brown border. You will add this content in the right column, directly beneath the search box you just created.

To create the links section:

1. Locate the search box you just created. Add a new <div> element with a class attribute set to "links" as shown.

```
<td align="center">
<div class="searchbox">
<h4>Search the Site</h4>
<form>
<input type="text" value="Enter search text..."
maxlength="25" size="18">
<p><input type="submit"></p>
</form>
```

```
</div>
<div class="links">
</div>
</td>
```

2. Within the new <div> element, add an image element that specifies the image "links_img.jpg." The image is 148 pixels wide by 106 pixels high. Add an appropriate alt attribute value as shown.

```
<div class="links">
<img src="links_img.jpg" width="148" height="106" alt="links dog
tag image" />
</div>
```

3. Save the file and view your work in the browser. Figure 13-26 shows the partially completed links section.

Figure 13-26

The partially completed links section

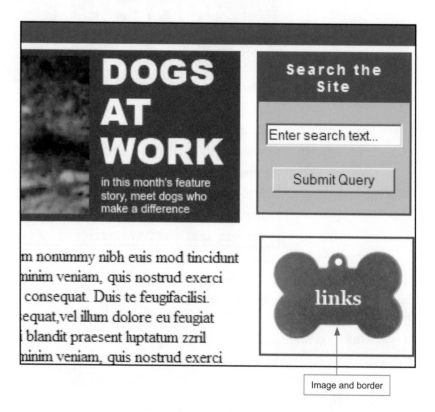

Image and border

4. After the image tag, add a set of hypertext links, each contained within its own <p> element. Like the links you added previously, these links do not have to actually link to a live page. Set the href value for all of the links to "index.htm."

```
<div class="links">
<img src="links_img.jpg" width="148" height="106" alt="links dog
tag image" />
```

```
<p><a href="index.htm">Pet Supplies</a></p>
<p><a href="index.htm">AKC</a></p>
<p><a href="index.htm">Westminster</a></p>
<p><a href="index.htm">Dog Blogs</a></p>
<p><a href="index.htm">Puppy Advice</a></p>
</div>
```

5. Add an <img> element that specifies the image file next_month.jpg at the bottom of the division, immediately after the hypertext links. The image is 131 pixels wide and 186 pixels high. Add an appropriate alt attribute value as shown.

```
<div class="links">
<img src="links_img.jpg" width="148" height="106" alt="links dog
tag image" />
<p><a href="index.htm">Pet Supplies</a></p>
<p><a href="index.htm">AKC</a></p>
<p><a href="index.htm">Westminster</a></p>
<p><a href="index.htm">Dog Blogs</a></p>
<p><a href="index.htm">Puppy Advice</a></p>
<img src="next_month.jpg" width="131" height="186" alt="Next
Month Feature Image" />
</div>
```

6. Write the style rule for the links division you just created. In the style sheet, add a rule that selects the links class. Set the width of the division to 152 pixels, and the height to auto. Add a border as shown and margin-left of 10 pixels. Also, center the contents of the links section with the text-align property.

```
.links {width: 152px;
   height: auto;
   border: thin solid #613838;
   margin-left: 10px;
   text-align: center}
```

7. Save the file and view the results in the browser. Figure 13-27 shows the page in Internet Explorer with the addition of the new right column content.

Figure 13-27

Page layout in Internet Explorer

Feature, links, and search completed

Controlling the Hypertext Link Styles

To complete the layout, the color and font of the hypertext links need to match the design of the site. You will also add a hover property to activate a background color when a user points a mouse to a hypertext link.

To style the hypertext links:

1. Add a new style rule to the style sheet that selects the <a> element. Set the font-size to 85%, font-weight to bold, and font-family to arial, sans-serif.

   ```
   a {font-size: 85%; font-weight: bold; font-family: arial, sans-serif}
   ```

2. Write another style rule that uses the link pseudo class to set the unvisited link color to match the brown color specified by the designer. Visited links can appear in the standard purple.

   ```
   a:link {color: #613838;}
   ```

3. Finally, write another style rule that uses the hover pseudo class to set the hover color to match the aqua color specified by the designer.

   ```
   a:hover {background-color: #93d4cd}
   ```

4. Save the file and view the results in the browser. The links are brown, and the aqua hover color appears when the user points the mouse to a link, as shown in Figure 13-28.

Figure 13-28
The hypertext link style

Completing the Web Page Design

You created a complete layout based on the graphic designer's original design. Although you have been testing the page in different browsers during the development process, it is a good idea to test a final time to make sure the pages are displayed properly.

Figures 13-29 and 13-30 show the page in a finished layout in Internet Explorer and Firefox, respectively. The page layout holds together well in both browsers.

Figure 13-29
The finished layout in
Internet Explorer

Figure 13-30 also shows the finished layout with the final column sizes used in the design. Using a combination of simple tables with CSS measurements lets you specify column widths and spacing to precise pixel amounts. The final column widths are calculated as shown in Table 13-1.

Column	Calculation
1	Smfeature division width + right margin = column width 190 + 15 = 205 pixels
2	Column width determined by dogs_at_work.jpg width = 599 pixels
3	Search box division width + left margin = column width 152 + 10 = 162 pixels

Table 13-1   Content table column width calculations

Figure 13-30

The finished page layout in Firefox with column widths

Finished Page Code

Following is the complete code for the page. Notice the CSS and HTML comments that identify each section of the style sheet and the table code. Remember that your style sheet rules can appear in a different order than shown here.

```
<html>
<head>
<title>Welcome to Dog World!</title>

<!-- Hex Color Codes
Brown: #613838
```

```
Red: #e32026
Green: #93d4cd
-->

<style type="text/css">


/* ------------ Small Feature Boxes in left column ------------ */
.smfeature {
width: 190;
height: auto;
border: thin solid;
border-color: #613838;
margin-bottom: 20px;
margin-right: 10px;}


.smfeature h4 {
font-family: arial;
font-size: 85%;
color: #fff;
background: #613838;
text-align: center;
letter-spacing: 2px;
padding: .5em;

margin-top: 0px;}

.smfeature p {
font-family:  arial;
color: 000;
margin: 10px;
font-size: 75%;}

/* ------------ Images in Small Feature Box  ------------ */
.smfeature img {float: left;
     margin-right: 5px; }

/* ------------ Bottom image in middle column  ------------ */

.feature2 {float:left; margin-right: 5px;}

/* ------------ Standard text style ------------ */
.bodycopy {margin-right: 10px;
font-size: 85%;
font-family: arial;
line-height: 1.25em}
```

```
/* ----------- Search box in right column ------------ */

.searchbox {
width: 152;
height: auto;
border: thin solid #613838;
margin-bottom: 20px;
margin-left: 10px;
background: #93d4cd;
text-align: center;}

.searchbox h4 {
font-family: arial;
font-size: 85%;
color: #fff;
background: #613838;
text-align: center;
letter-spacing: 2px;
padding: .5em;
margin-top: 0px;}

/* ------------ Links box in right column ------------ */
.links {
width: 152;
height: auto;
border: thin solid #613838;
margin-left: 10px;
text-align: center;}

/* ------------ Aligns text navigation bar ------------ */

.footer {text-align: center;}


/* ------------ Link colors and hover ------------ */
a {font-size: 85%; font-weight: bold; font-family: arial}
a:link {color: #613838;}
a:hover {background-color: #93d4cd}
</style>
</head>

<body>
<!-- Masthead Table -->
<table>
<tr>
<td><img src="masthead_green.jpg" width="975" height="95"
alt="DogWorld masthead image" >
```

```
</td>
</tr>
<tr>
<td><img src="brown_bar.jpg" width="975" height="20" alt="brown
bar image"></td>
</tr>
</table>

<!-- Content Table -->
<table width="975">
<tr valign="top">
<td>
<div class="smfeature">
<h4>Editorial</h4>

<p>
<img src="leftdog1.jpg" width="64"  alt="96" >
Lorem ipsum dolor sit ame, consectetuer
adipiscing elit, sed diem nonummy nibh euismod tincidunt ut
lacreet dolore magna aliguam erat volutpat.</p>
</div>

<div class="smfeature">
<h4>Dog Advice</h4>
<p>
<img src="leftdog2.jpg" width="64"  alt="79"  >Lorem ipsum dolor
sit ame, consectetuer
adipiscing elit, sed diem nonummy nibh euismod tincidunt ut
lacreet dolore magna aliguam erat volutpat.</p>
</div>

<div class="smfeature">
<h4>Your Email</h4>
<p>
<img src="leftdog3.jpg" width="64"  alt="57" > Lorem ipsum dolor
sit ame, consectetuer
adipiscing elit, sed diem nonummy nibh euismod tincidunt ut
lacreet dolore magna aliguam erat volutpat.</p>
</div>
</td>

<td><img src="dogs_at_work.jpg" width="599" height="163" alt="dogs
at work feature image" >
<p class="bodycopy">Lorem ipsum dolor sit amet,
consectetuer adipiscing elit, sed diem nonummy nibh
euis mod tincidunt ut lacreet dolore magna aliguam erat
volutpat. Ut wisis enim ad minim veniam, quis nostrud
```

```
exerci tution ullamcorper suscipit lobortis nisl ut
aliquip ex eacommodo consequat. Duis te feugifacilisi.
Duis autem dolor inhendrerit in vulputate velit esse
molestie consequat,vel illum dolore eu feugiat nulla
facilisis at vero eros et accumsan et iusto odio
dignissim qui blandit praesent luptatum zzril delenit au gue duis
dolore te feugat nulla facilisi. Ut wisi enim adminim veniam, quis
nostrud exerci taion ullamcorper
suscipit lobortis nisl ut aliquipex en commodo
consequat. </p>

<p class="bodycopy">Lorem ipsum dolor sit ame,consectetuer
adipiscing elit, sed diem nonummy nibh euismod tincidunt ut
lacreet dolore magna aliguam erat volutpat. Ut wisis enim ad minim
veniam, quis nostrud exerci tution
ullamcorper suscipit lobortis nisl ut aliquip ex
eacommodo consequat.</p>

<div align="center">
<img src="brown_rule.jpg">
</div>

<p class="bodycopy"><img src="bottomdog.jpg" width="100"  alt="dog
placeholder"  class="feature2">Lorem ipsum dolor sit
ame,consectetuer
adipiscing elit, sed diem nonummy nibh euismod tincidunt ut
lacreet dolore magna aliguam erat volutpat. Ut wisis enim ad minim
veniam, quis nostrud exerci tution
ullamcorper suscipit lobortis nisl ut aliquip ex
eacommodo consequat.</p>

<p class="bodycopy">Lorem ipsum dolor sit ame,consectetuer
adipiscing elit, sed diem nonummy nibh euismod tincidunt ut
lacreet dolore magna aliguam erat volutpat. Ut wisis enim ad minim
veniam, quis nostrud exerci tution
ullamcorper suscipit lobortis nisl ut aliquip ex
eacommodo consequat.</p>

<p class="footer">
<a href="index.htm">Editorial</a> | <a href="index.htm">Advice</a>
| <a href="index.htm">Your Email</a> | <a
href="index.htm">Training Tips</a> | <a
href="index.htm">Puppies</a> | <a href="index.htm">Breed List</a>
</p>
</td>
```

```
<td>
<div class="searchbox">
<h4>Search the Site</h4>
<form>
<input type="text" value="Enter search text..." maxlength="25"
size="18" >
<p><input type="submit" ></p>
</form>
</div>

<div class="links">
<img src="links_img.jpg"  width="148" height="106" alt="links dog
tag image"  >

<p><a href="index.htm">Pet Supplies</a></p>
<p><a href="index.htm">AKC</a></p>
<p><a href="index.htm">Westminster</a></p>
<p><a href="index.htm">Dog Blogs</a></p>
<p><a href="index.htm">Puppy Advice</a></p>

<img src="next_month.jpg" width="131" height="186" alt="Next Month
Feature Image">
</div>
</td>
</table>

</body>
</html>
```

Chapter Summary

In this chapter, you had the opportunity to use your CSS and HTML skills to build a complete mock-up of a page design for a fictional Web site. You saw that combining CSS with simple tables lets you build a Web design that follows good coding standards without sacrificing visually pleasing design. As you progressed through the building of the page, you saw how Web design is an interactive process that demands you continually test your work to ensure compatibility across different browser platforms.

▶ You can use CSS properties to create complex designs, such as the small feature boxes, without resorting to extra graphics.

▶ You can use CSS to control fonts, text alignment, color, and leading to gain complete control over your page typography.

▶ With CSS box model properties, you gain precise control over the white space within table columns and between different elements in a page design.

▶ Using simple tables to hold the page design together ensures that more users will see the Web page as you designed it for them.

Review Questions

1. What is the benefit of applying CSS rules to standard HTML markup?
2. What properties can you use to make standard heading elements, such as <h1> or <h2>, more distinctive?
3. In the small feature boxes section, what is the benefit of using descendant selection to style the elements that reside within the smfeature class division?
4. Why is it a good practice to state a background color for a Web page even when you are choosing white as the color?
5. What is the benefit of adding a line height setting to your standard content paragraphs, as you did in the feature article section?
6. When specifying a font family, what is the benefit of using a font substitution value?
7. What is the benefit of using the em as a measurement value, especially for fonts?
8. What is the benefit of working with a visible element or table borders when you are designing a Web page?

Hands-On Projects

1. Build the DogWorld page from this chapter using CSS positioning without the use of any tables. You can use the same graphics and content you used to build the table-based layout in this chapter. Refer to the "Building a Page Layout with Positioned Elements" section in Chapter 10 for ideas and guidance.
2. Build a different look for the DogWorld home page, using the graphics and content provided. How else can you arrange the layout to create an interesting and accessible design?

3. Build a secondary page for the DogWorld layout that is designed for reading rather than scanning. Use the graphical elements and content from the main page. Make sure to design for a smooth transition between pages, using some of the same look and feel that the main page exhibits.

Individual and Team Case Project

Finalize your project Web site by testing the finished design in multiple browsers and making any necessary adjustments or changes to support compatibility. If available, post your Web site to the class Web hosting area for live testing on the Internet. If you cannot post your Web site to the Web, prepare a CD or flash drive with your content to submit to your instructor.

If possible, enlist three to five people to review your Web site and fill out either your online or paper-based user feedback form. Compile the results and write a short paper detailing the results of your testing and what they indicate about the effectiveness of your design. Point out the areas that you feel could benefit from user recommendations. List any assumptions you made about the Web site and how users either confirmed or denied these assumptions.

If the time and format allows, prepare to present and defend your Web design to your fellow students. Prepare a short oral presentation (10–15 minutes) where you can present your design ideas and reasons for building the site. Be prepared to take questions and defend your design ideas.

Appendix A

XHTML Reference

This appendix includes element descriptions sorted both alphabetically and by category. The elements listed in this appendix are the ones you will use most often, including a list of the Core attributes allowed with the majority of XHTML elements and a complete list of character entities. Some elements are deprecated (obsolete) in XHTML but are still in common use in many Web sites. If you are creating XHTML-compliant Web pages, you should not use these deprecated elements. For more detailed information, visit the World Wide Web Consortium Web site at *www.w3.org*.

Core Attributes

The Core attributes are allowed within all of the elements listed in the element tables.

Attribute	Description
id	Specifies a document-wide unique identifier for an element
class	Specifies a class name for an element; the class name can be used to specify style sheet rules
style	Specifies a style sheet rule for the element
title	Specifies a title for the element; the content of the title is displayed in the browser as a pop-up

Table A-1   XHTML core attributes

Alphabetical XHTML Reference

Element	Description	Attributes
<!--comment text-->	Allows you to insert a comment in your code. Browsers do not display comments in the Web page. Place the comment within the tag, for example: <!-- This is a comment -->	None
<a>	Allows you to create a clickable hypertext anchor in a document; can be text or an image	Core attributes plus: • *href*—The target destination in a documen • *name*—The name of a fragment of the document • *target*—The window or frame in which the linked document is displayed
<b>	Allows you to boldface text	Core attributes
<base>	Sets the base URL or target for a page; this is an empty element	Core attributes plus: • *href*—The absolute or relative original • *url*—For the current document • *target*—The default window or frame in which links contained in the document are displayed
<basefont> (Deprecated)	Allows you to set a default size for the body text in the document	• *color*—The default text color • *face*—The default text face • *size*—The default text size for the document from 1 to 7; normal browser default is size 3
<blockquote>	Indents text on both the left and right margins	Core attributes
<body>	Identifies the body section of the Web page	Core attributes plus: • *alink*—The color for the currently selected link* • *background*—Points to the image file that is tiled across the background of the page* • *bgcolor*—The page background color* • *link*—The color for unvisited links* • *text*—The default text color* • *vlink*—The color for visited links* * Deprecated in XHTML
 	Inserts a line break, forcing text to the next line; this is an empty element	Core attributes plus: • *clear*—When used with a floating image, forces text to appear at *the bottom of the image*

Table A-2   Common XHTML elements

Element	Description	Attributes
<caption>	Indicates that the text appears as the caption of a table	Core attributes plus: • *align*—The alignment of the caption, either top or bottom; top is the default
<center> (Deprecated)	Centers text or images horizontally on the page	None
<div>	Indicates a division within the document	Core attributes plus: • *align*—The horizontal alignment of the contents of the division
<em>	Emphasizes text, usually as italic; browser determines the text style	Core attributes
<font> (Deprecated)	Allows you to specify the font size for any string of text; range of sizes is 1 to 7, with 3 being the default	• *size*—Sets the font size • *color*—Sets the text color • *face*—Sets the font typeface
<frame>	Defines specific information for each frame in the frameset	Core attributes plus: • *frameborder*—The width of the frame's border • *marginheight*—The margin height in pixels • *marginwidth*—The margin width in pixels • *noresize*—Prevents the user from resizing the frame by dragging the frame border • *name*—Sets a targeting name for the frame • *scrolling*—Determines whether scroll bars appear • *src*—Specifies the source XHTML file for the frame's content
<frameset>	Defines the column and row characteristics of the frames in the frameset	Core attributes plus: • *cols*—Separates the frameset into columns • *rows*—Separates the frameset into rows (Both of these attributes need percentage or pixel values to specify the frame width or height)
<h1> to <h6>	Defines text as a heading level; <h1> is the top-level heading and the largest text	Core attributes plus: • *align*—The alignment of the heading text
<head>	Identifies the head section of the Web page, which is reserved for information about the document, not document content	Three attributes that are not commonly used: • *profile*—Specifies the location of one or more metadata profiles about the document • *lang*—Specifies the base language for the document • *dir*—Specifies the default text direction

Table A-2 (*Continued*)   Common XHTML elements

Element	Description	Attributes
<hr>	Inserts a horizontal rule on the page; this is an empty element	Core attributes plus: • *width*—The length of the rule in pixels • *size*—The height of the rule in pixels • *align*—Horizontal rule alignment; default is center • *noshade*—Turns off the default 3-D shading of the rule
<html>	Identifies the file as an HTML file	None
<i>	Italicizes text	Core attributes
<img>	Inserts an image into a Web page	Core attributes plus: • *width*—Specifies the width of the image in pixels • *height*—Specifies the height of the image in pixels • *src*—The URL that points to the image file; this attribute is required • *align*—Allows you to wrap text around the image; valid values are left, middle, and right • *alt*—Allows you to specify an alternate string of text if the image cannot be displayed by the browser • *border*—The border for the image; set this attribute to zero (0) to remove a hypertext border on an anchor image • *hspace*—The horizontal white space in pixels on the left and right sides of an image • *vspace*—The vertical white space in pixels on the top and bottom of an image
<li>	Marks an individual list item; this is an empty tag Core attributes	
<link>	Defines a relationship between the document and external resources, such as a style sheet	Core attributes plus: • *type*—The type of external resource • *href*—The URL of the external resource • *rel*—Describes the relationship between the current document and the anchor specified by the href attribute
<meta>	Used within the document head to provide information	• *name*—The meta information name, such as keyword or description • *content*—The content of the named information type

Table A-2 (*Continued*) Common XHTML elements

Element	Description	Attributes
\<noframe\>	Contains content that is viewable by browsers that do not support frames	Core attributes
\<ol\>	Creates a numbered indented list	Core attributes
\<p\>	Marks the beginning of a new block of text	Core attributes plus: • *align*—The horizontal alignment of the paragraph content
\<pre\>	Preserves the formatting and spacing of text as typed in the source code; displays the text in a monospace font, different from the standard browser text	Core attributes
\<span\>	Serves as an inline division; used to apply a style class or rule to text	Core attributes
\<strong\>	Emphasizes text, usually as bold; browser determines the text style	Core attributes
\<style\>	Used within the head section to contain CSS style rules	• *type*—Specifies the type of style language; for CSS, use text/CSS as the value
\<sub\>	Subscripts text	Core attributes
\<sup\>	Superscripts text	Core attributes
\<table\>	Marks the beginning and end of a table	Core attributes plus: • *align*—Floats the table to the left or right of text* • *border*—Specifies whether a border is displayed for a table • *bgcolor*—The background color of the table* • *cellpadding*—The amount of space in pixels between the border of the cell and the cell content on all four sides • *cellspacing*—The amount of space in pixels between the table cells on all four sides • *height*—The height of the table* • *width*—The width of the table, either to a fixed pixel width or a percentage relative width* *Deprecated in XHTML
\<th\>	Forces the contents of a cell to be displayed as bold and centered	Core attributes plus: • *align*—The horizontal alignment for table cells within the table row • *valign*—The horizontal alignment for table cells within the row

Table A-2 (*Continued*)   Common XHTML elements

Element	Description	Attributes
		<ul><li>*bgcolor*—The background color of the table row*</li><li>*rowspan*—The number of rows spanned by a cell</li><li>*colspan*—The number of columns spanned by a cell</li></ul>*Deprecated in XHTML
<th>	Forces the contents of a cell to be displayed as bold and centered	Core attributes plus:
		<ul><li>*align*—The horizontal alignment for table cells within the table row</li><li>*valign*—The vertical alignment for table cells within the row</li><li>*bgcolor*—The background color of the table row*</li><li>*rowspan*—The number of rows spanned by a cell</li><li>*colspan*—The number of columns spanned by a cell</li></ul>*Deprecated in XHTML
<title>	Specifies the title of the Web page; title text appears in the browser title bar and as the bookmark or favorites text	Two attributes that are not commonly used:<ul><li>*lang*—Specifies the base language for the document</li><li>*dir*—Specifies the default text direction</li></ul>
<tr>	Marks a row of cells in a table	Core attributes plus:
		<ul><li>*align*—The horizontal alignment for table cells within the table row</li><li>*valign*—The vertical alignment for table cells within the row</li><li>*bgcolor*—The background color of the table row*</li></ul>*Deprecated in XHTML
<tt>	Specifies monospace text, us ually Courier	Core attributes
<u> (Deprecated)	Underlines text	Core attributes
<ul>	Creates a bulleted indented list	Core attributes

Table A-2 (*Continued*)   Common XHTML elements

Categorical XHTML Reference

The following is a quick reference list of the XHTML elements and attributes used in this book, listed by category.

Global Structure Elements

Element	Description	Attributes
`<body>`	Identifies the body section of the Web page	Core attributes plus: • *alink*—The color for the currently selected link* • *background*—Points to the image file that is tiled across the background of the page* • *bgcolor*—The page background color* • *link*—The color for unvisited links* • *text*—The default text color* • *vlink*—The color for visited links * Deprecated in XHTML
`<div>`	Indicates a division within the document	Core attributes plus: • *align*—The horizontal alignment of the contents of the division
`<h1>` to `<h6>`	Defines text as a heading level; `<h1>` is the top-level heading and the largest text	Core attributes plus: • *align*—The alignment of the heading text
`<head>`	Identifies the head section of the Web page, which is reserved for information about the document, not document content	Three attributes that are not commonly used: • *profile*—Specifies the location of one or more metadata profiles about the document • *lang*—Specifies the base language for the document • *dir*—Specifies the default text direction
`<html>`	Identifies the file as an HTML file	None
`<meta>`	Used within the document head to provide information	• *name*—The meta-information name, such as keywords or description • *content*—The content of the named information type
`<span>`	Serves as an inline division, used to apply a style class or rule to text	Core attributes
`<title>`	Specifies the title of the Web page; title text appears in the browser title bar and as the bookmark or favorites text	Two attributes that are not commonly used: • *lang*—Specifies the base language for the document • *dir*—Specifies the default text direction

Table A-3   XHTML structure elements

Text Elements

Element	Description	Attributes
<blockquote>	Indents text on both the left and right margins	Core attributes
 	Inserts a line break, forcing text to the next line; this is an emptyelement	Core attributes plus: • *clear*—When used with a floating image, forces text to appear at the bottom of the image
<em>	Emphasizes text, usually as italic; browser determines the text style	Core attributes
<p>	Marks the beginning of a new block of text	Core attributes plus: • *align*—The horizontal alignment of the paragraph content
<pre>	Preserves the formatting and spacing of text as typed in the source code; displays the text in a monospace font, different from the standard browser text	Core attributes
<strong>	Emphasizes text, usually as bold; browser determines the text style	Core attributes
<sub>	Subscripts text	Core attributes
<sup>	Superscripts text	Core attributes

Table A-4   XHTML text elements

List Elements

Element	Description	Attributes
<li>	Marks an individual list item; this is an empty tag	Core attributes
<ol>	Creates a numbered indented list	Core attributes
<ul>	Creates a bulleted indented list	Core attributes

Table A-5   XHTML list element

Table Elements

Element	Description	Attributes
<caption>	Indicates that the text appears as the caption of a table	Core attributes plus: • *align*—The alignment of the caption, either
<table>	Marks the beginning and end of a table	Core attributes plus: • *align*—Floats the table to the left or right of text* • *border*—Specifies whether a border is displayed for a table • *bgcolor*—The background color of the table* • *cellpadding*—The amount of space in pixels between the border of the cell and the cell content on all four sides • *cellspacing*—The amount of space in pixels between the table cells on all four sides • *height*—The height of the table* • *width*—The width of the table, either to a fixed pixel width or a percentage relative width *Deprecated in XHTML
<td>	Marks an individual table cell	Core attributes plus: • *align*—The horizontal alignment for table cells within the table row • *valign*—The vertical alignment for table cells within the row • *bgcolor*—The background color of the table row* • *rowspan*—The number of rows spanned by a cell • *colspan*—The number of columns spanned by a cell *Deprecated in XHTML
<th>	Forces the contents of a cell to be displayed as bold and centered	Core attributes plus: • *align*—The horizontal alignment for table cells within the table row • *valign*—The vertical alignment for table cells within the row • *bgcolor*—The background color of the table row* • *rowspan*—The number of rows spanned by a cell • *colspan*—The number of columns spanned by a cell *Deprecated in XHTML
<tr>	Marks a row of cells in a table	Core attributes plus: • *align*—The horizontal alignment for table cells within the table row • *valign*—The vertical alignment for table cells within the row • *bgcolor*—The background color of the table row* *Deprecated in XHTML

Table A-6   XHTML table elements

Link Elements

Element	Description	Attributes
`<a>`	Allows you to create a clickable hypertext anchor in a document; can be text or an image	Core attributes plus: • *href*—The target destination of the hypertext link • *name*—Names a fragment of the document • *target*—The window or frame in which the linked document is displayed
`<base>`	Sets the base URL or target for a page; this is an empty element	Core attributes plus: • *href*—The absolute or relative original URL for the current document • *target*—The default window or frame in which links contained in the document are displayed
`<link>`	Defines a relationship between the document and external resources, such as a style sheet	Core attributes plus: • *type*—The type of external resource • *href*—The URL of the external resource

Table A-7   XHTML link elements

Inclusion Element

Element	Description	Attributes
`<img>`	Inserts an image into a Web page	Core attributes plus: • *width*—Specifies the width of the image in pixels • *height*—Specifies the height of the image in pixels • *src*—The URL that points to the image file; attribute is required • *align*—Allows you to wrap text around the image; valid values are left, middle, and right • *alt*—Allows you to specify an alternate string of text if the image cannot be displayed by the browser • *border*—The border for the image; set this attribute to zero (0) to remove a hypertext border on an anchor image • *hspace*—The horizontal white space in pixels on the left and right sides of an image • *vspace*—The vertical white space in pixels on the top and bottom of an image

Table A-8   XHTML inclusion element

Style Sheet Element

Element	Description	Attributes
`<style>`	Used within the headsection to contain CSS style rules	• *type*—Specifies the type of style language; for CSS, use text/CSS as the value

Table A-9   Style sheet element

Formatting Elements

Element	Description	Attributes
<b>	Boldfaces text	Core attributes
<basefont> (Deprecated)	Allows you to set a default size for the body text in the document	• *color*—The default text color • *face*—The default text face • *size*—The default text size for the document from 1–7; the normal browser default is size 3
<center> (Deprecated)	Centers text or images horizontally on the page	None
<font> (Deprecated)	Allows you to specify the font size for any string of text; range of sizes is 1 to 7, with 3 being the default	• *size*—Sets the font size • *color*—Sets the text color • *face*—Sets the font typeface
<hr>	Inserts a horizontal rule on the page; this is an empty element	Core attributes plus: • *width*—The length of the rule in pixels • *size*—The height of the rule in pixels • *align*—Horizontal rule alignment; default is center • *noshade*—Turns off the default 3-D shading of the rule
<i>	Italicizes text	Core attributes
<tt>	Specifies monospace text, usually in Courier	Core attributes
<u> (Deprecated)	Underlines text	Core attributes

Table A-10 XHTML formatting elements

Frame Elements

Element	Description	Attributes
<frameset>	Defines the column and row characteristics of the frames in the frameset	• *cols*—Separates the frame set into columns • *rows*—Separates the frameset into rows (Both of these attributes need percentage or pixel values to specify the frame width or height)
<noframe>	Contains content that is viewable by browsers that do not support frames	Core attributes

Table A-11 XHTML frame elements

Numeric and Character Entities

Character	Character Entity	Numeric Entity	Description
"	&#34;	&quot;	Quotation mark
#	&#35;		Number sign
$	&#36;		Dollar sign
%	&#37;		Percent sign
&	&#38;	&amp;	Ampersand
'	&#39;		Apostrophe
(	&#40;		Left parenthesis
)	&#41;		Right parenthesis
*	&#42;		Asterisk
+	&#43;		Plus sign
,	&#44;		Comma
-	&#45;		Hyphen
.	&#46;		Period (full stop)
/	&#47;		Solidus (slash)
0	&#48;		Digit 0
1	&#49;		Digit 1
2	&#50;		Digit 2
3	&#51;		Digit 3
4	&#52;		Digit 4
5	&#53;		Digit 5
6	&#54;		Digit 6
7	&#55;		Digit 7
8	&#56;		Digit 8
9	&#57;		Digit 9
:	&#58;		Colon
;	&#59;		Semicolon
<	&#60;	&lt;	Less than sign
=	&#61;		Equals sign

Table A-12   Numeric and character entities

Character	Character Entity	Numeric Entity	Description
>	&#62;	&gt;	Greater than sign
?	&#63;		Question mark
@	&#64;		Commercial at
A–Z	&#65;		Uppercase letters A–Z
[	&#91;		Left square bracket
\	&#92;		Reverse solidus (backslash)
]	&#93;		Right square bracket
^	&#94;		Caret
_	&#95;		Horizontal bar (underscore)
`	&#96;		Grave accent
a–z	a - &#122		Lowercase letters a–z
{	&#123;		Left curly brace
|	|		Vertical bar
}	&#125;		Right curly brace
~	&#126;		Tilde
			Nonbreaking space
¡	&#161;	&iexcl;	Inverted exclamation mark
¢	&#162;	&cent;	Cent sign
£	&#163;	&pound;	British Pound sign
¤	&#164;	&curren;	Currency sign
¥	&#165;	&yen;	Yen sign
¦	&#166;	&brvbar;	Broken vertical bar
§	&#167;	&sect;	Section sign
¨	&#168;	&uml;	Spacing diaeresis
©	&#169;	&copy;	Copyright sign
ª	&#170;	&ordf;	Feminine ordinal indicator
«	&#171;	&laquo;	Left-pointing double angle quotation mark
¬	&#172;	&not;	Not sign
_	&#173;	&shy;	Soft hyphen

Table A-12 *(Continued)* Numeric and character entities

Appendix A

Character	Character Entity	Numeric Entity	Description
®	&#174;	&reg;	Registered trademark sign
‾	&#175;	&macr;	Macron overline
°	&#176;	&deg;	Degree sign
±	&#177;	&plusmn;	Plus-or-minus sign
2	&#178;	&sup2;	Superscript digit 2
3	&#179;	&sup3;	Superscript digit 3
´	&#180;	&acute;	Acute accent
µ	&#181;	&micro;	Micron sign
¶	&#182;	&para;	Paragraph sign
·	&#183;	&middot;	Middle dot
¸	&#184;	&cedil;	Cedilla
1	&#185;	&sup1;	Superscript digit 1
º	&#186;	&ordm;	Masculine ordinal indicator
»	&#187;	&raquo;	Right-pointing double angle quotation mark
¼	&#188;	&frac14;	Fraction one-quarter
½	&#189;	&frac12;	Fraction one-half
¾	&#190;	&frac34;	Fraction three-quarters
¿	&#191;	&iquest;	Inverted question mark
À	&#192;	&Agrave;	Capital letter A with grave
Á	&#193;	&Aacute;	Capital letter A with acute
Â	&#194;	&Acirc;	Capital letter A with circumflex
Ã	&#195;	&Atilde;	Capital letter A with tilde
Ä	&#196;	&Auml;	Capital letter A with diaeresis
Å	&#197;	&Aring;	Capital letter A with ring above
Æ	&#198;	&Aelig;	Capital letter AE
Ç	&#199;	&Ccedil;	Capital letter C with cedilla
È	&#200;	&Egrave;	Capital letter E with grave
É	&#201;	&Eacute;	Capital letter E with acute
Ê	&#202;	&Ecirc;	Capital letter E with circumflex

Table A-12 (Continued)   Numeric and character entities

Character	Character Entity	Numeric Entity	Description
Ë	&#203;	&Euml;	Capital letter E with diaeresis
Ì	&#204;	&Igrave;	Capital letter I with grave
Í	&#205;	&Iacute;	Capital letter I with acute
Î	&#206;	&Icirc;	Capital letter I with circumflex
Ï	&#207;	&Iuml;	Capital letter I with diaeresis
Ð	&#208;	&ETH;	Capital letter ETH
Ñ	&#209;	&Ntilde;	Capital letter N with tilde
Ò	&#210;	&Ograve;	Capital letter O with grave
Ó	&#211;	&Oacute;	Capital letter O with acute
Ô	&#212;	&Ocirc;	Capital letter O with circumflex
Õ	&#213;	&Otilde;	Capital letter O with tilde
Ö	&#214;	&Ouml;	Capital letter O with diaeresis
×	&#215;	&times;	Multiplication sign
Ø	&#216;	&Oslash;	Capital letter O with stroke
Ù	&#217;	&Ugrave;	Capital letter U with grave
Ú	&#218;	&Uacute;	Capital letter U with acute
Û	&#219;	&Ucirc;	Capital letter U with circumflex
Ü	&#220;	&Uuml;	Capital letter U with diaeresis
Ý	&#221;	&Yacute;	Capital letter Y with acute
Þ	&#222;	&THORN;	Capital letter THORN
ß	&#223;	&szlig;	Sz ligature
à	&#224;	&agrave;	Small letter a with grave
á	&#225;	&aacute;	Small letter a with acute
â	&#226;	&acirc;	Small letter a with circumflex
ã	&#227;	&atilde;	Small letter a with tilde
ä	&#228;	&auml;	Small letter a with diaeresis
å	&#229;	&aring;	Small letter a with ring above
æ	&#230;	&aelig;	Small letter ae
ç	&#231;	&ccedil;	Small letter c with cedilla

Table A-12 (Continued)   Numeric and character entities

Appendix A

Character	Character Entity	Numeric Entity	Description
è	&#232;	&egrave;	Small letter e with grave
é	&#233;	&eacute;	Small letter e with acute
ê	&#234;	&ecirc;	Small letter e with circumflex
ë	&#235;	&euml;	Small letter e with diaeresis
ì	&#236;	&igrave;	Small letter i with grave
í	&#237;	&iacute;	Small letter i with acute
î	&#238;	&icirc;	Small letter i with circumflex
ï	&#239;	&iuml;	Small letter i with diaeresis
ð	&#240;	&eth;	Small letter eth
ñ	&#241;	&ntilde;	Small letter n with tilde
ò	&#242;	&ograve;	Small letter o with grave
ó	&#243;	&oacute;	Small letter o with acute
ô	&#244;	&ocirc;	Small letter o with circumflex
õ	&#245;	&otilde;	Small letter o with tilde
ö	&#246;	&ouml;	Small letter o with diaeresis
÷	&#247;	&divide;	Division sign
o/	&#248;	&oslash;	Small letter o with stroke
ù	&#249;	&ugrave;	Small letter u with grave
ú	&#250;	&uacute;	Small letter u with acute
û	&#251;	&ucirc;	Small letter u with circumflex
ü	&#252;	&uuml;	Small letter u with diaeresis
ý	&#253;	&yacute;	Small letter y with acute
þ	&#254;	&thorn;	Small letter thorn
ÿ	&#255;	&yuml;	Small letter y with diaeresis

Table A-12 (Continued)   Numeric and character entities

Appendix B
CSS Reference

This appendix includes the most commonly used CSS property descriptions, sorted both alphabetically and by category. For more detailed information, visit the World Wide Web Consortium Web site at *www.w3.org.*

CSS Notation Reference

Notation	Definition
<>	Words between angle brackets specify a type of value; for example, <color> means to enter a color value such as red
|	A single vertical bar between values means one or the other must occur; for example, scroll | fixed means choose scroll or fixed
||	Two vertical bars separating values means one or the other or both values can occur; for example, <border-width> || <border-style> || <color> means any or all of the three values can occur
[]	Square brackets group parts of the property value together; for example, none | [underline || overline || line-through || blink] means the value is either none or one of the values within the square brackets

Table B-1   CSS notations

Alphabetical CSS Property Reference

Property	Values	Default	Applies to
Background (Shorthand property)	<background-color> || <background-image> || <background-repeat> || <background-attachment> || <background-position>	No default for shorthand properties	All elements
Background-attachment	scroll | fixed	scroll	All elements
Background-color	color name or hexadecimal value | transparent	transparent	All elements

Table B-2   CSS properties

Property	Values	Default	Applies to
Background-image	<url> | none	none	All elements
Background-position	[<percentage> | <length>] {1,2} | [top | center | bottom] || [left | center | right]	0% 0%	Block-level and replaced elements
Background-repeat	repeat | repeat-x | repeat-y | no-repeat	repeat	All elements
Border (Shorthand property)	<border-width> || <border-style> || <color>	No default for shorthand properties	All elements
Border-bottom	<border-bottom-width> || <border-style> || <color>	No default for shorthand properties	All elements
Border-bottom-color	<color>	The value of the color property	All elements
Border-bottom-style	none | dotted | dashed | solid | double | groove | ridge | inset | outset	none	All elements
Border-bottom-width	thin | medium | thick | <length>	medium	All elements
Border-color	<color>	The value of the color property	All elements
Border-left (Shorthand property)	<border-left-width> || <border-style> || <color>	No default for shorthand properties	All elements
Border-left-color	<color>	The value of the color property	All elements
Border-left-style	none | dotted | dashed | solid | double | groove | ridge | inset | outset	none	All elements
Border-left-width	thin | medium | thick | <length>	medium	All elements
Border-right (Shorthand property)	<border-right-width> || <border-style> || <color>	No default for shorthand properties	All elements
Border-right-color	<color>	The value of the color property	All elements
Border-right-style	none | dotted | dashed | solid | double | groove | ridge | inset | outset	none	All elements
Border-right-width	thin | medium | thick | <length>	medium	All elements
Border-style	none | dotted | dashed | solid | double | groove | ridge | inset | outset	none	All elements
Border-top (Shorthand property)	<border-top-width> || <border-style> || <color>	No default for shorthand properties	All elements

Table B-2 (Continued)   CSS properties

Property	Values	Default	Applies to
Border-top-color	<color>	The value of the color property	All elements
Border-top-style	none | dotted | dashed | solid | double | groove | ridge | inset | outset	none	All elements
Border-top-width	thin | medium | thick | <length>	medium	All elements
Border-width (Shorthand property)	[thin | medium | thick | <length>]	No default for shorthand properties	All elements
Bottom	<length> | <percentage> | auto	auto	Positioned elements
Clear	none | left | right | both	none	All elements
Color	<color>	Browser specific	All elements
Display	inline | block | list-item | run-in | compact | marker | table | inline-table | table-row-group | table-header-group | table-footer-group | table-row | table-column-group | table-column | table-cell | table-caption | none	inline	All elements
Float	left | right | none	none	All elements
Font (Shorthand property)	[<font-style> || <font-variant> || <font-weight>] <font-size> [/ <line-height>] <font-family>	No default for shorthand properties	All elements
Font-family	Font family name (such as Times) or generic family name (such as sans-serif)	Browser specific	All elements
Font-size	<absolute-size> | <relative-size> | <length> | <percentage>	medium	All elements
Font-stretch	normal | wider | narrower | ultra-condensed | extra-condensed | condensed | semi-condensed | semi-expanded | expanded | extra-expanded | ultra-expanded	normal	All elements
Font-style	normal | italic | oblique	normal	All elements
Font-variant	normal | small caps	normal	All elements
Font-weight	normal | bold | bolder | lighter | 100 | 200 | 300 | 400 | 500 | 600 | 700 | 800 | 900	normal	All elements
Height	<length> | <percentage> | auto	auto	Block-level and replaced elements; also all elements except inline images

Table B-2 (Continued)   CSS properties

Property	Values	Default	Applies to
Left	<length> | <percentage> | auto	auto	Positioned
Letter-spacing	normal | <length>	normal	All elements
Line-height	normal | <number> | <length> | <percentage>	normal	All elements
List-style (Shorthand property)	<keyword> || <position> || <url>	No default for shorthand properties	Elements with display value list-item
List-style-image	<url> | none	none	Elements with display value list-item
List-style-position	inside | outside	outside	Elements with display value list-item
List-style-type	disc | circle | square | decimal | lower-roman | upper-roman | lower-alpha | upper-alpha | none	Disc	Elements with display value list-item
Margin (Shorthand property)	[<length> | <percentage> | auto]	No default for shorthand properties	All elements
Margin-bottom	<length> | <percentage> | auto	0	All elements
Margin-left	<length> | <percentage> | auto	0	All elements
Margin-right	<length> | <percentage> | auto	0	All elements
Margin-top	<length> | <percentage> | auto	0	All elements
Padding	<length> | <percentage>	0	All elements
Padding-bottom	<length> | <percentage>	0	All elements
Padding-left	<length> | <percentage>	0	All elements
Padding-right	<length> | <percentage>	0	All elements
Padding-top	<length> | <percentage>	0	All elements
Position	static | relative | absolute | fixed	static	All elements except generated content
Right	<length> | <percentage> | auto	auto	Positioned elements
Text-align	left | right | center | justify	Depends on browser and language direction	Block-level elements
Text-decoration	none | [underline || overline || line-through || blink]	none	All elements
Text-indent	<length> | <percentage>	0	Block-level
Text-shadow	none | [<color> || <length> <length> <length>? ,]* [<color> ||<length> <length> <length>?]	none	All elements

Table B-2 (Continued)   CSS properties

Property	Values	Default	Applies to
Text-transform	capitalize | uppercase | lowercase | none	none	All elements
Top	<length> | <percentage> | auto	auto	Positioned
Vertical-align	baseline | sub | super | top | text-top | middle | bottom | text-bottom | <percentage>	baseline	Inline elements
White-space	normal | pre | nowrap	normal	Block-level elements
Width	<length> | <percentage> | auto	auto	Block-level and replaced elements; also all elements except inline elements
Word-spacing	normal | <length>	normal	All elements
Z-index	auto | integer	auto	Positioned elements

Table B-2 (Continued)   CSS properties

CSS Properties by Category

Property	Values	Default	Applies to
Color	<color>	Browser specific	All elements
Font (Shorthand property)	[<font-style> || <font-variant> || <font-weight>] <font-size> [/ <line-height>] <font-family>	No default for shorthand properties	All elements
Font-family	Font family name (such as Times) or generic family name (such as sans-serif)	Browser specific	All elements
Font-size	<absolute-size> | <relative-size> | <length> | <percentage>	medium	All elements
Font-style	normal | italic | oblique	normal	All elements
Font-stretch	normal | wider | narrower | ultra-condensed | extra-condensed | condensed | semi-condensed | semi-expanded | expanded | extra-expanded | ultra-expanded	normal	All elements
Font-variant	normal | small-caps	normal	All elements
Font-weight	normal | bold | bolder | lighter | 100 | 200 | 300 | 400 | 500 | 600 | 700 | 800 | 900	normal	All elements
Letter-spacing	normal | <length>	normal	All elements

Table B-3   Font and text properties

Property	Values	Default	Applies to
Line-height	normal | <number> | <length> | <percentage>	normal	All elements
Text-align	left | right | center | justify	Depends on browser and language direction	Block-level elements
Text-decoration	none | [underline || overline || line-through || blink]	none	All elements
Text-indent	<length> | <percentage>	0	Block-level elements
Text-shadow	none | [<color> || <length> <length> <length>? ,]* [<color> ||<length> <length> <length>?]	none	All elements
Text-transform	capitalize | uppercase | lowercase | none	none	All elements
Vertical-align	baseline | sub | super | top | text-top | middle | bottom | text-bottom | <percentage>	Baseline	Inline elements
Word-spacing	normal | <length>	normal	All elements

Table B-3 (*Continued*)   Font and text properties

Property	Values	Default	Applies to
Margin (Shorthand property)	[<length> | <percentage> | auto]	No default for shorthand properties	All elements
Margin-bottom	<length> | <percentage> | auto	0	All elements
Margin-left	<length> | <percentage> | auto	0	All elements
Margin-right	<length> | <percentage> | auto	0	All elements
Margin-top	<length> | <percentage> | auto	0	All elements
Padding	<length> | <percentage>	0	All elements
Padding-bottom	<length> | <percentage>	0	All elements
Padding-left	<length> | <percentage>	0	All elements
Padding-right	<length> | <percentage>	0	All elements
Padding-top	<length> | <percentage>	0	All elements
Border (Shorthand property)	border-width> || <border-style> || <color>	No default for shorthand properties	All elements
Border-bottom	<border-bottom-width> || <border-style> || <color>	No default for shorthand properties	All elements
Border-bottom-color	<color>	The value of the color property	All elements
Border-bottom-style	none | dotted | dashed | solid | double | groove | ridge | inset | outset	none	All elements

Table B-4   Box properties

Property	Values	Default	Applies to
Border-bottom-width	thin | medium | thick | <length>	medium	All elements
Border-color	<color>	The value of the color property	All elements
Border-left (Shorthand property)	<border-left-width> || <border-style> || <color>	No default for shorthand properties	All elements
Border-left-color	<color>	The value of the color property	All elements
Border-left-style	none | dotted | dashed | solid | double | groove | ridge | inset | outset	none	All elements
Border-left-width	thin | medium | thick | <length>	medium	All elements
Border-right (Shorthand property)	<border-right-width> || <border-style> || <color>	No default for shorthand properties	All elements
Border-right-color	<color>	The value of the color property	All elements
Border-right-style	none | dotted | dashed | solid | double | groove | ridge | inset | outset	none	All elements
Border-right-width	thin | medium | thick | <length>	medium	All elements
Border-style	none | dotted | dashed | solid | double | groove | ridge | inset | outset	none	All elements
Border-top (Shorthand property)	<border-top-width> || <border-style> || <color>	No default for shorthand properties	All elements
Border-top-color	<color>	The value of the color property	All elements
Border-top-style	none | dotted | dashed | solid | double | groove | ridge | inset | outset	none	All elements
Border-top-width	thin | medium | thick | <length>	medium	All elements
Border-width (Shorthand property)	[thin | medium | thick | <length>]	No default for shorthand properties	All elements
Clear	none | left | right | both	none	All elements
Float	left | right | none	none	All elements
Height	<length> | <percentage> | auto	auto	Block-level and replaced elements
Width	<length> | <percentage> | auto	auto	Block-level and replaced elements

Table B-4 (Continued)   Box properties

Property	Values	Default	Applies to
Background (Shorthand property)	<background-color> || <background-image> || <background-repeat> || <background-attachment> || <background-position>	No default for shorthand properties	All elements
Background-attachment	scroll | fixed	scroll	All elements
Background-color	color name or hexadecimal value | transparent	transparent	All elements
Background-image	<url> | none	none	All elements
Background-position	[<percentage> | <length>] {1,2} | [top | center | bottom] | [left | center | right]	0% 0%	Block-level and replaced elements
Background-repeat	repeat | repeat-x | repeat-y | no-repeat	Repeat	All elements

Table B-5   Background properties

Property	Values	Default	Applies to
Bottom	<length> | <percentage> | auto	auto	Positioned
Height	<length> | <percentage> | auto	auto	All elements
Left	<length> | <percentage> | auto	auto	Positioned
Position	static | relative | absolute | fixed	static	All elements except generated content
Right	<length> | <percentage> | auto	auto	Positioned elements
Top	<length> | <percentage> | auto	auto	Positioned elements
Width	<length> | <percentage> | auto	auto	All elements except inline elements
Z-index	auto | integer	auto	Positioned elements

Table B-6   Visual properties

Property	Values	Default	Applies to
Display	inline | block | list-item | run-in | compact | marker | table | inline-table | table-row-group | table-header-group | table-footer-group | table-row | table-column-group | table-column | table-cell | table-caption | none	inline	All elements
List-style-image	<url> | none	none	Elements with display value list-item
List-style-position	inside | outside	outside	Elements with display value list-item
List-style (Shorthand property)	<keyword> || <position> || <url>	No default for shorthand properties	Elements with display value list-item
List-style-type	disc | circle | square | decimal | lower-roman | upper-roman | lower-alpha | upper-alpha | none	disc	Elements with display value list-item
White-space	normal | pre | nowrap	normal	Block-level elements

Table B-7   Classification properties

CSS Measurement Units

Unit	Code Abbreviation	Description
Centimeter	cm	Standard metric centimeter
Em	em	The width of the capital M in the current font, usually the same as the font size
Ex	ex	The height of the letter x in the current font
Inch	in	Standard U.S. inch
Millimeter	mm	Standard metric millimeter
Pica	pc	Standard publishing unit equal to 12 points
Pixel	px	The size of a pixel on the current display
Point	pt	Standard publishing unit; 72 points in an inch
Relative	For example: 150%	Sets a font size relative to the base font size; 150% equals 1.5 times the base font size

Table B-8   CSS measurement codes

Glossary

!important—A CSS keyword that lets the user override the author's style setting for a particular element.

absolute URL—*See* complete URL.

active white space—White space used deliberately as an integral part of your design that provides structure and separates content.

audience definition—A profile of your average user.

banding—An effort to match the closest colors from the GIF's palette to the original colors in a photo.

box model—A CSS element that describes the rectangular boxes containing content on a Web page.

breadcrumb—One or more site navigation links, usually at the top of a Web page, that show the current page and any pages above it in the site hierarchy.

browser-safe colors—The 216 colors shared by PCs and Macintoshes. These colors are displayed properly across both platforms without dithering.

cache—The browser's temporary storage area for Web pages and images. There are two types of cache: memory cache and hard drive cache.

canvas area—The part of the browser window that displays the content of the Web page.

cascade—Style sheets originate from three sources: the author, the user, and the browser. The cascading feature of CSS lets these multiple style sheets and style rules interact in the same document.

Cascading Style Sheets (CSS)—A style language, created by the W3C, that allows complete specifications of style for HTML documents. CSS allows HTML authors to use over 50 properties that affect the display of Web pages. CSS style information is contained either within an HTML document, or in external documents called style sheets.

cell-level attribute—An attribute that affects one data cell in a table.

CGI—*See* Common Gateway Interface.

CGI script—A program that transfers form data to a server.

child element—An HTML element contained within another element.

color depth—The amount of data used to create color on a display. The three common color depths are 8-bit, 16-bit, and 24-bit. Not all displays support all color depths.

Common Gateway Interface (CGI)—The communications bridge between the Internet and the server. Using programs called scripts, CGI can collect data sent by a user via the Hypertext Transfer Protocol (HTTP) and transfer it to a variety of data processing programs including spreadsheets, databases, or other software running on the server.

complete URL—A complete Uniform Resource Locator (URL) is an address of documents and other resources on the Web that includes the protocol the browser uses to access the file, server or domain name, the relative path, and the filename.

containing box—The containing rectangle, or parent element, of any child element. The absolute containing element is the window area of the browser. All other elements are displayed within this containing box, which equates to the <body> element of an HTML document. Within <body>, elements such as <div> or <p> are parents, or containing boxes, for their child elements.

contextual link—A link that allows users to jump to related ideas or cross-references by clicking the word or item that interests them. You can embed contextual links directly in your content by choosing the key terms and concepts you anticipate your users will want to follow.

core attribute—One of the four attributes that can be used with any element. They include id, title, style, and class.

CSS—*See* Cascading Style Sheets.

CSS visual formatting model—A model that describes how CSS element content boxes should be displayed by the browser.

cursive—A generic value for the CSS font-family property. Cursive fonts are designed to resemble handwriting. Most browsers do not support this font family.

declaration—The declaration portion of a style rule consists of a property name and value. The browser applies the declaration to the selected element.

deprecated element—An element that the W3C has identified as obsolete in future releases of HTML.

dithering—This color mixing process occurs when a browser encounters a color on a Web page that it does not support. The browser is forced to mix the color. The resulting color may be grainy or unacceptable. To avoid dithering, work with browser-safe colors.

Document Type Definition (DTD)—A set of rules that contains all the elements, attributes, and usage rules for the markup language you are using.

DTD—*See* Document Type Definition.

em unit—In CSS, a unit equal to the font size of an element.

ex unit—In CSS, a unit equal to the height of the lowercase letter x in any given font.

Extensible Hypertext Markup Language (XHTML)—XHTML is HTML 4.01 reformulated as an application of XML.

extranet—A private part of a company's intranet that uses the Internet to share securely part of an organization's information.

fantasy—A generic value for the CSS font-family property. Fantasy fonts are primarily decorative. Most browsers do not support this font family.

File Transfer Protocol (FTP)—A standard communications protocol for transferring files over the Internet.

font—A typeface in a particular size, such as Times Roman 24 point.

form controls—These are the input elements that make up an HTML form, such as radio buttons, text boxes, and check boxes.

fragment identifier—The use of the <a> element and NAME attribute to name a segment of an HTML file. You then can reference the fragment name in a hypertext link.

frame—A section in canvas area of the browser that displays a separate, independent HTML document.

FTP—*See* File Transfer Protocol.

GIF—*See* Graphics Interchange Format.

global attribute—An attribute that affects an entire table.

Graphics Interchange Format (GIF)—The Graphic Interchange Format (GIF) is designed for online delivery of graphics. The color depth of GIF is 8-bit, allowing a palette of no more than 256colors. The GIF file format excels at compressing and displaying flat color areas, making it the logical choice for line art and graphics with simple colors.

grid—A layout device that organizes the Web page, providing visual consistency.

HTML—*See* Hypertext Markup Language.

hypertext—A nonlinear way of organizing information. When you are using a hypertext system, you can skip from one related topic to another, find the information that interests you, and then return to your starting point or move on to another related topic of interest.

Hypertext Markup Language (HTML)—The markup language that defines the structure and display properties of a Web page. The HTML code is interpreted by the browser to create the displayed results. HTML is an application of SGML. (*See* Standard Generalized Markup Language.)

inheritance—The order of CSS rules dictating child elements inherit rules from parent elements.

interlacing—The gradual display of a graphic in a series of passes as the data arrives in the browser. Each additional pass of data creates a clearer view of the image until the complete image is displayed. You can choose an interlacing process when you are creating GIFs.

Internet service provider (ISP)—A company that provides Internet access and Web site hosting services to individuals and organizations.

intranet—A private collection of networks contained within an organization. Intranet users gain access to the Internet through a firewall that prevents unauthorized users from getting in to the intranet.

ISP—*See* Internet service provider.

JavaScript—A client-side scripting language used with HTML forms.

Joint Photographic Experts Group (JPEG or JPG)—A file format, commonly shortened to JPG, designed for the transfer of photographic images over the Internet. JPGs are best for photos and images that contain feathering, complex shadows, or gradations.

JPEG—*See* Joint Photographic Experts Group.

JPG—*See* Joint Photographic Experts Group.

look and feel—The interface that the user must navigate on a Web site.

markup language—A structured language that lets you identify common elements of a document such as headings, paragraphs, and lists.

metalanguage—A language that lets you describe the characteristics of a markup language. The Extensible Markup Language (XML) is a metalanguage.

monospace—A generic value for the CSS font-family property. Monospace fonts are fixed-width fonts. Every letter has the same horizontal width.

nesting—The practice of placing one element within another element.

nesting tables—The practice of placing an entire table within a table cell.

parent element—An HTML element that contains child elements.

parser—A program built into a browser that interprets the markup tags in an HTML file and displays the results in the canvas area of the browser interface.

partial URL—A Uniform Resource Locator (URL) that omits the protocol and server name, and only specifies the path to the file relative to one another on the same server.

passive white space—The blank area that borders the screen or is the result of mismatched shapes.

plug-in—A helper application that assists a browser in rendering a special effect.

PNG—*See* Portable Network Graphic.

points of presence (POP)—Dial-up access points to your service provider's network. Your service provider should have at least one POP available so you can dial a local number to get access. Major ISPs such as AT&T have POPs throughout the United States, where a local ISP only will cover the area that includes their subscriber base.

POP—*See* points of presence.

Portable Network Graphic (PNG)—A graphics file format for the Web that supports many of the same features as GIF.

positioned layout—A CSS method that gives you control over the way element boxes are laid out in a Web page, allowing you to create complex page designs without tables.

processing instruction—A special type of XML element that contains information that doesn't fit into a standard XHTML structure.

property—A quality or characteristic stated in a style rule, such as color, font-size, or margin. The property is a part of the style rule declaration.

pseudo-class—An element that selects elements based on characteristics other than their element name.

pseudo-element—An element that lets you change other aspects of a document that are not classified by elements, such as applying style rules to the first letter or first line of a paragraph.

raster graphics—Images represented pixel-by-pixel for the entire image. GIFs and JPGs are raster formats.

rendering engine—A program contained in every browser that interprets the markup tags in an HTML file and displays the results in the browser.

row-level attribute—An attribute that affects an entire row in a table.

sans-serif—A generic value for the CSS font-family property. Sans-serif fonts have no serifs. The most common sans-serif fonts are Helvetica and Arial.

Scalable Vector Graphics (SVG)—A language for describing two-dimensional graphics using XML. SVG files can contain shapes such as lines and curves, images, text, animation, and interactive events.

screen resolution—The horizontal and vertical height and width of the computer screen in pixels. Currently, the two most common screen resolutions for Web design (traditionally expressed as width × height) are 800 × 600 and 1024 × 768.

script—A small program written with a scripting language such as JavaScript.

search engine—A software program that searches out and indexes Web sites in a catalog.

Secure Sockets Layer (SSL)—Communications software that allows transmission of encrypted secure messages over the Internet.

selector—The part of a style rule that determines which HTML element to match. Style rules are applied to any element in the document that matches the selector.

semantic markup—Descriptive markup that identifies the intended use of different document sections.

serif—A generic value for the CSS font-family property. Serif is the traditional printing letter form, with strokes (or serifs) that finish off the top and bottom of the letter. The most common serif fonts on the Web are Times and Times Roman.

SGML—*See* Standard Generalized Markup Language.

shareware—Software that is distributed free so users can try before they buy. Users then can register the software for a relatively small fee compared to software produced commercially. Shareware usually is developed by individuals or very small software companies, so registering the software is important.

site specification—The design document for your Web site.

SQL—*See* Structured Query Language.

SSL—*See* Secure Sockets Layer.

stacking level—The ordering of CSS elements on the z-axis.

stacking tables—The technique of building several successive small tables rather than one large one.

Standard Generalized Markup Language (SGML)—A standard system for specifying document structure using markup tags.

Structured Query Language (SQL)—A programming language that lets you select information from a database.

style rule—The basic unit of expression in CSS. A style rule is composed of two parts: a selector and a declaration. The style rule expresses the style information for an element.

style sheet—A set of style rules that describes a document's display characteristics. There are two types of style sheets: internal and external.

SVG—*See* Scalable Vector Graphics.

text property—A CSS property that lets you adjust the spacing around and within your text.

type selector—A CSS selector that applies a rule to every instance of the element in the document.

typeface—The name of type family, such as Times Roman or Futura Condensed.

Uniform Resource Locator (URL)—The global address of documents and other resources on the Web.

universal selector—A selector that lets you quickly select groups of elements and apply a style rule.

URL—*See* Uniform Resource Locator.

valid code—Markup code that conforms to the rules of the W3C.

value—The precise specification of a property in a style rule, based on the allowable values for the property.

vector graphics—Images represented as geometrical formulas, as compared with a raster graphics format, which represents images pixel by pixel for the entire image. GIFs and JPGs are raster formats. SVG is a vector graphic format. Vector graphics are scalable and cross-platform compatible.

W3C—*See* World Wide Web Consortium.

Web hosting service—Commercial service that provides Web server space only and may be more capable of hosting a more complex commercial site. This service does not include Internet access.

Web palette—The 216 colors shared by PCs and Macintoshes. These colors display properly across both platforms without dithering.

Web server—A computer connected to the Internet that runs server software. The software lets the computer use the Hypertext Transfer Protocol to serve HTML files to Web browser clients.

well-formed document—A syntactically correct XML or XHTML file.

World Wide Web Consortium (W3C)—Founded in 1994 at the Massachusetts Institute of Technology to standardize Web markup languages. The W3C, led by Tim Berners-Lee, sets standards for markup languages and provides an open, non-proprietary forum for industry and academic representatives to add to the evolution of HTML.

x-height—The height of the letter x in a particular font.

XHTML—*See* Extensible Hypertext Markup Language.

Index